LIBRARY OF NEW TESTAMENT STUDIES
408

formerly the *Journal for the Study of the New Testament* Supplement series

Editor
Mark Goodacre

Editorial Board
John M. G. Barclay, Craig Blomberg, R. Alan Culpepper,
James D. G. Dunn, Craig A. Evans, Stephen Fowl, Robert Fowler,
Simon J. Gathercole, John S. Kloppenborg, Michael Labahn, Robert Wall,
Steve Walton, Robert L. Webb, Catrin H. Williams

READING EPHESIANS

EXPLORING SOCIAL ENTREPRENEURSHIP IN THE TEXT

MINNA SHKUL

t&t clark

Published by T&T Clark International
A Continuum imprint
The Tower Building, 11 York Road, London SE1 7NX
80 Maiden Lane, Suite 704, New York, NY 10038

www.continuumbooks.com

British Library Cataloguing-in-Publication Data
A catalogue record for this book is available from the British Library

ISBN: 978–0–567–28777–9 (hardback)

Typeset by Data Standards Ltd, Frome, Somerset, UK
Printed in Great Britain by the MPG Books Group, Bodmin and King's Lynn

CONTENTS

This book is dedicated to
Pentti, Kaarina and Sampo Kaipanen

'Tiedän olevan hyvää ja kaunista, enemmän kuin unelma onnesta.'

Acknowledgements

First and foremost, I owe the deepest gratitude to the University of Sheffield for the generous funding for my doctoral studies and to everybody at the Department of Biblical Studies for supervision, inspiration and challenging me 'to find my voice and make it heard', particularly Professor Jorunn Økland, now in Oslo, Norway and Dr Barry Matlock. Secondly, I am grateful to the University of Wales Lampeter for my first academic post and much support at the completion of my PhD thesis from all my wonderful colleagues at the Theology and Religious Studies Department, particularly Dr Paul Middleton. Working with different religious communities in partnership with Lampeter continues to inspire my 'sociological imagination'. Thirdly, I am especially indebted to the Finnish Academy, University of Helsinki and 'Explaining Early Jewish and Christian Movements: Ritual, Memory and Identity' research group. The collaboration and dialogue with Professor Petri Luomanen, Professor Risto Uro, Dr Raimo Hakola, Dr Jutta Jokiranta and Mr Timo Vanhoja is priceless.

This book is a slightly revised version of my doctoral dissertation which was examined by Dr Edward Adams and Professor Loveday Alexander in December 2007. Both examiners offered invaluable, detailed assessments of my approach and readings, with helpful comments and criticisms. Needless to say, any shortcomings of this book are entirely my own. I also want to thank all who have interacted with my BNTC and SBL papers over the years, many of whom have become friends and conversation partners in an ongoing dialogue on methods, interpretations and other matters.

Finally, I want to thank a few people who are of special importance to this project and my doctorate. First, Professor Veli-Matti Kärkkäinen, who inspired and encouraged me to venture into Higher Education and Dr Andrew Davies of Mattersey Hall, who has also been hugely important on my student's journey, as has the college. I want to thank my fellow students, Dr Paul Nikkel, Dr Rafael Rodriguez and Dr Brian Lee, who enriched my PhD student experience with regular pub afternoons, wit and GSOH. I owe the deepest gratitude to my parents, Pentti and Kaarina, and brother Sampo, who shaped my primary socialization. I am grateful for learning what 'sisu' is (the resilience and fortitude Finns are made of) and how to find happiness. I want to thank all my friends who have kept me going, especially Jen, Dave, Outi, Piike, Päivi and Petri who have been wonderful, inspiring and so much fun! Lastly, thanks to Sergei, Evan and Ally at home; my everything.

PREFACE

This study examines how Ephesians engages in social entrepreneurship, that is, the deliberate shaping of emerging Christianness by providing ideological and social paradigms for the community of Christ-followers. This includes positioning the group in a Jewish symbolic universe, which is reconfigured to make room for 'Jesus Christ' and his non-Israelite followers, and modelling the group after Israel as God's people. The eclectic theoretical framework and Deutero-Pauline reading position used in this work have two particular purposes which seek to advance Ephesians Scholarship. The first aim is to offer diversified, theoretically informed social-scientific readings that illustrate extensive socio-ideological shaping in the discourse, and underline how the writer negotiates different group processes throughout the letter. The second aim is to examine emerging Christianness in the text, testing its ideological and social contours and its reforms upon Jewish traditions, based on interpretations of the Christ-event without the theological presupposition of assuming that something was wrong with the Judaism(s) of the day. Instead, these readings of Ephesians examine how a late first-century Christ-follower understood Jesus' Messiahship, its relation to the Jewish faith and its consequences for the non-Israelite community members in the Christ movement. Social entrepreneurship is used as an umbrella for a variety of social processes reflected in the text. These readings of Ephesians examine how the writer engages in a self-enhancing discourse that reinforces three basic components of communality. These include the construction of a positive in-group identity of Christ-followers, providing the group with ideological and social legitimating, and finally, establishing group norms and encouraging coherence that contributes to group aims.

Abbreviations

SNTSMS Society for New Testament Studies Monograph Series
SNTW   Studies of the New Testament and its World
WUNT   Wissenschaftliche Untersuchungen zum Neuen Testament
ZNW   *Zeitschrift für die neutestamentliche Wissenschaft*

PART ONE

CONSTRUCTING IDENTITY

Chapter 1

INTRODUCTION

This chapter introduces the questions explored in this study and provides selected readings from Ephesians 1 to lay the foundations for subsequent readings of the letter. Without exploring authorship issues in detail, this reading considers the epistle as a Deutero-Pauline text,[1] exploring how Ephesians adapts Pauline legacy for later situations.[2]

1. *Positioning Ephesians' Scholarship*[3]

Although matters of identity and 'what being a Christian means' have

---

1   The debate of the authorship of Ephesians is focused on its considerable verbal, thematic and theological differences with so-called undisputed Paulines. While some scholars simply state their position or outline their views briefly, others explore the issues in detail (cf. Lincoln 1990: lix–lxxiii; Best 1998: 6–36), but rarely with similar passion as Hoehner. Hoehner devotes 60 pages of his momentous commentary to the defence of Pauline authorship (Hoehner 2002: 2–61), which he then expands in 50 pages to introduction to the structure, setting and theology of the letter as Pauline (pp. 61–114), and finally includes 17 pages of bibliography on the authorship debate (pp. 114–30). Hoehner's survey on Ephesians' scholarship from the sixteenth century to 2001 demonstrates that 54 per cent of all scholars regard Ephesians as Pauline, while in the last ten years of his survey the opinion on Pauline and post-Pauline authorship is 50–50 (pp. 9–20). Despite this, other scholars suggest the authorship does not matter (to their particular question). Such readings often assume a post-Pauline stance but do not critically advance Deutero-Pauline scholarship, as will be discussed later.

2   Despite its parallels with Colossians, in particular, Ephesians is examined in its own right, making only occasional reference to other disputed Paulines. My forthcoming publications on the disputed Paulines will assess different texts in more detail. Naturally, a theoretical framework used in this study could be used from the traditional position, analysing how Paul shaped the community and his reputation through the letter to the Ephesians. Although I will adapt 'wandering viewpoints' to test different reading positions in Chapter 3 below, I will not do so with regards the authorship.

3   I use language of positioning to refer to different positions either in social or academic discourse; and/or for allocating something a particular discourse location and what this involves. I draw upon positioning theory which highlights ongoing construction of the self and identity through social discourse and how different positions are situated and interact in a discourse (Harré and Van Langenhove 1998b: 182; cf. 14–31).

long been acknowledged to be at the heart of the letter,[4] little systematic
attention has been previously devoted to the construction of social
identity in Ephesians. The precursors for exploring identity in Ephesians
include a number of major commentaries which have condensed the
purpose of the letter in terms of identity and meaning of group belonging
(e.g. Lincoln 1990: lxxv; Perkins 1997: 16; O'Brien 1999: 56–57;
MacDonald 2000: 22).[5] Scholars have observed traces of instability and
'insufficient identity' (Lincoln and Wedderburn 1993: 82–3) stressing
various elements of the discourse, such as the identity of the Church and
its relation to Christ (Schnackenburg 1991: 34); the cosmic reconciliation
(O'Brien 1999: 56–57); the meaning of baptism as an initial rite and a
point of transformation for Gentile believers (Dahl 1978: 133–43); or
appreciation of the meaning of salvation and living as 'worthy of the
heavenly calling' (Bruce 1961: 245). Martin Kitchen regards Ephesians as
a story of 'God's interaction with the world' and its moral consequences
for the *ekklēsia* (1994: 14). Andrew Lincoln reads the letter as an
exhortation to reinforce Christian commitment that incorporates a
distinctive lifestyle through the power of Christ and the Holy Spirit
(1991: lxxviii); and Harold Hoehner as exhortation to communal love
(2002: 106).[6] Other reflections on Ephesians' identity discourse include,

---

I apply basic assumptions of the positioning theory in exploring positionings in the text I
examine, as well as those I undertake as a reader, thus expanding the theory from the social
discourse I examine to that academic discourse in which I participate.

4 Although classic commentaries, such as Schlier (1957), interpreted Ephesians in the
light of Gnostic mythologies, in recent decades the emphasis has turned to Jewish influences
as the literature review below will demonstrate.

5 Previously matters of identity have often been part of theological exegesis of the letter.
For instance, although Lincoln uses traditional theological methods and terms he discusses
contours of identity rather perceptively. For example, he states that the Christology of
Ephesians is not swallowed up by ecclesiology, but its ecclesiology is thoroughly
Christological (Lincoln, 1990: xci). I would use more social-scientific terms to make the
same point: although communal matters of identity, social orientation and shared values are
important to Ephesians, they clearly derive from Christ, who is the core of communal
ideology and key for the members' shared identification as group members. Although there
are only a few references to the death of Christ (1.7; 2.13, 16; 5.2, 25), it nevertheless positions
Christ at the heart of the community. Ecclesiology, in other words, is Christological, as
Lincoln would say. Communal matters have been at the heart of Lincoln's theological
exegesis of Ephesians, who assumes that communal needs have prompted the occasion of
writing (cf. Lincoln (1981; 1990); Lincoln and Wedderburn (1993: 82–3)); contra Perkins,
who correctly challenges this assumption based on the mirror-reading method (1997: 16).

6 Hoehner's grand commentary on Ephesians responds with conservative ammunition to
the challenges posed by the Deutero-Pauline hypothesis. His thoroughgoing interpretation of
the letter in the light of this authorship conviction leads to harmonizing the letter with Paul.
For instance, his examination of the historical, social and political setting of Ephesus
involves chronological linking of Ephesians with Acts, and its ideological correlation with
other New Testament passages relating to Ephesus (e.g. 1 Tim. 1.5; Rev. 2.2-6). In my view,
this is not analysis of Ephesians, but rather general New Testament discussion related to

for instance, Arnold's suggestion that the language of identity targets the prominent textual relationship between the readers and the supernatural forces manifested in magic and witchcraft (1989: 165–71). Similarly, Ralph Martin connects Ephesians with Gnostic tendencies owing to its explicit claims of sharing the power and victory of the exalted Christ in a hostile universe of earthly powers (1991). Still others read Ephesians in the light of imperial rhetoric countering the language of the peace and wellbeing of the Roman Empire (Mussner 1982; Faust 1993; MacDonald 2004). Pheme Perkins concludes that Ephesians is concerned with a Pauline sense of Christian mission in a global perspective and God's plans to unite all things in Christ before the creation; thus envizaging human unity even beyond the scope of the imperial rhetoric (1997: 27–32).[7]

This leads to a significant conclusion that Ephesians' language of identity engages with Israelite, non-Israelite and imperial dialogue of identity.[8] Appropriate cultural performances are also an important part of Ephesians' language of identity and consequently its intercommunal relations.[9] For instance Larry Kreitzer suggests that Ephesians provides

---

Ephesus' location. Further examples from Hoehner's discussion of Ephesians' purpose further illustrate the same tendency. Although the theme of communal love is important to Ephesians as Hoehner demonstrates (pp. 104–5), his use of other New Testament texts may well have influenced his conclusion that: 'the purpose of Ephesians is to promote a love for one another that has the love of God and Christ as a basis … Possibly realizing that the Ephesians were starting to forsake their first love, Paul wrote this letter to encourage them to love both God and their fellow saints more deeply' (p. 106). Hoehner's reading position also causes him to disregard some interesting matters that would stress Ephesians' difference. For instance, although he does discuss ethnic reconciliation in Ephesians 2, he does not discuss its bearing on early Christian identity or its reflection of Jewish faith, or critically engage with Ephesians' distinctiveness on this particular topic, but reads Ephesians through the lens of a conservative Christian Church (Hoehner 2002: 374–7). Nor does he discuss the peculiarity of the portrayal of the Apostle Paul or examine interesting contrasts with 'typical Pauline thought', such as the lack of urgency for mission or expectation of the *parousia*, the pneumatology of Ephesians or the lack of interest in charismatic phenomena. Instead, he insists that 'theological features' are in agreement with the other Pauline letters throughout his commentary. In my view, Hoehner's study offers interesting Christian theological exegesis, but it does not examine Ephesians' distinctive features and development of Christianness in the text equally thoroughly.

7 However, as commonly acknowledged, the language of mission and evangelism is significantly absent from Ephesians. This does not need to prove Perkins wrong, though, as the language of mission can be seen as overall commissioning of Christ-followers and legitimation of their role as God's representatives; not with an agenda to go and multiply their number, and win converts from among the outsiders.

8 I use 'non-Israelite' instead of a traditional term 'Gentile', although I maintain 'Gentile' in selected quotations and allusions to scholars who use it to translate '*ta ethnē*', the nations in the NT. Both 'non-Israelite' and 'Gentile' maintain the NT categorization of ethnic diversity as Israelites or Judeans and 'other nations'.

9 I owe the phrase 'cultural performances' to David G. Horrell, who used it in his paper in the British New Testament Conference, Sheffield, in September 2006. See Lawrence (2005).

'the church [sic] ... with some practical advice on how to live as Christians in a socially-changing world where the temptation to lapse back into pagan ways was ever present' (1997: 48). Despite his use of anachronistic and inappropriate terms he is aptly sensitive to the social challenges the Christ-followers faced, as is Ernest Best, who regards Ephesians as an encouragement for the corporate maturity of believers which includes distance from the pagan world and commitment to the body of believers demonstrated by correct values and behaviours (1998: 74).[10]

In addition to works that engage with Ephesians' social influence on a surface level, Margaret MacDonald's commentary on Colossians and Ephesians offers a theoretically informed social-scientific study of the letter (2000) as does Daniel Darko in his study of the social function of Ephesians' *Haustafel* (2008). MacDonald suggests that Ephesians constructs a strong sectarian response to a post-Pauline situation where a community faced an increased threat of deviance and proposes that the identity discourse is designed to strengthen the group (2000: 21). MacDonald discusses different key components of identity, such as chosenness and ritual characteristics of the community; institutionalization of traditions and sectarian response to the surrounding social world; increasing social distance and erecting boundaries; and internal communal norms that reinforce acceptable behaviour by promoting peace, love and unity. It might appear that little is left for others to add. Nevertheless, I believe that different theoretical frameworks in this reading will open new avenues for exposition in dialogue with MacDonald and previous Ephesians' scholarship.

MacDonald suggests that Ephesians offers the fullest New Testament (NT) treatment of Christian identity (2000: 22). She reads the letter as a Deutero-Pauline text, which transfers Pauline legacy to a new generation (2000: 3). Although she does not want to be pinned down as an advocate for one specific purpose, it is probably fair to condense her discussion on Ephesians' goals to that of strengthening the community (2000: 20, 21). She argues that at the time of the writing of Ephesians, the Pauline churches had a fairly 'hardened' symbolic universe, which was adapted to the needs of a 'third generation' community by recalling the formative beginnings to address threats of deviance and growing integration with the surrounding social environment (2000: 208). This, according to MacDonald, includes ritual use of hymns to reinforce the sense of true identity, solidifying communal beliefs and values using images of

10   I use 'Christ-followers' for inhabitants of the text who identified the Palestinian Jesus with Israel's promised Messiah and allowed this belief to become socially significant, at least to the extent that it led to networking with the likeminded, who share in this identification. This, however, does not imply the divinity of Christ or exclusion of other beliefs or deities by default.

predestination and chosenness, baptism and sealing with the Holy Spirit in 1.3–14 (2000: 212). MacDonald assumes that the community experienced hostility in its social environment. For instance, she suggests the identification with Christ in 1.15–23 relativizes 'the experience of alienation and opposition that inevitably accompanies separation from a world dominated by evil' (2000: 226). This explains why Ephesians uses symbolic language and provides the community with reassurance from the belief that ultimately they belong to a heavenly assembly (2000: 226–7)[11]

MacDonald's reading of Ephesians comes with a well-informed discussion of the socio-historical context of early Christianities. However, this reading challenges her tendency to stress socio-historical causality of circumstances upon the text by accentuating the socio-ideological motivations of the writer.[12] I will proceed to argue that beliefs, values and norms are key components of identity and consequently there is no need to reconstruct particular socio-historical causes if the text does not explicitly discuss such factors. Instead, the distinctiveness of the Christ-following movement in itself was a sufficient cause to prompt the writing and offer the community further legitimation and socio-ideological guidance. For instance, while MacDonald correctly acknowledges the vulnerability of early Christ-followers and discusses the importance of a protective Jewish[13]

11　The same method of historical reconstruction of Ephesians' socio-religious context continues in M.Y. MacDonald's article, 'Politics of Identity in Ephesians' (2004). She argues that Ephesians 2.11-22 is best understood as reflecting the fate of the Jewish people under Domitian at the end of the first century CE, building an alternative society using architectural, military and familial images in order to appeal to and subvert imperial institutions with references to ultimate realities represented by Christ and the heavenly realm.

12　Although ideology is a part of, not separate from, what is 'social' I also use the term socio-ideological to stress the importance of the ideological values in the construction of Ephesians' social positioning and orientations, similarly to the emphatic use of socio-historical, socio-geographic and socio-economic.

13　I use 'Jewish' as an adjectival cultural definition that highlights diverse beliefs and practices that spring from the Hebrew Bible, despite Esler's discussion that promotes the term 'Judean' (Esler 2003: 64–71; cf. Campbell 2006: 3–10). I follow Nanos (2002: 20–1, n.6) and Cohen (1999: 69–106) who conclude that there is sufficient evidence that the term was used in the first century for 'religious life', despite difficulties of such categorization. It was used for specific practices and cultural performances, beyond the ethnic meaning of 'Judean', because certain ideological beliefs (or religion) and consequent praxis were also adapted by others beyond 'Judean' location or Israelite ethnic origin. 'Jewish' is used here in connection with 'Jewishness', which is an equivalent noun used for the formative identifications that are connected with the Hebrew Bible and the observance of Mosaic Law, despite a variation in their interpretation within different groups. I use 'Israel' and 'Israelite' to refer to ethnic Judeans and their descendants dispersed into different locations, who identify with a specific deity and his covenant with a specific ethnic group as in Deut. 6.4-9. I follow Anderson (1991), in taking such ethnic bond as 'imagined' rather than verified by people who perceive themselves as part of the same ethnic group for various reasons. For discussion of 'essential

umbrella for the group (2004),[14] one must ask if it is equally correct to conclude that the believers feel strongly threatened by external forces? (2000: 222–7; 257). Such reconstructive reasoning is fairly common in the social-scientific NT interpretation. Similarly, Philip Esler also assumes that the Deutero-Pauline language of Paul's imprisonment reflects external stress (2005b). He explains that imprisonment would have been part of the audience's experience, and a negative but powerful factor in their identity (2005b: 7). Although Esler correctly points to the bearing of harassment and persecution upon identity, it is beyond textual evidence to assume that this was part of communal life. Esler considers 'various types of harassment and persecution' echoed in Mark's Gospel, Acts and 1 Thessalonians (2005b: 7) which he then applies generally: 'harassment, persecution, imprisonment, trials and execution' were characteristic parts of the Deutero-Pauline era, and provided the background for imprisonment language (2005b: 17). In my view, the persecution setting may sometimes be a generic assumption rather than a specific feature addressed in a particular text in question.[15]

However, this is not to deny the relevance of the connection MacDonald and Esler draw between social circumstances and their bearing upon shaping group identity and social processes of a community. External pressure is a well-recognized factor in shaping communal identity, and often seen as the main catalyst for identity processes (Bauman 2001). So for instance Jeffrey Weeks, who argues that

> The strongest sense of community is in fact likely to come from those groups who find the premises of their collective existence threatened and who construct out of this a community of identity which provides a strong sense of resistance and empowerment. Seemingly unable to control the social relations in which they find themselves, people shrink the world to the size of their communities and act politically on that basis. The result, too often, is an obsessive particularism as a way of embracing or coping with contingency.[16]

Jewishness' and diversity of different Second Temple groups see e.g. Avery-Peck, Neusner and Chilton (2001); Grabbe (2000); Cohen (1989: 13–33; 1999) Trebilco (1991); Neusner (1987); Hakola (2005: 22–30; Jokiranta (2005: 39–52).

14   Darko dizagrees with MacDonald and suggests that hiding 'behind Jews' would have meant that the believers would have been 'ready to compromise their faith' and argues that MacDonald has not realized her hypothesis is 'contrary to what we know of the early church's attitude towards persecution' (Darko 2008: 14, n. 22). Darko seems to assume separation and strong sense of distinctiveness (uncompromising faith outside Jewish umbrella) contrary to MacDonald who assumes close ties with Jewish movements before 'the church' had developed faith that required separation. It should also be noted that Darko works with Pauline authorship and date (p. 25), which suggests he sees a very developed church very early in history.

15   See my response to Esler in the discussion of Ephesians 3.

16   Weeks (2000: 182, 240–3) as quoted in Bauman (2001: 100).

Therefore while MacDonald's and Esler's readings of Ephesians are sensitive to the persecution, its bearing on the letter may sometimes lack a specific textual base. In comparison with undisputed Paulines, Ephesians' lack of explicit contextual references makes it less useful for reconstruction of what the communal life may have been. Owing to the scant socio-historical 'data' in the letter, discussions of Ephesians' context tend to deal with the imagined milieu, that is, circumstances and socio-ideological currents we imagine to have been influential at the time.[17]

At its worst, the implicit reconstructive reading model can be rather uncritical: first, because vague textual components may lead to assumptions of specific circumstances, especially if such factors conform to one's idea of the 'general picture' of the NT Christianities; and secondly, because it may miss the possibility of influencing and reshaping social experience in and through the discourse by portraying social context in a particular way (to which I will return a little later).

Finally, Darko offers a recent example of theoretically informed analysis of Ephesians' identity discourse that combines traditional exegetical study with comparative analysis of Greco-Roman literature and insights from social identity theory in a discussion of the shaping of communal identity through ethical values.[18] Darko focuses on the rhetoric of differentiation between ingroupers and outgroupers in Ephesians 4.17–5.20 and on the social function of the household code in 5.21–6.9. His work offers a thorough exegesis of Ephesians and comparative analysis of Greco-Roman moral discourses from Greek, Roman and Jewish authors (cf. 2008: 13–19). Given Darko's conservative reading position, it would have been interesting to see closer interaction with Pauline scholarship reading Ephesians as Pauline. His work is characterized by the theological position that would have sometimes required further legitimation. For instance, who are the 'beloved children of God' and what about Israel as God's covenant people (cf. 2008: 104)? Darko speaks of 'the church' despite the fact that Paul is now widely regarded as faithful to his Jewishness and positioning him in the 'church' would have needed further substantiation.[19] Superimposing such loaded (and anachronistic) terms is

17 I use the term 'imagined' as meaning 'something as perceived, understood or believed to be', which does not exclude the possibility of verifiable classification as a true representation of something. 'Imagined' is used to stress interpretation that is always involved in the perception of reality, and underlining structures or presuppositions that lead us to 'imagine' things in a certain way.

18 Darko's work was published following the completion of my doctoral thesis and thus it does not feature in the dissertation, but offers its contribution to Ephesians' scholarship in this book.

19 Darko regards 'the church' as 'the macro "household of God"' (2008: 107). In my opinion, he views the 'household of God' through the lens of the Church, as he believes them to be 'Spirit-filled' believers in Christ.

more characteristic of Christian theological discourse than of social-scientific analysis of the early Christian identity.[20] This study is interested in the social influencing that began to shape minority views of certain Jews in the first century CE to such theological constructs, and amazed at the popularity these views gained among both Israelites and other ethnicities.

Ephesians' scholarship should engage with the relevant trends in Pauline scholarship. For instance, the 'New Perspective on Paul' is particularly relevant, given that it is essentially about issues of identity and culture and that it focuses upon the Jewishness of Paul and his role in negotiating inter- or intracommunal relations between early Christ-followers and other Israelites (Dunn 1982).[21] The most significant application of the 'New Perspective on Paul' to Ephesians is Tet-Lim Yee's reading of Ephesians entitled *Jews, Gentiles and Ethnic Reconciliation: Paul's Jewish Identity and Ephesians* (2005).[22] Yee deserves credit for exploring virtually unexplored territory as he draws upon the methodological insights of 'New Perspective on Paul' scholarship and highlights Ephesians' Jewish language.[23] He integrates reading Ephesians 2 with data on Jewish attitudes towards Gentiles[24] and argues that Ephesians is a thoroughly Jewish work which negotiates a new space for Gentiles in a relationship with Israel's God. Yee's detailed reading of Ephesians 2 in the light of other Jewish texts and New Perspective scholarship is commendable, but the key arguments of his work, the Jewishness of Ephesians, bringing in non-Israelites into Israel's *politeia*, and extending Israel's blessings to non-Israelites, are found in a rudimentary form in James Dunn's 1993 article (151–65).[25]

Despite its merits, Yee's work suffers from little theoretical basis for discussion of identity and ethnicity, as well as some lapses in critical

---

20   I have argued elsewhere that theoretical methods of the NT interpretation, such as social-scientific criticism, are often subservient to Christian theological presuppositions if we continue to ignore the diversity of the first-century context of the early Christ-movement and that its convictions about the Messiahship of Jesus and inclusion of non-Israelites were minority positions in the Jewish movement (Shkul 2008). This will be explored more fully throughout the study. For further dialogue with Darko's work, see Chapter 6.

21   Although I discuss what Jewish and Jewishness may involve, it is not my place to decide if something *is* Jewish, as I am an outsider to such complex cultural and ideological viewpoints and therefore cannot see myself as deciding what is Jewish and what may not be. Instead, I prefer to discuss how texts, values and beliefs compare with what I understand as essential Jewishness that involves upholding traditions of the Hebrew Bible, belief in divine (s)election and covenant, demonstrated by obedience to the Law of Moses.

22   For a more detailed discussion see the brief literature review for Ephesians 2 in the next chapter.

23   Less extensive studies on the topic include Weedman 2004.

24   Yee's preferred term that is retained here as indicative of his position.

25   Dunn was Yee's doctoral supervisor.

distance. The following three examples are indicative: first, while the title of the monograph refers to Paul's Jewish identity, Yee denies presupposing Pauline authorship for the Epistle (2005: 33). Nevertheless, the book reads as if Ephesians was assumed to be Pauline.[26] Secondly, Yee defines the author as a '(Christian) Jew, who never ceased to be a Jew' (2005: 33) but does not explain what '(Christian)' means; or how and when a Jew would cease to be a Jew. Thirdly, although the book focuses on ethnicity and inter-group relations, Yee does not engage in theoretical discussion at any significant length.[27] These limitations weaken his contribution to Deutero-Pauline studies and discussion of early Christianness[28] and its ethnic relations. Nevertheless, his monograph calls for a further discussion on identity and inter-group relations in Ephesians and disputed Paulines. This study responds to Yee by testing the author's Jewishness further.[29]

2. *Self-Positioning: Reading Ephesians as Social Entrepreneurship*

Given that Ephesians is ambiguous with regard its audience and its social setting, the text does not lend itself to social-scientific reconstruction of the community addressed. Instead, the theoretical framework is geared towards exploring Ephesians' constructions of identity and the social

26   Matters that one might expect to find in a Deutero-Pauline study of this topic, such as a discussion of the development of Pauline legacy, and evaluation of a post-Pauline socio-historical context and its bearing on early Christian identity, have not been given much discussion.

27   He explores intertextual resources in Jewish and Greco-Roman materials out of which he draws meaning into understanding Ephesians 2.11-22 as a community-enhancing text aimed at reducing social distance between different ethnicities.

28   I use 'Christianness' as an adjectival description of that identification of people and groups as Christ-followers, when Christ-followership is a socially formative core belief of such an individual or a group, despite their social location. In other words, Christianness is used to describe Christ-followership when that conviction becomes a primary identification that subjects all other cultural traditions and ideologies into re-evaluation. Consequently, I use Christianness to refer to a symbolic universe where 'Jesus Christ' is at the centre, and everything else is repositioned in the light of what this Messianic belief is understood to mean. It provides an analytical category to address those values and behaviours that were distinctive and later developed into Christianity. Furthermore, I regard titles of Jesus in the text as communal, subcultural designations in their original context. To highlight their subjective ideology I put them in inverted commas, such as 'Jesus Christ', 'Christ Jesus' and 'Saviour' when evaluating Ephesians' social entrepreneurship to remind myself and the reader that Jesus was seen as 'Christ' or 'Saviour' whether or not he was/is. Given that I explore social influencing in such an early stage of emerging Christianity I do not want to take these as 'agreed' titles, although they may be so for Christians. Instead, they would have been contested by many, negated by others and ignored by many at the time of the writing of Ephesians.

29   Yee's work provides an important conversation partner to the reading of Ephesians 2, where matters of identity, Jewishness and Christianness are discussed in more detail.

entrepreneurship of its author, that is, studying the way discursive positionings shape Christ-followership and explain its meanings in terms of communal values and group processes.[30] I propose that the full extent of Ephesians' social entrepreneurship – deliberate shaping of ideological beliefs and social orientations – can only be truly appreciated when we examine the letter as a whole, and how its different sections contribute to the same aim of shaping identity and social implications of Christ-followership.[31] Consequently, I use different social-scientific perspectives to examine how the social influencing is embedded in the text; how different parts of the letter contribute to the whole; and how the text asserts what Christ-followership means to the community.[32]

30 'Social entrepreneurship' is a relatively new concept, which typically refers to a business-like approach to addressing social problems and innovative solutions and projects to bring about beneficial social change. It has been embraced by business schools and universities as a robust way to combat social concerns, typically in socio-economic contexts. However, the terminology of entrepreneurship, such as 'identity entrepreneurship' and 'reputational entrepreneurship', has become well established in the social-scientific discourse and filtered into NT studies (cf. Esler 2003), including this one. I use the term social entrepreneurship to discuss different vehicles for social influencing, despite differences to its popular use and difficulties involved in using such a modern concept to describe something that we have only partial data from antiquity. The main difficulty with this phrase is not that the author of Ephesians may not have identified with today's social entrepreneurs' conscious approach to changing values and social circumstances, but that he did not share the activist stance towards social injustice of people in the ancient world, which typically characterizes today's social entrepreneurs' approach. Instead, Ephesians' writer is socially conservative, as readings of Ephesians 4–6 will discuss. For instance, Ephesians' moral discourse affirms slavery, which in my view is deeply unjust, exploitative and unlawful. Is it then fair to describe Ephesians' author as a social entrepreneur? This study will examine the extent of social influencing, mindful that this is ideological and cultural, rather than economically and structurally oriented.

31 However, the evaluation of Ephesians' social orientation in this study is selective and limited. I have deliberately concentrated on areas where my theoretical perspective will be most useful. I will also respond to some of the key works in recent scholarship that deal with Ephesians' socio-ideological contours and bring relevant themes from Pauline and early Christian studies to bear upon Ephesians' interpretation, particularly as Deutero-Pauline. This study will discuss 1) its identity construction using an eclectic theoretical framework and overarching model of social entrepreneurship; 2) reputations of Christ and Paul and the correlation between ideological and social, legitimation and remembering; and finally 3) communal social orientation expressed in prototypes and antitypes, discussing the negative consequences of ingroup self-enhancement in prejudiced stereotypes of outsiders. Although the readings will travel through the whole discourse, unfortunately some areas, like the household code and spiritual warfare, will be limited to a brief outline in the light of present theoretical frameworks.

32 Reading Ephesians uses a social-scientific theoretical framework to explore social and cultural dimensions of the text. For a discussion of the usefulness of the socio-scientific method among other forms of biblical criticisms, see John Elliott, who explores why social-scientific criticism might be useful (1995: 9–16); and surveys the history of the method (pp. 17–35); and outlines some of its presuppositions and procedures (pp. 36–59; 60–86). For

My reading position involves a number of assumptions that have risen from my research into Ephesians and literature on identity and group membership. Key approaches and theoretical frameworks must now be outlined in order to position the subsequent readings in the discursive landscape of social-scientific NT interpretation and the study of early Christianities. However, a more detailed theoretical discussion takes place in subsequent chapters, which explore how Ephesians builds its social entrepreneurship.

First, the concept of social entrepreneurship must be outlined briefly. To begin with, it is assumed that Ephesians engages in subjective reflections on the social life of early Christ-followers in a post-Pauline Greco-Roman context. However, the social circumstances, author's culture or that of the recipient group cannot be fully known from the letter, neither is it assumed that it would be objective in its stance towards social life or in the portrayal of early Christ-movement it addresses. The selectiveness of the author's treatment of social life suggests that he can be seen as an 'entrepreneur of identity', capable of providing individuals with a particular identity and bestowing that identity with meaning, purpose and value in the communal discourse (cf. Esler 2003: 38, 109). Further, the selectiveness of social reflection in the discourse means that the symbolic universe of the text should not be equated with the social universe of its embedded community. This would imply that ancient authors did not engage in world-shaping, but merely provided reactive responses to whatever the communities faced. It would also imply that every opposition and difficulty the text imagines had to be concrete and in the process of wrecking the community before the writer started to work. Instead, I would suggest that there was such a thing as early Christian social entrepreneurship, which involved deliberate shaping of beliefs and behaviours in the light of core values, as well as adapting communal discourse to evolving circumstances caused by external, material or economic forces.

The fact that Christ-followership was a minority position was sufficient enough to prompt writing of a legitimating discourse. First and foremost, reform movements and emerging groups require a discourse that explains the communality of the group and their difference from others and legitimates their distinctiveness as reasonable, correct and worthy of commitment.[33] Therefore, it was particularly in the beginning of

---

other discussions devoted to the discussion of the method and its impact, see Esler (1994); and Holmberg (1990); and for tracing the early Christian identity processes see, in particular, Lieu (2000; 2002a; 2002b; 2004).

33 My understanding of communal legitimation and social construction of the textual reality relies on Berger and Luckmann's classic work (1966: 110–46). My precursors in NT studies include e.g. Edward Adams, who explores how the construction of Pauline textual world provides compelling resources for communal discourse, aimed at transforming Christ-following communities to comprehensive social worlds 'providing structure and meaning for

Christianness, when the movement and its values and norms were in the process of formation, that ideological resources and guidance for identity negotiations had to be provided.[34] Otherwise the movement may have never got on its feet, and surely would not have emerged from the antiquity as a 'separate religion'. This assumption does not deny the fact that identity, its boundaries and group processes were undoubtedly negotiated within a diverse socio-ideological environment. But it stresses the need for socio-ideological resources and proposes that Ephesians constructs identity in the text in order to strengthen, shape and direct the movement.

In order to critically explore the socio-ideological manoeuvrings of the writer this study assumes key tenets of positioning theory. The theory highlights how social actors and textual characters are allocated certain value and roles in the discourse, which again is consequential for the communal life and social interaction (Harré and Van Langenhove 1999). Study of discourse positioning involves in Ephesians both positioning fictional characters in the text, and influencing social positioning of the recipient community in social interaction, while the former is seen as socio-ideologically designed to influence the latter. Ephesians' communal self-positioning involves naming and labelling, which derive from the way 'us' and 'others' are understood and constructed.[35] While naming may be imposed when a name or a label attached to the group may be contested, redefined or accepted by the group, it can also be self-ascribed (Lieu 2004: 239).

On one hand, naming 'others' involves a denial of their right to name and

---

every aspect of their lives' (Adams 2000: 245). This, he notes, was the initiation of Pauline world building, which continued long after the apostle provided its initial framework. This is exactly where I position Ephesians: utilizing and maintaining the Pauline construction of legitimating symbolic universe, whilst adapting it to a post-Pauline situation, continuing to build a compelling counter-reality that firmly grounds meanings of the Christ-event in the community and its members' consciousness.

34 I am mindful of James Crossley's critique of the tendency to overemphasize and defend theological/ideological aspects of the emergence of the movement, and he draws attention, fittingly, to social aspects of the movement's growth (Crossley 2006). Crossley does not deny the importance of ideology but downplays its importance over the broader socio-economic factors that attracted new members (p. 174). It is most likely that Christ-followership of non-Israelites resulted in tangible, socio-economic advantages. At the same time, the persuasion that strengthens their identification with the Christ-followers, and makes those communal networks attractive, is ideological, and cannot be overlooked in the discussion of emerging Christianities.

35 'Naming' and 'labelling' are here used interchangeably. Naming may be complimentary or injurious, negative or positive, depending on the perspective of identification. It is used in the service of both self-enhancement and fostering prejudice, and despite the common negative sentiment attached to labelling the process has both positive and negative potential. It is used both in self-descriptive identifications as well as categorization of others. It can be contested, rejected or adapted. Furthermore, even denigrating labels can be transformed into positive ones, rejecting negative associations and attaching positive notions instead.

define themselves (Pickering 2001: 73), which may be connected to silencing their voices in the discourse. For instance, Ephesians names the outsiders as 'nations' instead of making reference to actual groups and ethnicities. Consequently, naming seems to be used to silence and misrepresent 'others' in the discourse, which may lead to their biased treatment in the social discourse given that they are considered as social actors. However, on the other hand, as Butler has observed, 'in being called an injurious name, one is derogated and demeaned. But the name holds out another possibility as well: by being called a name, one is also, paradoxically, given a certain possibility of social existence' (1997: 2; cf. Pickering 2001: 73).

Positioning involves the process of the 'construction of the self through talk, particularly through "the discursive construction of personal stories that make a person's actions intelligible and relatively determinate as social acts and within which the members of the conversation have specific locations" [sic]' (Tan and Moghaddam 1999: 183). Names and labels carry inherent value judgments and social connotations, as well as rights and duties. Therefore it appears that the very act of naming is social and discursive positioning, which help us to analyse identifications and interpersonal attitudes. They also reveal how identities and group processes are negotiated (Tan and Moghaddam 1999: 178, 180). Naming and positioning are, therefore, among the basic social processes that bridge the identification, categorization and communal dialogue, facilitating further evaluation, discourse and other group processes. Consequently, names and labels have multiple functions in the social discourse. They provide tools for the powerful as well as for countercultural groups; they are descriptions that may be adapted in the service of majorities as well as minorities; official authorities, as well as minorities and reform movements. In this respect my reading follows Lieu, who focuses on the literary functions of labels as self-designation, examining how texts operate on different modes of categorization and redefinition (2004: 242, cf. 239–68).

The study of early Christianities can hardly avoid reference to contemporary terminology, concepts and theories that help us understand and conceptualize life in antiquity, but which are, at the same time, anachronistically superimposed onto the ancient world. The term religion, for instance, is habitually used in contemporary sociology to discuss specific aspects of social phenomena that relate to god(s) and their worship.[36] However, in antiquity what we today call religion was not recognized as a separate sphere of life, but its diverse expressions were

---

36 According to Elliott, 'religion' deals with 'attitude and behaviour that one is expected to display to those entities and forces which control one's existence and deity's various human representatives' (1995: 133).

part of identity, ethnicity,[37] geographical locations, as well as political regimes. Not only was religion a natural part of life, but what we now see as religious belief contributed perhaps more openly to social norms and cultural expressions, including ritual performances, both social and individual.[38] In this study religion is seen as a sub-category of ideology. Ideology carries the persuasive nature of religion: 'ideology is how the existing ensemble of social relations represents itself to individuals; it is the image a society gives of itself in order to perpetuate itself' (Nichols 1981, quoted in Cormack 1992: 9). Furthermore, ideology conveys selectivity and subjective motivation. It can even be seen as 'the production and dissemination of erroneous beliefs' whose inadequacies have social motivations (Lovell 1979 in Cormack 1992: 10). In a sense, ideology is the voice of the community represented by the writer, voicing those ideas, beliefs and values that are required for communal self-promotion on a competitive discursive field (Eagleton 1991: 28, 29). In the light of these definitions I use ideology for communal beliefs instead of theology, because beliefs about god(s) were interconnected with ethnicity and other socially formative beliefs.

This study does not focus on 'the sacred' or religion, but on the wider analysis of social, ideological and cultural aspects of the text. In other words, I take a cultural interest to matters of religion, following Beard, North and Price who regard religions as 'clusters of ideas, people and rituals, sharing some common identity across time and place' (1998: 249). Culture, in itself, is a socially shared way of life that includes a variety of factors, such as language, knowledge, beliefs, values, norms, sanctions, institutions, art, custom, traditions, interests and ideologies (Elliott 1995: 128). It is more than 'living expression' of a social life, but it links social experience and relations with meanings and feelings of the pleasure or displeasure we experience in them (Fiske 1982: 146). In other words, culture is the 'stuff' that makes communal belonging meaningful, and what separates those who share certain cultural similarity and those who are different (Barth 1969; Jenkins 2004: 22).

The socio-cultural approach in this study means that it may not prioritize matters of Christian theology. It is common that social-scientific NT scholars or socially informed readers distinguish between theology and the social, and insist on their equal importance (cf. Esler 1998: 40). So for instance, Atsuhiro Asano, who discusses the relationship between theology and sociological enquiry, raises a warning of placing too much

---

37 For a discussion of the importance of Judean ethnicity to religion see Campbell (2006a: 3–10; 2006b: 1, 17, n.2)

38 The religious messages of the biblical texts are inescapably historical as well as socially conditioned (Elliott 1995: 105). For a more detailed discussion on sociology and religion cf. Wilson (1982).

emphasis on either aspect. We must not, as Asano warns, ignore the social aspects of faith communities under 'theological reductionism', as this diminishes the importance of social phenomena in the interpretation of biblical texts, and categorizes reflections of social situations as religious dogma (2005: 17). Equally erroneous, he argues, is the reduction of theological text into purely social discourse (2005: 15–16). However, in my view, this is problematic. First, in what respect would the theological be any different from or gain a priority over other ideological beliefs?[39] Given that 'theological' is as anachronistic a term as 'religion', as it locates some elements of social dialogue into a separate sphere contrary to the ancient thought, why should one aspect of social life, that which deals with deities, worship and such like, be elevated into a position of priority from other aspects of social life? Perhaps for no other than 'theological reasons' that seek to maintain that which is 'sacred' as a distinct sphere of life, separate from other (purely) social influences. Secondly, would the priority of theology prevail in the discussion of other deities or for example neopaganism, or is it a priority for Christian theological matters?

Asano's stance seems to imply that 'social' and 'theological' are equally valid basic categories. This leads me to ask what about 'other faiths'?[40] Maybe we are more understanding towards the Abrahamic faiths, but how about Mormons, Jehovah's Witnesses, Hare Krishna devotees and their sacred texts, or neopagan groups? I have a suspicion that the legitimacy of other sacred texts and faith communities could easily be dismissed as purely social by many NT readers, given that 'we' tend to think that our faith is true and the others are not ... or even that 'other faiths' are social manipulation, imagined or erroneous.[41] Furthermore, if theological and social are basic categories, this would mean that humans are inevitably social and inevitably theological, which does not sound convincing given that there are plenty of humanists and atheists about.[42] Instead, faiths would appear to be matters resulting from e.g. particular ethnicity, socialization, experience and/or choice. In my view, prioritizing

39   See Crossley's critique of the use of the social sciences in NT scholarship (2006: 1–34, esp. 16).

40   The category 'other faiths' is often used with a meaning 'any other faiths but Christianity' which in itself is very interesting. For one thing, it does assume the plausible existence of one faith (Christianity) and others. However, the category of 'other faiths' is stereotypical and biased, as it denies differences between different faiths and points simply to their 'otherness' as they are not 'Christianity'.

41   This is inspired by Crossley's point that NT theologians/readers tend not to treat non-Christian religions with the same degree of openness. For instance, Crossley points to N. T. Wright's discussion on the resurrection (of Jesus), and questions why Wright regards some (other) resurrection narratives as fictitious, but NT texts are not subjected to scepticism (2006: 25).

42   Although some would dismiss them assuming that they have a 'God-shaped hole that only God can fill'.

(Christian) theology limits the discourse to the like-minded, which is unfitting for an academic disciple, particularly one self-categorized as social-scientific. In social-scientific work it is inappropriate to insist on principles that limit interaction with the wider cultural discourse, with adherents of different religions, humanists, atheists and the undecided or the disinterested.

Finally on the theological and theoretical approaches, one of the key benefits of the social-scientific perspective is that it allows a reader to penetrate into the discursive dynamics that have previously been unnoticed by scholarship approaching the texts as theology.[43] The theological approach to the NT falsely causes readers to imagine the authors of NT texts as 'saints' and/or 'theologians', whereas, in fact, they may be more appropriately seen as ideologically or socially motivated communal leaders.[44] Nevertheless, apart from a different self-positioning and choice of terms, my approach is similar to Esler's reading of Galatians, which assumes that theological aspects underline group processes. He explains Pauline theology as 'his understanding of God's plan for humanity and how his audience should align themselves with it' (1998: 39). This study shares Esler's basic assumption, but emphasizes that the text deals with what is said to be God's plan, which remains ultimately unknown to the recipients of the letter and to us. Furthermore, the discussion of what may be 'theological' to some is included in the evaluation of 'ideological', without any distinction, as the latter encompasses the former. Having said this, I have nothing against Christian proclamation or theology, as these serve important personal and social functions for believers both in the Church and academia.[45] However, this study reads Ephesians analysing ideological persuasion aimed at producing cultural similarity among members of a confessional community (cf. Boyarin 2004: 22).

It is also worth noting that although the theoretical perspectives used in this study have been formulated in the last few decades, it is assumed that similar social dynamics also characterized group belonging in antiquity. In my view, despite the chronological and cultural gap between texts and

---

43   There are, of course, scholars who discuss the NT from a non-theological perspective; literary, ideological, cultural, or other. This does not necessarily mean that the readings are not theological, as theological assumptions are often deeply rooted, as Crossley points out (2006). There are also theological critiques of the theological. So, for instance, Esler's 'communion and community' which sets out to challenge the way in which doctrines and theological principles have been extracted from the Scriptures, but his approach is no less theological, although it is more spiritual, encouraging us to view the NT writers as 'ancestors of faith' and exemplars (2005).

44   For the idea of veneration of biblical authors see Esler (2005: 196ff.).

45   Much of NT studies is of course self-enhancing Christian discourse, as I have argued previously (Shkul 2008; cf. Crossley 2006).

their twenty-first-century readers,[46] there is no need to assume that the NT authors and their texts would have been unaffected by what are now seen as cognitive, evaluative and emotional dimensions of intergroup relations (Tajfel 1978: 28; Esler 1998: 42–3, followed by Darko 2008), especially when text(s) like Ephesians display an explicit interest in group dynamics. At the same time, early Christians represented vastly different times and worldviews and it should not be assumed that they behaved exactly like the individuals in modern socio-scientific studies. However, in my opinion, the use of theoretical insights is justified: given that the NT authors, like that of Ephesians, seem to get involved in what we now classify as group processes, social-scientific perspective provides useful heuristic tools for exploring such discourses, their communal dynamics and potential social influencing.

Despite the fact that early Christian communities were largely illiterate they are likened in this study to 'textual communities', assuming that texts were socially formative for them.[47] There is considerable evidence to suggest that texts and their communal reading had important social functions for early Christians. In my view, this is an example of cultural transmission in and through the Jewish founders of the movement. For instance, Lieu asserts that texts were central to the shaping of Jewish identity within the Greco-Roman world (2004: 28–36). She outlines a number of textual means of 'world making' which include a) observing political history from a critical viewpoint, as *Maccabeans* does; b) the use of interpretation of earlier formative texts to conform to communal identity, as in *Pesher*; and c) experimenting with new literary styles, as, for instance, a dialogue of identity, as Joseph and Aseneth does (Lieu 2004: 34–35). Such evidence leads Lieu to argue that the rise of literacy and its democratization were crucial to the rise of Jewish movements and the

46 See Esler for the discussion of the 'past as ontologically alien' and negotiating cultural distance in order to increase intercultural understanding and communication of the biblical texts (2005a: 81–7).

47 The fact that the ancient world was predominantly illiterate does not reduce this assumption, but actually highlights the social power embedded in being in possession of texts, particularly if such texts, like Ephesians, claim to disclose divine truth for the community. The concept of early Christian groups as textual communities draws on Lieu's work (1996: 11–13; 2004). See, for example, the discussion on 'Text and Identity' (Lieu 2004: 27–61) and 'Texts and Communities' in the latter (2004: 300–302). It is correct, as Lieu observes, that the texts may have been resisted and there were those whose voices were silenced in the texts, as well as those who were implied as opponents (p. 301). Those whose identity and values were challenged have little hope but to conform or experience social distancing by the members of the ingroup if they internalized the text. 'Others' might have contested the values and propositions of the texts and chosen association with groups that represented their convictions and interests more closely. Thus NT writers' communal language and occasional uncompromising stance may have cultivated both ingroup orientation as well as diversity of adverse reactions.

intensification of identity from the mid second century BCE (2004: 36). Furthermore, it is clear that it was this 'biblically shaped literary culture' that gave birth to the literature of the Jesus movement and provided a basis for a communal legitimation and identity discourse as Jewish Christ-followers adopted, interpreted and expanded the corpus of Jewish Scriptures (Lieu 2004: 36, 37).[48]

However, the relationships between texts and social lives are multi-faceted and few explanatory notes on interrelated assumptions held in this reading are due. First, it is commonly acknowledged in contemporary NT scholarship that *texts did not float free from social experience.*[49] They are not 'autonomous literary worlds' drifting aimlessly upon the seas of Greco-Roman literature, disinterested in the social setting, social coun-terparts and ideological disputes of the day (Esler 1994: 18).[50] Although I view Ephesians as a deliberate creation, social entrepreneurship, it is important to acknowledge that it originated in a dialogue with their writers' social world, and their positive and negative experiences of it (Countryman 2003: 27).

Secondly, early Christian texts both 'reflect and construct social experience' (Lieu 2004: 27). Lieu explains,

> Their embeddedness and social functions are paradigmatic; but these become alive as we discover the way that texts construct readers and 'reality' through acts of power, by silence and marginalization, as well as by unarticulated assumptions, by the values and hierarchies engendered and by the authoritative voice claimed. (2004: 25)

In other words, texts both 'shape and are shaped by' communal identity (Lieu 2004: 27), as on the one hand, their design and composition is influenced by the author's social position and choices, and, on the other

---

48   I follow Berger and Luckmann in their use of the term 'legitimation' and its cognate terms (Berger and Luckmann 1966).

49   The fallacy of abstracting Paul's theology from its rhetorical and social setting was exposed by Holmberg (1978), propagated by Wright (1991), and followed by, for example, Esler, who continues to challenge the problem of analysing NT texts as socially disinterested literary art forms and argues that they are grounded in the discourses of their day (1994: 17–18; see also 1998: 25–28). 'Theologically' (Esler) or ideologically, NT texts are involved in the Christological persuasion that Jesus is the Messiah of Israel; and socially, they functioned as tools for constructing symbolic canopies and institutions that would provide meaning and a sense of belonging to their members in communities for whom they were written (Esler 1994: 18). Dunn's recent work also emphasizes the experience of faith in Jesus as the key motivation for early Christian communities and subsequently, their traditions and texts (Dunn 2003; 2005), thus linking social experience and the texts.

50   For discussion of different 'worlds' see Raimo Hakola, who follows Kari Syreeni and Matti Myllykoski in distinguishing between the social, literary and historical words of the fourth Gospel and how they contribute to a self-understanding of the community (Hakola 2005: 33–7, 110, 172).

hand, textually re-imagined reality can become formative for the reading community. Consequently, the ideological filtering of the text can become part of the 'reality' for the next generation and formative for their interpretation of their social experiences (Lieu 1996: 12, 199). Texts reflect their authors' values and experiences; and, in turn, influence their readers' responses to social circumstances in the world they experience, as they see their identity and position within the parameters of the symbolic universe of the text, which may involve significant counter-cultural elements or resocialization.

Thirdly, the authors, communities and their worlds remain unknown and are mediated through the text: although the author is part of the context of the writing, the context is separate, removed from the text, and the text similarly removed from its context (Adam 2000: 11). The authors and their communities are partially preserved in their literature, as ultimately only texts have survived with their textual reflection of social life. It is relatively common to interpret early Christian texts in the light of their 'background' and to assume that the socio-historical 'data' of the time and location help to unlock the text. However, caution is required. So for instance Jokiranta, who attempts to correct the tendency to over-emphasize the use of extratextual materials in her discussion of Qumran *Serakhim* and *Pesharim*:

> The events 'behind' the texts are only a part of understanding the texts and their world. It is equally important to explore the literary (textual) world and its internal 'rules' (e.g. rhetorical devices; intertextuality; potential meanings; symbolic world), as well as the socio-cultural premises for understanding the context in which these texts work. (2005: 25)

However, whether we know the 'events behind the texts' at all, or have reliable material to illuminate, the text must always be critically assessed. Consequently, it is vitally important to distinguish between the social world and that of the world of the discourse, as William Countryman points out:

> The text is a complex human artefact that carries with it much of the cultural and historical complexity in which it originated. Neither side of this complexity can be understood if severed from the other. The cultural and social environment in which a text was written did not so much determine people's beliefs and responses as it determined a world of discourse: which subjects were deemed important, where conceptual and ideological shoes pinched certain groups and gave advantage to others, what vocabulary was considered essential to discussion of a topic and therefore what would be novel in that context, what assumptions would be broadly recognized and accepted and therefore perhaps also most vulnerable to challenge, reversal or rejection. Any

ancient text will conceivably have meant somewhat different things to
different readers, even when they shared a common cultural context.
(2003: 65)

In the study of early Christianities, and Ephesians in particular, both the
contexts from which the texts rose and the contexts of their readers remain
largely unknown. Although we have reasons to assume that early
Christian texts were socially formative, the influence of the text within
the interpretive community remains ultimately unknown to us. Thus I will
explore Ephesians' textual world (not social world of its context) where it
positions Christ-followers, and analyse those social relations which the
text engages with.[51]

It is important that early Christian texts are not likened to 'case studies'
for social-scientific research, because when trying to gaze at the literary
texts we are likely to see 'the world' as constructed by their authors (Lieu
2004: 24).[52] In other words, the social and ideological contours of the
discourse are indicative of what the community (*ekklēsia*) meant to its
writer.[53] Although the text gives us access to the author's construction of
communal culture, its values and social relations, it does not give us access
to the mind of the author.[54] All we have is a discourse where identities,
values and social conflicts are ideologically positioned, whether or not
they reflect the positions of early Christian communities outside the text.
Instead, the community addressed in Ephesians is positioned in a fictive,
discursive location that should not be equated with the social context of
the (unknown) early Christian group in Ephesus, or thereabouts.[55] In

---

51   The interpretive history of the text and its use within particular faith communities
would also be an interesting exercise. However, a further study of Ephesians' use in social
influencing would require its own project.

52   Similarly Asano, who focuses on Paul's 'peculiar rhetoric [in Galatians] ... as a
representative of his own perspective' (2005: 25).

53   Anthony Cohen's *Symbolic Construction of the Community* argues that communities
can be best understood by focusing on their culture, what they feel that they have in
common, rather than communal structures (1985: 20). For the present purposes this means
assessing what is important to the writer. Its constructions of identity are likely to reflect
what Cohen describes as 'common interests' in a varied social playground (1985: 13).

54   The issue of authorial intention and its relation to social life will be developed further
in subsequent chapters.

55   The social location of the community is seen as 'fictive' as it reflects what is imagined
and perceived as significant, which does not necessarily reflect the actual social environs,
associations or power relations (cf. Cormack 1992: 88–97; Iser 1989: 270–5). For instance, the
treatment of ethno-religious conflict in Ephesians 2.11-22 suggests that the community
experienced hostility from Jewish communities or individuals. However, the text makes no
reference to interaction with Jewish groupings and it may be that the communal positioning
was designed to introduce selected key components the author required to validate the
community, without necessarily responding to social conflicts in his historical setting or that
of his audience.

other words, although Ephesians is an ideologically charged and socially interested literature, it should not be regarded as data for socio-historical reconstruction.

Hence literary texts should not be taken as mirroring external reality or the life of early Christians (cf. Barclay 1987). Instead, as Lieu suggests, the image (text) and the reality (surrounding the author) are both inaccessible without interpretation, but always subject to ideological colouring and subjectivity (1996: 2). For one thing, the reality is always a subjective experience depending on one's social positioning, and furthermore, this is re-presented, re-packaged and re-imaged in the text.[56] This echoes literary critical discussion of what the text does as well as to what it says (Iser 1993: 6). According to Wolfgang Iser, a text presents its author's reactions to and attitudes towards his social world; and these in turn constitute the world of a literary text (1989: 7). Further, the way the author has combined, modified and prioritized the representation of factors in the social world may illustrate intentionality of the text (Iser 1993: 6). However, this assumes that the author's social world is known or comparative sources exist. If so, it is useful to consider authorial selection from a variety of social, historical, cultural and literary systems, asking what factors receive focus and what kind of functions they have in the text to which they have been incorporated (Iser 1993: 5). Although limited specific data on Ephesians' author's world restricts the possibilities of exploring intentionality of authorial selection, the following broad cultural components may be useful points of reference: 1) meanings drawn from the Christ-event, 2) Hebrew traditions, and 3) the Greco-Roman world. I will consider how these are represented and repositioned in the text, and what functions reimagining social relations has in the discourse.[57]

The relationship between authorial intent and textual world-making features in Adams' examination of Pauline literary worlds, which differ from one letter to another (2000). For example, in Romans Paul constructs a world of conservative social ethos that endorses the existing socio-political order, appropriates the values of the wider society and promotes a universal view of salvation (2000: 220). However, 1 Corinthians uses *kosmos* as a negative term which challenges the dominant worldview outside the community, depicting *kosmos* as a hostile place destined for divine judgment and destruction (2000: 148).

---

56 Magnus Zetterholm also combines the examination of the social with literary-critical insights. He draws from Berger and Luckmann's 'social construction of reality', social-scientific theories and comparative material from antiquity, analysing how texts create meaning and what kind of a role readers play in the construction of meaning (Zetterholm 2003: 8–15, esp.13).

57 These three categories are by no means mutually exclusive, but have distinctive elements that illustrate cultural positioning of the Christ-followers in the text.

Consequently, salvation implies being rescued from the world, the construction of a distinctive counter-society and building strong communal boundaries to protect its distinctiveness (2000: 148, 149). Galatians also has spatio-temporal dualism that constructs opposition and 'new creation' identity; although the opposition is not towards society at large, but towards subcultural Jewishness, which exercised particular influence in the community (2000: 231). Finally, 2 Corinthians develops new referential worlds, like *sarx* and *kata sarka* (2000: 237). Adams' analysis demonstrates that words may carry different meanings in different texts and contexts and therefore their meaning must not simply be assumed from other contexts.[58] This is particularly important for Ephesians' (and other Deutero-Pauline) scholarship which all too often harmonize Ephesians (and other disputed letters) with the undisputed Paulines. Instead, it is important to analyse if Ephesians' textual world offers any significant adaptation of Pauline world-making and negotiation of Jewish and non-Israelite cultures.

Having outlined my reading position, I will now reflect on selected themes from Ephesians 1 from a social identity perspective in order to lay the foundations for the social-scientific readings which will be developed in the following chapters.[59] Social identity theory (SIT) highlights the importance of social context and sense of belonging to an individual's identity and focuses on social identification (us) and categorization (others), which characterizes Ephesians throughout the letter. However, in my view it needs to be supplemented by more detailed theoretical considerations in order to fully appreciate the contours of the discourse.[60] The following discussion of Ephesians 1 has been condensed to establish 1) key premises upon which social entrepreneurship is based and other theories and readings expanded upon and 2) to outline the magnitude of Jewish culture and traditions for the discourse.[61]

58   I will return to this point in the discussion of reforms on Jewish language and symbolic universe in Chapter 3.

59   Regrettably, the scope of the discussion does not allow for a detailed exegetical study. At the same time, such detailed treatment would quite possibly be more repetitive and less original, as thorough commentaries, such as Best (1998); Lincoln (1990); and Hoehner (2002), specialize in exploring exegetical details, as does Yee in reading Ephesians 2 (2005) and Darko in 4.17–6.9 (2008).

60   This is characteristic of Jenkins' approach to identity, which supplements SIT with other theoretical considerations (2004).

61   More detailed theoretical discussions precede the readings of Ephesians in subsequent sections of this book.

3. *Reading Ephesians 1: Social Identity Approach to Construction of Identity in the Text*

'Social' identity is defined by Henri Tajfel as 'that part of an individual's self concept which derives from his knowledge of his membership of a social group (or groups) together with the value and emotional significance attached to that membership' (1978: 63). SIT assumes that *social* identity is about perceiving oneself as similar to certain people and groups, and dissimilar to others (Tajfel 1978).[62] The basic assumptions for the use of the social identity approach in this study include the following points (cf. Jenkins 2004: 89–90):

- 'Social identity' is about internalization of collective identifications. This typically involves not only a shared description of who one is but also the appropriate behaviour attached to who one is.
- Such identifications are often stereotypical and commonly exaggerate both the similarities within the ingroup, as well as their differences stressing the dissimilarity between the ingroup and outsiders.
- Social identity is maintained by stereotypes and 'cognitive simplification' that help to manage the complexity of social life by production of simplifying stereotypes that enhance identifications. This simplifies interplay of internal similarity and external difference, which again reinforces communal identifications and identity. Other group processes that spring from social identity include, for instance, discrimination against other people for the purposes of self-enhancement and bolstering collective self-esteem. Similarly, when identification is unattractive it triggers the desire to attain positive identification via processes of social mobility, assimilation, innovation or competition.

To summarize, SIT refers to a shared identification within a collectivity, together with others who are seen as similar in some significant sense, which simultaneously defines those who lack the essential characteristic(s) or behaviour, who are therefore categorized as others or outsiders.[63]

---

62   This assumption has become so established that identity is often understood as social, by definition. So, for example, Jenkins, who argues that when identity is perceived as social, inseparable of its social context, the precursor 'social' becomes redundant (2004: 4). I follow Jenkins, assuming that even when individual and particular identity is in view it still remains social, under influences of its particular social location (unless a socially isolated person is in view).

63   Along with Jenkins, other significant social identity theorists consulted in this study include Robinson (1996); and Brown (2000). Robinson's volume contains essays from Tajfel's students and followers, and it offers more contemporary reflections on identity, group belonging, as well as on intragroup and intergroup processes. Rupert Brown contributes to the understanding of group membership and relationships within and between

Defining 'us' necessarily involves defining 'them', just as *in*clusion entails *ex*clusion (Jenkins 2004: 79). Consequently, this leads into a self-enhancing social process, which has both internal and external aspects, intra- and intercommunal dimensions.[64] Such social processes involve different levels of social influences as identity is in dialogue not only with its general social context, such as Greco-Roman antiquity, but it is nested within a particular subcultural context, such as social classes, networks and communities.[65]

The basic processes characteristic of SIT are evident in Ephesians. First, the community is understood as 'a group of people that have something significant in common; which distinguishes them from members of other putative groups' (Cohen 1985: 12). In Ephesians the community (or its writer) celebrates Christ-followership as the primary communal self-identification that defines people into 'us' and 'others' and thus provides them with distinctiveness and communality.[66] This is established in the letter opening which celebrates blessings and benefits that Christ-followership involves (1.3–14, see below). While the undisputed Paulines seem to use the formula of initial thanksgiving to introduce the main themes of the letter (Kitchen 1994: 52),[67] Ephesians does not relate the congratulatory address to the socio-historical setting of the embedded community. Instead, it opens with spiritual or symbolic language that celebrates relation with God(s) (Perkins 1997: 36):

---

groups, dealing with a rather comprehensive range of group membership ranging from group dynamics, its social processes, exercise of social influence within and between groups to group conflicts and collective dimensions of collective belonging. Jenkins inspires the eclectic method adapted in this study as his treatment of social identity discusses a variety of aspects of collective identification ranging from categorization of others to construction of boundaries, symbolic meanings of the community embedded in the social discourse, social predictability and institutionalization. For use of social-identity approach in understanding early Jewish and Christian movements, see for instance, Esler (1998: 40–57; 2003: 19–39); Lieu (2004: 98–108); Asano (2005: 52–3); Hakola (2005: 31–40); Jokiranta (2005: 16–20; cf. 276–84) and Luomanen, Pyysiäinen and Uro (2007).

64   For further discussion on self-enhancement see readings of Ephesians 4–6 in Chapter 6 below. For the importance of awareness of the other and external difference for identification see Jenkins, who maintains that ingroup identification and outgroup awareness are inseparable, basic components of identity (Jenkins 2004: 79–93).

65   As previously explained, in this reading the focus is on communal discourse, not on reconstructing the community, but on how the writer addresses them and seeks to shape their identity and social orientation.

66   This is then developed into the categorization of outsiders in subsequent chapters of the letter, where 'others' is a category used to exemplify what is central to identity, as the following readings of Ephesians proceed to argue.

67   This replaces a congratulatory address in Greco-Roman letters with a description of spiritual beliefs and benefits. See, for example, Rom. 1.8-15; Phil. 1.3-11; and also Col. 1.3-8 and 2 Cor. 1.3-11.

[1.3] Blessed be the God and Father of our Lord Jesus Christ, who has blessed us in Christ with every spiritual blessing in the heavenly places, [4] just as he chose us in Christ before the foundation of the world to be holy and blameless before him in love, [5] He destined us for adoption as his children through Jesus Christ, according to the good pleasure of his will, [6] To the praise of his glorious grace that he freely bestowed on us in the Beloved. [7] In him we have redemption through his blood, the forgiveness of our trespasses, according to the riches of his grace [8] that he lavished on us. With all the wisdom and insight [9] he has made known to us the mystery of his will, according to his good pleasure that he set forth in Christ, [10] as a plan for the fullness of time, to gather up all things in him, things in heaven and things on earth. [11] In Christ we have obtained an inheritance, having been destined according to the purpose of him who accomplishes all things according to his counsel and will, [12] so that we, who were the first to set out hope on Christ, might live for the praise of his glory. [13] In him you also, when you had heard the word of truth, the gospel of your salvation, and had believed in him, were marked with the seal of the promised Holy Spirit; [14] this is the pledge of our inheritance toward redemption as God's own people, to the praise of his glory.[68]

First, it is notable that imagining the community in the spiritual/symbolic world provides legitimating and ideological resources, cognitive, evaluative and emotional resources for social identification (cf. Tajfel 1978: 28), as well as cultural models. The discourse loads the references to 'saints' with communally meaningful descriptors.[69] For instance, the group is imagined as capable of experiencing divine spheres because the blessed Father 'has blessed them with every spiritual blessing in the heavenly places' (1.3).[70] The discourse implies that praise is the appropriate response to advantages bestowed, which cements the relationship between a powerful individual (here, God) and his beneficiaries (Perkins 1997: 36).[71] The experience of salvation is transformed into ideological

---

68   NT quotations are from NRSV, unless otherwise indicated.

69   It is important to bear in mind that terms and phrases receive their meaning in the communal discourse which loads them with intra-communal meaning, which may be independent of their use elsewhere (Cohen 1985: 74).

70   The identity and status of the members is articulated as certain as God's works are, until the writer adapts a more demanding voice in the second half of the letter, as I will explore in my reading of 4.17–5.20.

71   This has parallels with the Roman imperial rhetoric that celebrates the benefits brought by the empire, which also links citizenship with beneficiary status and recommends a reorientation embracing this relationship with gratitude. Such discourse is important in the identity construction, as a community that 'hears praises of its imperial – or, in this case divine – benefactor, of the peace and well-being that a benefactor's gracious use of power has bestowed on it, that community also comes to know itself in relationship to the benefactor' (Perkins 1997: 16).

resources by interweaving images of a beneficent God and 'Christ', with the glorious destiny of the believers. For instance, the believers are told that they have a divine purpose and destiny which was planned before the 'foundations of the world', when God chose believers 'in Christ', so that they would be 'holy and blameless in his sight' (1.4).[72] They have been 'sealed with the Holy Spirit' which serves as a spiritual guarantee of their identity, destiny and status (1.13; 4.30).[73]

I take the lack of specific reference to the life of the community or its members to indicate the letter is socially formative, rather than reflective or reactive.[74] For instance, the opening chapter describes their spiritual experience and beliefs, and it is much later in the discourse when we can

72   The sovereign purpose of God in choosing his people is a key idea in the Hebrew Bible (e.g. Deut. 7.6-8; 14.2), but it receives a Deutero-Pauline development in Ephesians (cf. Gal. 4.4-7; Rom. 8.15-23). For instance, Galatians 3 positions Christ as the seed of Abraham par excellence, taking over Israel's role as God's chosen and non-Israelites receive their position in him (Lincoln 1990: 23). Here, somewhat more directly, the non-Israelites are depicted as chosen and adopted, on the same Christological basis, but without typical Pauline theological reasoning as to how this takes place, and how this is justified in the light of Israel's chosenness and God's faithfulness to her. Perkins outlines Ephesians' similarities with the thought of the Dead Sea Scrolls, which similarly celebrate God's eternal plans to redeem humanity (CD 2.7; 1 QS 1.10-11, cf. Rom. 8.29-30) and that God's people walk the paths of righteousness that God has established for them and revealed to his faithful (Perkins 1997: 38, 40–1). However, here one of Ephesians' key differences with Jewish texts surfaces: Ephesians puts strong emphasis on non-Israelite participation in the status predominantly reserved for the children of Israel in other texts. This will be explored further in the course of the book.

73   Similar expression is found in 2 Cor. 1.21-22, which could reflect an early Christian conviction that the followers of Israel's Messiah experienced the fulfilment of Hebrew prophecy in their generous experience of the Spirit of God (Ezek. 36.26-27; 37.14; Joel 2.28-30). This seems to be a part of Ephesians' thought of fulfilment of things 'in Christ' alongside with the shift from Israelite to multi-ethnic community of God's people in him. In later Christian texts sealing is explicitly associated with baptism, as in some Dead Sea Scrolls (Perkins 1997: 43).

74   An argument to which I shall return in critique of reconstructive mirror-readings. The location of the believers 'in Ephesus' in the opening verse is textually dubious due to the uncertainty of the geographic pointer 'in Ephesus' in the most reliable ancient manuscripts. For a discussion of textual variants see for instance Best (1998: 98–101); Schnackenburg 1991: pp. 40–1), and especially Lincoln (1990: 1–4); and Hoehner (2002: 44–148). The uncertainty of geographic and social location 'in Ephesus' is less significant in readings that prioritize the text itself; but it does have its bearing on the possible reconstruction of the audience. The textual variants make the location of the community in Ephesus uncertain, which in turn, reduces the discussion of similarities between the text and the late first-century Ephesus into speculation (cf. Perkins 1997: 27–8). This, however, does not hinder Hoehner, who despite examining the matter with great care and detail nevertheless incorporates other NT data on Ephesus into his interpretation of the letter (Hoehner 2002: 78–97; 144–8). Kreitzer typifies a reader, who is weary of the Ephesus location, but nevertheless requires a hypothesis that positions the letter in a specific location, Hierapolis, assuming a network of churches (Kreitzer 1994: 30–48).

glean anything about their social persona. Even when some description occurs it is mere acknowledgement that they are 'non-Israelites' (2.11, 3.1). Instead, it is formative for the identity entrepreneurship that they are 'saints and believers in Christ Jesus' (1.1).[75] Thus the discourse is set in motion by the key communal identification: belief in 'Christ Jesus'. It is fundamental for Ephesians that its construction of identity is social: a shared identification between those who believe (1.1, 12, 13, 15). Although Ephesians virtually ignores communal activities, such as discussion of meetings or rituals, Christ-followership is nevertheless fostered within a community, as God's chosen people.[76]

It is also characteristic of Ephesians' social entrepreneurship to simplify social life in the text for communal purposes. Although identity is seen by contemporary theorists as fluid and negotiable, it is presented in Ephesians as a non-negotiable essence of those who have been divinely chosen and transformed by 'Christ'. This is achieved by using stereotypes, which are 'condensed symbols of collective identification' (Jenkins 2004: 128). For instance, members have been 'chosen in Christ' to be 'holy and blameless' (1.4), to live for God's glory (1.6). These positive ingroup stereotypes become resources for ingroup orientation 'involving the creation and maintenance of group values and ideologies and the positive valorisation of the ingroup' (Jenkins 2004: 128). In addition to positive ingroup symbols, stereotyping is used in constructing stigmatized identity of the outsiders using negative stereotypes (Jenkins 2004: 76). Ephesians uses two-dimensional stereotypes that accentuate positive features of being 'God's people' and accentuate the negative aspects of 'the nations' separation from him (e.g. 2.1-2, 11-12; 4.17-19, cf. 5.5-9).

The relationship of the believers and 'Christ' is depicted as fundamental for the life of the community. Ephesians' portrayal of their relationship makes a complementary contribution to the canonical Paul's gospel of the crucified and risen Christ (Lincoln 1990: xcvii). Indeed, the Deutero-Pauline perspective stresses the present incorporation of believers 'into Christ': the community is empowered with the same spirit God used to raise Jesus back to life (1.19-22); it is his body and fullness (1.23; 5.30), whom he nourishes and cares for (5.25-30) so that it would be transformed to reflect its divine head (4.15-16). Because believers are seen as Christ's body, it is not surprising that they are exalted in the heavenly places, too (2.5-6); although this imagination exceeds NT parallels that typically

75 The popular adjectival translation 'saints [who are] faithful', preferred by most commentators, little changes the meaning of the description, as the stress is on the congratulatory address, celebrating holiness and faith of the believers in Christ: those who are set apart for God in Christ Jesus, their Saviour. For the discussion of linguistic grounds for the above translation see Best (1998: 101) and Hoehner (2002: 141–3).
76 A theme which is developed through the letter.

envision experiencing heaven as an eschatological event fulfilled in the future.[77] In contrast, in the Revelation the Exalted 'Christ' promises: 'to the one who conquers I will give a place with me on my throne, just as I myself conquered and sat down with my Father on his throne' (3.21). Meanwhile, although Ephesians mentions an ethical challenge (4.17–5.20) and an ongoing spiritual battle (6.10-20), there is no uncertainty about believers' status, as the text celebrates the seating of the non-Israelite Christ-followers in God's presence. Ephesians' self-enhancing discourse involves the use of *sun*-compound words in the original Greek text (meaning 'with' or 'together'), which contribute to the communality of primary identification and build 'togetherness'.[78] *Sun*-compounds occur repeatedly in key ideological beliefs and moments of rhetorical import-ance throughout the letter. They are used to highlight what the community has together and what separates them from outsiders, reflecting the internal-external dynamics of the SIT. First, *sun*-language is used to *reinforce the communal bond with 'Christ'*, in phrases like 'made alive with Christ' (*sunezōopoiēsen*), exalted together with him (*sunēgeiren*) and seated together with him (*sunekathisen*) in the 'heavenlies' (2.5-6).[79] Secondly, *sun-compounds also make essential connections between the*

---

77   For instance, Paul fixed his eyes on the forthcoming eschatological fullness (1 Cor. 15, esp. 40, 42, 47–55 for bodily transformation and an imperishable body); and referred to a visionary experience (2. Cor. 12.1-4). However, Ephesians does not mimic the genre of apocalyptic imagination. It does not describe the appearance of God, Christ, believers or the surroundings in the heavenly space. Neither does it adapt images of heavenly visions and dreams typical to contemporary apocalypses, or visually describe the heaven(s). The heavenly location is not a special privilege and no heavenly secrets are passed on to the readers (contra Revelation, cf. 2 Corinthians 12.1-4). For further discussion of parallels in biblical Hebrew traditions, Qumran, and other Jewish and Gnostic texts see Perkins (1997: 62); MacDonald (2000: 235); and Lincoln (1990: 105–109). There are also opposing spiritual powers in the heavenly realms (2.2; 6.12; cf. Lincoln 1981: 140–1).

78   Campbell points out in his discussion of these compounds in Ephesians 2 that these phrases make explicitly clear that identity is social, not individual (Campbell 2006b: 10–11).

79   For similar language in other Deutero-Pauline social entrepreneurship see e.g. Colossians 2.11-13 where *sun*-compounds are used to refer to key communal processes of initiation and communal boundaries, in the context of spiritual circumcision and the 'circumcision of Christ'. Colossians refers to being buried together in baptism, being raised together and made alive together with Christ. Togetherness therefore deals with both communal experience and spiritual experience with Christ; whereas in Ephesians the *sun*-compounds are used for social communality with the ingroup. MacDonald stresses the similarity between the two pseudo-Paulines but fails to convince with her suggestion that being made alive is 'clearly' a baptismal reference (MacDonald 2000: 231). Although similar passages in Colossians negotiates communal rituals, initiation and communal boundaries, Ephesians does not. Although being made alive in Colossians follows 'dying together with Christ in baptism' and clearly has a baptismal context, the same should not be assumed in Ephesians, where being made alive together follows spiritual death (2.1) which deals with non-Israelite sin, separation from God and slavery to other spirits. See Lincoln 1990: 93 for discussion on spiritual death and sin.

community members, who are 'fellow citizens together' (*sumpolitai*) (2.19).[80] This is also seen in the descriptions of ongoing transformations on being 'joined together' (*sunarmologoumenē*) and 'built together' (*sunoikodomeisthe*) into God's spiritual dwelling (2.19, 20, 21).[81] Ephesians returns to the idea of transformation in the prototypical discourse, which outlines growth towards communal maturity as an essential group goal, described as 'being joined together closely' (*sunarmologoumenon*) and 'being united' (*sumbibazomevov*) in order to reflect 'Christ', the head of the community body (4.16).[82] They are also a 'joined body' as well as partakers together in the promise of 'Christ' (*sugklēronoma*, *sussōma* and *summetocha* in 3.6). Thirdly, *sun-compounds are used to stress their difference from outsiders*, as the members are told to 'not associate with' (*summetochoi*) the disobedient (5.7), or participate in the works of darkness together with them (*sugkoinōneite*, 5.11).

Ephesians' world-making is a typical example of self-enhancing discourse that celebrates communal membership. The discourse would not necessarily make sense to, or appeal to, outsiders (cf. Cohen 1985), but it assumes ideological agreement (= faith). Such intra-communal meaning is seen, for example, in the description of spiritual blessings (1.3); exaltation of believers (2.6); participation in 'Christ's victory' and being his body, his fullness (1.18-23); the classification as God's people according to the seal of the Spirit (1.13-14); and possessing knowledge of the love of 'Christ' that is beyond human ability to perceive and

---

80 For the language of non-Israelite status transformation see Hoehner (2002: 390–6); Yee (2005: 190–228) and subsequent reading of Ephesians 2 in Chapter 3 below.

81 Kreitzer makes a fascinating connection between Solomon's temple dedication and Ephesians' new spiritual temple of united people (2003: 501–2). He concludes Ephesians 'turns to the traditional descriptions of Solomon as a Temple-building king who ruled over a unified people in order to stress his point about the need for unity within the congregation he addresses' (2003: 502; cf. Campbell 2006b: 4–5). Solomon's prayer makes explicit reference to the 'foreign' and other, which Campbell reads in support of his reading of Ephesians that encourages multiple identities to unite, despite their ethnic differences (similarly to Dunn 1983: 65, 95–122; Yee 2005). However, the 'foreigners' prayer' does not talk about their incorporation, let alone their equal status, or their exclusive commitment to Israel's God (2 Chron. 6.32–33), which are key concepts to Ephesians. So although the language is similar, its intentions and meanings seem to be significantly different. Therefore, this is another example where Ephesians re-imagines the way things are (Lieu 1996: 199), using Jewish language with communally motivated revisions.

82 Social identity theorists have also shown that communities often relate their identities to significant individuals as prototypes or exemplars, imagined or actual community members who typify the communal identity (Haslam 2001: 66). Their antitypes are the individuals who exemplify the outsider as culturally inappropriate. Both types are usually biased and exaggerated, and they often appear in paired stereotypes, positive or negative. Ephesians uses both prototypical and antitypical stereotypes to symbolize belonging or otherness, respectively. Although these concepts occur throughout Ephesians they are most prominently present in chs 4–6.

understand (3.18-19). These are communally important symbols that develop the sense of group membership (Tajfel 1978: 28). Not only is the construction of communal identity in 1.3-14 loaded with symbolic meanings, Christ-followership is also prototypically portrayed in terms of strong ingroup orientation, as recognition of their faith and communal love '*for all the saints*' (1.15) demonstrates.[83] The power of such discourse that recounts positive aspects of group membership is acknowledged in social-scientific literature, as it benefits both the member(s) and the survival of the group.[84]

In my view, it is significant that the writer associated himself (in Paul's persona) with the community, stressing their communal 'togetherness' and shared status. I take the language or 1.3-14 as inclusive terminology stressing that all members of the community benefit from the abundant resources of God's grace without ethnic division.[85] If 'we'-language is taken to refer to Israelites and 'you'-language to non-Israelites it would result in a comparison of Jewish Christ-followers' blessedness and inferior status of the non-Israelite members, given that the descriptions of blessedness tend to use 'we'-language. If ethnic distinction is assumed here one should also consider if this continues throughout the letter. If yes, we would then find the two subgroup discourse, akin to Romans but the

---

83   This short exclamation between the eulogy and the first apostolic prayer in chapter 1 confirms the imagined nature of societal building blocks: the writer has *heard* about the faith and warm expressions of an ingroup orientation; not witnessed them first-hand. Many readers of Ephesians have discussed the element of personal distance between the author and the community addressed. Other contributing factors include the lack of personal greetings typical to the apostle Paul, and lack of reference to specific communal circumstances or issues. This verse is a classical instance that divides scholars into those who feel the need to defend the apostolic authorship, and those who don't. For instance, Hoehner, who maintains the Pauline authorship of the letter, explains that some time had passed since the apostle's ministry in Ephesus, and therefore the report was not mere hearsay, but rather an update on their present status as reported to Paul (Hoehner 2002: 248; contra Lincoln 1990: lx, 54 and Patzia 1984: 163–4). MacDonald concludes that the above factors suggest that the letter had multiple audiences in view. She notes that in the light of the first-century Mediterranean culture the writer acknowledges their honourable behaviour and commends them in response (MacDonald 2000: 222). In my view, the commendation is probably based on historical observation of approved behaviour in the community addressed. But the congratulatory acknowledgement of their appropriate character probably had a compelling force, as it implies a challenge that ingroup orientation must prevail.

84   A community like a 'collective insurance against individually confronted uncertainties' (Bauman 2001: 16).

85   Contra those who argue that Ephesians 1 distinguishes between Paul and the community; 'we' referring to Israelite members of Christ-movement, and 'you' to its non-Israelite affiliates (Campbell 2006b: 5; Barth 1974: 130–3; MacDonald 2000: 203–4; Lincoln 1990: 37–8). Schnackenburg (1991: 63–4); Perkins (1997: 42–3); Best (1998: 146–8); and Hoehner (2002: 231–3) take the language as inclusive, and the distinction as rhetorical change of address that stresses the later inclusion of the audience into Christ-movement.

discourse would not be about shared identity at all as the discourse would continually stress the non-Israelites' inferior affiliation and their need for resocialization. This is, of course, possible and would be very interesting social entrepreneurship, in fact. However, I will dismiss it from now on as unlikely, and read Ephesians as communal discourse without assuming ethnic use of pronouns, on the grounds that Ephesians makes explicit reference to non-Israelites where comparison is due. Elsewhere I take the distinction to imply the relationship between communal founder(s) as 'we' and the group as 'you'.[86] Having outlined SIT approach to textual construction of identity in Ephesians 1 some further considerations on social entrepreneurship, its design and cultural implications are due.

Because Ephesians imagines the community of Christ-followers as God's chosen people this leads to their labelling as 'holy ones',[87] which is loaded with symbolic meanings and social connotations.[88] First, it establishes the appropriate cultic status before God and connection with 'Christ', thus creating a sense of collective identification.[89] The community members are holy because they are set apart by God (1.4-5) and made

86 Similarly, I do not believe that the 'we'-terminology would be a code for 'mother-church' either, although it clearly makes a distinction between Paul/the writer, his associates and the audience. Kreitzer reads Ephesians in light of his three-communities hypothesis, which is implied in the we/you distinction (Kreitzer 1997: esp. 31–48). He argues that Ephesians is a letter from the 'mother church' in Colossae to a 'daughter church' as for instance 'you' -language in 1.1, 2, 13, 15, 16, 17, 18; 2.1, 2, 5, 8, 11, 12, 13, 19, 22 indicates (1997: 41). The terms describing 'mother church' are those expressions in the first person typically related with 'Paul' or the writer. Kreitzer takes general identity descriptors as describing a network of churches in the Lycus Valley (1997: 41). He identifies verses that I regard as community self-enhancing descriptors as relating to the network of churches (cf. 1997: 41-7). His reading is quite plausible as it does not push the text into categories that appear hostile to the dialogue, but appreciates Ephesians' community enhancing language. However, the three-church hypothesis is difficult to justify from the text. The lack of explicit network language is particularly interesting especially in comparison with the discussion of early Christian associations in undisputed Paulines and Colossians (e.g. Rom. 15.24-26; 2 Cor. 8, 9; Gal. 1.22-24; 1 Thess. 1.6-10; cf. Col. 2.1; 4.15-17). Despite NT evidence for the fact that Pauline churches networked and shared resources, Kreitzer fails to convince, although his theory illustrates how tempting readers find the reconstructive readings.

87 The labels 'holy' and 'saint' are used interchangeably to translate Greek *hagios*, which is used as a communal characteristic in the text. See 1.1, 4, 15, 18; 5.3, 6.18; and also cf. 2.19; 3.8, 18 for the stereotypes for 'holy' community.

88 Naming and labelling are used synonymously, as both refer essentially to the same thing, creating a simple definition to express social identification. See, for instance Jenkins (2004: 72–6) for discussion of the theory, and Pietersen (2004) and Still (1999) for its use in the NT studies. Negative labelling will be discussed in connection with the intercommunal relations, in Chapters 5 and 6 below.

89 In comparison, 1 and 2 Corinthians, 1 and 2 Thessalonians and Galatians address 'communities' (*ekklēsia*). 'Holiness' is an essential description of the community and prototypical value in Paul. For instance, 1 Corinthians states the community is 'called (to be) holy' (1.2), and Romans addresses them as 'God's beloved who are (called to be) saints' (1.7).

holy by redemption 'in Christ' (1.4-7). It functions as a positive ingroup stereotype which repeatedly reinforces the beneficial relationship the audience has with God, for example, in the images of the household of God and as his spiritual temple (2.21); and in describing the community as 'the bride of Christ'; flawless in purity and perfection (5.27).[90] This has important communal aspects because labelling of 'holy ones' helps to define and position 'self' and 'others' for the purposes of discourse,[91] as it provides basic categories for the letter that builds on this identification providing guidance for social orientation (chs 4–6). It seems that being holy is a primary metaphor for the community, which becomes a societal label, which is expanded upon using positive descriptors and character-istics, and stressing their difference from 'outsiders' (cf. part 3).[92]

Secondly, the concept of holiness seems to be more than mere 'impression management strategy' (Jenkins 2004: 20) but the idea of holiness likens the community with Israel, as it resembles Israel's appointment as a holy nation in Exodus 19.6.[93] In my view, this demonstrates that the author positions the discussion of Christ-follower-ship in the Jewish symbolic universe. Ephesians draws on Jewish ideas of holiness as the fundamental characteristic of God's people and its counterpart, un-holiness of the nations and outsiders.[94] Furthermore, because Ephesians imagines that 'nations' are included among the people of God 'in Christ' (1.4-5; 2.19-22) it has to deal with the stereotype of non-Israelite sinfulness to legitimate their inclusion.[95]

Finally, Jenkins' distinction between nominal and virtual aspects of identity further explains the use of labels like 'the holy ones' in the communal rhetoric.[96] The nominal identification is about names while the virtual identification is what that identification comes to mean to its bearer (Jenkins 2004: 76–7). So, what really matters to communal life is the virtual identity and 'the difference it makes in individual lives'

---

90   The only exceptions are found in the description of the apostles (3.5) or the spirit (1.13; 4.30).

91   It is worth noting that naming results from either ingroup identification or categorization of outsiders. It opens up a discourse where meanings of names may be exemplified and expanded upon.

92   Cf. 1.15; 2.19; 3.8, 18; 4.12; 5.3; 6.18. Ephesians also uses 'all [the] saints' in 3.8, 18 and 6.18.

93   For the use of Israelite discourse of chosenness in modern constructions of nationhood, see Hastings (1997).

94   See, for instance, self-enhancing Israelite texts that stress their holiness as God's chosen people (e.g. Exod. 19.6, 31.13; Lev. 11.44-45; Deut. 7.6, 26.19, 28.9-10).

95   The 'People of God' is used as a conceptual model for the community in a benevolent relationship with God.

96   Ephesians exemplifies this with 'holy', 'uncircumcised' or the 'nations' as I will establish in the subsequent readings.

(Jenkins 2004: 77).[97] For example, communal holiness is a nominal identification which is later developed in different metaphors, projected as its appropriate virtual identifications. So, for example, the community is seen as a collective space of sacred worship that transcends worship in temples and shrines and they must be communally oriented and culturally distinct from the Greco-Roman world (2.19-22; 4.1-16, 4.17–5.20).[98]

In addition to adapting suitable cultural narratives for the purposes of the new community, Ephesians also engages in inventing traditions, for instance, the Messiahship of Jesus.[99] Ephesians' communal self-identification as God's chosen people 'in Christ' is neither ideologically nor socially as simple as it may appear to twenty-first-century readers. The discourse of identity builds on a highly contested claim that that Galilean Jesus was Israel's Messiah, despite his execution as an insurgent.[100] Nevertheless, Ephesians positions 'Jesus Christ' as the ideological core of communal identity, making him formative for communal membership, beliefs and values. First of all, it functions throughout the letter as a key feature of social identification that legitimates non-Israelite inclusion and enables non-Israelites to 'connect' with Israel's God and have legitimating 'spiritual' experiences and empowerment (1.13-14; 2.4-6; 5.18-20).[101] In addition, it is used to provide guidance for communal social orientation, as for example, communal solidarity is based on the Christ-event (2.11-22; 4.1-6, 13-16; 6.18, 23) which imposes certain ethical demands (4.1; 5.1), to which I will return later.[102]

97   For example, Ephesians 2.11-22 can be seen as responding to nominal identification and external labelling. The label of 'uncircumcised' demonstrates unfavourable categorization, while the passage seeks to provide new nominal and virtual identifications and remove any stigma of former labels. Elsewhere Ephesians uses both nominal and virtual identifiers to distance the community from antitypical outsiders.

98   Being God's dwelling implies a counter-cultural reversal of status as it was the socially powerful who were associated with impressive buildings and residences, and likens the community to priests and oracles associated with temples and shrines.

99   For theory on invented traditions see theory in Chapter 2, and readings of Ephesians chapters 2 and 3, in particular. Naturally, this does not mean that the concept was literally invented by the Deutero-Pauline writer, but he offers his own version of the story of 'Christ' to the community. Its level of innovation could be compared to other NT traditions, and surviving non-canonical early Christian texts, but that is beside the point. The point is that as far as Jewish traditions go, the Messiahship of Jesus was a new, invented tradition.

100   Ephesians does not include any legitimation of Jesus' Messiahship or a discussion of how Israel's Messiah is also the Saviour of the nations. In all likelihood these were included in the initial stages of communal membership or recruitment (cf. 1.15; 2.8; 4.20-24).

101   Whatever these are remains unclear.

102   Petersen suggests that 'being in Christ' is a counter-cultural component of a Pauline symbolic universe: 'Being in Christ or being in the Lord is a state of social being that governs the relationships between believers even outside the spatial and temporal boundaries of the church. Being in Christ/the Lord, therefore, excludes all other forms of social being for those who are "in" *him*. And this state of being is the norm which determined the behaviour, the

Although 'Jesus Christ' is central to identity construction, it is important to note that adding a belief in Jesus as Israel's Messiah into either a Jewish symbolic universe or a Greco-Roman pantheon would not necessarily mean Christ-followership would be an exclusive or distinctive identity.[103] Despite the contested Messianic identification of Jesus, Christ-followership becomes the key identification for the community. It provides the basis of social identification and categorization as belief 'in Christ' as a salvific agent of God which defines the members (Eph. 1) and outsiders (Eph. 2, 4, 5). Interestingly, 'Jesus Christ' is depicted as a communal hero. He is imagined as a cosmic sovereign (1.20-23) and his foremost role is that of God's agent who accomplishes his eternal plans.[104] He is celebrated as the mediator of communal salvation and the source of blessings, grace, gifts, exaltation and communal virtues as explored above. These passages anchor the members' identity 'in Christ' as a divinely authorized and the vindicated founder of the community.

Ephesians' construction of the community also involves inventing a myth of divine origin. Ephesians likens the community of Christ-followers to Israel, a nation of God's people characterized by holiness and separation from the surrounding nations (Smith 2003, esp. 19–33; 44–58) and invents a myth of divine origin when it imagines the community as 'chosen and called' by God (1.4, 5).[105] Divine chosenness is fundamental to Jewish identity, as Moses is believed to proclaim, 'you are a people holy to the LORD your God; the LORD your God has chosen you out of all the peoples on earth to be his people, his treasured possession' (Deut. 7.6; 14.2). Despite of its non-Israelite membership Ephesians adapts the author's heritage here inventing a non-Israelite myth of divine origin, imagining that Christ-followers are 'members of God's household', and 'his beloved children', bought with the precious price of Christ's death, as

---

form of social relations, that is appropriate, indeed, required, between believers' (Petersen 1985: 289). Similarly in Ephesians, 'being in Christ' becomes a socially formative primary identification.

103   It is easy to forget that naming Jesus as 'Christ' was contested and different labels may have a different feel to them. For instance, should I have chosen to label Jesus as 'the Messiah' in my study it may have resembled the Hebrew traditions more closely. Therefore labelling Jesus as the Messiah could make the reading appear more continuous with Jewishness, as somebody noted in response to my 2006 SBL paper. In my view, this could have had the adverse effect, suggesting that I personally believe that Jesus is Israel's Messiah, and not that I explore such naming in the text. Again, if I called Jesus '*Yeshua*' as Shulam and Le Cornu do (Shulam and Le Cornu 1997: 36) I may have achieved the rhetorical aim of stressing Jesus' Jewishness. In labelling 'Jesus Christ' I have expressed caution and stressed Ephesians' subjectivity and ideological bias of Messianic description.

104   Cf. 1.5, 9, 12; 2.7, 10, 20; 3.4, 6, 8, 11; 5.32.

105   Stories of being chosen and legitimated by God are common in the myths of ethnic and religious election that feature frequently in constructions of identity and communal stories (Smith 2003: 255).

'a fragrant offering and sacrifice to God' (2.19; 5.1, 2).[106] Furthermore, it mimics Israel's covenant and mission (Exod. 19.1-6; Deut. 26.16-19) developing counter symbolism of non-Israelite covenant, sealed with the sign of God's spirit (1.13-14),[107] and their commission as a manifestation of divine wisdom (3.10). Like Israel, the community is also distinct from the 'nations', as the writer imagines people who walk in predestined good works (2.10).[108]

Finally, the importance of Ephesians' symbolic language for the socio-ideological positioning of the community is worth brief consideration, particularly as the letter opens with a view to 'heavenly realms' not to synagogues, temples, market places or any actual social setting in the Greco-Roman antiquity. Ephesians 1 transfers the discourse of identity from the socio-political realm to a spiritual and ideological symbolic universe where 'Christ' reigns and 'earthly principles' and status markers do not apply:[109]

> God ... raised him [Christ] from the dead and seated him at his right
> hand in the heavenly places, far above all rule and authority and power

---

106 I take Israel as a cultural model in broad terms: modelling is not about details or original meanings, but about adapting and reinterpreting cultural elements important to the writer. The use of Israel as a cultural model also has interesting political connotations. As previously noted, the letter calls for gratitude and loyalty to the new deity and other imperial concepts, such as Lordship, citizenship, benefits of correct relation with the ruling powers, peace and civic rights, are formative to construction of *ekklēsia* identity in Chapter 2. See, for instance, MacDonald (2004: 419–44; esp.420–22; 442–44) and also Campbell, who regards Ephesians as the most political text within the NT (2006b: 7). Although language of citizenship and the Empire would have been common discourse at the time of writing, Ephesians' political overtones do not need to imply that identity was perceived in dialogue with the Empire, particularly as Ephesians makes explicit reference to *politeia* (citizenship) of Israel (2.12; see discussion in Chapter 3). Instead, it may be part of responding to Israel's chosenness and citizenship, which involves the exclusion of the nations (e.g. Pss. 80, 105; Deut. 5.1-3; Isa. 65.9). Therefore, engaging with Israel's citizenship and alienation of the nations seems to be another legitimating imperative. However, the reference is more ideological than social; it is about reasoning the inclusion of non-Israelites, not about relations between non-Israelites and Israelite *politeia*, which is notably absent.

107 Ephesians follows Paul in using the idea of legitimating the Holy Spirit (Rom. 8.12-17, 28-30; Gal. 4.5-7). See MacDonald 2000: 198–9, and Perkins 1997: 38–9, for discussion of other Jewish parallels.

108 See discussion of Ephesians 4–6 below.

109 It remains speculative if the celebration of Christ-followers' status results from ideological reasons, as belief in the extension of Israel's *politeia*, or from social reasons, if for instance the members were recruited largely from among the lower classes. It is possible that the discourse emphasized spiritual benefits to give the group 'something to feel good about' if they faced oppression or insufficient status in real life and opportunities for social mobility were limited. It is easy to imagine that the language of citizenship and status could evoke positive emotive responses among lower classes, in particular. However, this remains speculative.

and dominion, and above every name that is named, not only in this age
but also in the age to come. And he has put all things under his feet and
has made him head over all things for the *ekklēsia*,[110] which is his body,
the fullness of him who fills all in all. (1.20-23)

Not only is 'Christ' exalted but the community is also imagined to be
seated with him 'in heavenly places' (2.6). The spiritual vantage point in
'God's presence' seems to provide the platform of (ultimate) superiority,
from which the relations with the social world are then observed.
Furthermore, lifting the discourse from the social plane to the symbolic
universe also allows for culturally radical claims. Because communal
beliefs and values are contested, the symbolic discourse position avoids
conflict and social competition: the discourse uses a well-established
symbolic universe where God's reign is taken as given, and constructs a
legitimating counter reality for the community 'in Christ' (see Chapters 2–
4 below). Thus, the symbolic universe in which the spiritual reality locates
becomes the primary referent to identity.[111]

Consequently, Ephesians' symbolic universe is a community-enhancing
counter-reality where the Christ-followers are positioned for the purposes
of the discourse. Instead of observing the social influences in their socio-
geographic location, Ephesians gives the community new frames of
reference, where God and 'Christ' reign, and the socio-political environs
are considered less consequential. In other words, as MacDonald
observes, Ephesians' highly flexible and adaptable metaphorical imagery
has the power to transcend the historical referents of the community
(2000: 254).[112] This is typical of legitimating communal discourse that

110   I do use *ekklēsia* or 'community' instead of 'church' in English translations of the
NT.

111   Yee suggests that 'inferior powers' (1.21; 3.10; 6.12) are a code for socio-political
powers (2005: 24–8). If so, Ephesians' symbolism would also imply counter-political rhetoric.
However, whether socio-political powers can be seen as holding people in captivity, luring
them into sin and immorality is uncertain (2.2.). Although different cultures, political powers
and social or economic benefits they offer could lure people into life that the writer sees as
compromising. However, it is equally possible that 2.2 and other related passages refer to
spiritual beings, according to ancient belief that spirits and deities were believed to influence
human life. See Perkins (1997: 59–60) and Best (1998: 201–7), for ancient beliefs in
astrological and supernatural, spiritual influences.

112   In addition to the 'saints', citizenship of Israel and other nations (2.11-12), the
characters in Ephesians' symbolic universe include for example God, his spirit, 'Jesus Christ'
and Paul, whose portrayals will be discussed in due course. It also manifests elusive
authorities, powers, cosmic forces (1.21-22; 2.2; 3.10; 6.12), holy apostles and prophets (3.5)
and other communal leaders (4.11-12), the devil who is quite militant and wants more room
(4.27; 6.11), stereotypical outsiders (4.17-19, 25-28; 5.3-7, 11-17), wives, husbands, children,
parents, slaves and masters (5.21–6.9) and finally in closing remarks it introduces Tychicus,
who is a 'dear brother and faithful minister' and a reliable source of instruction who will be
able to tell the community 'everything' during his anticipated visit (6.21-22). Much could be

integrates different provinces of meaning, ideological, cosmological, spiritual and social, which simplifies the diversity of the social order in symbolic arrangements that convey divine order and totality (Berger and Luckmann 1966: 113; Petersen 1985: 59).

The symbolic universe provides the overall frame of reference for conceiving human experience within a given 'universe' (Berger and Luckmann 1966: 76; Berger 1969: 26).[113] It may involve both selection and deselection of social and ideological factors, but this does not necessarily imply discontinuity with the social milieu. Furthermore, it may be designed to provide compelling counter-reality: the symbolic universe based on spiritual realities is the ultimate reality that challenges social relations and social hierarchies (Petersen 1985). Construction of a symbolic universe could be motivated by social reasons, as for example, conflicts that the author poses a resolution to, or to explain why certain behaviours are commendable and others are not.[114] Or it could be used to

---

said about Ephesians' (and other NT) portrayal of Israel's God, who has become a largely passive deity. For instance, the God of Ephesians' symbolic universe is presented as the pre-existent divinity, probably *YHWH* of the Hebrew Scriptures. However, Ephesians simply outlines his beneficiary role to the community of Christ-followers: he has predestined salvation for the nations in Christ before the foundation of the world (1.4, 5) and prepared good works for them to accomplish (2.10). He has, for some reason, decided that his might is best displayed through Christ-followers (3.10). He seems to accept both Israelites and people from other nations on the basis of Christ's reconciliatory death (2.13-16) but he has no voice to comment on his relationship with Israel, who previously enjoyed an exclusive relationship with him. His relationship with Israel is met with (perhaps awkward) silence. Neither are we told what was his reaction when his Son abolished the law he had previously assigned to Israel as a sign of covenant (2.15). While the idea of a conflict between the actions of the 'liberating Christ' and Israel's God may be intriguing, it is only speculation as Ephesians neither explains cultural reforms nor discusses contrasting traditions. It is as if the ancient God has become a 'Christian', too: he has adopted the believers (1.5), who call him 'Father' (e.g. 1.2; 2.18; 3.14; 5.20; 6.23) and sit in his presence (2.6), which exceeds much of the Hebrew imagination (1 QH 11.9-29; 19.10-12; 4Q 521, 2.6-7, 12; cf. Hoehner 2002: 335; Perkins 1997: 62). He anointed Jesus, who died a reconciliatory death that pleased God who exalted him (1.20) and promised to assign him a cosmic reign in the future (1.10), and after this he commissioned Paul (3.2-9). Although Christ receives much of the writer's adoration, one should make no mistake, God is (still) able to accomplish profusely more than one could ask or imagine (3.20). So God considers and plans, but he does not speak or act. Perhaps this is one of his weaknesses as the Deutero-Pauline writer steps up and speaks on his behalf (cf. Ephesians 3 in particular).

113   Other NT scholars who engage with Berger and Luckmann include, for example, Luomanen (1998); MacDonald (2000); Adams (2000); and Zetterholm (2003).

114   MacDonald's equivalent to the symbolic universe is the building of an alternative society that she calls a 'new international movement – the universal *ekklēsia*' (2004: 444). This movement, as MacDonald puts it, encourages spiritual transcendence and opposition to the surrounding society. In my view, the former is more important than the latter: any resistance or social separation is subtle and mainly ideological and moral, as the spiritual warfare demonstrates. See my reading of 6.10-20.

give a platform to alternative thought, for ideological reasons. In addition, symbolic universes have a self-enhancing function: they provide 'sheltering canopies' for both institutional order as well as individual biography, which individuals and communities employ to position themselves socially (Berger and Luckmann 1966: 120).[115]

The construction of Ephesians' symbolic universe develops in subsequent chapters of the letter, but it essentially involves supreme powers (God and 'Christ') that legitimate the movement. Symbolic universes provide ideological and social resources for the community and its members (cf. Cohen 1985: 98; Jenkins 2004: 112). For example, it allowed early Christian imagination to position the exalted Christ alongside Israel's God. It provides the discursive field where communal ideology meets social reality, as ideological principles and recommended social orientations are discussed in a particular environment where unwanted challenges and social complications are deselected and disregarded.[116] This has two important facets. First, Ephesians interacts with the real world through a symbolic counter-reality that provides the ultimate legitimation of social institutions because it integrates all provinces of meaning: ideological, spiritual, cosmic and social (Petersen 1985: 59). In other words, the creation of a symbolic universe provides the all-embracing frame of reference and all human experience can be imagined as taking place within it (Berger and Luckmann 1966: 76). Secondly, the symbolic counter-reality provides an image of reality as everyday life is positioned against other referential fields, in this case, spiritual realities (Berger and Luckmann 1966: 59). Because Ephesians positions itself as explaining God's will and eternal mysteries, it is therefore difficult to render it as unreal or invalid. It positions the community as recipients of divine wisdom, supernatural knowledge and God's eternal mystery (1.18;

115   See Berger's work on 'sacred canopy' (1969), for 'religious' legitimating canopies.

116   This would have strengthened communal identification and shaped social reality (Lieu 2004: 39). Ephesians' use of the symbolic is an example of what Berger and Luckmann describe as language that transcends the reality of everyday life (1966: 54–5). The discourse creates togetherness and communality based on the underlying spiritual interpretation of reality when it is reflected 'within' that particular symbolic universe. Therefore the community can be real although the communality of its members would be imagined or ideal. Such ideologically legitimated worldviews are typical of religious communities. According to Berger and Luckmann religious worldviews can be seen as transposing reality by creating a spiritual enclave which has specific values, norms and orientations, and typically requires commitment in response to 'knowing god' or his revelation (1966: 54–5). Due to the symbolic universe, Ephesians construction of a community appears in the discourse as 'given, unalterable and self-evident' (1966: 77). It develops a 'canopy of legitimations, stretching over it a protective cover of both cognitive and normative interpretation' (1966: 79), which has the power to transform and shape the individual and their collectivity, and generate identifications, so that the member(s) come to know themselves in a particular universe (1966: 84–5).

3.8-9, 18).[117] It strengthens the connection between the imagined divine origins and their realization in the community in appropriate virtual identifications. This is one of the key ways by which Ephesians gains its persuasiveness, which makes the discourse a compelling resource for social and ideological orientation among the likeminded who accept its claims for truth and revelation.

The construction of Ephesians' symbolic universe is of fundamental importance for the identity and survival of the group, as it provides the basis and paradigms for its members' social relations and group processes. Berger and Luckmann suggest that how compelling a symbolic universe is determines how powerful its constructions of identity and intergroup relations are: the firmer the symbolic universe, the stronger the members' commitment to it (1966: 174). Given that Ephesians is a sub-cultural discourse addressing non-Israelite Christ-followers, it is unlikely that the community benefited from firm structures or institutions. Instead, they had to reconcile ideologically novel communal values in a diverse Greco-Roman environment, while aspirations of independence from either Jewish movements or denouncement of polytheistic worship would have been treated with suspicion.[118] Bearing these factors in mind it is easy to imagine that Ephesians' symbolic universe and language of divine legitimation would have been particularly compelling, as will be explored in the subsequent readings. The language of divine legitimation was needed to position the community firmly in the minds of its members. In other words, where the social foundations for the community were weak and socially unstable, it would be all the more important to

117   The prayer request that God would 'open the eyes of the hearts' may derive from common Jewish thought although the phrase does not have direct biblical antecedents (Perkins 1997: 48).

118   For the evaluation of cross cultural challenge and its bearing on early Christianities, see for instance MacDonald (2004) and Zetterholm (2003). It seems that the negotiation of identity and cultural performances were of fundamental importance for the development of early Christianities and possible causes for their ultimate separation from Jewish groups. So, for example Zetterholm, who suggests that it was the inability of the emerging Christianness to develop a common identity for Jewish and non-Jewish adherents of the Christ-movement that eventually caused the break between Judaism and Christianity (Zetterholm 2003: 7). He believes that the messianic faith demanded adherents to abandon both traditional (Greco-Roman) religions and Torah observance (2003: 5). Further, he suggests that the social consequences for a Jew attached to a messianic synagogue in an urban diaspora community were probably not very profound at all and had little impact on the person's social and religious identity, unlike for instance, joining some other Jewish movement, like a monastic Qumran sect (2003: 6). However, it was specifically the non-Israelite believers that had to face far more serious social and cognitive consequences (2003: 6).

compensate this by boosting the ideological foundations for communal identity.[119]

The symbolic resources would contribute to its reality in the lives of its members. The symbolic universe would offer 'a mask of similarity' which implies that 1) community membership depends upon the symbolic construction and signification of a mask of similarity which all can wear; an umbrella of solidarity under which all can shelter; 2) the similarity of communal membership is thus imagined (e.g. that each member is called and adopted by God and redeemed 'in Christ'); and 3) the community, however, would have a potent symbolic presence in people's lives and thus it would not be imaginary although its construction components, ideology and religious symbolism would be (Jenkins 2004: 110; Cohen 1985; 2002). As Jenkins points out, 'a mask of similarity' does not actually guarantee socio-cultural equivalence, but people appear socially and ideologically similar (2004: 110). So, if the Ephesians' community members reorganized their world(s) in the light of Christ-centred convictions and shared values drawn from the symbolic universe, they would appear similar to a considerable degree, despite individual difference and variance. Furthermore, although both communal similarity and difference with outsiders could be imagined and constructed, their consequences, however, would be real and not imaginary given that virtual identifications, ingroup preference and negative attitudes toward outsiders would be real and bring the community into real social experience too.

At this point in our exploration of Ephesians' construction of communal identity it begins to emerge that the letter makes use of a number of ideological vehicles which simplify social life, in order to promote particular orientations and worldview (cf. Davis 1987: 24). For instance, the characters, God, Jesus, Paul, 'the circumcised', 'the saints' and the sinful 'nations', are textual generalizations whom the author uses to make ideological statements or provide social guidance.[120] Therefore, ideology is not a mere theory or a foreign perspective through which we might gaze into the text, but matters of faith and worldviews are vital parts of a social movement (Zetterholm 2003: 182). The functions of ideology in a communal discourse may include mobilization, challenge to authorities and the use of ideological components as resources of the community (d'Anjou 1996 in Zetterholm 2003: 182). In my view, one important function of ideology must be added to the above list, namely

119   It is reasonable to assume that the discourse was well received in the implied community and beyond, given that the text was preserved and quickly assumed an apostolic status, leading to its later canonization. For the discussion of early allusions to Ephesians, Patristic references and its canonization see Best (1998: 14–17) and Hoehner (2002: 2–6).

120   Literature, as Eagleton suggests, gives a privileged view to the ideological structures of its writer, as we can observe his/her ideological manoeuvres (1976: 101).

that of setting paradigms for belief and behaviour in a discourse of communal boundaries.

4. *Conclusions*

In this chapter I have undertaken self-positioning discussing my reading position. Although the prominence of identity has been a key theme of Ephesians in recent scholarship, a more theoretically informed reading will illustrate the extent of negotiation of identity and group processes in Ephesians' thought. This study takes social entrepreneurship as an essential social process for emerging groups that require legitimating. Consequently, the text is not seen as mirroring social circumstances or a response to them but rather it is seen as a vehicle for social influencing to shape the world of their recipients by providing particular frameworks through which social life is to be interpreted. The need for social entrepreneurship and providing self-enhancing, legitimating discourse is seen as a natural step in the emergence of new movements that seek distance from the socio-ideological surrounds.

Ephesians' social entrepreneurship is seen as involving adapting cultural heritage, such as the author's Jewish heritage; inventing traditions, such as the divine origin of the community and the Messiahship of Jesus; as well as shaping social remembering and setting paradigms for social orientation, which will be explored in later chapters of this study. This chapter surveyed themes emerging from Ephesians 1 outlining why a social-scientific approach is useful for this particular text, and how it seems to conform to the basic assumption of the SIT, as it addresses that aspect of identity which is socially shared, and it separates that group from others. According to the SIT, internal-external dialectic of comparing 'us' and 'others' is formative to the way community members come to view themselves and interpret their social reality. This is evident in the way Ephesians promotes a sense of self (being a Christ-follower) and sense of communality (in *ekklēsia* of God's people) and difference from others. Ephesians' opening suggests that the letter is a self-enhancing communal discourse that is geared towards strengthening communal identity, as celebration of 'being in Christ' in 1.3-14 illustrates. It has two communal functions of strengthening identification and encouraging loyalty to the divine benefactor. This provides the foundations for social entrepreneurship which develops the meanings of communal membership and proceeds to impose particular cultural assumptions and ideological convictions upon the group, as further chapters of this study will examine.

Furthermore, Ephesians 1 also demonstrates that the author positions the discourse and the community in a Jewish symbolic universe, which is

adapted to make room for 'Jesus Christ' and his followers. It adapts the
story of Israel's election and chosenness thereby reinventing God's chosen
people 'in Christ' and providing them with a myth of divine origin (1.4-5,
11). It also adapts the idea of covenant as non-Israelite Christ-followers
are made God's people 'through Christ', redemption and forgiveness, and
sealed with the Holy Spirit as a sign of being God's people, his chosen
possession (1.7, 14). Although the discourse of identity relates to both
Jewish and Greco-Roman worlds, the descriptions of social life in
Ephesians are scarce and as the letter opening demonstrates, the discourse
is based on symbolic counter-reality and the spiritual relationship with the
divine. Social entrepreneurship begins with and continues to develop
ideological statements that describe relations with God, meanings of the
Christ-event and their bearing on identity. This has two important
functions: communal legitimation and provision of appropriate cultural
models that reflect the holiness of Israel and God.

   To summarize, Ephesians' construction of identity is firmly established
in the opening chapter. It is about explaining why and how the
community of Christ-followers assumes Israelite privileges, like divine
calling and chosenness, a covenant with God and being set apart as his
people, separated from the rest. This involves a re-definition of the
Hebrew concept of what the people of God means: the following readings
of Ephesians will demonstrate that God's people are no longer defined by
the election of ethnic Israel and her covenant with God, but by faith 'in
Christ'. Having outlined key manoeuvres in Ephesians' identity construction in the opening chapter, its most striking feature in my opinion is the
extent of cultural models it draws from Jewish traditions. The following
chapters explore how the social entrepreneur develops communal identity
by legitimating non-Israelite Christ-followership and bolstering communal ideology by social remembering (Part Two); and what social
consequences being God's chosen people has for non-Israelites (Part
Three), integrating social-scientific theory with readings of the letter.

PART TWO:
LEGITIMATING IDENTITY

Chapter 2

THEORETICAL FRAMEWORK FOR EXPLORING
SOCIAL REMEMBERING AND COMMUNAL LEGITIMATION

1. *Introduction to Readings of Ephesians 2 and 3*

Having outlined how 'being in Christ' functions as the key component of
Ephesians' construction of identity this study proceeds to consider other
textual features that shape communal identity and how social entrepreneurship continues to adapt Jewish traditions in the service of non-
Israelite Christ-followers. Part Two explores how deeply embedded self-
enhancing communal motivations are for the discourse, particularly in
terms of explaining the community as legitimate and inaugurated by God.
It begins with a discussion of literature on social remembering, followed
by readings of Ephesians in the light of this theoretical framework.
Readings of Ephesians 2 and 3 explore how the writer shapes reputations
of Jesus and Paul to provide a novel identity with a positive sense of
historical continuity and to justify the socio-ideological positions of the
discourse. I will examine how the writer loads the death of Christ with
communal significance in order to validate the Christ-followers' ingroup
culture; and how he legitimates the community using Paul's unique role in
making known of the 'mystery' of God, which is the inclusion of the
nations (*ta ethnē*) among his holy people. Having outlined the main goals
of the section, this chapter will proceed to briefly survey the most relevant
examples of Ephesians 2 and 3 scholarship and outline relevant theoretical
paradigms for exploring social remembering in subsequent readings.

1a. *Engaging with Ephesians' Scholarship*

The main aim of this study is to advance Ephesians' scholarship by
offering a systematic social-scientific reading that engages with the
discussion of Ephesians' contribution to the development of early
Christianities. Some of the research questions formative for this study
respond to Yee (2005).[1] Yee penetrates into the historical context of

---

1   See brief review of Yee in the introduction.

Ephesians and Pauline letters,[2] and highlights the extent of Jewish cultural traditions that impregnate the text. Despite building on Dunn (1993) he breaks new ground in terms of a meticulous evaluation of Ephesians' Jewishness, which has not been previously explored in such detail, possibly owing to the lack of urgency its classification as 'pseudo-Pauline' has caused.[3] At first, he tests the new perspective on Eph. 2.1-10, which he regards as a typical Jewish attitude to 'Gentile sinners'.[4] Then Yee proceeds to closely evaluate Eph. 2.11-22. He examines 'Jewish covenantal ethnocentrism', arguing that the purpose of 2.11-13 is to surmount the social distance between Jews and Gentiles (2005: 72; 111–21). Yee likens Ephesians to typical Jewish 'polemic against the Gentiles' (2005: 35, 40, 49). He sees Ephesians juxtaposing Jewish exclusivism with the 'magnanimity of Christ' that is hailed as replacing exclusivism by inclusivism and acceptance (2005: 188).[5] Then he proceeds to discuss how Jew and Gentile could be one, exploring the implications of *pax Christi* for the Christian Gentiles and their relationship with the Jews (2005: 140–4). In short, Yee argues that the Jews perceived Gentiles through the 'grid' of covenantal ethnocentrism, which meant that the identification between Jewish ethnicity and religion was too close. Yee labels this as 'closed-ethnic religion', which made Gentile inclusion impossible unless Israel is drastically redefined (2005: 71, 111–21). This, he suggests, takes place avoiding an explicit reference to 'ethnocentric Israel', but joining the Gentiles into 'holy ones' (2.19), when the exclusive 'body-politic of Israel' is transposed into 'an inclusive community body' (2005: 216). Therefore, Yee suggests that Ephesians coins the positive term 'holy ones' to eliminate the negative connotations of Israel, which is ethnocentrically tainted (2005: 190–8). Ephesians 2 thus offers 'society-refining' metaphors such as 'one new man' and a corporate personality of the reconciled humanity that overcomes the polarization of Jews and Gentiles (2005: 221).

Yee demonstrates interestingly and with great detail that the author's 'thought processes are thoroughly impregnated with characteristic Jewish

---

2   See Yee (2005: 2–3) for an outline of his research questions, and pp. 3–33 for a fuller explanation of the aims of his study.

3   I owe this inference to Dr R. Barry Matlock who supervised the early stages of my doctoral research.

4   Yee presumes that negative remarks are scripturally inspired and widely spread, although Paul's explicitly Jewish comments, such as 'we are Jews – not Gentile sinners' (Gal. 2.15) are absent from Ephesians.

5   Yee seems perfectly unaware of any communal and ideological requirements involved in Christ-followership and ingroup dynamics of social inclusion and exclusiveness, insisting on 'undisguised inclusivism' of Christ's reconciliation 2005: 190, 197, 198, 211). Such ingroup dynamics are discussed in more detail in the following chapter, which develops, for instance, the notion of social exclusiveness and the intolerance of Ephesians' ingroup culture.

thought and manners of speech' (2005: 29). However, in my opinion Yee does not fully explore what is the relationship of Ephesians' Jewishness and its Christianness; or to which extent each term describes the contours of the discourse.[6] While I similarly believe that Ephesians is positioned in a Jewish cultural environment, I disagree with Yee's underlying assumption that a similar cultural framework would guarantee and necessarily assume ideological and/or social likeness. The key for the Jewishness of Ephesians, when Jewishness is understood as a social description, is to explore the communal and social dimensions of identity, and virtual, as well as nominal, facets of such a label. Similarly, use of Jewish discourse components does not necessarily mean that they would remain primordial and unchanged when they are transported into a new literary or communal location. Consequently, it is important to consider how the language of Ephesians portrays its writer's Jewishness, and how this relates to the community of Christ-followers in their socio-historical context.

In my view, it is crucial to consider the following questions when discussing Ephesians' Jewishness: how does the text present and represent Jewish values and beliefs; how might these have been modified – and for what reasons might this occur? Furthermore, do the beliefs, values and identity in the text strengthen Jewish identity and social relations with Jewish groupings in the late first-century context? And finally, is the letter faithful to what could be defined as 'essential Jewishness' or does the text suggest that some level of theoretical and/or ideological distancing from Jewishness is occurring? While Yee skilfully demonstrates Ephesians' Jewish literary characteristics, he does not show equal endeavour and detail in discussing possible reasons as to why, how and to what extent the author's conviction of Christ might challenge Jewish assumptions at the time of writing; or if such instances are in line with the undisputed Paul; and what might they mean for the depiction of early Christianities. Despite its merits, it is unfortunate that Yee's work is focused on the discussion of 'Jewish identity' on a 'theological' or 'literary' level without giving due attention to the social implications of the text.

Yee's ideological explorations focus predominantly on the affirmative, presenting how the author 'perceives the world as a Jew' (2005: 45) and thus, stressing the continuity between Israel and the Church (2005: 3, 213–19). Thus, while the monograph offers interesting discussion of Ephesians' Jewishness, it fails to fully explore how the text functions as a representative of the Christ-movement. For instance, Yee reasons that in Ephesians 2.14-15 'Jews still remain Jews' and only the ethnocentric use of the Law is abolished (2005: 166), but he does not explore what this

6 He mentions the relationship between Israel and 'the church' in his topics for further research (2005: 221).

would mean to the addressed community or their social networks and relations. In my view, Yee seems to focus on affirming Jewish identity instead of offering a more critical study of the ideological terrain of the letter. For some scholars, continuity with Paul goes together with the authorship of the letter.[7] However, if one does not presuppose Pauline authorship, the need to ascertain continuity with Paul or his Jewish identity similarly disappears.

At times, Yee's 'new perspective' sounds rather negative. For instance, he prescribes Christ as 'the antidote' to 'the exclusivistic Jewish attitude which led to ethnic alienation' (2005: 32, cf. 186). In all fairness, the suggestion that Judaism needed an antidote is quite inappropriate, especially if this comes from a cultural outsider, chronologically distanced from the world he critiques. Ephesians is a minority voice from antiquity that negotiates specific cultural boundaries in the light of a particular ideology. It should be approached as communally driven literature, mindful of its creative composition and socially driven goals. Consequently, reading Ephesians should not lead to a labelling of 'Jewish covenantal ethnocentrism' (2005: 87), as this denies the validity of Jewish covenant in the Hebrew Bible (pp. 71–2) and it seems to imply that 'God of Israel' was a bad idea from the start. It becomes evident that Yee responds negatively to the Jewish covenant, i.e. 'Jewish ethnic exclusiveness' (2005: 87–111) and takes Ephesians' ethnic discourse as a problem that the writer conveniently resolves via Christ: 'the author's aim is primarily to construct a new space for the Gentiles who were marginalized by the Jews who practised ethnocentrity' (2005: 120). He critiques 'self-confident Judaism which is bold enough to situate the Gentiles at the "extremities" of its own "world"' and their 'antagonistic attitudes' (2005: 120, 143).[8]

Wasn't Jewishness exactly what Yee was looking for? Why then should Jewish identity be a problem? Or its boundaries? Discussion of Ephesians' Jewishness or social processes should cause us to objectively analyse subjective ingroup dynamics even if they are not shared by the writer (or reader), even if they would be critiqued in the text itself. Jewish values sprang from communal traditions and sacred texts that affirmed the origin of their ethnic selection as God's prerogative (Exod. 20; Deut. 5.6-7; 6; 7.6, 7-11), even if Ephesians' author would take them negatively.[9]

7   Hoehner has to be the best example (2002). His commentary on Ephesians passionately defends the apostolic authorship of the letter and consequently establishing strong conformity between Ephesians and Pauline thought is of great importance for the argument throughout.

8   I assume Yee critiques Jewish 'ethnocentrism' from Ephesians, retelling what he perceives to be Ephesians' responses to Jewishness. Nevertheless, negative language about ancient Jews seems to be a critical lapse, particularly so in a New Perspective reading.

9   For intertextual parallels in other Jewish texts for Israel's chosenness and God's covenant with her see e.g. Shulam and Le Cornu (1997: 325–92) on Romans 9–11.

Furthermore, the more weight one puts on the divine in the instigation and sanctioning of Israel's communal values, the less offensive it should be to observe people's commitment to their God and sacred traditions. In my view, a NT reader or scholar should try to avoid making ethnic judgments. Besides, ironically, how wouldn't one denouncing Israel's God-endorsed 'set apart-ness' be guilty of ethnic or religious superiority him/herself? Yee may narrowly avoid my criticisms by presuming that there was '*a certain stream of Judaism*' which 'narrows the scope of the divine grace and so limits membership [of God's people] to what constitutes the "body politic" ethnocentrically to include only ethnic "Israel"/Jews or a much smaller group than the whole humankind' (2005: 122). In my view, Yee should have provided a rationale to convincingly explain at which point this social innovation took place and when did (presumably) God-given ethnic covenant go wrong? When did the God-inaugurated symbols and boundary processes turn into exclusivist rituals against 'his eternal plans'?

Further, Yee regards Ephesians as a renewal movement 'breaking through the boundaries within one Judaism (not all) of the first century which is marked characteristically by covenantal ethnocentrism' (2005: 228). This is still problematic. It illustrates a wider problem in the NT scholarship that needs 'a Jew' to blame, or some kind of a 'Jewish problem' to explain Christian texts (Shkul 2008). But why do we need to imagine such a group? Did they ever exist? Were they fictional characters in Ephesians' literary construction, to serve the discourse of identity? No, they are not; Ephesians does not have criticisms of Israelites, let alone a specific 'misunderstood' socio-ideological view of ethnicities.[10] Could it be that the falsely ethnocentric are just scholarly imagination? Their 'real' existence could be loosely inspired by readings of 2.11 (not in Yee, cf. 2005: 83–7), or theological default setting and persistent models in previous scholarship. Interestingly, Yee has now installed – or tried to install – misguided Jewish ethnocentrics into our worldview (as his readers) and into 'our' memories of Second Temple Judaism.

Far from appreciating the contours of ideologically loaded ancient texts engaged in social competition and their interesting reflection of social processes, some of Yee's observations are biased and problematic in my view. For example, arguing that the ethnocentric Jews had unhealthy or confused attitudes toward other ethnicities (2005: 142, 176).[11] The fact that Yee is prepared to criticize first-century Jews on the basis of

---

10   Even if it had, one only needs to consider the presentation of the non-Israelites to realize characters and events serve socio-ideological purposes of the text.

11   Although Yee sets out to offer a 'new perspective' reading, some of his observations are not far from theologically arrogant as he keeps referring to God's original plans and resolutions described to us in Christian texts. I will return to this subsequently. For the

Ephesians suggests that for him Ephesians is not just a viewpoint of a Jewish Christ-follower who reasons with the values and boundaries of emerging Christianness, but the text seems to have incontestable authority to him. Yee perceives the writer of Ephesians in terms of a Jewish cultural critic, who challenges the concept of the ethnic election of Israel with the election of believers in Christ: 'He presumably is denouncing the disposition of the Jews who concerned themselves exclusively with the question of their ethnic and religious identity but ignored the overall plan of God to include both Jews and Gentiles as his own people' (2005: 189). The most important question is how does Yee know 'the overall plan of God'? Does he substantiate his claim from the Hebrew Scriptures; or acknowledge conflicting voices in different Jewish texts? No.[12] He refers to Ephesians 1.3-14 where God's plans are disclosed.[13] Is Ephesians early Christian social persuasion or *the* word of God? Less of the former and more of the latter for Yee, it seems.[14] Yee's views on the will of God are not problematic if we 'do' Christian theology, which is a self-enhancing communal discourse on a large scale. However, for a discussion of Jewishness this is odd and unconvincing in my view, as it begs the question whether Ephesians really is the best source for understanding the plans and intentions of Israel's God.[15] Moreover, for a discussion of identity and cultural boundaries, this is ill-informed and lacks the spirit of appreciation, enquiry and objectivity that one would expect of social sciences.

Claiming that Jewish people 'ignored the plan of God' assumes that Ephesians' (or similar) view of non-Israelite inclusion was widely known, considered and then rejected. This is problematic as it ignores the models Jewish communities had for non-Israelite inclusion, and related scholarship. If the initiation processes in Jewish communities were highly distinctive in the wider cultural context of the Greco-Roman world, socially (and otherwise) painful, and therefore not popular, is beside the point. It is bizarre for academic discussion on Second Temple Judaism to

---

discussion of theological supercessionism see, for example, Donaldson (1997: 238–9), and particularly Kelley, who highlights racism embedded in Christian theology (2002). Similarly, Buell (2005), Penner (2008) and Crossley (2008).

12   It is rather surprising that Yee does not discuss the Hebrew Bible when discussing the plans of Israel's God, like Dunn who aptly compares 'universalist Judaism' with a similar thought in Paul and Ephesians (1993: 151–65, esp. 159).

13   Yee believes that Jews' self-understanding had 'injurious social consequences' and compares them with God's original plan for Israel as expressed in Ephesians 1.4; 3.5-6, 8-9 (2005: 101; cf. pp. 121, 123, 140).

14   Exactly the same for Darko (2008: 110, 114), to whom I shall return in due course. Naturally the question could be answered, both/and, as social persuasion and Christian view to the authority of Scripture do not need to collide, and the role of rhetoric, or social persuasion in the more recent scholarship, is well acknowledged.

15   See also Chapter 3 below.

dismiss these processes and God's role in them, in my view (contra e.g. Shaye Cohen; Nanos; Donaldson, etc.). Although Yee promises to give the old question (of the Law) 'a fresh look which sets the question about the Law firmly against the backcloth of a Jewish perspective' (2005: 156), his argument is weakened by criticism of Jewish values and orientations. He focuses on the negative aspects of the Law and speaks of its role in consolidating Jewish identity as a negative 'tool of estrangement' (2005: 158) and critiques 'Jewish tendency to divide or factionalise' (2005: 164).

In my view, Christian readers of the NT are often theologically predisposed to identify some faults in Judaism to explain texts' distinctiveness, or methodologically misguided to notice there is anything wrong with it. For example, when Yee proceeds to take a negative view of community boundaries that separated Israel from other nations, he contradicts his aim to observe the 'Jewish perspective'. Similarly, he takes 'Israel' as a symbol for the people of God, but critiques the social consequences of the ethnic chosenness, which he frequently labels 'ethnocentrism' that 'estranged' the Gentiles (2005: 174, cf. 90). In my view, the key to Ephesians is its Christianness, that is, values drawn from the Christ-event, not faults with Jewishness or with any Jewish groups. The ideological factors that prompted Ephesians' reforms on Jewish culture and adaptation of Pauline traditions could include the importance of the Christ-event and its various interpretations, and the social influences probably included the popularity of Pauline mission. Whether the Christ-event is causal for the writer's claims for distinctiveness or a convenient means of legitimating reformist ideology born for social reasons remains unknown.

However, do we have to reconstruct a 'wrong' Judaism from Ephesians who is then to blame for what the text seems to critique? In my view a negative assessment of the first-century Jewish people implies devaluing their traditions and Hebrew Scripture. Instead, exploring Ephesians as a distinctive voice, i.e. social influencing with its own communal goals, offers a more critical and suitable heuristic tool for understanding early Christ-movement. In addition, if one is mindful of the text's own social goals there is no urgency to point the finger at anybody else for its views. I am convinced that we can (and must be able to) understand early Christian literature without constructing an Israelite error, fault or negative attitude to explain the text and its disposition (Shkul 2008). Instead, the key is the subjective interpretation of the Christ-event, and how formative this is to the writer and consequently to the discourse. As it stands, Yee's labelling of 'Israel' as a negative, ethnocentric term is unsatisfactory as it is not based on his assumption of a wrong sense of ethno-cultural communality, as he seems to find Israel's ethnic covenant problematic. The reading of Ephesians 2 in this chapter proceeds to challenge such a criticism of Israel, which seems to be a 'Christian', etic perspective.

Along with Yee, Timothy Gombis (2005) provides another recent example of interaction with the Jewish literary features in Ephesians. Gombis' doctoral dissertation proposes that Ephesians' key theme is 'the Triumph of God'.[16] He outlines the following components of a Divine Warrior motif in Ephesians: the triumphs of the exalted Christ (1.19–2.22); the triumph of God in the imprisonment of Paul (ch. 3); the triumph of 'Christ' and the empowering of the Church: embodying the triumph of God 'in Christ' (4.1-16); and the Church waging divine warfare against the powers (4.17–6.9).[17] The consistency of the 'triumph of God' motif throughout the letter is central for Gombis' argument that 'reading the letter through the lens of the ideology of divine warfare from the ANE, developed in the OT [sic] and utilized throughout the NT, brings to light the argument of Ephesians and reveals its overall coherence' (2005: 4; cf. 9–35).[18] This, according to Gombis, provides a solution to the well-assessed problem of Ephesians' composition in a motif that binds together the two seemingly different halves of the letter.[19]

The main difficulty in Gombis' study is that the discussion of God's triumph over the Law implies positioning the Law as God's enemy. This is clearly problematic. In my view, he fails to provide a convincing argument for Ephesians 2, albeit correctly highlighting the obvious motif of Christ's accomplishment in the passage.[20] He claims that the credentials of Christ, who has been installed as cosmic lord in 1.20-23, are vindicated by a display of his credentials as universal sovereign, his triumphs over all competing powers – here, the hostile powers and the Law – i.e. 'the

---

16   Gombis' research follows the publication of Yoder Neufeld's *Put on the Armour of God* and others, who have discussed the idea of divine warfare in ancient texts and Ephesians' adaptation of the motif (cf. Lincoln 1990: 432–41;1995: 99–114; Perkins 1997: 142–4).

17   Gombis' discussion of 'the church as waging divine warfare against the powers' excludes the explicit warfare passage of Ephesians 6.10-20, referring to Neufeld's study that focuses on the divine warrior motif in Isaiah 59, Wisdom of Solomon 59, 1 Thessalonians 5, and Ephesians 6 (2005a: 7).

18   Gombis uses 'Old Testament' instead of e.g. 'Jewish Scriptures' or the 'Hebrew Bible'. This, in my view, implies an unnecessary language of replacement or succession typical of Christian tradition.

19   Gombis (2005a: 1–2); cf. Schwindt (2002: 46–7); Muddiman (2001: 7); Gnilka (1971: 13–21). I view social entrepreneurship as an overarching model, of which the divine warrior motif is one example of positioning the discourse in the Jewish symbolic universe. It is used to stress God's supremacy and the fulfilment of his works in the life of the community.

20   According to Gombis, the conflict-victory scheme in Ephesians 2 contains the following elements: threat (2.1-3); triumph over the powers (2.4-6); the purpose of God in his triumph (2.7-10); threat (2.11-12); triumph over the Law (2.13-16); victory shout (2.17); celebration (2.18); temple-building (2.20-22). In other words, Gombis identifies two triumphs of the exalted Christ, over powers and over the Law (Gombis 2005a: 61–84).

powers that rule the present evil age' (2005: 52) is difficult. Gombis, as Yee discussed earlier, assumes that the fundamental division created by the Law means that Israel had turned the Law into something that it was not (2005a: 76–7).[21]

In my view, Yee and Gombis seem to be listening to Ephesians rather than critically analysing its ideological manoeuvrings. This, again, is a perfectly valid theological exercise. This study seeks to demonstrate that Ephesians is ideologically and socially predisposed in order to achieve its communal goals of compelling the identity construction and resocialization of non-Israelites. I propose that exploring Ephesians' social entrepreneurship avoids such pitfalls as blaming (ancient) Israelites for falsifying the Law or failing to be what God intended them to be, 'the light for the Gentiles' (Gombis 2005a: 76). Nevertheless, despite the theological differences of our reading positions and their almost inevitable conclusions, Gombis' study demonstrates that the idea of the triumph of God, his Son and his people through his spirit, is indeed a key theme of the letter and an essential component of the believers' identity. This study is in agreement with Gombis' view that the sense of God's supremacy, the empowerment of believers and their identification with 'Christ' and Paul are essential components of the identity of God's people that the community is called to imitate their moral and spiritual battle.

1b. *Engaging with Scholarship on Early Christianities*

Meanwhile, other readings of Pauline and other early Christian texts offering a positive contribution to discussion of emerging Christianness have emerged.[22] For example, MacDonald (2004) and Zetterholm (2003) have provided important perspectives on the study of the internal and intercommunity relations of the early Christ-movement and its varied socio-historical circumstances. Both draw attention to the fact that non-Israelite believers (like those addressed in Ephesians) enjoyed the protection of the Israelite communities in the polytheistic Greco-Roman context.[23] This would have been natural, given that in the early stages

---

21   He does not discuss the status of Israel, or for instance, note the distinctions in attitudes toward Israel and the Law between Romans and Ephesians, or engage with the problematics of negative portrayal of the Law.

22   Important evaluations of ideological and social complexities of Jewishness of Early Christianities include e.g. Mark Nanos' work (1996; 2000: 146–59; 2002); Gager (2000); and Becker and Reed (2003).

23   This does not mean that they were cowardly or compromising: as Darko reads from MacDonald and defends early Christians who did not 'hide behind Jews' (Darko 2008: 113, n. 22). This seems to imply a negative attitude towards early stages of the movement when it nested in its Jewish basis, perhaps because the NT contains some criticisms relating to negotiation of non-Israelite inclusion in that period; or that overemphasizes their sense of distinctiveness and fails to appreciate the period when Christ followers weren't a 'church' yet.

Christ-movement would have shared the Jewish symbolic universe. However, given that the messianic conviction was debated and it became socially formative, a process of distancing began. Jewish origins offered social stability in terms of avoiding a charge of rejecting local religions and being seen as turning into an illicit religion. While MacDonald highlights the importance of a protective umbrella of association with Jewish communities (2004: 422), Zetterholm's distinctive contribution highlights the non-Israelite Jesus-movement's desire to establish independence at a relatively early date (2003: 15). He draws attention to the discursive dynamics of an intra-communal dialogue between 'Jesus-believing Gentiles' who wanted to dissociate themselves from the 'Jesus-believing Jews' within the Jesus movement. Although Zetterholm views the early Jesus-movement as a messianic but still Jewish community, he highlights the importance of identity negotiation and group processes which led to the eventual development of the movement into '*a new non- and even anti-Jewish Gentile religion*' (2003: 7). He draws attention to the fact that Ignatius of Antioch articulated Christian dogma from outside Judaism as early as at the turn of the century and sharply contrasted Judaism and Christianity (2003: 3, cf. 203–11). This causes Zetterholm to question how it can be that a member of an originally Jewish messianic movement about eighty years later finds Judaism incompatible with the movement he belongs to (2003: 3).

Zetterholm's attentive questioning brings balance to the study of early Christianities as it seeks to understand the development from an Israelite messianic movement to a non-Israelite religion. In my opinion, he raises highly important questions relevant for the discussion of Ephesians, its ideology and social orientation, which similarly addresses intra-Christian discourse and assumes the legitimacy of Christ's work as God's redeeming agent. Furthermore, it is commendable that Zetterholm treads carefully and avoids blaming other Jewish groups for not upholding a Christ-centred reformist view. Instead, he argues,

> it is assumed that the audience addressed in Paul's letters are Gentiles. Consequently, discourses where the contradiction between the torah and belief in Christ are salient are not applicable to the situation of the Jewish believers at all but are part of a rhetorical discourse aimed at preventing Gentiles from becoming Jews (2003: 5).[24]

MacDonald and Zetterholm discuss the period when distinctiveness gained ground and distancing from Jewish groups began to take place. It would have taken longer still for the groups to establish independence and to be recognized by their wider social context as a separate entity.

24   Cf. Gal. 3.10-11; Rom. 3.20, 9.31; 2 Cor. 3.4-18 and Ephesians 2.14-16. Zetterholm presumes with Gager (2000) that Paul imagined separate ways for salvation for Jews and Gentiles (2003: 5).

The negotiation of non-Israelite inclusion is a separate question and there is no need to assume that the covenant boundaries of Israel are also discussed.[25] In my opinion, in a social-scientific study of early Christian identity negotiations and community formation, there is no need (or excuse) to dismiss the validity of the Hebrew canon in favour of upholding early Christian texts, or argue why they might be correct. This would be part of theological exercise but not social-scientific, which should be mindful of the fact that communal discourses are typically meaningful to insiders, not others, and self-enhancing, upholding what is deemed communally important.

While Yee's assessment of ancient Jewishness seems to be inspired by his reading of Ephesians disclosing the 'eternal plan of God', Zetterholm is more mindful of the complexity of pre-Christian understandings of non-Israelite salvation in Jewish eschatology, and the diversity of responses to the social conflicts around the non-Israelite inclusion. He offers a superior, non-apologetic discussion of the ethnic conflict and the terms of non-Israelite inclusion: he describes the solution the messianic movement embraced as a radical resolution when ideology was transformed to (accommodate) social reality (2003: 140).[26] According to Zetterholm, the salvation of non-Israelites meant that they had to be included in the covenant precisely as Gentiles, not as circumcised proselytes, or otherwise Israel's God would continue to be 'the God of the Jews' rather than the God of all nations and ethnicities (2003: 156). He suggests that the apostle James saw no need for Paul's 'soteriological innovation' but held that the Jesus-believing non-Israelites were saved as god-fearers or righteous-Gentiles (2003: 161, 166).[27] It was the difficulties of amalgamating these two groups that led to their separate groupings, which Zetterholm sees as 'the embryo of what later became a virtual separation between Jews and Gentiles, between Judaism and Christianity' (2003: 166, cf. 222–4). He correctly points to the social causes of Paul's ideological innovation, which in all likelihood provides the foundation on which Ephesians' notion of equality at the cross is based.

---

25 Even if they were, we should not insists upon their correctness. It is common in social-scientific studies to acknowledge that one can be critical of their traditions for various reasons while group memberships, identities and their meanings are constantly evolving and negotiated.

26 Crossley (2006) similarly points to the social causes for 'why Christianity happened'.

27 The relationship between God's oneness, universal salvation and non-Israelite inclusion is also central to Nanos' view: 'Gentiles are forbidden to become Jews not because becoming Jewish and keeping the Torah is no longer a valid act of faith; they are forbidden because to do so would be to deny the universalistic oneness of God (he is the One God of all nations), which would implicitly deny the election of Israel and the privilege of the Torah, because if he is not the One God of all outside of Israel who believe in him then he is not the One God of Israel; he is not the One God at all' (Nanos 1996: 184).

Therefore, in my view, Zetterholm's discussion offers a more balanced discussion of the ideological and social complexity of early Christian thought. However, a few other important models for understanding early Christian texts and their ideological reflection of social complexity must be briefly outlined. The understanding of socio-ideological legitimation and communal oriented reputations of 'Christ' (2.11-22) and Paul (3.1-13) draws from the discussion of Paul's Christological core and non-Israelite inclusion. For instance, Terence Donaldson highlights the importance of Christ in the re-mapping of the apostle's convictional framework: Paul's worldview changed as Christ replaced the Torah as the key signifier of the community membership (1997: 215, 236–48).[28] The key to a re-configured Israel, he suggests, is the Christ-event, which is seen as re-configuring his Jewish convictional world:

> The result of his Damascus experience was that Christ came to occupy the position in his convictional world previously occupied by the Torah. Consequently the reconfigured convictional world is structurally similar in many ways to the native world, except that Christ has replaced Torah at the center. The most important similarity has to do with the Gentiles: Paul continues to believe that the only hope of salvation for Gentiles lies in their becoming proselytes to Israel prior to the *eschaton*, but his Damascus experience has led him to redefine Israel (and thus proselytism) in terms of Christ'. (1997: 236)

While Zetterholm stresses the social aspects of the ideological shift, Donaldson emphasizes the importance of the religious experience in Paul's ideological reformation, and the NT texts substantiate the importance of both factors in early Christian faith and experience. The re-mapping of the convictional world is a useful paradigm to understanding why Ephesians is so Jewish, but at the same time, quite different due to the Christ-event and its socio-ideological consequences.[29] Donaldson correctly identifies the extent of Jewishness in Pauline thought, and 'the Israel-centred' nature of Paul's missionary conceptions in particular.[30] The subsequent readings explore how these Pauline concepts feature in Ephesians, analysing its Jewishness and its Christ-based revisions.

28 See also Esler (1998).

29 Donaldson likens Paul's Gentile mission to Jewish proselytism, where the eschatological salvation of the nations depends on their proselyte conversion in this age (Donaldson 1997: 242, 248).

30 Donaldson rightly connects Paul's apostolic conscience and Jewishness, The term 'apostle to the Gentiles' (Rom. 11.13) ... betrays a decidedly Jewish vantage point on the world. Moreover, to characterize his role Paul draws heavily on the model of the prophets of Israel, the Servant of Isaiah and the priests of the Temple. He goes to the Gentiles, then, not simply as an individual Jew, but as a representative of Israel, sharing Israel's spiritual blessings with the nations. (1997: 260).

Similarly, Nanos (1996, 2002) and Esler provide important perspectives for the discussion of Pauline ideology and Ephesians' reforms of Jewishness. Both discuss early Christianities assuming a close association with other Jewish movements before any separation between the church and synagogue had taken place.[31] Esler, to begin with, proposes that Paul was an entrepreneur of identity who sought to establish a common identity to reduce conflicts between Judean and non-Judean (Esler's preferred terms) Christ-followers by establishing a common superordinate identity while maintaining former subgroup identities (2003: 30–31, 38). Thus Paul provides a common identification without erasing or challenging ethnic identities. Esler explains, 'the participants must not be encouraged to abandon their original (sub)group identities entirely, since if they consider that their original identities are threatened they might react strongly to preserve them, a result that can intensify animosity or bias toward members of the other (sub)group' (2003: 178). The olive tree metaphor in Romans 11.16-24 serves to illustrate Esler's analysis of the 'recategorization' or 'common ingroup identity' model (2003: 29–30): the tree is formed of Israelite and non-Israelite parts, cultivated and wild olive branches, while the image preserves the differentiation without erasing the distinctiveness of the two subgroups or the salience of subgroup identities (2003: 298–305). I will discuss if Ephesians, too, maintains subgroup identities or whether it proposes a new identity for both collectivities; and what implications this may have for Deutero-Pauline study and relations between Christianness and Jewishness at the time of writing.

Nanos reasons that Paul's apostleship was motivated by seeing Jesus as Israel's Christ and Saviour of the world (1996: 9, 15). It was a mission of bringing in 'righteous Gentiles' into the worship of One God, joining them with the historical faith of Israel (1996: 36–7), providing specific *halakhah* to ensure their minimal purity and appropriate lifestyle in 'obedience of faith' (1996: 35), without the necessity of a proselyte conversion and subsequent submission to Torah obedience.[32] Nanos points out that Galatians and Romans confront different sides of arrogant triumphalism, on the part of Israelite and non-Israelite believers, respectively (1996: 370). He analyses intra- and inter-Jewish disputes around the legitimacy of the status of non-Israelites without a proselyte conversion and discusses why Paul's inclusion of 'righteous Gentiles' was an issue within Jewish subgroups. His monograph on Galatians discusses the competition

31   Along with, for example, Boyarin (1994; 2004).

32   Nanos suggests that Paul saw the eschatological promises of the restoration of Israel and gathering of the nations in messianic faith cf. Rom. 11.25-32; 15.4-21 (Nanos 1996: 37). 'Christian Gentiles' ought to submit to synagogue authority and 'the operative *halakhot*' that defined a proper socio-religious code for 'righteous Gentiles' such as the apostolic degree and Noachian Commandments (1996: 75).

between Paul's communal politics and other social control agents, who
operated within the Jewish synagogue community (2002: 12). Their role
included maintaining internal community politics within the Jewish
movement, facilitating proselyte conversion, ensuring their legitimate
status within the Jewish group and consequential communal protection,
as well as looking after their communal interests and vulnerable position
as a religious minority within the Greco-Roman society, in compliance
with established norms and practices (2002: 14, 318).

Nanos draws attention to the idea of multiple identities and that diverse
communal praxis in Jewish groups is embedded in the concept of
'righteous Gentiles', which explains how non-Israelites could be considered righteous without obeying the Torah, without undergoing
proselyte conversion and circumcision. The concept of 'righteous
Gentiles' and Noachian decrees could offer a model that balances both
Paul's Jewishness and salvation of the nations in Christ under a different
regime, thus reducing his radical discontinuity from other Jewish
teachers.[33] As Nanos explains, 'while the early Christian Gentiles were
not expected to become Jews, they were expected to obey the operative
first-century halakhah for the "righteous Gentile" worshipping the One
God in the midst of the Jewish community, for God is holy' (1996: 187).
Therefore, the halakhic code for non-Israelite affiliates was an ideological
extension of the Hebrew canon that facilitated social interaction with
associates from other ethnic groups and cultures. The concept of the
'righteous Gentiles' facilitates the discussion of messianic origins of the
Christ-movement by a) providing earlier examples of a successful non-
Israelite affiliation with the Jewish movement and social processes that
made this possible and by b) reducing the assumption of originality of
Christ-following communities and their social integration of non-
Israelites.

2. *Theoretical Framework*

The reading of Ephesians 2 and 3 is based on theoretical perspectives on
communal legitimation and social memory theory. First, the legitimating
functions of the discourse.

---

33   However, it is difficult to assess if the concept was a later development or how popular
it would have been in the first century CE and whether it actually provided a plausible model
for early Christian thought, despite the attractiveness of subsequently interpreting Gentile as
a parallel phenomenon on reconciling universality and particularity. See, for instance,
Donaldson 1997: 230–6, who remains unconvinced of the righteous Gentile approaches,
unlike Gaston (1987); Lapide and Stuhlmacher (1984: 69); Fredriksen (1988: 165–76); Segal
(1990: 204); Nanos (1996: 51–5, 163–4, 166–70, 226–7), and others.

2a. *Legitimating the Community, Ideology and Identity*

Legitimation refers to those aspects of a discourse that provide explanation and justification for beliefs, values, social structures or boundaries, as well as stories and communal remembering. To quote Berger and Luckmann, 'the legitimation "explains" the institutional order by ascribing cognitive validity to its objectivated meanings' and 'justifies' it 'by giving a normative dignity to its practical imperatives' (Berger and Luckmann 1966: 111). Legitimation is highly important for communities and group processes, particularly in the case of new and emerging groups. Esler discusses the importance of legitimation for social transformation of a reform movement when it departs from its cultural matrix and forms an independent sect (1994: 13–14). Esler is correct, although the process does not require sectarian separation: any significant social distancing calls for reformists or reform groups to legitimate themselves, their distinctiveness and reforms on the parent group/religion or previous traditions.[34] This, according to Esler, is achieved by putting into place 'a symbolic universe in which the new institutional order will have identity and meaning' (1994: 14). Consequently this new institutional order can be designed to provide a reform group with a distinctive identity and sense of communality, as subsequent readings argue, happens in Ephesians.

A communal discourse has multiple levels: oral, written, authoritative, minority, accepted, contested, rejected. All of these may contribute to dialogue of communal legitimation, although in the NT we only find its authoritative and presumably accepted forms. Communal discourses have many functions ranging from furthering and strengthening communal construction, to its legitimation and members' identification process, and discussion of values and behaviours that foster ingroup communality, establish coherence and discourage deviance. It may also contain different levels of communal legitimation: 1) incipient legitimation, simple traditional affirmations, pre-theoretical and self-evident knowledge; 2) theoretical propositions in a rudimentary form, such as proverbs, legends and folk tales; 3) explicit theories developed by specialized personnel who transmit them through formalized initiation procedures; and 4) symbolic universes that integrate different provinces of meaning and encompass the institutional order in a symbolic totality (Berger and Luckmann 1966: 112–13). Such symbolic processes of signification are particularly relevant in the discussion of spiritual realities embedded in the religious texts, as in

---

34 The terms 'sect', 'sectarianism' and 'sectarianist' are used broadly to reflect the minority stance of Ephesians (and other early Christian texts) and its subcultural stance, without implying rigid correspondence of any particular type. Similarly, in their Diaspora contexts Jewish movements were subcultural with regards the diversity of Greco-Roman cultures. Thus Ephesians is a minority voice within larger and established, but still subcultural, Jewishness.

our study. Alternative realities and their legitimation cannot be experienced or legitimated in the same way as everyday experiences (1966: 113). They can only be experienced 'theoretically' (believed) or spiritually (through some communally accepted forms).

As previously established, Ephesians' communal worldview is positioned in the symbolic universe, that is, (imagined) spiritual framework for the discourse and communal experience. Its legitimation, therefore, deals with spiritual experience, which, in essence, means imaginative connections between experiences and beliefs. Berger and Luckmann acknowledge the power of the legitimation of identity in a symbolic universe and its role in providing a safe haven for communality against its social challenges:

> Identity is ultimately legitimated by placing it within the context of a symbolic universe. Mythologically speaking, the individual's 'real' name is the one given to him by his god. The individual may 'know who he is' by anchoring his identity in a cosmic reality protected from both the contingencies of socialization and the malevolent self-transformations of marginal experience. (1966: 118)

Furthermore, alternative symbolic universes imply a threat as they cast doubt on the inevitability of one's preferred or current symbolic universe (1996: 126). This is why communal discourse may project a legitimating vacuum, without any sign of social negotiation, conflict or alternatives to communal distinctiveness which are, despite their silencing in the discourse, likely to be present in social interaction.

Having briefly outlined key perspectives for exploring communal legitimation, further theoretical frameworks are required in order to understand how various aspects of the discourse contribute to this aim. The complexity of Ephesians' social influencing cannot be fully appreciated without exploring social memory theory that illuminates how the discourse is loaded with communal meanings,[35] given that it is particularly the way 'Jesus Christ' and Paul are remembered that justifies the ideological and social positions of the community.

2b. *Social Remembering and Communal Memories*
Along with SIT based approaches, social or collective memory perspective is a diverse and vibrant discourse in sociology and social psychology. It began with Maurice Halbwachs (1877–1945), who distinguished between collective and individual memories and argued that memory is always

---

35 Different collective and social memory studies use different terms and definitions. Here, 'communal memory' refers to memories held by a particular group and 'communal remembering' to the process, while 'social memory' refers to the bearing of a social context in the processes of remembering (cf. Rodriguez (2004; 2005).

socially constructed and constrained.[36] Remembering is essentially and inevitably social, just as individuals are always social and cultural, inseparable from social setting and constraints of social life (Halbwachs 1992: 40; Jenkins 2004: 4).[37] Remembering is an integral part of identity and consequently, an ever-present part of the social experience. Similarly, both individual and collective memories are always human constructs that are drawn in the identification process, by both individuals and social collectivities (Jenkins 2004: 26). However, underlining the social dynamics of remembering does not reduce the fact remembering is at the same time individual as well as social activity, 'while the collective memory endures and draws strength from its base in a coherent body of people, it is individuals as group members who remember' (Halbwachs 1950: 48). Furthermore, we may, strictly speaking, only discuss memories in a group, not memory of a group (Esler 2005b: 13). There is no communal mind, and even if there had been a uniform base for collective remembering, the only source for discussing early Christian remembering are memories embedded in the literature, which illustrate either the writers' memories or the way they deliberately shape remembering, not memories of members of those collectivities.

However, the communal context for remembering provides a powerful connection with the (imagined) communal past: 'being social presupposes the ability to experience things that happened to the groups to which we belong long before we joined them as if they were part of our personal past' (E. Zerubavel 2003: 3).[38] Furthermore, remembering and social context are in a dialectic interaction; just as a social setting has its bearing on remembering and memories, remembering and memories provide connections and networks, as well as psychological and ideological components for social life.[39] Schwartz suggests that collective memory operates on two sources, '*history* and *commemoration*. Collective memory is a representation of the past embodied in *both* historical evidence and

---

36   For an introduction to Halbwachs see Coser (1992) and Misztal (2003) and for its use in biblical studies see introduction by Duling (2006); and contributions by Crossan 1998: 45–89); and Kirk and Thatcher (2005).

37   Coser is the editor of selected Halbwachs' writings on collective memory (1992), which includes edited chapters translated from *Les cadres sociaux de la mémoire*.

38   Individual connection with the communal past may be imagined and is often beyond verification.

39   Collective memories and social remembering operate under the same interactive dynamics as texts. For instance, they are simultaneously influenced by social location, its ideological and cultural components, while being influential in shaping and constructive for the social location as some elements are raised into significance and the significance of other factors is supressed.

commemorative symbolism' (2000: 9, italics original).[40] This is particularly important for considering memories embedded in a text, as writing
combines selective ideas about the past with present judgments and
emotive responses, and presents them in a specific written context, which
provides further constraints on remembering.

2c. *Social Memory and Ideology*

Remembering does not take place in a vacuum, neither are memories free
from their hybrid social location, whether stored individually or collect-
ively, shared by individuals in groups.[41] Consequently, ideological
motivations are commonly understood as formative for communal
remembering.[42] In addition to social context, ideology also contributes
to paradigms that guide how social entrepreneurs draw memories from
the past, how the group relates to its past and how they filter information,
interpret experiences and deal with social competition.

This leads to a very important point: we cannot access the past, but
memories are representations of the past that are shaped by ideological
and social constraints. The past is not stored and preserved as it
happened.[43] As Michael-Rolph Trouillot says, the 'storage model of the
past is therefore unacceptable in the light of social memory theory; the
past does not exist independently, as fixed storage of historical residue,
from which collectivities or individuals may draw consistent and
unchanging deposits' (1995: 14–15). The fact that memories are preserved
is important: the events and interactions themselves do not remain but

---

40   For further discussion on the politics of collective memory and its cultural aspects, see
Schwartz (2000: 1–25). I use 'ideological' parallel to Schwartz's 'political', referring to
persuasive functions of remembering in the promotion of communal ethos.

41   Remembering also requires the positive disposition of the remembering community;
as Halbwachs argued, 'every collective memory requires the support of the group delimited in
time and space' (1950: 84).

42   To reiterate, ideology is understood as those beliefs that justify social arrangements
and explain the way things are or ought to be. It refers to ideas, beliefs and values that are
required for communal self-promotion, which often involves a dialogue with opposing ideas
(Eagleton 1991: 28, 29). Ideology and culture are therefore closely related, while the ideology
is particularly interested in signs, meaning and values encoded in culture (1991: 28).
Consequently, communal ideology clarifies the worldview, values and aspirations of the
group and explains what is important for them, how they differ from others and what their
aspirations are.

43   To quote Halbwachs, '... memories are repetitions, because they are successively
engaged in very different systems of notions, at different periods of our lives, they have lost
the form and the appearance they once had. They are not intact vertebra of follies animals
which would in themselves permit reconstruction of the entities of which they were once a
part' (Halbwachs 1992: 47).

memories contain elements of them.[44] However, memories themselves may also evolve or be forgotten.

Perhaps the ideological colouring of memories makes them even more useful in the construction of identity. Halbwachs acknowledged that memories perpetuate our sense of identity (1992: 47), for example by explaining the founding of the group (and communal identity), providing it with a sense of purpose and destiny as well as legitimating it by providing ideological significance and self-enhancing factors. Identity construction negotiates ideological and mnemonic components, selecting and deselecting suitable elements. It is also important for the preservation of the collective memories that a community succeeds in controlling communal remembering, preventing communally harmful memories from emerging and decomposing existing memories that do not conform to the ideology of the group.[45] The shaping and controlling of remembering is an essential part of religious communal discourse.[46]

A social approach to remembering involves taking into consideration the dialectics involved in gazing into the past through the spectacles of the present. The 'presentness' of the viewpoint for which reminiscing of the past is simply unavoidable, as is its social nature. As Halbwachs suggested, 'collective memory is essentially a reconstruction of the past [that] adapts the image of historical facts to the beliefs and spiritual needs of the present' (quoted in Schwartz 2000: 5). In other words, the ideological constraints of the present viewpoint affect the processing of the past into meaningful communal rhetoric. At the same time, the contours of the present viewpoint are shaped by the bearing of the past on the present social context. As Lewis Coser notes, 'the present generation may rewrite history but it does not write it on a blank page' (1992: 34).[47] Instead, social beliefs and values, despite their origin – religious or not – have a dual character: they are simultaneously 'collective traditions or

44 In my view, memories are like stored food products – they can be stored in a variety of forms: frozen, liquefied, cooked, pickled, etc. They contain the essence of a given item, but no matter how they are stored, they cannot be reconstructed or their original form cannot be recreated. They are both discontinuous and continuous, authentic and different. Memories embedded in literature are preserved in a particular way, and to what extent that remains fluid and open for different influences varies from text to text, and perhaps, from reader to reader.

45 See Halbwachs' discussion of safeguarding permitted memories and controlling alternative memories in the context of emerging Christianness (1992: 94).

46 Although some early Christian texts explicitly discuss alternative views and provide socio-ideologically loaded counter memories, such negotiation of conflicting views is absent from Ephesians. Instead, even its selection of mnemonic components features typical deselection and silencing of anything challenging. See readings of Ephesians 3, 4, 5.

47 This is significant for discussing the Jewishness of Ephesians as it facilitates the discussion of cultural continuity of its symbolic universe and its relation to ideological revisions embedded in the collective memories. See the discussion in Chapters 3 and 4 below.

recollections, but they are also ideas or conventions that result from a knowledge of the present' (Halbwachs 1992: 188).

So, despite my rejection of a reconstructive agenda in this study, one must acknowledge that ideological and social conditions affect the way communities draw from and interpret the past, and therefore circumstances may have both direct and indirect bearing on social entrepreneurship. However, those circumstances cannot be recreated from the text. Instead, my focus is on how traditional material is used and intertwined with new ideas in support of communal agenda and beliefs.[48] This does not mean that the social entrepreneur would be ill-intentioned or fraudulent: rather the ideological interest expand and stretch the material so that its 'original underlying structures may lose their coherence' (Kunin 2005: 182–3). Therefore memories provide powerful resources for communal legitimation, as Schwartz acknowledges in his discussion of 'the politics of memory', discussing memory, social power and political struggles, and emergence of 'a new kind of society, one where the minorities and the powerless enjoy more dignity and rights than ever before' (Schwartz 2000: 14).

Consequently, the political or ideological shaping is an important element of social memory studies. Schwartz acknowledges that collective memory is not merely a function of social power, but it also operates as a symbolic filter, 'through which experience – political and otherwise – is apprehended' (2000: 18). His understanding of ideological and social functions of collective memory is worth quoting in full as it illustrates how important this theoretical perspective is for understanding social entrepreneurship and how the past may feature in the formation of communal identity and its legitimation.

The past is matched to the present as a model *of* society and a model *for* society. As a model of society, collective memory reflects past events in terms of the needs, interests, fears and aspirations of the present. As a model *for* the society, collective memory performs two functions: it embodies a *template* that organizes and animates behaviour and a *frame* within which people locate and find meaning for their present experience. Collective memory affects social reality by *reflecting, shaping and framing* it (2000: 18, italics original). [49]

Such reflecting, shaping and framing of social experience is part of what Marco Cinnirella calls creation of 'meaningful stories', when identity

---

48 See Kunin's discussion of the process of ideological transformation of a traditional myth (2005: 179–204, esp. 182).

49 However, the distinction between 'model *of*' and 'model *for*' is an analytical tool, as Schwartz points out; both aspects of collective memory operate in every act of remembering (Schwartz 2000: 18, italics original).

construction combines past and present resources (1998: 243).[50] This is common in early Christian literature that combines traditional and reformist values. Such stories recreate and interpret the past as a 'model of community' reflecting their communal needs and 'model for community', providing ideological paradigms for the group that facilitate framing communal mindset and locate its meaning in its social context (Schwartz 2000: 18). Therefore, communal remembering is, like identity, subject to ongoing social processes, which may cause the past events to be glorified, altered or devalued depending on the present needs and orientations of the community.[51] In other words, communal discourse and acts of public commemoration operate strategic inscription as well as exclusion, remembering and forgetting, depending on communal ideology and operative social entrepreneurship. At the same time, given that collective memories are linked with communal aims and ideology, they may be in direct contrast with another group: what is remembered by one group may be exactly the event that another group seeks to forget.

2d. *Invented Traditions*

Social memory studies assume that all memories are socially constructed and there is always some element of creative projection or filtering. This is particularly important in our discipline of NT studies where mirror reading and reconstruction of the past from the text are a commonplace and the historical accuracy of the textual traditions is often a non-negotiable matter of faith and conviction. [52] Despite this tendency the theoretical literature suggests it is unviable to assume that communal memories embedded in the texts would be correct, factual, historical and unbiased by default. Although all memories are socially constructed, I find Eric Hobsbawm and Terence Ranger's theory on invention of

---

50   Similarly, Esler, who makes an important observation on the fluidity of social identity and communal concept of 'possible selves' (Esler 2005: 9–10). Cf. Condor (1996: 285–315, esp. 302–3).

51   So-called retrospective interpretation of the past is one example by which memories of earlier events are reinterpreted in the light of later events and values. This may alter the conception of a person or a circumstance significantly, depending on more recent events and values. Retrospective reinterpretation may increase continuity between the past and the present or provide explanations as to why things progressed in a certain way. Thereby a person or a collective avoids having inconsistent memories, but harmonizes their memories and value judgments that accompany remembering.

52   The theological interest in historical accuracy in the biblical past, or for instance, its 'truthfulness' features in scholarly works. So, for instance, Hoehner who takes Ephesians' 'interest in truth' as evidence for apostolic authenticity (Hoehner 2002: 49), as does O'Brien (1999: 43–4). This illustrates communal processes discussed in this study: Christian faithful have a genuine theological/communal need to affirm reliability of Scripture, hence affirmative interpretations receive stress in their works.

tradition an important addition to social memory perspective in this study. Hobsbawm explains invented traditions as 'responses to novel situations which take the form of reference to old situations', which give any change or innovation the sanction of continuity, presenting it as unchanging and invariant, or dressing up novelty as antiquity (1983: 2).[53] For our purposes, inventing traditions includes providing a novel concept, identity or a group with a historical story. This may have a variety of functions ranging from providing continuity and historical longevity; explaining the adaptation of a pre-existing symbolic universe; boosting communal identity by meaning and stability drawn from the past, and for instance, reducing the attractiveness of an alternative group or their ideology in the context of social competition.[54]

Some theorists emphasize the invention and creativity, whilst others stress the authentic core of traditions and memories. For instance, Trouillot argues that although traditions and collective memories may be imagined or fictional, this does not need to mean that they would be fake, as people in all societies are concerned with historical accuracy and authenticity (1995: 8). Similarly, Arjun Appadurai argues that societies and cultures have a universal interest in the accuracy of history and operate what he calls the rules of the 'debatability of the past' (1981: 201–19). There would be no reason to assume that ideological influencers could malevolently fake and falsify either historical accounts or their connections with groups and societies. Instead, the invention is subtle: the use of the past may be so selective, the connections between certain events or people in the past might be debatable, or the meanings imposed upon past proceedings or figures may be so subjective, that the use of the past seems so distorted, selective and ideological that it is best described as imagined, invented or fictional. For instance, the lives of Jesus or Paul may be historical facts, but their memories in early Christian texts may not.[55] So

53   For a further discussion of ways of remembering and inventing traditions in early Christian texts see Judith Lieu's discussion of 'History, Memory and the Invention of Tradition' (Lieu 2004: 62–97).

54   Jesus' Aryan origins exemplify ideologically motivated reworking of an existing historical story and invention of alternative traditions. Crossley provides shocking examples of involvement of the Nazi party members in German theological works and Nazi pamphlets, which argued for Jesus' non-Jewish origins. They illustrate fictionality and ideological shaping of religious – and in this case, ethnic and political – discourses. 'If such scholars did not deliberately lie, they sure came very close', Crossley comments (2005: 19).

55   This, however, does not mean that they are false but that they are sometimes used in ideological contexts where their historical accuracy perhaps matters less than legitimating authority. This is part of what Trouillot calls 'constructionist dilemma' with regard to history: while constructionists may point to the generally acknowledged fact of biased and subjective invented and/or fictional stories, it is much harder to prove that any single narrative is produced and fictional (Trouillot 1995: 13). Similarly, while the historicity of Jesus and Paul may be acceptable, the historicity of their memories may be hard to verify.

for example Wayne Meeks, who suggests that there is a certain historical core, which has been ideologically embellished: 'although history is always fictive, it does not make up its story as a whole. It interprets something that, however dimly we may perceive it, really happened' (2003: 160). Also, the ideological or political use of social memory in the service of a particular agenda does not need to imply negative intentions or conscious manipulations by the leaders and/or social entrepreneurs: they may consider themselves as genuinely representing the 'truth' – possibly even unaware of its contested nature, or that it could be misguided or understood differently (Bodnar 1992: 20; Schwartz 2000: 16, 254).

However, others stress the ideological agenda and inventive use of traditions. So, for instance, Schwartz, who argues that invented traditions are vehicles for power that 'symbolise societal cohesion, legitimate new institutions, statuses and relations of authority, and inculcate new beliefs and values'; and further, they are 'invented' in the sense of being 'deliberately designed and produced with a view to sustaining order' (2000: 14–15). Ideological colouring of social remembering may, indeed, mean that alternative, conflicting and even false histories and historical legitimations may be produced.[56] This problematizes the concept of tradition, which instead of being understood as 'a conception or practice unwittingly transmitted across generations' now 'becomes a conscious strategy adopted by political or ideological regimes to reinforce their authority' (Schwartz 2000: 15). It follows that an evaluation of social dynamics, influences and power relations should be part of a discussion of traditions, memories and remembering.

Such multifaceted perspective characterizes Crossley and Karner's edited volume *Writing History, Constructing Religion* (2005), which offers a fascinating discussion of the intricate relations between religion(s), history and texts. The following questions are characteristic of their approach:

> Are the official histories of a given religion narratives of power that marginalize or exclude alternative versions and subversive voices? Who controls what we are told about the past? Are the writing of history and the construction of religion so immersed in ideology that nothing of the past can be known to the historian of a given religion? Should anyone even care? How might we critically engage with (academic) theories of religions and histories as well as with the very concepts they utilize in all-too-often non-reflective manner? (2005: 4)

56 As Crossley observes, historicity is now anybody's business. '[T]his makes it possible for histories of anything and everything to be written, inspired by a wide range of ideologies and beliefs. The idea of writing of a history what some might regard obscure is hardly new, particularly in the Marxist tradition, and it has continued to flourish not least due to the impact of postmodernism' (Crossley 2005: 21).

These questions must not be limited to 'official histories' alone, although it is commonly assumed that the past is transmitted through lines of authority and those in positions of political, cultural and/or societal leadership. However, political or ideological promotion using reconfigurations of the past is not, by any means, restricted to official authorities, although a majority of social memory studies discuss 'official' memory manipulation by the elites. Nevertheless, different narratives, conflicting memories and contrasting reputations may exist among minorities as well as among majority groupings; among those with power and influence; as well as among the marginalized or oppressed, and different subgroups among both sides of the power divide. Although the present study considers a text that may represent 'official' Christian thought that has gained (almost) unchallenged acceptance and a normative status in canonical Christianity, the reading nevertheless places the text back in the diverse ideological matrix of its day when its contents were contested. Instead of keeping Ephesians on the pedestal of divine inspiration, it is placed in the late first-century CE context, among diverse cultural and ideological currents of emerging Jewishness and the polytheistic Roman Empire. This facilitates critical analysis of the social entrepreneurship, before the text was fixed among the canonical books, mindful of the fact that despite its minority/subcultural origins Ephesians seems to be heavily ideologically loaded and display tendencies to marginalize, exclude and extinguish subversive voices, which I proceed to test in the following readings.

2e. *Reputational Entrepreneurship*

In addition to previously explored perspectives, literature on reputational entrepreneurship further exemplifies how communities remember. Communal legitimation often expands on its historical founders who are credited with shaping the community and other figures in the communal past. Barry Schwartz and Gary Alan Fine are key sociologists on reputational narratives. Both explore the process of shaping reputations and their social construction by other figures of communal significance. In other words, while a person may contribute their reputation by their values and achievements, our focus here is on later acts of reputational entrepreneurship, whereby someone else (often posthumously) considers their reputation for the purposes of communal rhetoric, and subjects his or her values and achievement to reputational shaping.[57] Mmemonic narratives of such figures and events of communal

---

57 Reputational entrepreneurship is seen as a sub-function of social entrepreneurship; part of a bigger picture, along with identity construction, its legitimation and establishing of communal norms.

founding are also seen as subject to socio-ideological shaping as the reputational narratives are ideologically constructed, when some facts are chosen, some exaggerated, and others ignored in reputation construction.[58] Like any communal memories, reputations are equally idealistic, ideological and driven by the current needs of the community given the importance of creating an image of a person that closely and meaningfully connects communal leaders and their (faithful) followers.[59] For instance, all early Christian texts commemorate Jesus, despite controversial aspects of the reputation of the executed Palestinian Jew, and they label him as the Messiah, celebrate his connection with his followers and invest momentous value upon his teachings and activities, not to mention his death and alleged resurrection. The stigma of his arrest and execution is reinterpreted in at least martyrological, if not soteriological language, which exalts his role in God's plans and his guilt is transferred upon those who decided his fate. Similarly, Deutero-Pauline stories of Paul diminish difficult aspects of his reputation and embellish his role for the Christ-movement.[60]

According to Schwartz, the task of the reputational entrepreneur is 'to make an ordinary person great, or more commonly, to bring the person's greatness to public attention' (2000: 67). Fine regards a reputation as 'a socially reorganized persona' and 'a shared image...connected to the forms of communication embedded within a community' (2001: 2–3). For example, neither Jesus, nor Paul, or any of the apostles are known to later generations of Christians, but believers still identify with their embellished reputations. The following reading of Ephesians argues that their presentation is 'socially reorganized' and deliberately constructed in discourses to promote certain ideological principles and successfully so, as Christians still identify with these figures because their reputations correlate with their beliefs and values.

Fine distinguishes two interrelated tasks in the constitution of a reputation: 1) 'to propose...a resonant reputation, linked to the cultural

58 Reputations – as any aspect of social remembering and history – are interpretations of 'truth', that is, 'truth' as discursively reported, subjective, but not entirely subjective (Ben-Yehuda 1995: 276).

59 Although reputations may be either positive (heroes, prototypes, exemplars) or negative (villains, outsiders) the focus in this study is on the reputation of positive figures in the absence of specific villains in the discourse, while the outsiders and antitypes are projected stereotypically in Ephesians.

60 My current and future projects consider Deutero-Pauline texts as a group as well as later early Christian texts. The social memory perspective is still useful for those who wish to read the disputed letters as Pauline, but they would approach the texts as autobiographical, which would in some ways be all the more striking, as one would find Paul quite shamelessly promoting himself and his exemplary role 'in God's economy'.

logic; and 2) 'to make that image stick' (1996: 1177).[61] In the NT studies we are not exploring recruitment texts aimed at explaining the basis of Christ-followership to an audience to whom he is presumed to be unknown. Instead, the intended audience, in most texts, is already familiar with the figure whose reputation is being constituted, and reputational entrepreneurship is rather about enhancing and explaining the meaning and full significance of a reputation, not establishing one from nothing.[62] Therefore, the reputational entrepreneurship in NT texts, as in Ephesians, utilizes a pre-existing positive orientation toward that person (cf. Eph. 1.15; 4.20-24).

It is very important to notice that a successful reputational entrepreneurship requires certain communal and structural dynamics. To begin with, the person must be seen as commendable and their reputation worth considering for successful implantation of collective memories into societal discourse (Schwartz 2000: 297). However, even though a group may deem a person commendable, their reputations may still be fabricated or significantly overstated. Nevertheless, there are some constraints that hinder reputation shaping. First, there are ideological paradigms or cultural logic that limits the shaping of reputations. Communities are predisposed with certain social and ideological filters that cannot be manipulated beyond their limits. Secondly, there are also constraints on the credibility of the reputation and communal predisposition.[63] It must be accepted as genuine – otherwise its acceptance would be undermined (Y. Zerubavel 1995: 232). Consequently the success of any proposed interpretation of the past or a construction of a reputation depends on the likelihood of the community to accept it within their cultural and ideological paradigms. As Fine points out, the cultural sameness of the reputational entrepreneur increases the likelihood of the construction of a reputation that will be accepted, receives a place in the collective memory of a group and gains a position of potential influence in

61   The way in which reputations link with the cultural logic of communities and 'stick' may transcend time, for instance, the way reputations of biblical heroes do.

62   With the possible exception of Luke–Acts, the NT texts are usually written to believing communities, although they may contain recruitment sections, which make reference to or narrate introducing new audiences to an enhanced reputation of Jesus. The book of Acts contains numerous narrative sections in which the enhanced reputation of Jesus is explained to either an Israelite audience, who might be familiar with other forms of his reputation; or to non-Israelites, especially in a non-Palestinian setting, which contain elements of making an ordinary (Jewish) man great in their eyes. For instance, Acts 17 contains examples of reputational entrepreneurship to both Israelite and non-Israelite audiences.

63   Even though many studies on collective remembering (including this one) stress the function of the ideological agenda and the creative use of traditions and memories in communal discourse, the agenda alone, even when coupled with the creativity of the entrepreneur – or manipulative intent – cannot guarantee the results.

their social experience (1996: 1182).[64] Similarly, Schwartz also distinguishes between social entrepreneurs who share their audience's socio-ideological location and those who represent different social positions and values (2000: 254). The latter may also engage in social entrepreneurship and induce their audience to adopt other or to some extent revised values and memories (2000: 254). The former are self-enhancing while the latter are socially influencing and transforming.

Reputational entrepreneurship may utilize existing reputations, that is, figures already positioned on a pedestal. This features in Schwartz's analysis of the construction of Abraham Lincoln's reputation that had significant links with the existing reputation of George Washington:

> By the century's end Abraham Lincoln's reputation, according to all indicators, exceeded that of every president except George Washington. Yet the relation between the two figures was complex. On the one hand, the inertia of Washington's fame was difficult for Lincoln to overcome. On the other hand, Washington's memory was a resource from which Lincoln's memory gained strength. The more often Lincoln was paired with Washington, the more his reputation grew and the more widespread his commemoration became. (2000: 102–103)

Therefore Washington's reputation functioned like a pedestal upon which Lincoln was lifted to raise his profile, and similarly, Lincoln's reputation is now used accordingly to raise profiles of later figures of significance, including the 44th President of the USA.[65] Using existing reputations is not uncommon in early Christian writings either, which often use the established reputations of Israelite heroes, such as Moses, Abraham and others, in enhancing the reputation of 'Christ' or decorating the portrayal of his followers.[66]

64 Among early Christian texts, e.g. Galatians bears witness to competing and/or conflicting social entrepreneurship (e.g. 1.6, 8-9; 2.4, 11ff.; 3.1; 4.10-11, 16-20; 5.7-12; 6.12-13, 17), while Ephesians brushes complications to its views under the carpet and credits itself with divine authority.

65 The election and inauguration of the current US president has witnessed deliberate use of rich symbolism and loaded historical connections as Barack Obama has been linked with Dr Martin Luther King and dreams of the American civil rights movement, as well as with Abraham Lincoln. Much of the historical symbolism is deliberate self-positioning as e.g. arrival of the President Obama to his inauguration tracing Lincoln's train journey from Philadelphia to Washington DC. Further symbolic acts included his visit to Lincoln memorial, voluntary work on Martin Luther King Day preceding his inauguration, and perhaps most significantly, the use of Lincoln's inauguration Bible from 1861.

66 This point is fundamental to my Master's dissertation, where I argue that the Fourth Gospel uses Moses' reputation to establish Jesus' greatness: Jesus is placed on a pedestal by comparing him to Moses, whose legacy is firmly established among the Jewish recipients of the text. Not only is Jesus likened to Moses, but he is pronounced superior, and thus the writer adapts Jewish traditions to promote subcultural beliefs (1.17, 45; 5.45, 46; 7.19, 22, 23; 8.5; 9.28, 29). The use of legendary Israelites is widespread in the NT and offers further

Different times and changing social locations may provide different opportunities for reputational entrepreneurs. Schwartz considers the later growth of Lincoln's reputation after its poor start in his own generation, suggesting that his reputation was elevated because he suited the concerns of the later generations, giving their aspirations tangible expression (2000: 295). Two further points from Schwartz's discussion are worth considering: sometimes reputational entrepreneurs are ideologically motivated by the interests of the current society (or the subgroup they represent) and therefore their reputational constructs are more likely to reflect the values of their social location and thus sustain and strengthen collective memory (2000: 295). If, however, social entrepreneurs have an ideological motivation of their own that is significantly different from their social location, or they represent an alternative viewpoint, their constructs are likely to create collective memories and mould diversified and different reputations which aim at changing existing memories (2000: 295).

Reputational entrepreneurship may be either positive or negative, providing prototypes or antitypes. In other words, reputation construction may involve both people who typify insiders and exemplify the values and behaviours of the group; or outsiders, who serve as warning examples of vices and villains, outside the group (Haslam 2001: 66). The prototypes (imagined ideal members of the community) and exemplars (historical figures with a reputation of being ideal members) serve as positive role models and exemplary figures for others to follow.[67] The construction of either positive or negative role models uses similar methods with opposite values. For instance, communal antitypes embody the use of negative stereotypes while the prototypes and exemplars are constructed using positive ingroup stereotypes, of which they are representative. The group discourse may use prototypes and exemplars, for instance, in explaining communal values, practices or identity; endorsing the value of the community in contexts of social competition and in negotiating communal processes and boundaries; while antitypes provide their negative

---

research opportunities for studies of reputational entrepreneurship and social remembering (cf. Gal. 3.6-18; Rom. 4; Jas 2.20-25; 1 Jn 3.12-13, and Hebrews 3, 5–9, 11, 12). For instance, Paul's use of Abraham as the ancestor of Christ-followers in Romans 4 and in Galatians 3, 4 is very interesting, as it challenges established myth of genealogical ancestry and invents counter tradition of ideological continuity. Thus it exemplifies the fact that different groups can use the same historical prototypes differently, or contest for their ownership (Lk. 3.8). For further discussion of the use of Israelite figures in early Christian rhetoric see e.g. Esler (1998: 191–7; 2003: 171–94; 2005b: 8–9; 2006: 23–39); Nanos (1996: 139–43, 189; 2002: 62–70; 154–5); and Asano (2005: 149–79).

67   The terms 'prototype' and 'exemplar' are often used without any distinction, while the former often encompasses what is defined here as the latter. This is often accompanied with and/or results from the lack of distinction whether the figures who do typify positive communal values are real or fictive. For an example of their accurate use, see Esler (2003: 171–94; 2005b).

counterparts exemplifying outsiders and deviance. Finally, both positive and negative reputations may be deliberately constructed, ideologically coloured and designed for social influencing.

2f. *Diverse Reading Positions and the Reader's Dialogue with the Discourse*
Finally, having considered social construction and social memory perspectives, a brief discussion of some ideas drawn from cultural theory and literary criticism will be useful in exploring complexities of Ephesians and its scholarship. First, the discourse involves a *deliberate selection and deselection* of materials, in order to constitute suitable collective memories that shape communal identity in a preferred direction. For instance, the discourse chooses the hostility between Israelites and others, and offers a resolution extending the beneficial status of Israel to include others 'in Christ'. This is self-enhancing and communally constructive. But at the same time, the discourse withholds important information about Israel, communal values and behaviour; and, as the history of interpretation demonstrates, readers have provided different projections for processing the meaning of the text. For example, Ephesians does not discuss Israelites who weren't in ideological agreement with Jesus being Israel's Christ. Furthermore, the explicit consequences of 'abolishing the Law' in 2.15 to Israelite believers are not detailed, neither is the author's view to the role and purpose of the Law in general, outside 'Christ'.

In my view, the deselection of the fuller treatment of Israel and the Law suggests that the writer limits the discussion to issues that matter most to the community. This simplifies the discourse and creates an illusion of 'truthfulness' (or divine revelation) in the absence of alternative world-views. Such essentialism is still commonplace in social identities that often present 'for example' faith or ethnicity as immutable and unchanging, rather than parts of an ordinary and changing social experience. To quote Bauman,

> Ethnic identity and its practical outshoot, ethnopolitics, base their authority on bonds of blood and descent, and even the bonds of language and culture are treated as if they were natural facts. This essentialist position does not hold water; far from being a natural identity, ethnicity is carefully cultivated, and not seldom a manipulated, strategy of social action led by unelected elites who often exploit or mislead their supposed beneficiaries. Religion, on the other hand, provides no unchanging identities. While believers think of their faith as unchanging, religions are more like highly context-sensitive sextants than like the tied and tagged luggage of unified groups. (1999: 136–7)

Similarly, Ephesians leads its recipients to think of the communal faith as unchanging and God-warranted and thus by implication, beyond socio-cultural contest or change. Therefore, the deselection of complexities, promotion of communal ideology and language of divine verification (both implicit and explicit) operate as a legitimating foundation for the communal discourse. Furthermore, it is also important to consider what bearing essentialism has on collective remembering and how it affects the community, especially with regard to her relations with other Jewish groupings. For instance, one could ask whether the social entrepreneurship remembers 'Jesus Christ' in a way that strengthens communal relations with Israelites. How does it remember common nominators it shares with other Jewish groups? Does it focus on broad common themes or subcultural, distinctive elements peculiar for the community? These questions will continue to be explored.

However, we are not faced with simple explanations or a solution to Ephesians' relations with/within Jewishness. Instead, the text allows for different readings and even contrasting interpretations depending on the readers' cultural and ideological positioning and their prejudices and preferences. I propose that Ephesians could be either a text that projects Jewishness or seems to establish Christianness, depending on the reader's position and interpretation of the textual components. In my view, the role of the biblical critic is not to provide solutions to the weaknesses of the text, or to protect the audience from its complexities – although it is relatively common for NT interpreters to conform with theologically familiar interpretation, prompted by their own socio-religious inclination; when a reader identifies with the wider Christian discourse its theological imperatives lead one to conform with self-enhancing interpretations.[68] Dissenting and uncomfortable voices should rather, like Crossley suggests, be 'explained not silenced' (2005: 21). However, no reader could fully explain possible meanings of the text in question, or voices within. Rather one could offer well-informed explanations in terms of critically engaging with the complexities of the text.[69] Hence this reading

---

68 Communities, like the Church, offer a meaningful location to anchor individual identity and provide community enhancing discourse which its members naturally identify with. For example, Darko uses *'extra ecclesiam nulla salus* (outside the church there is no salvation)' in his discussion of Ephesians' moral discourse (Darko 2008: 68). I imply no criticism of his discussion in the context, but I find his use of such dogmatic Latinism unhelpful and rather too theological, given that he is explaining non-Israelites social orientation in the first century.

69 This reading seeks to avoid 'interpretive supercessionism', that is, assuming the 'correctness' of one's viewpoint without properly acknowledging a plurality of reading positions and interpretations. Fowl notes this phenomenon (1998). He points out that sometimes 'even those biblical scholars who recognize the theoretical validity of a variety of interpretive methods and approaches tend in practice to be quite monistic, implicitly regarding their own approach as superior to alternatives' (p. 34). He categorizes reading strategies into three groups: 1) determinate, 2) anti-determinate and 3) underdetermined. Determinate readings endeavour to produce or discover the meaning of the text; while the

aims to examine possible difficulties within the text and in diverse interpretations,[70] and highlight complexities and alternative explanations as to why dissenting and uncomfortable voices occur. It is not in my interest to establish what *the* meaning of the text is, as if one could distil the pure meaning in the process of interpretation. Therefore, this reading highlights communicative processes as much as meanings of the discourse; and discusses interpretive aims, interests and practices as well as the contours of the text (Fowl 1998: 56, 58), and its socio-ideological aspects.[71]

Different reading positions result in different perspectives and, inevitably, different readings. Zetterholm has brought Wolfgang Iser's 'gaps in the text' to bear on a study of early Christian texts and uses it to explore the complexity of scholarship. He argues that the 'gaps in the text' are filled by the reader using different assumptions and thus result in different interpretations, when, in Zetterholm's words, 'the meaning arrived at through the reading process is dependent on what the gaps in the text are being filled with' (2003: 8). It follows that different 'fillings' produce different meanings. The reader exercises freedom and prerogative by

---

second, anti-determinate, is directly parasitic to the first, aiming to deconstruct interpretive certainties and avoid mastering the texts (pp. 10, 32–3). Anti-determinate readings engage in a double interpretation in dialogue with the text as well as with their dominant interpretations (pp. 42–3). Unlike determinate readings, they denounce fixed meanings and remain characteristically open to further interpretation (p. 55). Such a pluralistic mode of discourse of diverse interpretations and the claim that Scripture would lack coherent meaning can be seen as unacceptable for the Christian faith, a complexity also discussed by Francis Watson in his discussion of texts, reading communities and meanings (cf. Watson 1994; 1997: 97). Although the mode of interpretation here acknowledges the value of determinate interpretations to faith communities and their members, it seeks to engage with diverse viewpoints, reading positions and interpretations, akin to Fowl's third category, 'under-determined' interpretation (Fowl 1998: 32–3; 56–61). Such an approach recognizes and engages with 'a plurality of interpretive practices and results without necessarily granting epistemological priority to any of these' (p. 33).

70 In my view, the socio-ideological focus does not clash with the importance of acknowledging different reading positions, but if anything, makes their evaluation all the more important.

71 That said, it is important to explore the complexity of the discourse and its reception a little farther. While the group of original and early Christian readers of Ephesians may have accepted the textual symbolic universe and its polarization of ethnoreligious interaction and other ideological matters, its contemporary critics may not necessarily do so. In addition, cultural and chronological distance between the world of the text and that of its present-day reader adds to the complexity of the reading and processing of its meaning. Consequently, affirmative readings can be accompanied and/or challenged by critical readings, which may not share or accept textual symbolic universe. In today's biblical criticism a plurality of readings is inevitable and recognized as it is connected with diverse reading positions that enrich the scholarship in the twenty-first century and should increasingly do so. However, most of the NT readers still come from the Church or the academia (most of which comes from the Church) which still keeps the readings and approaches quite limited.

positioning him/herself and the text, its author, characters and content. Consequently the interpretation is inseparable from the intricate combination of positionings by the reader.[72]

It is useful to explore Iser's theory a little deeper. The 'gaps' or 'blanks' stimulate the reader to fill them in with projections, giving life to what is unsaid or implied as it expands to take a greater significance (1978: 168). When the unseen joints and textual perspectives imagined by the reader are connected, the 'blanks' disappear (1978: 183).[73] Although the author has provided textual constraints to guide meaning-making and filling the blanks of the text, a reader has his/her choice in the reading and interpretation process. The text can also be read from multiple positions, a process that Iser calls a 'wandering viewpoint'. testing different gap fillers and examining a multiplicity of possible meanings (1978: 109). The following chapter will continue to use a wandering viewpoint in order to provide a critical reading of 'the abolition of the Law' (2.15).

The above dynamics of legitimation in communal discourse, social remembering and construction of communally significant reputations provide the basic framework for analysing Ephesians 2 and 3, their presentation of Jesus and Paul as communal heroes and how their reputations provide a) communal legitimation and b) paradigms for members' identity and social orientation, onto which we shall now turn.

72 Naturally this is socially and psychologically conditioned, based on the reader's values, resources, constraints, etc., which Iser describes as referential background for processing meaning (1978: 38).

73 Iser's later works, *Prospecting* and *'The Fictive and the Imaginary*, develop these concepts further in a more theoretical discussion of functions of literature and literary anthropology.

Chapter 3

READING EPHESIANS 2:
'REMEMBERING CHRIST' AND ITS COMMUNAL FUNCTIONS

The following two chapters will explore how Ephesians shapes the reputations of Jesus and Paul and how these memories shape how the community understands itself, providing both social and ideological justification with the language of divine legitimation. First, I will show that these figures are interlinked in legitimation of the group, explained as the culmination of God's eternal purpose. Secondly, I will demonstrate how the text makes explicit reference to the social and ideological distinctiveness of Christianness using remembrance of 'Christ' and Paul; and discuss what this means to the community and our understanding of Deutero-Pauline Christianities. This is connected with two key ideological positionings: reforms on Jewish Law and reconfiguring the revelation of God's will. To begin with, this chapter will consider how Ephesians explains the meaning of Jesus' death. The following reading will examine in detail what may be Ephesians' most crucial social claim, that 'Christ has abolished the Law' (2.15) and tests what implications this has for the community and our understanding of early Christianities. I take 2.15 to be decisive for the textual ideology and community relations and therefore critical for Ephesians' interpretation.

1. *Ephesians 2 and the Socio-Ideological Positioning of the Discourse*

Ephesians 2 encourages the community to grasp the full significance of the Christ-event, and the marvellous status transformation it brought to non-Israelites. It explains how the community is legitimated as God's people using collective memories of what God has achieved in Christ for the community. This section is particularly interesting for our examination of Ephesians' social entrepreneurship because it demonstrates how the author intertwines the core historical event (life of Jesus) with its ideological interpretation. Furthermore, it negotiates traditions and reforms: this is where Jewish symbolic universe and culture find their strongest expressions in Ephesians, as well as their uncompromising reforms at the cross.

Ephesians 2 builds on the letter opening, where the communal interpretation of the past events began. The retrospective interpretation of the Christ-event is similar to the construction of Christianness and communal identity in the opening chapter, when the blessedness of the believers was commemorated by looking back to their salvation and beyond (1.3-14),[1] and Christ-followership was explained as God's eternal purpose, designed 'before the foundations of the world' (1.4). In chapter 2 the interpretation of the Christ-event is related to the communal legitimation: 'Christ' is portrayed as a mediator who removes the social burden of a restrictive code of Law and the burden of proselyte conversion with rites of initiation that non-Israelite affiliates to Jewish groupings may have found uninviting.[2] He also facilitates communal spirituality: believers experience exaltation and abundant power in him (2.6, cf. 1.19-20).[3] In my view, the implanting of the redemption 'in Christ' firmly into the communal memory and explaining its meaning using diverse metaphors throughout the letter seems to be one of the chief aims of the writer's social entrepreneurship.[4] At times it is celebrated, as in the *berakah* above, but here it develops into processing the past into resocializing communal discourse, as the implied community is repositioned and devalued in the symbolic universe, in order to highlight the value of the Christ-event. This is achieved by articulating the plight of humankind both in universal and ethnic terms, in Ephesians 2.1-10 and 2.11-22, respectively.

The ideological reinterpretation of the past enhances the reputation of

---

1   Descriptions of calling, adoption, redemption and being sealed with the Spirit may appear simply self-enhancing rhetoric rather than a spiritual experience of God to a critical reader, although their reality (and therefore, their legitimating function) is widely accepted in Christian communities.

2   In my discussion of the Jewish covenant I imply no value judgment and reject negative view to 'Jewish exclusivism' (cf. Yee 2005). 'Exclusivism' seems to be a somewhat unfair notion given that, as the NT texts imply, Jewish communities did accommodate non-Israelites and had initiation processes in place. In addition, I reject the tendency to project Jewish faith as burdensome or use associated negative stereotypes. It seems plausible that when one has or assumes a Jewish ideological position and embraces its religious discourse, Jewish faith (ancient or present) can be meaningful and its practices are important expressions of belonging and orientation toward God. Overtly negative interpretation of Jewish traditions by Christians and NT critics goes together with failing to appreciate ongoing legitimacy of the Jewish traditions, which are preferred as providing legitimation and history story from which Christianity began. The same applies to 'other' faiths: when one rejects the discourse that explains the faith, community and its socio-ideological position, it tends to result in rejecting the validity of religious behaviours and practices.

3   See readings of 4.11 for discussion of spiritual and social powers in Ephesians.

4   Other significant contributions in remembering Christ in Ephesians are found in chapter 1 with its soteriological and cosmic interpretations of his transcendent persona; and in 5.25-33 where his love and sacrificial self-giving are in focus, along with the symbolic union between him and his followers.

'Christ' and communal dependence on him: the Christ-event is made more meaningful by stressing the non-Israelites' spiritual death (2.1-5) and social conflict (2.11-16) that supposedly characterized life before 'Christ'. First, the lostness of humankind, and non-Israelites in particular, is planted in the past so that the redemption would simultaneously increase in value:

> [2.1] You were dead through the trespasses and sins in which you once lived ... [4] But God, who is rich in mercy, out of the great love with which he loved us even when we were dead through our trespasses, [5] made us alive together with Christ – by grace you have been saved. [6] ... and raised us up with him and seated us with him in the heavenly places in Christ Jesus.

Secondly, in the same way, stressing the alienation of non-Israelites, labelling them as 'foreign' and 'alien' further heightens their status improvement 'in Christ':

> [2.11] So then, remember that at one time you non-Israelites by birth ... [12] remember that you were at that time without Christ, being aliens from Israel, and strangers to the covenants of promise, having no hope and without Christ in the world. [13] But now in Christ Jesus you who once were far off have been brought near by the blood of Christ... [2.19] So then you are no longer foreigners and aliens but you are fellow citizens with the saints and also co-members of the household of God.

Both status-improving discursive manoeuvrings above are ideological. Spiritual death and foreignness would hardly have been characteristic non-Israelite self-descriptions, but they are invented negative characteristics superimposed upon them by the writer. Therefore, where the construction of Christianness in Ephesians 1 is based on the presumption of a shared past experience, 2.1-22 is not. Instead it is an interpretation of the past that repositions the community spiritually, culturally and ethnically inferior in order to redefine their membership and their status as members of God's people.

At first the characterization of the non-Israelite life before 'Christ' appears stereotypical, emphasizing the sinfulness of the 'Gentile other': 'You were dead through the trespasses and sins in which you once lived, following the course of this world, following the ruler of the power of the air, the spirit that is now at work among those who are disobedient' (2.1-2). Yee suggests that the author's language is 'a clear reflection of traditional Jewish polemic against the Gentiles with respect to the moral standard of the latter' (2005: 40).[5] It utilizes the concept of spiritual death familiar from the Hebrew Bible and Paul, which often occurs in

---

5   His examples for 'traditional' polemic include Isa. 1.17-25; 41.8-9; 44.9.20; Job 18.21; Ps. 79.6; Jer. 10.25; 1 Macc. 1.27; 3 Macc. 4.16; Wis. 13.1; 14.23-26; 2 Esd. 7.48; Judith 8.20; and Rom. 1.21-25; 1 Thess. 4.5 and 2 Thess. 1.8 (Yee 2005: 40). He suggests that the polemic

ideological criticism of a lifestyle neglecting God's commands.[6] However, this could be more than 'typical Jewishness' and begin to demonstrate Ephesians' reformed viewpoint: the writer puts aside for a moment the assumption of Israel's blessedness and positions all humanity as equally lost: 'All of us once lived among them in the passions of our flesh, following the desires of flesh and senses, and we were by nature children of wrath, like everyone else' (2.3). There is sufficient evidence to assume that the author is Jewish, but he does not stress their better status before God here, but the discourse seems to imply that Israelites – like he – are also in need of God like 'the rest'. They have the covenant, as he will soon point out, but despite that they are projected here as transgressors along with the others, who are together made alive 'with Christ' (2.4).[7] This suggests that what Israel means for the Deutero-Pauline writer could also be redefined and in service of communal discourse; positioning Israelites as slaves to sin, sons of disobedience and the 'children of wrath' betrays a reformist viewpoint (2.3) which could be likened to prophetic criticism in other Jewish texts.[8]

Gerd Bauman points out that culture is not like a giant photocopying machine that keeps churning identical images (1999: 25). Consequently, neither was Jewish cultural heritage copied to all Second Temple Jewish groups in identical forms nor would different communities and their influencers be culturally and ideologically identical, but great variation occurred. Although the basic components of the symbolic could have been shared and key terms repeated in various communal contexts, their meanings were diverse. The multiplicity of influences in pluralistic social environs resulted in variegated forms of early Judaism(s) as widely acknowledged.[9] For instance, the Dead Sea Scrolls (DSS) suggest great cultural and ideological distinctiveness by writers who identified their communities as true Israelites and sharply critiqued Israelites outside the boundaries of their community.[10] Similarly, the writer of Ephesians maintains the Jewish symbolic universe and its cultural assumptions; but

---

represents a 'typical' condemnation of 'Gentile sinfulness'. For other evaluations of Jewish attitudes to their ethnoreligious 'other', see Donaldson (1997: 52–4) and MacDonald (2000: 228–31, 234–40; 2004: 422–3).

6 Gen. 2.15-17; Deut. 30.11-20; Ezek. 3.19-20; 18.21-24, 26-27; 33.8-9, 13-16, 18-19. See also Rom. 5.12, 21; 6.23; 7.10, 24; 8.10; and Col. 2.13.

7 This reduces the possibility of 'two way salvation' in Ephesians and two covenants, for Israelites and others.

8 See e.g. Isa. 30.9-14; 59.12-13; 63.10; Jer. 7.16-20; Ezek. 22.1-4.

9 See e.g. Sanders (1977); Boyarin (1994); Baumgarten (1997); Avery-Peck et al. (2001); Grabbe; (2000; 2007: 114–32); and Nickelsburg (2003).

10 Dr Rafael Rodriguez made a very interesting comment in response to my 2006 SBL paper, pointing to the fact that NT scholars automatically categorize NT texts as 'Christian' although other reform texts of the period, such as DSS, are automatically assumed to be Jewish, despite their sharp critique of Jewish customs and different interpretations of

redefines its conceptions perceived essential to his Christ-followership, including Israelite redemption 'in Christ'.[11]

Yee reasons that Ephesians' extensive use of the Jewish scripture shows 'that the Jewish scripture had become part of the author's tacit dimension, forming the "grid" of his theological and ethnical weaving' (2005: 43). In light of the above, I suggest that the author's Jewish cultural heritage is christologically reformed – and it is the reformed Christ-centred Jewishness which forms the framework for the discourse, as following readings will seek to further substantiate. The Hebrew Scriptures and other cultural influences together form the writer's cultural environment, but it is hugely important to note that he regards this conceptual world as fluid and flexible as it can be adapted in the light of recent ideas and circumstances.[12] Ephesians' understanding of Christ includes his tran-scendence, reconciling death on the cross and exaltation and triumph, which illustrates a flexible combination of cultural elements drawn from different Messianic beliefs, combined with apocalyptic imagination of divine triumph, which again, is not necessarily non-Jewish as all these factors have some parallels in Jewish thought of the period.[13] Perhaps the only difficult idea is the historical identification of Jesus and his wide rejection by Jewish people.

In my view, what happens in 2.1-3 does not measure distance between the author and 'the Gentiles' as Yee suggests (2005: 53), but rather the author stands alongside the non-Israelites and emphasizes the transgres-sions that separate all people and God.[14] Despite parallels of prophetic criticism and spiritual death in Jewish traditions, the positioning of Israelites alongside non-Israelites implied in Ephesians is interesting.[15]

---

formative scriptures. This highlights the default setting and theological conditioning of the NT scholarship. For further discussion of DSS see Lim and Collins (forthcoming); Chalcraft (2007); and Jokiranta (2005).

11   Pauline traditions follow Jewish thought where God's wrath is typically linked to deviance, as for instance Rom. 1.18-32 elaborates. Note that Paul engaged with the complexity of the Law, transgressions and human plight more fully than Ephesians does (Rom. 2–3; cf. Eph. 2.1-10, 11-15).

12   This is not the same as the Hebrew Bible as the 'substructure' of the author's theology (Dodd, 1952: 127; Yee 2005: 43, n. 40).

13   But I would not say it is Jewish or it is not, because I am a cultural outsider to Judaism and making such decisions is not part of my reading process.

14   It is true that the writer does position non-Israelites as outsiders 'to measure the religious and social distance' (Yee 2005: 53), but this happens in 2.11ff., not here.

15   Yee does note the 'self-indictment' of the 'insatiable desires which are forbidden by the Law' and finds parallels to author's admission of his sinfulness, mainly from the NT (Yee 2005: 57-8). Yee does not differentiate between NT and 'other' Jewish texts, but cites both as examples of Jewish thought. While otherness of NT texts shouldn't be assumed, there is something dubious and problematic in citing as Jewish texts that the Jewish communities have not embraced. Similarly, when he refers to the writer and 'his people' (p. 58) he does not

Fine suggests that for a negative reputation to be prominent the entrepreneurship of a positive image is either missing or has failed in its attempt (1996: 1173). Consequently, discursive positioning of the Israelites as 'the children of wrath' would suggest that they were either not part of the communal dialogue or were not influential enough to overturn their categorization alongside the non-Israelites; or they agreed with the writer's view that they indeed needed a solution for their passions and desires that led to trespasses and God's wrath (2.2-5). Similarly, the traces of the 'Gentile sinners' stereotype in Pauline and Deutero-Pauline texts suggests that either non-Israelite Christ-followers did not defend their status or succeed in their possible attempt to (re-)install value of their heritage. Alternatively, perhaps they became convinced that e.g. Ephesians' retrospective interpretation of their past as wholly negative is appropriate, in the light of new beliefs.[16]

Furthermore, cultures are not a baggage of unchanging truths that travel with individuals to different social locations, where they are unpacked, unchanged and used again. Instead, they are rather like navigation systems that depend upon position in time and social setting (Bauman 1999: 90). This social re-navigation and cultural flexibility meant that alterations to *beliefs and values were possible* as the apostolic age passed, the movement grew and its social composition and circumstances changed.[17] Ephesians has adapted its ideological paradigms to include the salvation of the nations and their election 'in Christ', while still maintaining his cultural position and core elements of the Jewish symbolic universe. For instance, although the non-Israelite inclusion, their election (1.4, 5; 2.10), and their equality with Israelites seem to be to the fore (2.11-22), and even if their salvation is projected as the climax of God's plans (3.5-11), 'Jesus Christ' is still perceived as operating within Jewish conceptional frames, bringing the sacred elect of the nations into a worship of Israel's God. Therefore, Ephesians' attitude to the 'non-Israelite other' offers means for their association (like god-fearers and proselytes in other texts) without altering the basic stereotype of their difference. This demonstrates that the author's symbolic universe was a

---

discuss this in the light of the relationship between the Jewish people and the Christ-followers. This suggests that the weight of the writer's ingroup orientation with the Christ-following community seems to go unnoticed by Yee.

16 The survival of the text and its eventual canonization does not mean that its views were not contested at all. But it allows us to assume that its socio-ideological positions gained prominence within the recipient community and among early Christians beyond the core ingroup.

17 This flexibility was one of the author's values and it does not mean that Ephesians' views would have been embraced by others in the spirit of plural society and faith. It is quite likely that its view would have either been contested or dismissed as minority views.

socially constructed entity where the presence of the ancient benevolent deity and the selection, consecration and holiness of his people appear as given and unalterable assumptions, with which the salvation of other nations is negotiated.

It is also important to notice that we do not learn from Ephesians what the non-Israelites actually were like, but we can only observe their socio-ideologically motivated portrayal that reflects inter-ethnic and inter-communal positionings of the writer. Because Ephesians is a subcultural, minority text which manifests some tension with its social basis, critiques other cultures and proposes alternative models it resonates with the basic ideas of sociology of sectarianism, from Max Weber's church-sect typology to Wilson's basic classification of a sectarian movement to ideal types (1975), Stark and Bainbridge (1979, 1985), and others.[18] Like many other early Christian texts, Ephesians has been examined in the light of Wilson's sectarian types (1975, cf. Esler 1994: 70–91; MacDonald 1988: 32–9; 2000: 174–7; 236–40).[19] However, as MacDonald correctly acknowledges, Ephesians does not neatly fit into any seven types in Wilson's categorization, namely revolutionist, conversionist, introversionist, manipulationist, thaumathurgical, reformist or utopian (1975).[20] Nevertheless, the ideas of transformation (Ephesians 1, 2), correctness of its own view (3.5-6), and the socio-ideological distance from the surrounding sinful world is important for Ephesians, as we see in the condemnation of the past life in 2.1-10 and setting socio-ideological paradigms through prototypes and antitypes in 4.17–5.20. So it clearly manifests a reformist stance and strong ingroup orientation typical of

18   David Chalcraft's edited volume *Sectarianism in Early Judaism* was published roughly when I submitted my doctoral work, and I will engage 'sociological imagination' reflecting his work in my forthcoming projects. Chalcraft (2007) offers useful discussion of Weberian sociology of sects with a particular reference to Second Temple Judaism in Part 1 of the volume (2–105) followed by a relevant Weber bibliography (106–11); and a collection of essays discussing sectarianism by different sociologists.

19   According to Esler, two of the most relevant heuristic models for understanding early Christianities are those of revolutionist and conversionist, while the others are less frequent (Esler 1994: 72–3).

20   See MacDonald (2004: 237–8). Ephesians has a number of parallels with attitudes and social processes discussed in Wilson's typology. For instance, it manifests some revolutionist ideology that presumes the intervention of some supernatural prophesied event and subsequent restoration, since only a divine action can change the evil proceedings of the world or dominant society (Wilson 1975: 23). Similarly, Ephesians seems to hold a conversionist belief that God will change humans, but it does not fit the ideal type as it does not mobilize conversionist mission, which typically characterizes such movements (1975: 23). It also manifests idealistic introversionist tendency as it is preoccupied with the holiness of the separated community, but again, there are no practical instructions for withdrawal from the world (1975: 23–4). While Ephesians is not a perfect specimen of any of Wilson's ideal types, they are helpful in highlighting different responses to social environment perceived negatively, along with other models from sociology of sectarianism.

sectarianism and offers plenty of material for further reflection in Ephesians and Deutero-Pauline scholarship. Different types and models demonstrate that groups and communities frequently combine different strategies in their sectarian responses to their cultural location. It seems that just as identities fluctuate and resist categorization, social expressions of different sectarian models overlap and different tendencies are reflected in the same groups and communal discourses.[21]

For instance, on the one hand, it is characteristic of Ephesians' social entrepreneurship to denounce the surrounding (social) world due to its sinfulness and distance from God (2.1-3; 4.17ff.). This epitomizes how Ephesians manipulates its readers by selective, ideologically coloured remembering as well as by not-remembering. Both communal forgetting as well as communal remembering are important; forgetting any value of non-Israelite heritage, culture and life 'before Christ'; and remembering the past as reinterpreted in the light of the Christ-event. Therefore Ephesians seems to operate an ideological framework that filters individual and collective memories so that past lifestyle would be devalued and characterized as detestable purely on the grounds of the absence of Christ from it.[22]

However, on the other hand, although Ephesians undervalues the non-Israelite social setting of the community and established Jewish boundaries (2.15), it does not promote isolating the community as a monastic or isolated movement.[23] This suggests that any social distancing is ideological, value-based, and perhaps psychological, rather than actual and socio-economic. Negative labelling of outsiders accentuates the difference between community and non-members, as seen in the 'sons of disobedience' and 'children of wrath' (2.2-3). Ephesians reinforces devaluation of their cultural setting and strengthening their communal orientation

---

21 Cf. Grabbe (2007).

22 It may be peculiar that some memories should be negatively transformed in self-loathing, denying the value of life before Christ. However, similar processes do still take place in different movements, especially religious. For instance, members of evangelical groups often emphasize their 'testimony', exaggerating their (alleged) condemnation, struggle or lostness before they were 'saved' and stressing the change that occurred with belief in Christ. This highlights the salvific and other value of their experience of (or belief in) a spiritual transformation, which is often accompanied by outlining evidence for moral transformation. In my view, the transformation seems to stand for the acceptance of new cultural logic, values and beliefs, which come with new social orientation and ethic paradigms that the person adheres to and, therefore, is transformed by.

23 The readings of Ephesians 4–6 examine more closely its social orientation. For discussion of parallels with Jewish sectarian thought see, for example, MacDonald (2000: 237–40), and Perkins (1997: *passim*).

(cf. 4.1-3).[24] This may result from external pressure on the community as, for instance, MacDonald suggests. She argues that in 2.1-10 the writer responds to external threats and recalls the rejection of the outside world and entry into the community (2000: 238–9). Indeed, Ephesians builds communal identity by portraying the powers of the world outside as threatening and stressing the believers' partaking in Christ's victory (2.1-3, 4-6). The writer then intertwines a set of Pauline ideas and reinterprets them to linking God's initiative in their salvation and their lifestyle: 'For by grace you have been saved through faith, and this is not your own doing; it is the gift of God – not the result of works, so that no one may boast. For we are what he has made us, created in Christ Jesus for good works, which God prepared in advance to be our way of life' (2.8-10). This is an example of adaptation of religious symbols that may be modified from their original context to convey certain meanings to new generations of communal members (MacDonald 2000: 239; cf. 1988: 90–1). For instance, here the meaning of 'faith v. works' has been transformed; having lost its original, Pauline connotation which negotiates the 'Gentile inclusion' and Torah observance, it has become a general symbol for God's initiative in salvation (MacDonald 2000: 240), and 'good works' has become a metaphor for a God ordained, virtuous lifestyle.[25]

It seems to me that the Deutero-Pauline writer has simplified complex Pauline traditions and distilled the debates of the apostle to simple and memorable statements that stretch a 'legitimating canopy' over social conflicts and debates, silenced in the discourse.[26]

Finally, although the Jewish symbolic universe is reformed with meanings drawn from the Christ-event, it seems that social entrepreneurship still reflects ethnic stereotypes (contrary to Yee).[27] Having introduced the self-enhancing comparison between the deficient past and blessed communal present the discourse builds on the ideas of non-Israelite

24   Communal possession of salvation is typical of Wilson's 'introversionist sect' (1975: 23–4; cf. Eph. 4.17-33). Ephesians' encouragement for separation whilst (presumably) retaining (at least some of) her original social networks is a typical example of tension between introversion and engagement in introversionist groups (1988: 32–42; 2004: 423–7).

25   See Chapter 6 for a more detailed exploration of the prototypical lifestyle Ephesians promotes.

26   For theoretical perspective on legitimation see Berger and Luckmann's discussion of institutionalization and sedimentation of traditions (1966: 70–89).

27   Negotiation of multi-ethnic Christianness is central to Romans and Galatians. However, unlike Paul, Ephesians reasons in an idealistic fashion. This has led Yee to categorize the community as a representative of 'a Jewish messianic inclusivistic movement which transcends covenantal ethnocentrism' and believes that 'Messiah Jesus' surmounted the social distance between Jews and Gentiles (Yee 2005: 228). However, both classifying Ephesians as 'inclusivistic' and Jesus as 'Messiah' are problematic as this study continues to explore.

otherness, compared to covenant Israel, and their status improvement (2.11-22).[28]

1a. *Non-Israelite Status Transformation in 2.11-22*

This section will discuss the social implications of the ethnic reconciliation in 2.11-22 and how this contributes to communal legitimation. Here the innovative hermeneutics of the social entrepreneur continue to develop the idea of non-Israelite believers' status improvement based on ideologically loaded remembering of the Christ-event. This continues his flexible use of Jewish traditions in communal self-enhancement and further illustrates the licence of reworking he assumes. Ephesians' textual 'world-making' continues building on the symbolic counter-reality where social realities and cultural values are reinterpreted.[29] Here the non-Israelites' status transformation involves political and religious overtones that stress the reign of 'Christ' and its beneficial consequences to those who were formerly outside God's kingdom:

> [2.11] So then, remember that at one time you non-Israelites by birth, called 'the uncircumcision' by those who are called 'the circumcision' – a physical circumcision made in the flesh by human hands – [12] remember that you were at that time without Christ, being aliens Israel, and strangers to the covenants of promise, having no hope and without God in the world. [13] But now in Christ Jesus you who once were far off have been brought near by the blood of Christ. [14] For he is our peace; in his flesh he has made both groups into one and has broken down the dividing wall, that is, the hostility between us.[15] He has abolished the Law with its commandments and ordinances, that he might create in himself one new humanity in place of two, thus making peace, [16] and might reconcile both groups to God in one body through the cross, thus putting to death that hostility through it. [17] So he came and proclaimed peace to you who were far off and peace to those who were near; [18] for through him both of us have access in one Spirit to the Father. [19] So then you are no longer strangers and aliens, but you are citizens with the

28   For then–now (*pote–nun*) comparison see Tachau (1972: 21–70; 134–43); and Lincoln (1990: 86–8).

29   Iser adapts Goodman's 'world-making' for a selective, fictional *modus operandi* resulting in a paradigmatic dimension to real life (Iser 1989: 270). As noted before Ephesians' world-making differs from Paul's in its exclusion of dialogue with outsiders, but the 'significant others' are either positioned outside the community and/or in the past or as enticing agents of moral decline (2.1-3, 11, 12; 4.17-19; 5.5ff.). Potential conflict is also presented in symbolic terms, as if it involved spiritual realities, not people and social conflict (6.12). However, the (non-Israelite) sins are expressed as moral and 'real', not as works of hostile or deceiving spirits, but as an expression of moral decline or rebellion, which a believer must reject (cf. 4.17–5.20 *passim*). See Chapter 6 below.

saints and also members of the household of God, [20] built on the foundation of the apostles and prophets, with Christ Jesus himself as the cornerstone. [21] In him the whole structure is joined together and grows into a holy temple in the Lord; [22] in whom you also are built together spiritually into a dwelling place for God.

It is regrettable that this study cannot offer a close reading of 2.11-22, because this, as Yee demonstrates, would be a project on its own. Nevertheless, an outline of its discursive positionings and a brief consideration of its broad mnemonic manoeuvres are important to set the scene for closer examination of its central ideological statements and social rearrangements. The passage involves discursive re-positioning of the non-Israelites, which integrates them in worship of God in the Jewish symbolic universe. The writer continues to ignore the traditions of his fictional characters and typecasts them as non-Israelites. They are further stereotyped as foreigners and outsiders (2.12a) according to a view that accentuates Israel's blessing and covenant position (2.12b) and as a consequence, apportions sin and separation for others, expressed in negative representation and stereotyping.[30] This is where shaping Jesus' reputation meets communal interests. Remembering 'Jesus Christ' includes transforming the status of the non-Israelite believers by the negation of social conflicts they may experience in the process of their incorporation into Jewish community. The writer builds an ideological bridge upon which 'those who were far off have been brought near', eradicating the nation's social distance 'in Christ' and 'by his blood' (2.13). The widely established early Christian symbols of Jesus' death, his blood and the cross are retained in Ephesians' communal memory, but here they become symbols of ethic reconciliation and solutions for social conflict (2.13-15). Although non-Israelite inclusion 'in Christ' was probably a matter of much debate, Ephesians imagines it to be an act of peace, thus transforming existing memory with subcultural counter-mnemonics: 'Christ' made the divided groups into one (2.14a), breaking down the divisive wall of hostility (2.14b),[31] abolishing the law (2.15a), creating one new humanity and making peace (2.15b), and reconciling both groups to God and putting to death hostility between them (2.16). Communal remembering of Jesus' reconciling reiterates concepts of peace

30   For the discussion of Jewish and Greco-Roman influences on Ephesians 2.12 see Hoehner (2002: 356–61).

31   I take the dividing wall in 2.14 as a metaphor for a social boundary separating Israel and other nations. The best explanation for the creation and maintaining of such a persistent social boundary is the Mosaic Law (e.g. Lincoln 1990: 141–2; Schnackenburg 1991: 114; Hoehner 2002: 370–1). Other interpretations include a 'cosmic wall' and a divisive marker at the Jerusalem Temple (cf. MacDonald 2004: 244–5). For further discussion see e.g. Yee (2005: 144–51); Barth (1959: 33–45); Perkins (1997: 71–3); and Hoehner (2002: 366–74).

with God and access to him, which both Israelites and non-Israelites now share. He grants non-Israelites citizenship and membership in God's family (2.19).

Although Ephesians unites and reconciles 'both groups', Israelites and non-Israelites (2.14, 16), this experience is a vital part of its Christianness, as it is embedded in remembering the death of 'Christ' on the cross. Therefore it seems most convincing that the reconciliation refers only to those representatives of both groups who identify by faith with this concept, the saving death of 'Jesus Christ' on the cross.[32] This is further indicated in the fact that the community members 'have been built on the foundation of the apostles and prophets, with Christ Jesus himself' as the central structure (2.20). Ephesians makes no attempt to explain how this relates to Israel's position as God's people and 'unbelieving Israel' – so, although this would not be popular with the 'new perspective', Ephesians forgets Israel as God's chosen people, as the covenant people have awkward boundaries.

The cultural re-navigation in this passage includes two basic steps: 1) the evaluation of non-Israelite otherness and its reversal in 'Christ', as non-ethnic members are joined into the people of God; 2) the removal of socio-ethnic hostility by 'Christ', which includes removing hostility, abolishing the Law and the creation of a new humanity from divided ethnicities. Here Ephesians' social entrepreneurship – and the symbolic language in which social influence is coded – differs significantly from Romans: Romans describes a tree that consists of non-Israelite branches grafted into a cultivated olive tree of Israel, thus maintaining a distinction between the two groups (Esler 2004: 30–1, 298–307). In contrast, in Ephesians the community likened to a spiritual temple is not constructed of distinct Israelite and foreign components, but of new creations (2.15).[33] This leads me to disagree with Yee who suggests that 'Jews remained Jews and Gentiles, too [remained Gentiles]' (2005: 166).[34] Instead, Ephesians

---

32   Ephesians makes few references to the death of Jesus, as in 1.20 and the language of sacrifice in 5.2. However, it does not develop atonement theology or any systematic discussion of its significance except reconciliation in this passage. Ephesians may follow Colossians which similarly stresses peace and reconciliation at the cross (cf. Col. 1.20, 22; 2.14). The point of mentioning his death or the way he died is not so much of historical but of communal value, as the communal body was redeemed and came to existence at his death (Best 1998: 266).

33   Though Ephesians does intertwine different metaphors, some of which highlight differences among the members and others their similarity. For instance, the metaphor of divine gifting makes a distinction between different functions and roles among the members (4.11, 15-16). Similarly, the household code differentiates statuses and roles (5.21–6.9). However, the *ekklēsia*-body and divine warrior metaphors stress their togetherness and common positions (5.25-32; 6.12).

34   Cf. Yee 2005: 144. Yee takes the 'new humanity' as a 'new corporate identity of an eschatological humankind' that marks the beginning of the transformation of the whole

installs creation of 'new humanity' in communal memory. It causes its community to remember that the newness is not created '*ex nihilo*' like Darko points out, but out of division (2008: 110).[35]

1b. *Diverse Reading Positions and the Socio-Ideological Positioning of the Discourse*

Ephesians 2.11-22 has traditionally been read in opposition to 'Judaism' (anachronism has often played a significant role) and its remarks on the Law have been seen as evidence for a separation of inter-religious disputes. Though it could be assumed that other communal discourses may have ensured that, for example, 2.15 was neither intended nor understood as a total dismissal of the law in its time and original recipient community. However, the matter is more complicated with the post-Pauline date, as the movement shifted from its Jewish origins and grew in independence by the second century CE, as e.g. Lieu and Zetterholm have demonstrated, and thus close association with the Jewish movement can no longer be assumed. But the separation is not the only hermeneutical possibility. The Deutero-Pauline comments can be seen as expressions of social and religious competition, not fixed and defined attitudes directed against 'Judaism'.[36]

In order to understand the community embedded in the text its relations

---

cosmos (p. 188); similarly Schnackenburg 1991: 115–16; and Best, who notes the realized eschatology involved in the idea, given that in the Jewish thought creation of a new man belonged to the end of time (1998: 261–3). MacDonald follows Lincoln, who discusses the similarity of Ephesians with Paul's Adam Christology, which similarly makes Christ the representative of 'the new order' who symbolically incorporates believers into himself and transcends old divisions, cf. 1 Cor. 12.12, 13; 15.22, 45-49; Gal. 3.27-28; Rom. 12.5; Col. 3.10-11 (MacDonald 2000: 245–6; cf. Lincoln 1990: 143). Hoehner concludes that the new humanity means that Gentiles did not become like Jews in terms of a proselyte conversion, but both become new (Hoehner 2002: 378–80). Indeed, even if, as Lincoln points out, Ephesians would be making use of proselyte terminology, as in Joseph and Asenath (61.4, 5), the idea has been reformed, as a new creation is not about proselytes joining into Israelite community, but the newness of both Jews and Gentiles (Lincoln 1990: 144). However, a third entity is not entirely free of ethnic influences, as I will argue in Chapter 6 below.

35 Ephesians' election of non-Israelites and the language of 'new humanity' borders on ethnic reasoning where Christianness is imagined as a wholly new entity, in comparison to Greeks, Romans and Israel. Although the language of a 'third race' does not dominate Pauline thought, it finds a precursor in 1 Cor. 10.32 where Paul refers to Jews, Greeks and the 'Church of God'. Other parallels include the concept of 'spiritual Israel' and language of spiritual renewal as 'new creation' (Gal. 6.15), and being the true children of Abraham (Rom. 4, 9; Gal. 3–4). For Jewish parallels of 'newness' of proselyte converts see Lincoln (1990: 144) and for post-NT ethnic reasoning see Buell (2005).

36 So, for instance, Dunn who concludes that 'the Deutero-Paulines are characteristically lacking in overt or even in clearly implicit anti-Judaism', with the possible exception of Titus (1993: 165). Instead, he argues, the Deutero-Paulines reflect a syncretistic context, where Jewish elements featured considerably (165).

to Israel are particularly important. It is important to test whether Ephesians upholds the role of Israel as God's elect and extends Israel's blessings to non-Israelites, or whether it conveys a rudimentary idea of replacement, substituting Israel with *ekklēsia*.[37] This reading will focus particularly upon the claim that 'Christ has abolished the Law' in 2.15 for two main reasons: 1) first, because this verse is critical for understanding communal identity, boundaries and intergroup relations; and 2) secondly, because it is crucial for understanding Ephesians' place in the development of early Christianities and Pauline theology.[38]

In terms of its social aspects: depending on the interpretation of 2.15, Ephesians can be seen as culturally continuous with essential Jewishness, or socially different, denouncing what appears to have been the key symbol of Jewish identity, or at least its socio-ideological significance, and therefore, discontinuous. The verse is equally important for understanding Ephesians within the early Christian movement: if one views the Pauline and other earliest Jesus-movement as maintaining fellowship with other Jewish groupings, then the Christ-followers' claims for independence by articulation of a distinctive community orientation (without the Law) would seem to be in contrast with the apostolic teaching and origins of the movement.[39] If so, the difference between Paul and a later independent 'non-Israelite Christianity' could be explained by identifying elements of separation in pseudo-Pauline writings, here Ephesians, that

37 For a considered view on Ephesians' socio-ideological positioning both Jewishness and Christianness of the text and its writer's manoeuvrings have to be considered. In order to achieve this social-scientific theoretical framework will be supplemented with theoretical models from literary criticism, to which I shall shortly return.

38 It is inevitable that this study will exclude plenty of interesting material on Ephesians and merely outline what for me are key moves of Ephesians' social entrepreneurship. From here forth 'Christ has abolished the law' functions as shorthand for 2.15 in this study. It is possible that the phrase *tōn entolōn en dogmasin* qualifies and limits the aspects of the law that were abolished (e.g. Barth 1974: 287–91), especially as there is no other critique of the law. However, it is assumed here that the phrase does not limit what is abolished, but rather emphasizes the divisiveness of the law in the context of hostility (cf. Lincoln 1990: 141–3; MacDonald 2000: 245), given that Ephesians' focus is particularly on socially divisive practices. Ephesians does not differentiate different aspects of the law; it does not uphold the importance of some aspects of the law, or explain its significance to Israel, but is dismissed as negative. The writer focuses on circumcision as a boundary process and oneness of the reconciled community in 2.11-22, and the fact that he does not engage in a discussion of Sabbath observance, food laws or other rituals, unlike for example Col. 2.14-23, may be indicative of different social locations. I will discuss this in my forthcoming work on the Deutero-Paulines.

39 In addition to epistles commonly seen as post-Pauline, 1 Thess. 2.13-16 is frequently taken as Deutero-Pauline interpolation due to its accusations against the Jews, contra Setzer (1994: 9–25).

'pushed the boat out' with apostolic authority and legitimated the ideologically different viewpoint as Pauline tradition.[40]

Nevertheless, although Ephesians and other Deutero-Paulines exhibit a lack of interest in discussion of Israel's role and relationship with the communities implied, any evidence for social separation is less clear. In my view, the separation between early Christian and Jewish thought has been an essential part of the interpretive history without being an integral component of the text as the chapter proceeds to argue. For example, the idea of a separation between 'Judaism and Christianity' has traditionally been the dominant approach and this has produced readings that conform to such an assumption. However, in the last decades readings that stress the Jewishness of early Christianities have begun to overturn that paradigm.[41] The texts have not changed but the readings have. Therefore, given that the discussion of early Christianities is based on texts, it is important to be sensitive to the dynamics of reading and processing meanings of texts that allow for diverse interpretations, and facilitate critical engagement with different readings. For instance, a survey of Ephesians 2.15 scholarship suggests that different readers have provided different explanations for textual complexities and ambiguities, and arrived at different solutions because the text does not explicitly provide detailed answers to our socio-ideological (or theological) questions. Thus, a further discussion of a reading strategy is due in order to critically engage with the complexities of the text. Because I regard 2.15 as crucial for Ephesians' interpretation I will explore it in the light of some literary-critical models which are not part of explicit discussion throughout this study or usually combined with socio-scientific methods.[42] Naturally, literary-critical evaluation of different reading positions, presuppositions and, even more importantly, their bearing on the study of early Christianities is always of vital importance.[43]

---

40   This does not need to imply abuse of communal leadership or deception, but e.g. that Pauline view on the law was genuinely believed to mean that the law was brought to an end and no longer important.

41   Jewish texts that have recently become available have contributed to understanding of the diversity of the Second Temple Judaism(s), and parallels with the NT thought.

42   Testing different readings is particularly fitting for Ephesians due to disputes on the authorship of the letter, consequent ambiguity of its date and uncertainty of the socio-historical setting of its audience. Although uncritical speculation of such factors that lead the reading as conforming in a certain direction would be problematic, there is a fine line between assumptions that almost inevitably lead to certain interpretations and research preferences that exclude certain interpretive possibilities. For example, reading position and research questions I have chosen in this study focus on testing the Deutero-Pauline authorship and its socio-ideological contours. Thus I do not devote time into readings from other possible angles although they would offer interesting avenues to explore.

43   Although such perspectives are important the reading process is not equally detailed elsewhere in this study.

I suggest that the meaning of the claim that 'Christ has abolished the Law' (2.15) is particularly sensitive to external links, presuppositions and gap fillers. This verse is decisive for the ideological and social aspects of the text, as well as for understanding the development of early Christianities: 2.15 is critical for understanding the Jewishness/ Christianness of the text, its social orientation and communal relations, both within the group and with outsiders. For instance, it is at this verse where a reader is drawn to decide what kind of early Christianity the text represents and what kind of Christianness it was developing; whether it maintained an association with Torah-observant Jewish Christianities or whether it contributed to a process of separation that gradually resulted in separate Christianity and Judaism. In other words, whether the community maintained a close connection with Israelites or whether their ideological position suggests a separate social location. Furthermore, the verse is also decisive for hermeneutical observations on the development of Deutero-Pauline Christianities depending whether the post-Pauline development is seen as continuous or a rather more radical adaptation of his legacy.

This is where fresh readings of Ephesians are a significant contribution to its scholarship. The discussion of Jewishness of early Christianities made its way to Ephesians scholarship, too. Consequently, many recent projections on Ephesians fill the 'gaps' with evidence of Jewishness.[44] Yee (2005) is the most detailed example, which explores the Jewishness of Ephesians following Dunn, who highlighted the Jewish worldview of the author and what he describes as a surprising lack of anti-Semitism in the pseudo-Paulines (1993: 151–2). Although Yee's 'New Perspective' reading deserves credit for calling further attention to Paul's – or Ephesians' – Jewishness, it fails to fully explain what 'Jewishness' means to the letter. Like Lieu and others have pointed out, it is insufficient to suggest that the textual evidence of Jewishness would disprove anti-Jewishness (2001: 127); or perhaps more correctly, that linguistic similarity would automatically mean social or cultural agreement. Similarly Raimo Hakola, who discusses 'essential Jewishness' and its selective expressions in the Fourth Gospel and suggests that it makes diverse Jewish traditions contribute to the development of a 'non-Jewish Christian identity' as it negates some basic aspects of Jewish identity (2005: 32). Hence the author's terms, their meanings and social effects deserve detailed attention: if the author's literary style and the main components of the textual symbolic universe seemed characteristically Jewish, it does not exclude the possibility that they were used in service of reformist values and convictions. Similarly, if the text was immersed with Paul-like

---

44   In addition to Yee, MacDonald also highlights Ephesians' significant engagement with Jewish people (MacDonald 2004), as Perkins (1997) has done previously.

expressions and rhetorical moves (whichever way one understands Paul), it does not follow that Ephesians is necessarily in agreement with Paul in the undisputed letters. Therefore, both Jewishness and Christianness deserve detailed investigation, along with the factors that contribute to hermeneutical decisions and convictions over matters of interpretation.

2. *'Christ Has Abolished the Law' as a Socio-Ideological Test for Readings of Ephesians*

Ephesians' social entrepreneurship comes across as innovative adaptation of Pauline legacy. Here it offers a unique interpretation of the work of 'Christ', as it regards ethnic reconciliation and reforms of the Law (and implicitly, God's covenant with his people) as essential meanings of his death.[45] This is a prime example of the shaping of communal identity with ideologically shaped memories which link the historical core, present concerns (over ethnic hostility) and ideological convictions (about communal boundaries). By doing so, the discourse shapes how the community should remember 'Christ' and what his death is said to have achieved. Consequently, I would suggest that the claim that 'Christ has abolished the Law with its commandments and ordinances' (2.15) is of key importance to the ingroup identity and communal ideology, and because it deals with the law and appropriate cultural performances it has its bearing upon their intra- and intergroup relations. Thus 2.15 connects the historical past and communal present.

The reading 'the abolishment of the Law' as a test case for Jewishness and/or Christianness involves two hermeneutically different possibilities, which in my view, are decisive for arriving at coherent interpretations for the letter as a whole.[46] The two alternatives imply a significantly different social orientation and different perspectives on communal identity, which in turn result in the construction of different collective memories and

45   Like its post-Pauline counterpart in Col. 2.13-14, 'And when you were dead in trespasses and the uncircumcision of your flesh, God made you alive together with him, when he forgave us all our trespasses, erasing the record that stood against us with its legal demands. He set this aside, nailing it to the cross'. Both centralize the removal of the Law code at the cross, which Colossians links with spiritual transformation, forgiveness, regeneration and baptism (MacDonald 2000: 102, 106–8). In Colossians, Baptism functions as a counter-ritual to circumcision as a boundary marker that draws the line between God's people and 'others': 'In him also you were circumcised with a spiritual circumcision, by putting off the body of the flesh in the circumcision of Christ; when you were buried with him in baptism… (2.11-12). Therefore the removal of one boundary process is clearly replaced with another in Colossians, unlike in Ephesians.

46   For traditional interpretations and the key representatives of maximalist (dispensational denial of the Law) and minimalist interpretations (upholding the value of the Law generally, denying its 'divisive function') see Yee 2005: 154–5, ns. 112–13) and the discussion

interpretations of 'Christ'. The two interpretive possibilities for the phrase 'Christ has abolished the Law' are an abandonment of Torah observance 1) as a rejection of the traditional boundary for 'God's people', which distinguished between Israelites and non-Israelites, whilst allowing for the ongoing validity of the Torah for Israelites; and 2) as an articulation of distinctive boundaries for 'the people of God in Christ' and renouncing the validity of the Torah altogether.

2a. *Readings that Maintain the Validity of the Torah*
This view assumes that in 2.11-22:[47]

1) The separated non-Israelite status is evaluated from a Jewish cultural position and characterized by communal privileges expressed in the covenant(s) and its sign, circumcision.
2) The blessings now received by non-Israelites in 'Christ' are equivalent to the covenant blessings of Israel, namely peace, access to God and citizenship. Israel has not been cast off but non-Israelites are brought in to share in their blessings, and the symbolism of a sacred location is transposed to the community as a whole in terms of being a spiritual temple.
3) All that has taken place is that the barrier that kept the non-Israelites out has been broken down and the distinction between Israel and foreigners summed up in the question of circumcision, the dividing line between ethnicities, is abolished. As the principle of division is removed the Israelites and foreigners are now 'one new human being' (2.15).

The following ideas typify the interpretation of 'the abolition of the Law' along with this view: This view assumes that the Torah was a symbol for the covenant that only Israelites were God's covenant people and thus its abolishing meant that others could now be included as full members of the community, as well. The concept of God's people was extended and universalized at the messianic era when non-Israelite Christ-followers were also included into his people and thus the former ethnic characteristic no longer applies. Consequently, in this view of Pauline traditions, the law, which was a sign of ethnic covenant no longer applies. Therefore the principles of ethnic covenant and circumcision that signified this

---

below. A quest for a coherent reading of the text as a whole is, of course, just one way of engaging with the letter, among multiple reading strategies. However, it is important for this study that focuses on communal ideology and its bearing on identity and social relations.

47 As proposed by Dunn (1993: 157–9) followed by Yee in his more detailed analysis (2005: 71–212).

covenant are no longer valid signs for the totality of God's people.[48] The circumcision no longer demonstrates who is a member of the people of God, which includes uncircumcised non-Israelite followers of 'Jesus Christ'. Thus, this view assumes that the Christ-event inaugurated reforms in God's people and their boundary processes. For instance, Yee argues that Israel is radically redefined and their ethnic covenant is transformed as Ephesians constructs a new space for the non-Israelites (2005: 71–72),[49] Israel is then transposed 'into an inclusive community-body' (2005: 71–72, 91).[50]

However, the Pauline view was not the only approach to non-Israelite inclusion. Nanos discusses the social role of Paul's opponents in Galatia, who were 'social control agents', concerned with the communal distinctiveness and relations of the Israelites with the surrounding society (2002: 12). Naturally, when they came into contact with Pauline disciples claiming a full membership without going through the standard process of initiation through circumcision a conflict was bound to occur. The conflicts arose as Jewish Christ-following minorities sought to identify outsiders as the righteous members of the people of God without approved initiation rites (2002: 8). Paul's ideology indicates that Galatian addressees were persuaded and accepted the dominant Jewish communal norms and boundaries, and wanted to (re-)establish a communal status of righteousness before God, which, according to Paul, they had already achieved in Christ (2002: 12). It was therefore particularly at the boundaries of Jewishness where social entrepreneurs and non-Israelite Christ-followers negotiated communal characteristics (membership in the people of God marked by righteousness) and belonging (through circumcision as a symbol of faith, covenant and membership).

The negotiation of communal boundaries is one of the key factors in constructing communal identity, as the boundary defines similarity (who is a member) and excludes difference (who is an outsider); and makes explicit on what basis, whether ethnic, cultural, ideological or social, these divisions occur (Jenkins 2004: 94–107, 108–23). Social boundaries are communal processes that have important functions in preserving the

---

48   I am avoiding Yee's 'covenantal ethnocentrism' (cf. 2005: 71, 91, 112–13, 121–2, 186–7, 215–16, 219, 221, 228).

49   Let's put the negative language aside for a moment and footnote accompanying references to 'exclusive disposition of the Jews' and the 'exclusive, ethnic-oriented body politic of Israel' (Yee 2005: 71–2).

50   Yee gets very close to being socially aware when he concludes that 'the boundaries between Jews and Gentiles were socially innovated' (2005: 123), if it wasn't part of his criticism for ignoring God's plans (2005: 123) and 'little-mindedness of the Jews' and their 'less than healthy attitudes' (2005: 126, 143).

group and its identity as well as in recruiting new members.[51] It is true that communities and their boundaries imply certain roles and social person-alities that an individual may assume (Barth 1969: 17) and therefore they may seem restrictive to outsiders. This, however, should provide no basis for etic judgments.[52] Although Ephesians includes the removal of the law, the discussion of communal boundaries is far from clear and systematic. The writer does not engage in boundary marking by describing initiation, rules and norms, punishments, excommunication or exit rituals; but the key values are embedded in the ideological discourse more discretely.[53] Nevertheless, regardless of how a reader engages with the text some boundary negotiations are rather obvious and relatively undisputed. Such is, for example, the importance of Christ and participation 'in him' that defines communal togetherness and functions as an implicit primary identification throughout the letter.[54]

51   For Yee's discussion of the function of the Law in Israel's cross-ethnic relation see 2005: 78–83; 154–61.

52   Rather, a critical examination of social functions of the boundary processes should also discuss other aspects of communal identity and group processes. Although this study includes a wider discussion of Ephesians' view to Christ-following community, unfortunately the scope of this book does not allow for evaluation of other Jewish and early Christian movements, although they would be both relevant and interesting to this study.

53   It is notable that social entrepreneurship excluded any discussion of behaviours that would lead to a formal rebuke, or possible exit and the excommunication of deviant members. In my view, this is typical of Ephesians, which silences social conflicts, and to some extent, also the possibility of deviant behaviour. In 4.17–5.20 the writer condemns deviance, but does not explain what happens to a member if their 'Gentile sinfulness' reoccurs. This is also ideologically complex as Ephesians regards deviance as slavery to hostile spirits, while believers ought to obey and serve God who has designed good works for them to accomplish according to God's power operative in their lives (1.19; 3.20).

54   Sometimes being 'in Christ' is assumed to lead into transformation that would remove previous identities and their deviance. So for instance Schweitzer: 'For [Paul] every manifestation of the life of the baptized man is conditioned by his being in Christ. Grafted into corporeity of Christ he loses his creatively individual existence and his natural personality. Henceforth he is only a form of manifestation of the personality of Jesus Christ, which dominates that corporeity' (Schweitzer 1998: 125). However, from social-scientific perspective being a Christian is psychological, social and ideological matter, both individual and corporate, while the evidence for any spiritual transformation is largely unverifiable as any cultural change may result from different community, values and beliefs, without spiritual catalyst. Therefore a Christian remains his own man – or woman or child – despite their belief in Jesus as Christ and Saviour. The early Christian social entrepreneurship was acutely aware of the fact that Christ-followers required guidance and motivation so that their lifestyle would be culturally appropriate, fitting for the corporate body of God's people. Among those who correctly stress the complexity of Christian identity in the NT are e.g. Campbell (2006a: 163), and his student Brian Tucker. Tucker discusses the use of 'in Christ' language in Pauline identity formation in 1 Corinthians, and correctly points to the unifying centre of Christ-followers' identity (Tucker 2007: 10–11). Paul's social entrepreneurship in 1 Corinthians offers a multifaceted discussion of Christ-followership as it negotiates Christianness, Jewishness and Greco-Roman identities. This, as Tucker interestingly argues,

To reiterate the first point: it was the Israelite covenant-identity that sanctioned the exclusive ingroup orientation and separation from non-Israelites. This had to change if non-Israelite Christ-followers were now included among God's people and Israel had to be ideologically enlarged to make room for non-Israelites. However, this view assumes continuity of Israel in 'Christ' and the 'Church'.[55] However, the renewed Israel is no longer defined exclusively by Israelite traditions, but 'in Christ', when even 'foreigners and aliens' are included. This has significant implications for communal remembering. For instance, redefinitions on Israel included transferring the communal social memory from the Exodus to the Cross. In addition, former membership symbols receive new counterparts (if not replacements) as the circumcision of the non-Israelites no longer signifies membership and baptism is introduced as a new sign of the membership for non-Israelites.[56]

The second important premise of this view is that Israelites continue to observe the Torah because Ephesians does not state otherwise. This is a key example of 'filling the gaps' whereby a reader provides the meaning based on extratextual factors. According to this view only the dividing function of the Law is annulled (Dunn 1993: 159). The Law is made inoperative by nullifying the divisive beliefs associated with (Yee 2005: 154, 157),

> The author has spoken critically of the Law, but this by no means amounts to a personal attack. Rather he is speaking from an insider's perspective on the Law which Jews had deemed significant but used as an instrument of division in order to reinforce their distinctive identity ... and the 'body politic based on a particular *ethnos*. This enmity between Jews and Gentiles lies not with the Torah *per se* but with the human attitude that perverted the gifts of God into signs of separation

---

involves multiple identities that are secondary to being 'in Christ' (2007: 11, 17). Ephesians' positioning of Jewishness and Christ-followership seems to operate on similar grounds, while the attitude to cultural bearing of Greco-Roman identities is not welcomed in the same manner; see Chapter 6 below.

55   It is assumed that in the NT *ekklēsia* refers, primarily and predominantly, to a local community addressed by an author, or a fellowship of certain communities, not anachronically to 'church' as a fixed institution and independent of its Jewish origins. Although it is specifically in Ephesians where we find a more universal 'church' in terms of its reference to a translocal unity of believers as opposed to outsiders it is also viewed in a cosmic context. However, the idea of a fixed institution would still be anachronic and the term 'community' probably better describes the social context of the believers addressed, contra Darko (2008). For Paul's use of *ekklēsia* cf. Nanos (2002: 75–6, n. 1).

56   Ephesians 4.5 assumes that the baptism ritual was one of the key communal tenets. Although Ephesians gives no details of this practice it is probable that both Israelite and non-Israelite members underwent this ritual, given that the practice that goes back to the earliest Christ-following movement was evidenced widely in the NT.

and exclusiveness ... [T]he Law ...which therefore occasioned ethnic enmity, is now abolished through the death of Christ (Yee 2005: 160-1).

Therefore, it is the divisive function of the Law that has been abolished by 'Christ', and it cannot any longer be used in 'aiding the Jews to distance themselves from the Gentiles' (Yee 2005: 160). Consequently, the old ethnic forms of identification and allegiance are no longer appropriate and are replaced by inclusive attitudes promoted in 2.11-22 (Yee 2005: 188).

Having read Ephesians from Dunn and Yee's angle, the 'wandering viewpoint' will shift to consider some of the assumptions and difficulties involved in taking 'the abolition of the Law' as the abandonment of ethnic division among the people of God, assuming that Israel's Torah observance is maintained. The following considerations arise from the reading of Ephesians.

2b. *Textual Elements that Challenge these Readings*
Instead of discussing multiple identities under a umbrella of common Christianness, Ephesians seems to be concerned with the changes involved in the non-Israelite inclusion and their resocialization – it details neither the consequences of alterations to Jewish symbolic universes nor social complexity resulting from the non-Israelite inclusion into fellowship with Israelites; neither does it provide socio-ideological guidance to Jewish Christ-followers, or their concerns over the Law abolishment in 2.15, or non-believing fellow Israelites and their relationship with God and the community. Two textual factors are of crucial importance here: first, the text does not explicitly maintain subgroup identities or cater for them, and secondly, the new creation of the 'new person' in 2.15b conveys their replacement, 'He has abolished the Law with its commandments and ordinances, that he might create in himself one new person (*anthrōpos*) in place of the two, thus making peace....'.

First, the issue of multiple identities. The removal of ethnic favouritism suggests that 'belief in Christ was additional to, not in substitution for Israelite Law and identity' (Esler 2003: 276; cf. Dunn 1990: 196). As a consequence, if Torah observance continues, while it no longer functions as the symbol for the whole people of God, Christ-believers would have multiple identities as ethnic distinctions categorizing members according to the Law of Moses would prevail.[57] Therefore it would be perfectly plausible that the community could include Torah-obedient Israelites and non-Israelites who would presumably be subject to some basic guidelines to facilitate social interaction. The

---

57   This is central to Campbell's view of Christian identity in Paul (2006a: 10, 49, 52, 57, 66, 147, 166, 168, 174).

Deutero-Pauline community would then operate similarly with Pauline communities: Paul did not abrogate the identity of Israel or their observance of the Torah but negotiated the terms of non-Israelite inclusion under the covenant of Christ (Nanos 1996: 178; 2002: 9). Nanos discusses in detail the ideological and social factors involved in attaching non-Israelite believers to the Jewish Jesus-believing groups that inevitably required negotiation of communal values, with regard to membership symbols, and other norms that facilitated interaction within the group (cf. 1996: 166–238).

Esler's model for reduction of subgroup conflict by recategorization proves useful in understanding the community dynamics in early Christianities (2003: 30–3). According to this view, once both subgroups are positioned together against other groups they will value their ingroup members although their differences remain (2003: 30). In addition, the social contact within the group will facilitate communication between groups and reduce devaluation and conflict further (2003: 30). Literature on SIT and group processes assumes that communal discourse gives guidance to members' interaction with other social actors in everyday life. Moreover, the success of such a mixed community depends on its social entrepreneurship: how deep a mutual tolerance it generates and how powerful the overarching common identity may prove to be. The common ingroup identity model could explain the extravagant language of Ephesians: its self-enhancing tone could be geared to highlighting the superiority of the ingroup over possible rival communities and outgroups, such as Israelites who do not associate with Christ-believers or Christ-believing Israelites who do not associate with non-Israelites and non-Israelite groups (cf. Esler 2003: 275). It is also true that Ephesians clearly constructs a unifying ingroup identity, as seen in the symbolic counter-reality where the believers are positioned enjoying the benefits of the divine election, preordained good works, abundant blessings, exalted status and access to God, his power and protection as well as different gifts, functions and social positions allocated by 'Christ'. It makes good sense of the ethnic reconciliation (so Campbell 2006b). Similarly, the two prayers also convey the notion of superior identity and spiritual experience, as does the idea of possessing a superior revelation (1.17-23; 3.1-6; 3.14-21). However, these passages do not require multiple identities, as they make perfect sense as communally enhancing identity construction for non-Israelite community, given that the discourse requires resocialization of them, and wants them to be culturally adopted into Jewish symbolic universe and distanced from the Greco-Roman world.

Although the Ephesians 2.13-22 reconciliation scene may suggest an idyllic image of a harmonious community the reality was probably less so. Although Ephesians does not really describe Israelite membership in its fictional community, one could imagine that Israelite members in any community with different sub-identities (Israelite and non-Israelite) and cultural performances (Torah-obedient and others) had to undergo a significant cultural adjustment. The non-Israelite members faced a significant social challenge of re-orientation, too. However, the text gives no guidelines how to make the diversity work. Therefore the main difficulty of reading Ephesians in the light of Nanos and Esler (2003) is that the crucial elements and complexities of multicultural social entrepreneurship are not explicit in the text, as they are in the undisputed Paulines. For example, the negotiation of coexistence with Israel and the presence of Israelite Christ-followers are both missing, as is an explanation of the Law's ongoing validity. It is important to note that the presence of Israelites in the community and the fictional characters in the letter are two separate things (2.14-22). I take the latter to be part of Ephesians' idealism because they or their concerns are not addressed in the letter at all. In my view, if 'the annulment of the Law' left the community with two ethnic groups who had a history of social conflict, and an internal division between Torah-obedient Israelites and other members inside its bounds, it is quite likely that some social conflict would eventually (if not immediately) reappear. If only the principle of Israelite ethnic superiority is cancelled 'in Jesus' name', further social entrepreneurship is required to diminish conflict among remaining different subgroups.

The social entrepreneurship does not provide ideological resources or guidance for negotiating multiple identities and cultural performances that would vary so considerably in a community which would include Torah-observant members and ethnic others who follow different *halakhah*. Could communal harmony be achieved or maintained without any cognitive, evaluative or emotive tools to appreciate diversity? If the author's intentionality can be evaluated in the light of his/her selection and deselection of different discourse components and cultural influences (Iser 1993: 6), then the deselection of halakhic discourse and Torah observance would not suggest that the community addressed included both Israelite and non-Israelite Christ-followers. In my view, in the absence of an explicit discussion of diversity and guidance for making it operative in the community, it is highly unlikely that Ephesians' social entrepreneurship would have envisaged multiple identities, despite how compelling the model is for other early Christian texts.

Although Paul might have envisaged a more hybrid identity, as Zetterholm points out, the presumption of a common new Christian identity for both Jewish and Gentile believers is difficult from a social-psychological viewpoint (2003: 6). Their starting points were significantly different and creation of a common culture that accommodated both would have required cultural adaptation from both groups. It is difficult to imagine how the complexity of multiple identities and cultures would be sustainable without appropriate discourse, which Paul offers in Romans and 1 Corinthians (so Esler 2003; Tucker 2007); and as the Pauline correspondence demonstrates, the negotiation of shared communal values was difficult. In light of Pauline controversies and history of early Christianities it seems that the model of multiple identities was socially unsustainable, and eventually overcome. Given that the multiple identities or negotiation of communal culture do not feature in Ephesians as they do in the undisputed letters suggests that it adapted Pauline traditions in the light of different social circumstances. In my view, one could reason from Ephesians that the period of mixed communities was already history in the Deutero-Pauline period, as it does not provide guidance and socio-ideological resources for such complexity of communality. It is also significant to note that in Ephesians there is no reference to Jewish social networks that suggests that some distancing is intended. Also, this would explain why devaluing or revising Jewish cultural boundaries was possible.[58]

The above readings examined the plausibility of Christ-followers' multiple identities in Ephesians. Nanos' model of 'righteous Gentiles' concerning the inclusion of ethnic strangers into the Israelite community provides a possible explanation for how the distinctive subgroups and multiple identities would work (1996). Nanos portrays Paul as a faithful Jew committed to Israel's restoration and commissioned to accelerate the ingathering of the nations that has already begun (1996: 18). He suggests that Paul and other apostles adapted the Law and Israelite customs for foreign believers according to the idea of 'righteous Gentiles' attached to the synagogue movement (Acts 15.19-20), providing them with a model of 'righteous behaviour' which demonstrates their respect for Israel's faith and monotheistic worship (1996: 35). The dispute over the historicity of the Acts 15 narrative does not reduce from the fact that it demonstrates Nanos' model convincingly: the apostolic council considered the inclusion of non-Israelite Christ-followers and initiated socio-ideological reforms

---

58   In my view, there is a difference between Pauline and Deutero-Pauline positions in their reflection of Jewishness. While Paul renegotiated Jewishness to facilitate non-Israelite exclusion, he probably wasn't ready to have the Law 'abolished' altogether. While Yee could be seen as overemphasizing Jewishness, Heikki Räisänen, on the contrary, could be overestimating Paul's affiliation with the non-Israelites. Räisänen speaks of Paul who had 'fully internalized the Gentile point of view and identified himself with it' (1986: 258), which seems to assume quite extensive socio-ideological distance to Israel. In my view, identification with non-Israelites happens later (so e.g. Zetterholm 2003; Buell 2005). Despite its dismissal of the Law, even Ephesians has not *fully* identified with the non-Israelite position. For a discussion of Paul's Christological reforms on Jewishness without leaving it behind see for example Asano (2005: 82–9).

on Law and communal boundaries marking the 'people of God', attaching non-Israelite followers of 'Christ' into a community of Jewish Christ-followers under a different regime validated by Israel's Messiah (esp. 15.19-20; 28-9). This was legitimated by Peter's argument that appealed to the work of the Holy Spirit and regeneration of Gentiles (15.7-11) that Paul and Barnabas confirmed with their testimony (15.12). Then the assembly considered James' social entrepreneurship that transformed the report of common cultural (spiritual) experience into a legitimating myth as a fulfilment of prophecy for nations' worship of Israel's God (15.13-21), and non-burdensome rules of purity and conduct were agreed upon. This is similar to association of the 'righteous Gentiles' in the wider synagogue movement, which expected them to obey certain customs and avoid idolatry (Cohen 1989: 22).[59] The inclusion of the 'righteous Gentiles' is therefore a plausible Jewish model to explain how non-Israelites could have been affiliated to Israelite groups, so also Donaldson (1997: 230–6). The presence of 'righteous Gentiles' did not touch upon the validity of the Torah as non-Israelites were connected with Israel without obligation to fulfil the Torah or to impinge on their covenant or challenge Israel's status.

This has a number of possible parallels with Ephesians, which is predominantly concerned with the social aspects of the non-Israelite inclusion. First, their legitimacy of their inclusion is established in the positive identity construction in Ephesians 1. Secondly, the obstacles for their social inclusion are removed in chapter 2, which also offers identity-enhancing discourse of their equality as members of God's people and 'fellow citizens with saints' (2.19). Thirdly, the community is historically legitimated in chapter 3 as it is linked to Paul's legacy and apostolic early Christian movement (see Chapter 4 below). Fourthly, Ephesians' concern for holiness and anxiety about the 'pagan' deviance is substantial: even though the text proclaims a new creation (chs 1; 2.4-10, 14-15) and offered two intercessions for their spiritual transformation (1.17-23; 3.14-21), the author defaults back to his stereotypical view of their cultural tendency to misdemeanour in 4.17ff., as if he doubted their 'newness' (or their ability to change their ways) despite his earlier identity entrepreneurship (see Chapter 6 below). In light of this, a 'righteous Gentile' model could explain how Ephesians likens non-Israelite Christ-followers to Israel and sanctions non-Torah-observant guidelines for appropriate behaviour to facilitate networking.

In my view the idea of 'righteous Gentiles' is a highly relevant model for

---

59   It is quite likely that the rabbinic Noachian Commandments reflect earlier practices and boundary negotiations addressing social challenges faced by the Diaspora communities (Nanos 1996: 169ff.; Cohen 1989: 13–33).

understanding the bigger picture of Israelite and other Christ-followers' relations, and their association with the Jewish Diaspora groups. It provides a highly plausible hermeneutical model for the community relations and continuity between Jewishness and Christianness, providing a compelling explanation for Pauline liberty to position non-Israelites outside the Law, whilst justifying Paul's ongoing observance of the Torah, as well as the challenge from other Israelites, who regarded the 'righteous Gentiles' as 'potential Jews', who should be led to full initiation rights (Nanos 1996: 54). However, despite its attractiveness, whether it is a credible theory for Ephesians is another matter. The 'righteous Gentile' theory could explain the partial abolishing of the Law, meaning that the requirement of the Law observance was no longer required to facilitate networking and communal relations between Israelites and other ethnicities. However, it raises some of the same questions as the partial abolishing of the Law in Ephesians discussed above. In particular, if the social entrepreneur had an operational 'righteous Gentiles' policy in mind there would have been no need to speak about the invalidation of the Law, but a language of comfortable *halakhah* could have been used as in Acts 15.

There are a number of textual components which make the 'righteous Gentile' association model less likely for Ephesians. These demonstrate that although this model may have been operative in early Christian movement as we could glean from Acts and undisputed Paulines, Ephesians' social entrepreneurship operates with a different socio-ideological framework. For instance, there is little evidence for what kind of status the 'righteous Gentiles' would have enjoyed within Jewish social networks. Ephesians' declaration of their equal status may have exceeded what was typical for such associations given that the Jewish community was based on an ethnic covenant between the (imaginary) nation and their God.[60] Because the membership consisted largely of culturally similar members – or wore a mask of similarity so that the focus

60 I use 'imaginary nationhood' to highlight a concept of nationality or ethnicity that is not measured by documentation or location, as in the case of Diasporic Israel. It describes formative use of a myth of common origins to explain social and ideological commonality, which creates a sense of identification despite the lack of political independence or shared geographic location, when Diasporic members would equally feel part of the group (Anderson 1991: 6–7). The biblical portrayal of Israel provides a striking illustration for what Anderson describes as a community 'confident in their unique sacredness' (1991: 13). This is akin to Smith's examination of sacred foundations of national identity, for which he takes ancient Israel as 'a prototype of covenantal kind of chosenness' (Smith 2003: 7, 44–65; 66–94). The chosenness is an important part of their communal discourses, and therefore the distinction between 'hereditary' and other affiliates is understandable. The nationality (peoplehood) and faith are considered inseparable. Similarly, the discourses of nationhood and faith are intrinsically intertwined: for instance, the addition of new members is described in terms of religious conversion and confirmed by appropriate spiritual rituals (2003: 20).

is not on individual variation – it was comprehensible that members who joined the group on their voluntary initiative – not by birth/primary socialization – were a minority and distinguished as such. Although their association with Israelite communities and rejection of Greco-Roman culture or polytheistic worship might have caused them to be labelled 'Jews' by outsiders, the community affairs were such that they were labelled as non-ethnic affiliates, for instance, proselytes by the group itself. According to Cohen, for a non-Israelite member in the Jewish community the nearest status to an Israelite was that of a proselyte, while reasonable doubt remains that they were classed as somewhat subordinate (1989: 26–30). Their distinctive classification, and thus different identity applied to them, is evident in the use of labels like 'God-fearer', 'proselyte' or 'God-fearing Gentile'.[61] Such labels either emphasize their initiation, or categorize them as ethnic 'other' to the natives, who were seen as the core members or primary members of 'God's people', based on the ethnic election, imagined nationhood and the myth of divine origin.[62] In discussion of social affiliation and identity it is important to distinguish between categorization, which would be how Israelites viewed non-Israelite associates, and self-identification, which would be the labels and meanings non-Israelites attached to themselves. The data in our case is probably of categorization. However, it is possible that the constraints of communal discourse did not approve or encourage non-Israelite associates to identify themselves as Israelites or God's people, for whatever reason. This could be particularly the case of 'God-fearers', who were negotiating different cultures and social networks, without full entry into a Jewish community as circumcised and Law-obedient members. Therefore their self-categorization could have adopted dominant labelling and strengthened use of distinguishing labels.[63]

Although Paul and Ephesians seem to represent Universalist Jewishness it cannot be known for sure how typical universalism was in contemporary Jewish movements, and what status non-Israelite associates enjoyed.[64]

Furthermore, both utilize the same historical myths and their communal remembering highlights the distinctive heritage of the group (2003: 21). For further discussion on nationhood and identity, see e.g. Anderson (1991); Hastings (1997); and Smith (2003).

61 Cf. Mt. 23.15; Acts 2.11; 6.5; 10.2, 22; 13.16, 26, 43; 17.4; 18.7; cf. Donaldson (1997: 65–7).

62 The chosenness of Israelites is inseparable of the otherness of the nations. Yee makes a pertinent observation that the sense of chosenness caused Israelites to engage in 'rhetoric of otherness' to explain the Gentile world through Israelite parameters which stressed their impiousness (Yee 2005: 56, 110–11).

63 Relevant to today's immigrant discourses, how the foreigners are labelled and how they categorize themselves.

64 The equality of nations alongside Israel is a familiar concept in Pauline texts. For instance, his language of 'heirs according to promise', 'children of Abraham' and 'sons of God', positions non-Israelites as full members in the 'people of God' among Israelites (e.g.

Although the literary evidence for 'righteous Gentiles' and 'god fearers' at the time of Ephesians is scarce, it does suggest that distinguished labelling of non-ethnic members did occur and that such affiliates were not considered equal to Israelites. Ephesians' language of a new humanity, non-Israelite status and membership in God's people and spiritual temple, along with communal blessings, spiritual experiences and fixing communal identity 'in Christ' suggest that non-Israelites are not just peripheral members but the constitution of covenant has been revised.[65]

In addition, the language of new creation from both past identities would be superfluous if Ephesians' social entrepreneurship only assumed transformation of non-Israelites in 'Christ'. Instead it envisages that 'Christ' 'made both groups one … that he might create in himself one new humanity in place of the two' (2.14-15). The discourse connects antinomian stance and the new community; just as hostility is removed by abolishing the Law the inequality and ethnic division are gone because of the new humanity, God's people. The language of new humanity cannot be insignificant, as it imagines Christ-followers as God's new creation and installs another metaphor into communal discourse, reinforcing the earlier ideas of their divine origin. Furthermore, the metaphor of new humanity sketches the outsiders against whom the 'people of God' are defined. The outsiders, people of circumcision and of uncircumcision are in the past and as Lieu writes, 'represent a way of being that "we" have left behind' (2004: 314). In addition, due to the weight of enmity and hostility in the discourse it is unlikely that the old groups and the new would coexist in the reconciled community of saints.[66]

Gal. 3.28, 29; 4.4-7, 28; cf. Rom. 3.22-24; 9.30; 10.9-13). For a discussion of the equality of non-Israelites in Paul and the socio-ideological challenges involved in their attachment to the Jewish community, see, for example, Nanos (2002: 203–83), and Donaldson (1997: 230–48). However, in my view, Romans 11 gives an insight to primacy of Israel, which may still have been part of his Paul's thought, although his letters are mostly concerned with non-Israelite matters, as in Ephesians.

65 As noted before, Ephesians focuses on the positive identity construction and simplified ideological discourse by making no reference to disputes or opposing viewpoints. Nevertheless, it is most likely that Ephesians' view of non-Israelite equality would probably have been challenged in a similar fashion with the Galatian controversy, when Paul advocated Gentiles' full inclusion without circumcision and proselyte status, which was contested by other Israelites (cf. Nanos 2002: 318). Similarly, distancing from the Greco-Roman culture would have inevitably resulted in social pressure (cf. MacDonald 2004: 434–5, 442). Hence, for instance, Josephus negotiates civic loyalty and religious interests of the culturally and ideologically different Jewish people (2004: 428–32).

66 The coexistence of diverse groupings, Jesus-believing Law-observant Israelites and others is a hypothetical possibility in the first place, as the text does not explain the coexistence or diversity of cultural origins of the community members. The possibility rises from the reading process, as a possible alternative, particularly in connection with an early date and the unlikelihood of a separate non-Israelite group of Christ-followers.

The idea of amalgamation of groups into communal 'we-ness' first appears in 2.14: 'He is our peace; having made the two [groups] into one and having broken the middle wall of partition, which is hostility, in his flesh'. The oneness and newness are achieved when obstacles of the separating middle wall, the hostility, the Law with its commandments and regulations and enmity are destroyed.

In my view on 2.11-22 it is unlikely that the new *anthrōpos*, new communal identity, would be an overarching concept that maintains past identities and their differences regarding the Law.[67] The new *anthrōpos* rises from the context of past divisions and the image of a new humanity transcends old divisions, which suggests to me that the division has been dealt with along with its causes and issues, and past hostility has been exterminated (2.16). Therefore it appears that the social entrepreneurship is geared towards shaping the identity and behaviour of the new *anthrōpos*. However, multiple identities would maintain the base for categorization between 'them' and 'us', 'the circumcised' and 'uncircumcised'. Thus it would seem that plurality without appropriate discourse and legitimating could result in a conflict all over again.

Furthermore, if the author wanted to negotiate the social location and sacred space for the non-Israelites only, there would have been no urgency for a new creation in place of the two.[68] While the discussion of non-Israelite inclusion, its theological, social and ethical implications, dominates, Ephesians does suggest that Israelites undergo some transformation, as well, along with others. It is important to note that the author identifies with Christ-followers, not with Jewish people outside the boundaries of faith in 'Christ'. Therefore the writer does not represent his Jewish traditions, as such, but what he makes Jewishness to be, while the evidence of the messianic event has spilled all over his symbolic universe.[69] For instance, he does not identify with those whom he labels 'the circumcision' (2.11), and the Jewish cultural boundaries are reduced to disputes and social conflict around circumcision (2.11-16). On the contrary, it seems that the likeminded Israelites are made new in 'Christ' (2.15), reconciled to God along with non-Israelite saints (2.16) and established on 'the foundation of apostles and prophets' (2.20).

---

67   The symbolism of the body as a communal metaphor re-appears in 4.24 when believers are told to 'put on the new *anthrōpos*, created in God's likeness in true righteousness and holiness'. This reinforces the idea of oneness of the new person, and her holiness.

68   MacDonald highlights the connection between 2.15 and 2.10 (2000: 245). The concept of a new creation is a powerful communal metaphor: not only does it speak for the unity of the believers despite their ethnic origin and social setting, but it also proclaims the culmination of God's plan in Christ and the destiny of the believers manifesting God's glory and might.

69   As noted before, the author does not directly identify with Israel. See further discussion of 'silencing Israel' below.

Therefore there is more to renegotiation of the traditions than just the inclusion of the righteous Gentiles. This has significant consequences for communal identity and social remembering, as reconciliation, removal of the Law and new creation are constitutive parts of communal identity that are remembered as consequences of Christ's death.[70]

It is important to note the negative socio-ideological positioning of the Torah observance. If Ephesians does indeed engage in identity construction it cannot be accidental that the text constructs a negative portrayal of the Law in 2.11-22. The observance of the Law is remembered in a negative – not covenant – context; while the text positions Israel as the covenant people, it does not honour the Torah as it honours 'the covenants of the promise' (2.12). In contrast, the only reference to the observance of the Law is the 'circumcision' in 2.11 where what was perhaps the most essential aspect of the Torah observance is positioned in the context of an ethnoreligious conflict. This ignores communal functions of the law, as it would have symbolized belonging and otherness, and reinforced covenant-identity to its members. This suggests that the writer no longer views the observance of the law from a typical Israelite position, but from another place, where different socio-ideological concerns matter. This does not necessarily position him outside its boundaries, but at the edges, as he connects with the non-Israelite world and negotiates their membership. Furthermore, the circumcision appears as the sign of division, not membership; it is referred to in the context of past divisions and the practice is not endorsed. Besides, the circumcision is described as 'a physical circumcision made in the flesh by human hands (*cheiropoiētou*)' (2.11b), which hardly adds to the status of the ritual. It has traditionally been taken as evidence of devaluation, possibly implying the Pauline idea of 'true, spiritual circumcision' (Rom. 2.28-29; Phil. 3.2-3, cf. Col. 2.11).[71] In my view, it is quite possible that the 'made by hands' is a shorthand for controversies of circumcision, especially as the comment stands in the

---

70 Halbwachs makes an interesting point on social remembering of Jewishness, 'circumcision and the many ritual interdictions [of the Jewish cult] are dead memories that have no more relation to the present' (1992: 96). He refers to later separation of Jewishness and Christianness (not in those terms). However, circumcision is not a dead memory to the writer of Ephesians, but rather a reminder of social conflicts and its inevitable causes.

71 So, for instance, Bruce (1984: 293); Lincoln (1990: 136) and Hoehner (2002: 354–5). The distancing of the writer from the 'circumcision' group stands despite what meaning one attributes to its further description *cheiropoiētou* (2.11). Hoehner stresses the negative meanings which suggest that the term carries disapproving connotations of a human will as opposed to God's will referring to Isa. 2.18; 10.11 (2002: 354). On the contrary, Yee disagrees and argues 2.11 was neither polemical nor negative verse and *cheiropoiētou* could refer to circumcision (Gen. 17.9-14; Lev. 12.3), although it frequently implies negative connotations (Yee 2005: 84, 85). For the discussion of a meaning of 'circumcision' as a key Israelite symbol for their self-definition as the People of God at the time of writing Ephesians see for example Yee (2005: 78–83) and Best (1992: 48).

context of hostility and conflict. It underlines the conflicting views linked with the question of circumcision in the boundary negotiations.

Ephesians demonstrates lack of social entrepreneurship to facilitate *halakhic* diversity and explain multiple identities. There is no defence of the Law and/or its ongoing legitimacy. If the community began among Israelite Christ-followers whom non-Israelite believers have joined, one could expect some reference to the influence of Israelite agents of circumcision or negotiations of required behaviour in the community, since the declaration of equal status of non-Israelites without proselyte conversion would have been disputed by the wider Israelite community (Nanos 2002: 317f.). It is possible that the community was already considerably distanced from influencers who sought to establish 'essential Jewishness' or a *halakhic* code for non-Israelites. Alternatively, one could assume that the community had a fixed and functioning code for non-Israelite members. However, this is unlikely considering the author's repeated frustration with the heathen lifestyle, unless he is stereotypically occupied without any reason (4.17–5.20). Ephesians does not appeal to the Law in its ethnic reasoning, except for parental philosophy in its appeal to children (6.1-3). Obedience to parents promises a reward, as does humble servitude of the slaves to their masters (6.5-8). This proves that the Torah has some value to the writer. However, the appeal to 'the first commandment with a promise' could be an example of a general mindset of recompense, which imagines that those who do good will be rewarded. It is also possible that this is an example of a selective use of the Hebrew Scripture, as it was believed to disclose God's covenant with humankind (now extended to non-Israelites) but cultural performances related to Torah observance were deemed as irrelevant. This would substantiate my suggestion that Ephesians uses Israel and her sacred traditions to legitimate Christian community, and here, its ideology and social orientation.

Finally, the social consequences of the simultaneous abolition of the ethnic division of the Law and maintenance of its regulations appear complex and would have required some explanation. As discussed above, given that Ephesians was particularly mindful of the hostilities and division caused by Israelite boundaries, would it be sufficient to suggest that the problems caused by the ethnoreligious Law could be uprooted with a mere Christological statement, if divisive cultural performances were to continue? Or, if we consider text as providing ideological and social paradigms to the community, why would the social entrepreneur assert that the Law is abolished if it is still to be practised by Christ-following (and other) Israelites? It would seem rather pointless to pronounce the abolition of the Law while maintaining its ongoing praxis. Similarly, it would be meaningless to disapprove the social consequences of the Law, as Ephesians clearly does, and simultaneously, maintain its use, as the Law and its social implications are inseparable to each other.

Finally, the communal consequences of the claim that 'Christ Abolished the Law' are considerable. Regardless of the writer's intention, there is a possibility that the declaration became associated with its literal interpretation, spelling the end of Torah observance among God's people (contra Yee, Dunn, Campbell and others). This may give some indication for the process when close ties with the synagogue movement gradually turned into claims of distinctiveness, and eventually led to the formation of separate communities. Lieu acknowledges textual selectiveness and the potential discourses have for social construction. For one thing, a textual image may be a selective reflection of the reality or a fictional, ideological aspiration (2004: 53). It may project a socially independent and innovative concept, while the reality it negotiates and presents may be considerably different (Lieu 1996: 12). In addition, a selective, ideologically guided reflection of social reality, or an aspiration of what reality should be like, may get a life of its own in the communal discourse. The text may thus become formative for the recipients, shaping their worldview and social identity – beyond the reality or communal praxis it may have originally sprung from. Then what was composed or imagined as a part of a fictional, symbolic universe will become part of the reality.[72] Therefore it is possible that textual images, such as 'Christ abolishing the Law', contribute to the processes which led to eventual separation, as the text constructs Christianness by shaping the symbolic world of its readers (Lieu 2004: 61).

Furthermore, if we assume that the text provides the ideological paradigms for the community, this would seem to insinuate that the abolition of the Law became a rather central conviction as it is explicitly linked with the community defining Christ-event (2.14-16). Consequently, it would follow that the abolition of the Law may have caused division rather than harmonious unity if the passage was seen as providing apostolic legitimation for separation from Jewishness. In addition, Ephesians' 'image' of the harmonious Church (2.14-22) come across as ideological rather than an accurate reflection of the 'reality' of the diverse and contested intra- and intercommunal relations of the Christ-followers in the late first century CE.

In the light of the social-scientific perspective in this study, I would therefore suggest that even if the author was as Jewish as Paul, his social entrepreneurship probably failed because it does not provide ideological resources for valuing Jewish traditions and associated cultural perform- ances. However, it is more likely that these are lacking because they were

---

72 The shaping of the world by discourse is a grounding assumption of, for instance, Berger and Luckmann (1969); Iser (1978); Lieu (1996); and Zetterholm (2003).

not consequential enough to the author. Nevertheless, Jewishness clearly has a crucial legitimating function as Ephesians positions Christ-followers within the Jewish symbolic universe, redefined in the light of the Christ-event and its socio-ideological meanings, and assumes to them Israel's status. Therefore, it is more likely that the writer values Israel's supreme and powerful God, rather than Jewish social networks and cultural expressions. This would explain why Ephesians uses Israelite traditions for communal legitimation but subjects it to social and ideological reforms by abolishing the Law.

To recap, if the expression 'Christ has abolished the Law' was directed at non-Israelites, while Israelite Christ-followers still obeyed the Law, then there would be a positive sense of continuity between Jewishness, 'New Perspective' Paul and Ephesians. However, in addition to textual positions of the discourse, there are a number of socio-ideological issues to consider, which go together with this reading of 2.15. While both multiple identities of Christ-followers (Esler) and inclusion of 'righteous Gentiles' (Nanos) offer plausible explanations for texts reflecting Pauline Christianity, neither of these models fits Ephesians comfortably, when the complexity of its socio-ideological cluster is closely examined. The discourse does not provide ideological resources for maintaining harmony of multiple identities, as there is no 'olive tree metaphor' to imagine plurality (Rom. 11.13-24). On the contrary, one must not ignore that as far as Ephesians is concerned the conflicts and hostility ultimately result from multiple identities, Israelite and other, who are now made one. Ephesians 2.11-22 speaks of the creation of new community of God's people 'in Christ' and permanent removal of social conflict. Having considered some of the identity negotiations of early Christianities reflected in Ephesians 2, one thing is certain; the non-Israelite inclusion was a very intricate affair and it is equally certain that this was eventually costly to the early Christian movement. Zetterholm is probably correct in suggesting that the complexities of non-Israelite inclusion and the negotiation of their status became consequential for the eventual separation of Jewishness and Christianness.[73]

Having observed different models for a partial abolishing of the Law, multiple subgroup identities and inclusion of 'righteous Gentiles', we must now consider the more traditional interpretation for abolishing the Law in 2.15, which implies that the Law has been dismissed and all 'people of God' now operate a different regime. However, I want to distance the following reading from anachronistic supercessionism that promotes

---

73   Zetterholm argues that in the post-Pauline situation non-Israelites were reduced into the position of 'God-fearers', which triggered the movement of social separation frustrated at the Jesus-believing Jewish leadership, who did not maintain or agree with the status the Gentiles had assumed in Pauline mission (2003: 207).

different dispensations of Moses and of Christ, march out as a voice of 'Gentile Christianity', or speak for 'the universal church'. Instead the claim that 'Christ abolished the Law' is explored as a part of Ephesians' ideology, not mine. Furthermore, it is seen as an articulation of distinctive Christianness without assuming that it would represent ideologically or socially fixed 'Christianity' or what was right or wrong with Judaism(s). Furthermore, it is taken as a self-enhancing minority voice focused on promoting community of non-Israelite Christ-followers. The reading will now proceed to evaluate Ephesians' Christianness and discuss those discursive manoeuvrings that seem to distance the community from Jewishness.

2c. The Abolition of the Law in the Articulation of Distinctive Christianness
To reiterate the hypothesis of this study, I propose that Ephesians engages in social entrepreneurship, by deliberately shaping identity and social orientation according to the ideological parameters it links with the Christ-event. I suggest that Ephesians shapes the remembering of 'Jesus Christ' by linking present social concerns with his death, which then validates the socio-ideological positioning of the community. In other words, the death of 'Jesus Christ' legitimates his non-Israelite followers and provides resolutions to problems involved in their classification as the people of God. Reading 2.11-22 from this position results in three basic principles:

1) the discourse provides ideological resources for understanding the social conflict between the Israelite people of God and others, due to ethnic covenant ideology and culture (2.11-12).
2) past social conflict and antagonism are no longer threatening the community because of the ideological reforms Christ inaugurated, which accommodate the saints from other nations. This implies that God has inaugurated new, messianic constitution for his people, who are the 'new humanity in Christ' (2.13-16).
3) The status improvement that 'Christ' brought guarantees spiritual and social improvements, such as fellowship with God plus communal unity and equality, instead of enmity and divisions of ethnically hostile and divided humanity (2.17-22).

Exploring Christianness within the social-scientific framework takes 'the abolition of the Law' as a cancellation of the ethnic marker, which was relevant for Israel, but as ethnic Israel is no longer 'the people of God' (according to Ephesians) – but Christ-followers are chosen and predestined – the Law is no longer obeyed either, in order to eliminate its divisive function (2.14-15). I will first consider a number of literary, ideological and social elements in the text that substantiate this reading. Then I will employ a different 'wandering viewpoint' and discuss the weaknesses of this view and the interpretive process that it requires.

To begin with, it is important to notice that revisions upon the Law are part of self-enhancing ingroup discourse, shared with the like-minded, ignoring alternative solutions. As noted previously, the text distances itself (and its readers) from the challenges and disputes its Christ-centred views may trigger. The silencing of alternative voices is a discursive technique peculiar to Ephesians, which differs from Pauline and other Deutero-Pauline texts.[74] The importance of silencing the alternatives and distancing the community from disputes contributes to effectiveness of the socio-ideological discourse. These discursive manoeuvres are crucial to the intention of the text, as they demonstrate how the text interacts with its social context and ideological diversity of its environment. As Iser suggests,

> If we are to uncover the intention of a text, our best chance lies not in the study or the author's life, dreams, and beliefs but in those manifestations of intentionality expressed in the fictional text itself through its selection of and from extratextual systems. The intentionality of the text thus consists in the way it breaks down and distances itself from those systems to which it has linked itself. The intention, therefore, is not to be found in the world to which the text refers, nor is it simply something imaginary; it is the preparation of an imaginary quality for use – a use that remains dependent on the given situation within which it is to be applied. (1993: 6)

I explore relationship between communal beliefs and social orientations, and how these are installed in the discourse in the light of Iser's 'preparation of an imaginary quality for use'. I take Ephesians' ideological components as imaginary in a sense that they are beyond verification and highly contestable. For example, passionate and value-loaded assumptions, like the exaltation of 'Christ', the election of the believers, that 'Christ' abolished the Law, or that non-Israelites are morally inferior are examples of Ephesians' ideological imagination, that is, installing community enhancing values and explanations into the discourse and thus into the communal worldview.

Intentionality reveals how the text interacts with the world it reflects, that which it portrays and that of its readers. This is highly significant as Ephesians' textual distancing creates an illusion of social distance, and then builds on this assumption with cultural revisions and ingroup orientation.

Textual distancing is particularly important in discussing the relations

---

74   In contrast to, for example, Paul's polemic against Peter (Gal. 2.11-14) or more general, stereotypical complaints about alternative views or their proponents (e.g. Gal. 1.6-8; 4.17; 2 Cor. 11; Col. 2; 1 Tim. 1.3-11; 6.3-5; 2 Tim 3.1-9).

of the community and Israel.[75] Even though Ephesians does attack neither Israelite traditions nor Israelites it frames the Torah negatively and distances itself from Jewishness and Jewish groupings:

1) The text does not acknowledge Israel outside the community of believers or a division among Israelites over 'Christ' but in basic terms equates the community with Israel.[76] Ephesians offers no explanation as to how the ethnic Israel became the community of Christ-followers where the non-Israelite 'saints' are fellow citizens, and what is the relationship between the two.

2) The text does not uphold the idea of the righteousness of Israel but positions Israelites alongside 'Gentile sinners' (2.3), equally sinful and equally in need of saving. In 2.11-22 the conflict is not caused by their moral deprivation but by 1) the Law, particularly in terms of the boundary question of circumcision, and 2) the simple fact that they were outsiders as a consequence of Israel's election.

3) The text does not honour the Law or make any explanation for its ongoing validity. Instead, the Law is linked with social conflict and 'Christ' is presented as a hero who solved the problem for those regarded as outsiders from a Jewish viewpoint.

4) The text does not refer to association with any Israelite believers, or other Israelites apart from stereotypically as 'the circumcised' (2.11). There is no reference to Jewish social networks or synagogue setting. Similarly, contrary to the Gospels, Paul and even other Disputed Paulines, Ephesians ignores Jewish customs, such as food Laws or Sabbath observance and other customs, which would be natural components in the cross-ethnic social intercourse among early Christianities.

5) The text does not honour any Israelite believers. There are no other prototypes than archetypal Paul and (Asian) Tychicus (6.12). Here Paul is not 'Hebrew of Hebrews' but the unique bearer of Christian revelation (3.1-13), and his Jewishness hardly features in the construction of his memory in Ephesians, as even the image of a prophet is transformed and linked with the Christ-movement (cf. Eph. 3; 4.1-16).

Consequently the concerns of the Christ-followers (*ekklēsia*) dominate the discourse. The group is not constructed of distinguishable Israelite and foreign components (Romans 11), but of new creations (2.15). While the body metaphor makes a distinction of gifting and function among members (4.15-16) Ephesians does not differentiate ethnically or ideologically, between Christ-followers and other Israelites. Thus Ephesians

---

75 For distancing from the Greco-Roman context see 4.17–5.20, Chapter 6 below.
76 MacDonald (2004: 433).

has positioned 'Jesus Christ' and his followers at the very heart of the Jewish symbolic universe adapted to facilitate their inclusion.

Lieu offers another very important perspective on understanding early Christian texts and their reflections on Jews and Christ-followers. She describes the 'Jew of the text' as a literary creation who exists because of the author's decision, to serve whatever viewpoint is allocated in the text (1996: 12). Consequently, as Ephesians 1 and 2 demonstrate, Israel provides the community with a legitimating story and makes the community appear historically continuous with Israel's traditions. In my opinion, the textual distancing is all the more outstanding the closer association we expect the writer and his recipients to have had with the synagogue communities.[77] However, Ephesians is not only silent about Israel, but it fails to explain or uphold the importance of Israel's ethnic covenant and her distinctive culture. Instead there seems to be an implicit diminishing of Israel or her value to the community,[78] and some tendency to claim true ownership of the Hebrew traditions, which developed relatively early in Christianness along with the claim for being the true Israel.[79] The writer assumes that Jewish traditions are flexible and they may be renegotiated in the light of 'Christ' and fuller revelation to which it makes explicit claims (3.4-6). Therefore it seems that Ephesians is not classed as a Deutero-Pauline development from the apostolic thought without a reason, and the Israelite heritage of the author is not a fixed grid but allows for considerable ideological and social distance fluidity towards its Jewish origins. This does not need to imply any supercessionist tendencies, though, as contrasting and even polemical use of the same traditions is typical of social competition, particularly among religious groups.

I propose that the understanding of Ephesians' relation to Israel goes

---

77   Particularly assuming Pauline authorship and reading Paul in the light of the New Perspective scholarship.

78   In my view, there are a number of discourse elements that diminish the value of some central Jewish concepts. For instance, the election of Christ-followers diminishes Israel's chosenness and seems to dismiss Israel's status, given that there is no defence of Israel's covenant or its ongoing validity. The social entrepreneur celebrates that God 'chose us in Christ before the foundations of the world' and 'destined us for adoption as his sons' (1.4, 5 lit.). Assuming chosenness and 'being sons of God' take over hugely important concepts from the Hebrew Bible (e.g. Exod. 4.22; Deut. 7.6-7, 32.6; 1 Kgs 3.8; Isa. 64.8; Jer. 3.19, 31.9). Similarly, the saints are exalted and seated with Christ 'in heavenly places' (2.6). Although the text does not say that Israelites are not there, it makes no reference to any Israelite saints that might have seats there, although we expect this to be the case. When it comes to the text itself, it does not explicitly say this. Furthermore, given that those who are seated there do so 'in Christ Jesus' could make the position of those Israelites who rejected his Messiahship rather awkward.

79   See the discussion of Ephesians' positioning of Paul as the rightful interpreter of God's word in Chapter 4 below.

together with the interpretation of the 2.15 claim 'Christ has abolished the Law'. While it seems quite clear that Ephesians did not require non-Israelite Christ-followers to obey the Torah, it remains possible, in theory, that reducing the communal significance of the Law represents the removal of the requirement of Torah obedience to non-Israelite community and has little to do with Israelites and God's covenant with them, who are not even part of the group. What remains is that although Israel is acknowledged as the 'people of the covenants and promise' in 2.12, she has been deselected in communal remembering, as explored above. Therefore, I suggest that Israel is the most crucial 'gap' in the text. She is neither dismissed nor endorsed, and she is barely even acknowledged; but we can hardly engage with the text without thinking about Israel, and thus she remains as a silent character in the symbolic universe at the mercy of readers and interpreters. Most importantly, it is clear that ethnic Israel is not equated with God's people. On the contrary, MacDonald argues that Ephesians 'equates the church with Israel without acknowledging a split within Israel itself, and the existence of Jews outside of the church (or even explicitly acknowledging their presence within the audience)' (2004: 433).[80]

Nevertheless, because Israel conveys a relationship with God and its 'covenants of promise' (2.12) a reader may well be drawn to imagine that Israel can not disappear, but continues its existence because it is almost inconceivable that God's covenants should be broken and Israel should become irrelevant. Even though the writer regards Hebrew traditions Israel receives no further mention beyond 2.12. There is little doubt that (at least) some of the Israelites are included with 'non-Israelite' citizens in the metaphor of a spiritual temple, '...you are no longer strangers and aliens, but you are citizens with the saints and also members of the household of God' (2.19, cf. 3.18). The identity of 'saints' in 2.19 offers two interpretive alternatives. First, Ephesians could refer to joining of non-Israelite believers onto ethnic Israel, linking 2.12 and 2.19. This would mean that God's people would combine three kinds of saints, Israelites who are Christ-followers, Israelites who are not Christ-followers, and non-Israelite 'in Christ'. In other words, whether Israelites would be Christ-followers or not would be irrelevant, as they would benefit of lasting covenant with God, according to the two-covenant model (cf. Gaston 1987; Gager 1983). However, while this offers a very plausible solution to resolve the NT complexities on non-Israelite inclusion, it is not without its difficulties. For instance, the early Christian discourses typically heighten the importance of 'faith in Christ' and its importance

---

80   See also MacDonald (2000: 251–9) and Darko who reads Ephesians through the lens of the church (2008).

to all people, including Jewish (cf. Eph. 2.1-7).[81] Secondly and conversely, it could be argued that these 'saints' here mean Israelite Christ-followers. This is more likely as Ephesians proceeds to explain that citizens of God's Israel are 'built on the foundation of the apostles and prophets with Christ Jesus himself as the cornerstone' (2.20) and insists that communal descriptions make explicit references to 'Christ'.

Furthermore, Ephesians clearly understands the community as a Christ-following group: 'a holy temple in the Lord' which is joined together 'in Christ', and built together in him (2.21-22).[82] The absence of differentiation between those who are 'in Christ' and ethnic Israel indicates that the community seen as God's people assumed a shared primary identification of Christ-followership, although members may come from culturally and ethnically diverse groups. This is highly significant as Ephesians envisages that it is the *ekklēsia*, not Israel, which 'manifests God's wisdom' and fulfils his eternal purposes (3.10). Instead, I argue that Israel serves legitimating purposes while communal experience is imagined in a community of reconciled Christ-followers, who enjoy peace and access to God (2.18).

In light of the above, there are two ways of understanding Ephesians' construction of the people of God: either 1) the citizenship of Israel remains legitimate and her covenant continues, but the people of God is extended with the inclusion of the nations 'in Jesus', or 2) the people of God is redefined and consists of Christ-followers. In addition to hermeneutical complexities, both options also involve social and ideological difficulties, including the affiliation of 'proselytes' and 'righteous gentiles' in option 1. Although this sounds hugely speculative, this model would seem to imply the membership of both Christ-following non-Israelites, (some of whom) do not obey the Torah (e.g. those from 'Acts/ Pauline Christianities') AND other non-Israelites who would undergo

81   Although this offers an alternative solution for NT interpretation, the two-covenant view is, like many aspects of Christian theology, only conceivable as Christian intra-communal discourse meaningful to the community who agrees with its messianic principle. It would not have worked as an over-arching view to negotiate relations with other Jewish communities in the antiquity (who would not agree 'Jesus Christ' as Israel's Messiah); neither does it resolve theological difficulties in today's Jewish-Christian relations. In my view, its main difficulty is that it assumes 'our' decision on who is Israel's Messiah, who is included in God's people and how to reconcile the nations 'in Christ'. Assuming this as a solution for interreligious relations would border theologically arrogant, although the view works as a legible alternative for what the early Christians may have thought and offers Christians a possible explanation of how to legitimate both 'us' and Israel, despite its criticisms by traditional theology.

82   This reading finds further plausibility in the fact that the communal characteristics, being 'in Christ' and all the benefits resulting of his grace, are described using inclusive 'we'-language that refers to those who are united by their faith in 'Jesus Christ', as discussed in Chapter 1.

Jewish initiation rites and obey the Torah, as normal. This would seem to undermine the idea that Jesus is 'the saviour of the nations', unless there would be a dispensational change so that all new non-Israelite members would join 'in Jesus'.[83] But this complication reduces the likelihood of option 1. However, the point is that Ephesians does not figure these out for its readers. It is a communal discourse and the writer does not digress to matters beyond the ingroup, or provide explanations for issues that are of no immediate communal significance.[84] If anything, keeping things simple was probably good social entrepreneurship.

All things considered, Ephesians leaves a number of 'gaps' in its positioning of the ingroup and Israel: 1) it explains neither the continuity nor discontinuity of Israelites in the community; 2) it does not use 'remnant' language, make explicit that only some Israelites were included or anticipate a future restoration of Israel; 3) criticism or rejection of ethnic Israel, or any other Jewish grouping, is also missing.[85] As noted before, a reader can then fill the gaps with different fillings and arrive with different meanings. Consequently, Israel as a fictional character in the text is at the mercy of the readers who might easily dismiss the community of Israelites, even if their traditions are seized and identified as legitimating discourse for the 'new humanity in Christ'. Alternatively, readers may uphold the continuity between 'the church' and Israel based largely on the lack of explicit dismissal or critique. In other words, Israel is positioned according to how the textual gaps are filled: either stressing lack of legitimation of Israel (as above) or dismissal of Israel, as I proceed to explain.[86] However, it is important to note that reading Ephesians against the two-covenant model, i.e. assuming separate covenants for Israel (ethnic election and covenant) and for non-Israelite Christ-followers (election and salvation in Christ) involves a major difficulty in terms of the

---

83 It seems possible that different communities existing synchronically in different places had different code for non-Israelite affiliation. However, the important thing is that it is particularly when we consider the presence of other non-Israelites that the difficulty with this otherwise simple model becomes evident. In the light of the missing evidence for option 1 this is pure speculation, and seems both unlikely and unconvincing and I wonder if any social entrepreneurship would make this a plausible communal model.

84 On the contrary, while the absence of Israel in the text is striking, the Greco-Roman social setting is seen as threatening, as Chapter 6 demonstrates. This could lead us to speculate that for the Deutero-Pauline writer, the non-Israelite inclusion into Jewish movement was no longer a cause of dispute, as it was to the apostle who defended their salvation 'in Christ' as a separate covenant, not under the rubric of the Mosaic covenant and the Torah observance that characterizes the members of that community.

85 This is unusual as communal disputes often collide on contested topics and refute alternative views.

86 However, given that Ephesians is a religious text we might use our own opinion (gap-filling exercise) as legitimated 'biblical view to Israel' that may go on to influence our worldview and beyond.

social orientation the text provides to its recipient community: namely that Ephesians does not legitimate Israel as God's people in her own right or provide ideological tools to either understand this or engage with it. Also, there is no explanation for her ongoing relationship with God.

Consequently, I propose that Israel's function is to offer legitimation, historical story and cultural models for the social entrepreneur, who imagines the community purely in terms of Christ-followers. Israel provides a standard for God's people and legitimation for ongoing categorization of people to members and outsiders, given that God makes beneficial covenants with those he has chosen. This contributes to communal orientation and ingroup preference in members' identity and their social relations. Furthermore, Israel provides a model for blessings that go together with being God's chosen possession. This is seen in the characterization of non-Israelites according to their 'have-nots'; neither do they have the sign of circumcision, nor 'the covenants of promise', hope or God (2.12). Further still, have-nots of other nations combined with the special status given to Israel involve a level of dissatisfaction or conflict: Ephesians positions Israelites and others not as dismissive groups disinterested in each other, but rather as negatively oriented toward each other, as the status differences entail a negative orientation, 'hostility' between Israelites and others (2.14).[87] Although Ephesians negates this conflict, it maintains the group dynamics as it assumes a difference between God's people and outsiders and social distancing as reading of 4.17–5.20 will explore.

---

87   It remains unclear if the social hostility is actual or fictional; whether it is something that the writer is aware of, or whether it actually has significant bearing on the lives of the community members. Given the theoretical rather than narrative reference to actual incidences of conflict, it could be just the author's judgment of intercommunal relations, based on his social location and experience, which is not (necessarily) the same as that of the audience he has in mind, or the community embedded in the text. Similarly, Macdonald suggests that the text simply 'resists being pinned down to any historical situation' (MacDonald 2000: 252). Consequently, she believes that understanding Ephesians 2.11-22 as dealing with 'specific tensions between Jewish and Gentile Christians' probably goes beyond the evidence (2000: 253). MacDonald offers the following suggestions, either that the passage deals with 'Gentile arrogance' or that it reflects tensions involved in the incorporation of non-Israelites into the church, and may be encouraging harmonious relations (2000: 253). In my opinion, rather than discussing which was more likely to have greater influence on Ephesians, the social circumstances or the development of ideas and ideological creativity of a writer, it is better to acknowledge that these issues are interlinked rather than separate influences in the development of early Christianities. Nevertheless, the description of the hostility and 'the dividing wall' (2.14) suggests that socio-religious or ethnic differences are a real concern for the writer, and it is unnecessary to assume that his concern was purely ideological, but it presumably had its roots in social experience, although that might not have been shared between him and the non-Israelites addressed – especially as he reports the hostility to the non-Israelites, who might have been unmoved by estimations by Israelites outside their immediate, day-to-day social context.

So, in my view, Israel provides socio-ideological models for the people of God and a close relationship with God, as well as the negotiation of communal boundaries in the dialectic process of external categorization and internal identification between insiders and outsiders. It is another example of Ephesians' flexible cultural renavigation: the author chooses relevant elements that serve the purposes of his communal values and builds his own socio-ideological cluster. It is precisely because it is a communal discourse, not theological treatise, that s/he has no need to explain his decisions or complications deselected. The importance of such internal-external dialectic for identity and identification process is central to social identity theory (e.g. Jenkins 1996, 2004) and Asano offers a relevant Pauline studies example in his study of Galatians (2005: 36–53; cf. Esler 1998). Asano concludes that Paul reckoned that his days with 'Judaism' were past (Gal. 1.13-14), and adapted his traditions for a 'recreated worldview' that served as an ideological framework for the community and its internal legitimation (2005: 226–9). Although one may not agree with his view on Paul, similar processes clearly operate in the Deutero-Pauline Ephesians as we can glean from its ideological framework that adapts Israelite culture and narratives for communal benefit, placing the community of Christ-followers, not Israelites, at the heart of the discourse.

This is further evident in the textual birth of the new person (*anthrōpos*) 'in Christ' (2.15). This image symbolizes the new community of God's people. This is significant, for at least in the early stages of Pauline mission he formed the Christ-following groups along in closer affiliation with Israelite groupings, most evidently seen in the Acts narrative. This is also true in Galatians, where a non-Israelite converts to this messianic new faith but seemed to take this as joining Judaism (Wan 2000: 126), and had dealings with other communal members with different views on their initiation. Wan suggests that instead of subsuming all [ethnic] differences under Jewish homogeneity he amalgamates differences between groups and ethnicities whilst maintaining cultural characteristics (2000: 125).[88]

---

88 Wan makes an important insight when he argues that Paul 'deconstructs [his traditional] ethnocentrism by relativising his own prerogatives as a Jew in this new community' (Wan 2000: 107–31, esp. 126). Paul does not erase ethnic differences in Galatians, nor do his later epistles use a 'blanket of erasure of differences' (cf. 2 Cor. 11.22; Phil. 3.5-6; Rom. 9.1-5; 11.1). Wan proceeds to argue that instead of erasing differences the new 'people' are reconfigured by 'combining these differences into a hybrid existence' (2000: 126). He explains that the new identity for the Galatian community is 'a combination of both Jewish and Hellenistic traits' and 'an amalgam of two district varieties' (2000: 126). This means that each group must accept the difference of others and presume no claim to power or dominance over others, but different groups could retain their cultural integrity (2000: 126). He paraphrases Gal. 3.28 in the light of post-colonial Asian-American hermeneutics as 'you are both Jew and Greek, both free and slave, both male and female, for

However, in Ephesians the cultural other (non-Israelite) does not maintain one's former identity but has to undergo adoption, transformation and join into Israelite saints, and Israelite symbolism characterizes their new identity. Furthermore, identification with their past or non-Israelite culture in general is demonized and strongly discouraged (4.17ff.). It seems that Ephesians wants to both erase cultural difference, as well as remove the culturally different (Pickering 2001: 213). Therefore, although some aspects of Jewishness have been redefined and perhaps 'compromised' (such as the Torah observance), other are passionately upheld (holiness and distance from others), and the contours of Ephesians' identity discourse are both flexible and rigid; flexible in terms of legitimation of 'Jesus Christ' seen as 'the saviour of the nations' and inflexible in terms of non-Israelite influences and its stance towards members' lifestyle. Thus Ephesians is a discourse of power; while the writer assumes flexibility others are given socio-ideologically restrictive paradigms, on to which I will return in the discussion of 4.17–5.20.

Based on the discussion above it may be concluded that the Deutero-Pauline model of abolishing the Law and devaluing Jewish culture reinterpreting its symbols continues to distance Pauline traditions from Pauline and Jewish Christianities. Ephesians' communal legitimation uses socio-ideological components that derive from Jewish heritage, observed through Christ-followers' spectacles. First, the ideological legitimation of the community is based on 'Christ', who paved the way for the saints into God's presence, abolished the Law and removed social hostility between members from divergent ethnicities (2.14-16). Secondly, the legitimation links the group with Israel, who provides legitimation for the followers of 'Israel's messiah'. However, this is ideological and mnemonic, rather than social, as it utilizes symbolism and discourse components but does not provide guidance of social relations or facilitate close social positioning. Consequently, Israel supplies the novel community with historical antiquity.

The legitimating mnemonics (use of communal memories to provide legitimating historical story) continues Ephesians' characteristic use of complex and intertwined images. This is seen in the characterization and positioning of the audience: their ethnic otherness is reversed not only granting them 'citizenship' (2.12, 19); but also by creating a new humanity that replaces the 'uncircumcised' and the 'circumcised' and their problematic history (2.15), imagining that this dispels social difference. Whether the creation of a 'new humanity in Christ' actually augments or reduces Israel's legitimating function is an interesting question. It may

---

you are all one in Christ Jesus' and he explains that 'in this dialectic conception, universality is upheld, but it is universality that is predicated on, requires and is erected on the foundation of cultural and ethnic particularities (Wan 2000: 127).

reduce the role of Israel because the new creation speaks the novelty of the community and newness of both 'Jew and Gentile'. However, the new humanity seems to be a secondary metaphor, which is not built on elsewhere in the discourse. Its meaning or birth (how it rises from Israel) receives no explanation, and inexplicably it seems to fade into insignificance as the rest of the discourse continues to develop meanings of the non-Israelite origins of the readers, not their newness. This indicates that the writer emphasizes their cultural otherness rather than their new creation by God 'in Christ'. For Ephesians both understanding 'the historical disadvantage' of being a non-Israelite and that status transformation are essential components of communal identity. The writer labours to establish that the ethnic disadvantage is continuing in terms of unwanted cultural baggage, and warns they could lose their new status by living like 'pagans' (4.17–5.20).

Furthermore, the attention given to the development of reputations of Jesus and Paul may also provide a level of continuity with Israel. However, whether this is the case is another intricate matter, where the reading positions and meanings associated with – or imported into – the text matter a great deal. For instance, many NT critics – especially those for whom the Jewishness of early Christianities is a default setting – easily see 'Israelite' signals in mentions of either Jesus or Paul.[89] However, although general models of 'messiah' and 'prophet' derive from Israel they are used to promote Christianness, as discussed in this chapter and the following. The writer must have been aware of how contested the reputations of these figures are presented according to the writer's conviction and any dispute is silenced: 'Jesus Christ' and Paul are presented as communal heroes and the discourse protects the community from alternative elements. Such silencing epitomizes how communal mnemonic engineering installs memories in the community in a particular shape. Fine distinguishes between three types of difficult reputations: 1) negative, stigmatized and relatively fixed reputations; 2) contested, which are very much in negotiation, usually for a period of time before a certain reputation gains wider acceptance, or becomes e.g. 3) a subgroup reputation, in case of people who have more than multiple reputations held by different groups of people, as some reputations are solidified in different forms by conflicting subcultural groups (2001: 10–11). Considering Jesus, while the first type was probably fairly common in many circles (if they had ever heard of him); the second type belonged to the earliest Jesus-movement and as reflected in the Acts narrative, for example; and the third type is found in Pauline disputes and post-

---

89 The concept of a 'default setting' and the implicit paradigms presuppositions set for NT readings derives from Dunn who discusses readers' cultural conditioning and its inevitable reflection onto the text (Dunn 2005: 79–125).

Paulines; and eventually Jesus' reputation transformed from 'difficult to dominant' (Rodriguez 2004). Ephesians' treatment of contested Israelites could be a means of challenging a negative reputation prevalent in other groups and in discourses of competing social entrepreneurs.

However, when discussing the Jewishness of Jesus and Paul it is important to consider again both their Jewishness and Christianness. First, the historicity of Jesus receives no attention in the text that focuses on his role as God's agent (contra Hoehner 2002: 464). The discourse is designed for community members who already accept Jesus as Israel's Christ, and have decided to follow him in socio-cultural obedience, and perhaps 'potential members', who are not particularly addressed. The letter is not aimed for recruitment which has been achieved earlier by (the preaching of) the gospel in which the story of Jesus might have been more important (1.13, 15; 4.20-4). Similarly, Ephesians does no historical positioning for Paul's reputation, or inclusion among the 'apostles and prophets' (3.5; cf. 2.20; 4.11);[90] but turns him into both apostle and a prophet *par excellence*. Thus although the discourse draws from Jewish imagination, both represent the novel movement, and serve social construction of the non-Israelite Christ-following community.

Therefore having considered a variety of textual positionings, the relationship between Israel and the community remains difficult because of the silence in the text on the matter. In this study the socio-ideological reforms are observed exploring Ephesians' construction as a subgroup social engineering, without signing up to its socio-ideological positionings or upholding their correctness today. In my view the community of Christ-followers is seen as operating separately, and although Israel's 'covenants of promise' is recognized it is of no consequence to the life of the community due to their minority position. Other explanations may stress the ideological differences and 'matters of faith'. A reader may assume that the community of Christ-followers 'takes over' from Israel, and enjoys the relationship with God according to the current terms of the contract, 'in Christ' while Israel is dismissed. For example, Dahl analyses skilfully both the importance of Jewishness to the discourse and its subcultural orientation, 'I see no way to avoid the conclusion that the author of Ephesians had a keen interest in the Jewish roots and origins of the church but failed to show any concern for the relationship of his

---

90 Paul is presented as 'the apostle' as the chapter proceeds to argue, despite the contested nature of this claim (cf. withholding the title 'apostle' from Paul in the Acts of the Apostles). It is a commonplace to take the references to 'apostles and prophets' in Ephesians as authoritative positions within the movement, as e.g. MacDonald (2000: 262–3), and Hoehner (2002: 441–4) explain, discussing a wide range of linguistic and theological aspects of the phrase.

audience to contemporary Jews outside the church' (2000: 446).[91] Darko may exemplify readers who stress the concerns of 'the church' that typically disconnect Ephesians (and the church) from its Jewishness: he stresses the newness of 'the church' as 'a brand new entity' and sees no continuity with Israel, arguing that the Jewish people would join on the same terms with Gentiles (2008: 113, n. 21). Furthermore, he argues that 'Ephesians does not trace the foundation of the church to Jewish heritage ... Its identity and essence are shaped by this sense of newness embedded in the work of God through Christ' (2008: 114) failing to note the extent of Jewish imagination and its legitimating function.

My readings aim to show that such disconnection with Jewishness is not the case, and nuance understanding of both Jewishness and Christianness of Ephesians. It is important to note that Ephesians builds on Jewish ideological and symbolic resources and honours her covenants and ancient God as well as her reputation with a view to sinful nations, despite dismissing social relations from the discourse.

To summarize, Israel's traditions have a legitimating function in Ephesians, although Israelites are peripheral as the *ekklēsia* receives full attention as the dominant fictional character in the discourse. The discourse of ethnic reconciliation has, as Yee puts it, 'society-creating and community-redefining' aspects: it is meant to 'reframe the notion of the people of God' (2005: 126). When the discourse is understood as social entrepreneurship, the extent of cultural re-navigation and mnemonic engineering become clearer. We find the writer's traditions (Jewishness) are redefined in the light of new values (Christ-event) which amalgamates new ideology and new collective memories used to shape new identity and culture (Christianness) of non-Israelite Christ-followers, whose culture is dismissed.

This means that despite the Jewishness of its symbolic universe, Ephesians constructs distinctive communal identity and boundaries. The idea of a community implies simultaneous similarity and difference, defining its members, outsiders, boundary markers and processes that distinguish the groups from one another (Cohen 1985: 12).[92] As previously established, Ephesians' communality is established with/in 'Christ' (esp. in Eph. 1–2). What easily goes unnoticed is that once the election and communal membership are embedded 'in Christ', a boundary is drawn between the believers and those who don't share their faith in 'Jesus Christ'. Consequently, whatever the text associates with Christ becomes a matter of identity that defines the community, its members and outsiders. Thus communal symbols, values and rituals highlight the

---

91   Similarly Sanders (1993: 200–1).

92   See Lieu for a thorough analysis on boundary processes in Jewish and early Christian texts (2004: 98–146).

'we-ness' of the group and provide ideological tools for enforcing their communality and ingroup orientation. Such group symbols, boundary markers and processes can be meaningless to outsiders, but their private dimension is idiosyncratic with loaded symbolic meaning, established by the culture which characterizes the members and binds them together (Cohen 1985: 74; cf. Jenkins 2004: 113, 117; Asano 2005: 39–40). For instance, Ephesians' Christ-connection, symbolic language of sacred 'heavenly' space (2.6), being God's holy temple (2.21), his dwelling (2.22) or the body of Christ (4.15-16; 5.30) are only meaningful in communal dialogue and probably meaningless to outsiders.[93] Cohen's discussion highlights their function as communal boundaries:

> People become aware of their culture when they stand at its boundaries: when they encounter other culture, or when they become aware of other ways of doing things, or merely of contradictions of their own culture. The norm is the boundary ... Since people become most sensitive to their own culture when they encounter others', the apposite place at which to find their attitudes to their culture (or their imputation of meaning to their community) is at its boundaries. (1985: 69, 70)

Therefore, Ephesians' discursive 'boundary locations' are those where the writer distinguishes the ingroup from the surrounding socio-ideological context, even if the terms in itself would be neutral as the focus is on their subcultural, communal meaning (in Christ). These include, for instance, 1) communal Christ-orientation; 2) baptism (4.5); 3) spirituality (1.13-14, 19; 5.18-20); 4) strong community focus (1.15; 2.15-22; 4.1-6; 5.21) and 5) cultural separation (e.g. 4.17; 5.5, 6, 7). It is cultural processes such as these that distinguish the group by constructing both them and the 'others' (Cohen 1985: 12). It is important to note that for the purposes of communal stability these features are typically presented as non-negotiable and fixed in social entrepreneurship, despite the fact that in real life boundaries are checkpoints where negotiation and testing occurs.[94] For

---

93   Their parallels in other literature would illustrate what they mean in other contexts and communities. The point is not whether the terminology, experiences, values and norms would be unique to the community, but how these function in the communal social processes. It is the symbolic, idiosyncratic Christ-centred interpretation that makes them things that distinguish the group. For further discussion see Cohen on 'communities of meaning' (1985: 70–96) and Jenkins, who explores 'symbolising belonging' (Jenkins 2004: 108–23).

94   Although boundary processes can be routinized or institutionalized, the processes of identification are temporary checkpoints rather than concrete walls – and even the latter are permanent only in the makers' conceit, as in our textual social entrepreneurship (Jenkins 2004: 103). Bauman points out that communal culture is not like a collective inheritance that would automatically replicate itself – nor a mould that shapes peoples' lives (1999: 25). The fluidity of social identity as well as boundary processes are widely acknowledged in social-scientific literature. See, for instance, Barth (1969), whose ground-breaking proposal was that ethnic identities are not primordial and immutable; but they are processes which allow

example, Ephesians projects idealized resocialization that produces holy and communally oriented Christ-followers, who are characterized by prototypical communal values (Bauman 1999: 25). [95]

Coming back to the implications this has on 2.11-22, and 2.15 in particular; Israel is not set aside as such, but the discourse clearly provides a constitution of a new community and new people of God. The text remembers 'Jesus Christ' linking societal values and meanings to his death thus legitimating the construction of the new people of God and their social orientation, which leaves the Law behind. Ephesians re-negotiates crucial boundary processes that divide Israel and other nations in communally coloured memories of circumcision, *politeia* of Israel, covenants and the Law. After the reconciliation (2.13-18), Israel embraces the non-Israelite believers (2.19), and the community is labelled as the 'new humanity' and symbolized as God's dwelling (2.15, 22).[96] As noted before, the continuity of God's covenant with Israel is neither affirmed nor rejected, but the writer transfers key concepts to 'Christ' regime: 'the nations have become joint heirs, co-members of the same body, and co-sharers in the promise in Christ Jesus' (3.6, literal translation). The membership 'in Christ' is shared between ethnicities and the 'covenants of promise' (2.12) finds a communal counterpart in the 'promise in Christ Jesus through the Gospel' (3.6). Thus Israel's self-definitions and boundary markers are reinterpreted or replaced as non-Israelite believers are predestined to manifest God's wisdom, and circumcision loses its function as a symbol for God's people as it is remembered as socially divisive.[97]

It is not unthinkable that Israelite boundary processes were

---

moving in and out of them. His understanding of ethnicities as transactional and flexible has become a basic anthropological model, although it does not escape criticisms (Jenkins 2004: 99–104).

95 Ephesians' social entrepreneur operates like a cultural leader who 'preaches the essentialist theory', while what he practises is the processual theory (Bauman 1999: 91). He essentializes the discourse as 'immutable sacred texts rather than the convictions of living and changeable people' (1999: 67). In other words, the text projects permanent, God-legitimated 'facts', while its values and norms would be contested and subject to different responses, faithful and less so.

96 Ephesians does not refer to communal worship much with the exception of 5.18-20 which describes the thanksgiving and singing of hymns, in the fullness of the Spirit (contra 1 Cor.). Instead we find language of an intimate spiritual connection with the divine. In my view, this is another distancing device that presents the group in a superior relationship with the divine than, for example, synagogue or cultic associations. It also dismisses internal disputes and conflicts.

97 Note, however, that Ephesians does not attack circumcision (Phil. 3.2), spiritualize it (Rom. 2.29), explain it (Gal. 5.6; 6.15) or negotiate another ritual to replace circumcision (Col. 2.11-12), which in my view is a major difference between Ephesians and the above texts. Unlike Paul, Ephesians does not install Abraham in the communal legitimation despite how

re-evaluated because ethnic Israel is no more regarded as the people of God, who are now defined by faith in 'Christ' and their possession of the spirit, not by the covenant with Moses. Given that the social entrepreneur desires a harmonious, united community, but knows that circumcision could be a divisive issue and agitate cross-ethnic relations, it seems that there would be no option but to propose alternative norms and follow more lenient initiation processes.[98] This is achieved when 'the Law and its commandments and ordinances' are abolished (2.15) and the community is distanced from proselyte-praxis and the disputes characterizing the Pauline period. It is important that the language of reforms is definite, unconditional and aggressive: not only is the Law abolished but the social hostility is killed by 'Christ'; an image which gives a bizarre twist into remembering Jesus in the NT. This reading position has assumed that the Law is completely abolished in Ephesians' view. How likely, then, would the permanent removal of hostility be if ethnic divisions over Torah observance are retained and coexist in the community? If diverse practices or multiple identities exist within one community, further tools for negotiating the complexity would be urgently required – otherwise diversity would be unsustainable or unharmonious, before long.

Finally, if one considers that the discourse is world-shaping, the literal reading of the abolition of the Law could have been highly significant for intergroup processes as it could have promoted intolerance toward Israelite believers as well as the synagogue movement. Secondly, it has its consequences for Deutero-Pauline hermeneutics: the distancing from Jewish culture would set this writing apart from the New Perspective's Paul: if the Law is abolished without guidance for multiple identities, the writer is clearly disinterested in social relations with Israel but focused on providing his group with the required ideological legitimation. This is achieved in 2.11-22 which offers a licence for new communal processes and by the replacement metaphor of the new humanity. It is striking that in Ephesians the Law is associated with 'the circumcised' and like the ethnoreligious Israel, the Law seems to have lost its position as a characteristic of God's people.

---

convenient it would be that he lived before the Law was given. Ephesians' emphasis could be part of his different social position, a lesser influence of Israelite relations in connection with its non-Israelite context and chronological distance from the apostle.

98   Again, while the writer is concerned about hostile relations he does not discuss or refer to ethnic disputes in/affecting the group. The text is not about life of the community but its fictional character: if the community was in a non-Israelite location it is possible that the circumcision dispute or ethnic hostility may not have affected the group at all. But it certainly was a concern for the writer and the alternative solution required the legitimating authority of Christ himself.

2d. *Textual Elements that Challenge these Readings*

However, textual complexities and factors that impact this reading position must also be examined. It is important to acknowledge that both contrasting interpretations of the 'abolition of the Law' engage with the text as well as with the gaps in the text; and the reading process involves both factors imported into the text as well as disregarding some textual features. Therefore, the following factors, which may challenge the interpretation of abolishing the Law as an articulation of distinctive Christianness, must be considered.

As noted before, the fact that non-Israelite believers are joined 'with the saints' suggests that these saints represent at least some Israelites and, in the absence of evidence to the contrary, Torah observing people of God. While 2.15 envisaged the reconciled groups as a 'new humanity', 2.19 could be interpreted as meaning that Christ-following 'Israelite saints' are still regarded as a separate entity or that non-Israelite saints are joined with the historical Israel, just as the category of 'the nations' continues to feature in Ephesians' social guidance.[99] This has its bearing upon Ephesians' view to early Christianities and so-called early 'Jewish Christian' relations; as the former would convey multiple identities, and the latter two ways of salvation. In my view, the reader's role in processing the meaning of 2.19 is crucial: readings either stress oneness of the 'new humanity' and 'being in Christ' as primary identification; or stress ongoing ethnic identifications that still distinguish between Israelites and others. Whichever concept is given priority depends on a reader's choice, as arguments can be constructed for and against both hermeneutical alternatives (cf. Yee 2005: 196–7; contra Lincoln 1991: 151; Perkins 1997: 75; MacDonald 2000: 249).

The 'saints' in 2.19 could be taken as either 'all believers' (regardless of ethnic origins), 'Israelite Christ-followers' or 'historical Israel', respectively. First, the 'all believers' reading finds support elsewhere in the letter Ephesians uses 'saints (holy ones)' exclusively as a label for those who are 'in Christ'. In favour of 'Israelite Christ-followers' is that Ephesians' stress on changes to the non-Israelite status could imply that Israelite citizens (*politeia*) would feature among the fellow-citizens (*sumpolitēs*).[100] This allows for two different conclusions: either taking 'saints' referring to Christ-following Israelites, given that in Ephesians' saint-identity is

---

99 The interpretations for 'fellow-citizens with saints' also include an alternative translation for *tōn hagiōn* as a reference to angels as 'holy ones' (Gnilka 1971: 154; cf. MacDonald 2000: 249). Although there are contemporary Jewish parallels for such use (cf. Yee 2005: 195–8), this is, in my view, unlikely as labelling 'saints' is an important literary device in the text and there is no reference to angelic beings in God's presence, contrary to opposing spiritual powers and beings (1.21; 2.2; 6.12).

100 The connection between *politai* (2.12) and *sympolites* (2.19) is significant. Cf. MacDonald, who notes this but still takes the phrase as referring to 'all believers' (2000: 286–

explicitly linked with 'Christ'; or, in favour of ethnic Israelite 'saints' given that the *tēs politeias tou Israēl* refers to Israel *per se* in 2.12, the 'saints' could be a reference to Israelites and part of the 'language of inclusion' which extends benefits of citizenship to non-Israelites. Ephesians acknowledges that the core members of the Christ-following movement were Israelite Christians, represented by the figure of Paul and his associates (1.12), in contrast with the subsequent non-Israelite believers (1.13). Therefore, although Ephesians focuses predominantly upon believers' shared and unifying Christ-followership, the social entrepreneur nevertheless remembers the fact that they do come from different ethnic backgrounds.

It is important to consider the positive communal functions of the Law. Why should the ethnic Law be abolished if the dissociation from the non-Israelite world is crucial for believers, as Ephesians 4 and 5 demonstrate? Why is it that although Israelites saw the Law as a protective fence around the nation, its divisive function dominates the discussion in Ephesians (Perkins 1997: 71–3), even though the distance between 'the people of God' and other cultures is still fundamental? Although the Law has been abolished the community must be, like Israel, characterized by holiness, glorify God with their lifestyle and dissociate themselves from the surrounding cultures (e.g. 2.10; 3.10; 4.22-4; 5.1-3). The writer seeks to create a parallel community that similarly distances itself from the surrounding world; or to be 'Israel' maintaining holiness without the ethnic characteristics of the Law observance, depending on how the reader positions Ephesians on the 'Jewish Christian relations' continuum. Therefore, the dedication for God as culturally distinctive models Christianness and provides the standard for the people of God, that is, according to Ephesians, new humanity 'in Christ'.

There are some hermeneutical obstacles for discontinuity with Paul. The more one stresses the continuity of Israel's faith in Ephesians, the easier it is to harmonize the text with Paul under the 'New Perspective' umbrella. This is important to Yee's reading of the Jewishness of Ephesians, who devotes less attention to comparing different nuances or discussing how these might reflect a later date, different setting, another author or dissimilar beliefs or values.[101] In my view, it is appropriate and

---

7). According to Yee, 'Gentiles and "holy ones" are a structural pair similar to uncircumcision/circumcision, while the author specifically avoided reference to the historical Israel due to their ethnocentrism' (Yee 2005: 196–7).

101   Yee positions himself with Deutero-Pauline scholars, dissociating himself from the question (Yee 2005: 33, n.149). As it stands his work could almost be read in the light of Pauline authorship, not least by its title. The implicit 'Paul wrote Ephesians' view could explain why its continuity with 'Paul of the new perspective' is so important to him. Although Gombis leans towards Pauline authorship (2005: 7, 13) he (perhaps reluctantly) positions himself among the Deutero-Pauline scholars, similarly to Darko (2008: 25).

in most cases necessary to dismiss the authorship discussion with brief definitions; it is not equally justified to dismiss all discussion of the author, failing to engage with his socio-ideological positionings and discursive manoeuvrings. In some cases the 'writer' or 'author' is in practical terms synonymous for 'Paul' if readings fail to explore the Deutero-Pauline developments and distinctiveness of the text. Studies that pay lip service to the Deutero-Pauline hypothesis but avoid discussing its implications often echo the concerns of traditional scholarship despite suggesting that one has moved on with the times. However, this is unhelpful if indeed 50 per cent of scholars dispute the letter's apostolic origin (Hoehner 2002: 9–19). This suggests that at least half of Ephesians scholars would be receptive to the critical study of the authorship and therefore ongoing dismissal of matters relating to the development of post-Pauline Christianities is poor scholarship. It is quite regrettable if scholarship labelled as Deutero-Pauline refuses to discuss the Deutero-Pauline issues.

The position of this study with regard to Paul and possible Deutero-Pauline developments can be summarized as follows. Paul is viewed as a pioneering figure in the early Christ movement (Donaldson 1997: 303) who challenged the proselyte-practices and argued for full membership for non-Israelites among God's people without proselyte conversion rites, without the necessity of Law observance, and also without challenging Israelite obedience of the Law (Nanos 1996: 3–20; Westerholm 1988; 2004). Interestingly, the Acts of the Apostles portrays Paul as Law-observant throughout the narrative, which suggests that this was an important aspect of his legacy and reputation.[102] The rejection of Jewish Torah obedience is often explained in the light of Paul's call (or conversion). For instance, Donaldson argues that Paul went through a paradigm shift, when the realization of the resurrection caused him to rethink Jewish traditions and reorganize his conceptional framework and placing Christ at its centre. Consequently for Paul, it was Christ, not the Torah, that determined membership in God's people (1997: 304). Ephesians follows by offering a simplification of the Pauline discussion of the relevance of the Torah for Christ-followers in 2.15 claiming that 'Christ has abolished the Law'. It is most probable that this view was socially motivated, developing those elements of Pauline tradition that dispute the need for Christ-followers to obey the Law. These could include, for instance, arguments for the saving efficacy of Christ's death and being made right with God through it; the temporality of the Law until Christ; or that covenants of the Law and of Christ are oppositional

---

102 The historicity of the narrative is less important here: what matters here is the construction of Paul's reputation, not its historical accuracy. It is most likely, though, that Paul's Jewishness in Acts reflects the historical core of his reputation.

and that a new creation reigns over the Law.[103] Nevertheless, such convictions would have grown in dialogue with social experience and reflecting the popularity of the Christ-following movement among non-Israelites. Possible social causes of revisions on Jewish Law may have included a critique of Israelite chosenness, conflict over the Law-free non-Israelite inclusion, or a disagreement about Jesus as 'the Christ' and participation of the nations in the people of God through him.[104]

The early separation from Israel would be socio-historical improbability. To begin with, the characterization of the community as consisting of non-Israelites is more difficult if one assumes early Pauline authorship. Although Ephesians 2.14-22 has a view of a mixed congregation, in fact only non-Israelites are addressed and the author's concerns about their ethnic 'otherness' seem to dominate. In my view, the lack of synagogue attachment and consequentially, the ease with which to pronounce the Law abolished becomes more plausible the later the discourse is thought to have been written. Given that early Christian writers in the second century could denounce 'Judaism', claim to possess a superior understanding of Hebrew Scriptures and assume to be among the rightful heirs of Israel's invaluable heritage (Zetterholm 2003: 224, cf. 203–24); it is worth considering the journey from Paul to Ephesians to Ignatius. It could well be that Ephesians could be ideologically positioned among developing Christianities rather than in the early Jewish Christ-movement.

One can hardly dismiss the fact that an early 'elimination of the Law' would be historically unlikely as the community would have struggled to legitimize itself outside the protective umbrella of Jewishness. So, for instance, MacDonald, who has raised a legitimate objection against the assumption that the Ephesian community would have been socially as independent as the ideological positioning of the discourse might suggest. It is quite likely, as she proposes, that the Jewish communities provided early Christianity an umbrella with a legitimate social status and protection in the eyes of the imperial government (2004: 435). She suggests that it was Christians like those reflected in Ephesians that drew the attention of Emperor Domitian, who was concerned with those who

103   As, for instance, in Rom. 3.23-24; 5.9, 10; 10.4; Gal. 2.16; 3.23-26; 5.2-4; 6.15. It is most likely that identity politics and non-Israelite inclusion were central to Pauline mission, and would have formed a firm ideological framework for his associates and followers. They would be ideological disciples of Paul, for whom, as Westerholm argues, '[i]t is wrong to impose particularly Jewish aspects of the Sinaitic Law on Gentile believers when it is clear that the Law cannot provide the basis on which sinners may find favour with God' (2004: 442).

104   Westerholm argues that instead of the other factors mentioned, it was specifically the idea of the inability of the Law to deal with human sin that led to the construal of the Law's validity and purpose as limited (2004: 441).

'followed the Jewish way of life without professing Judaism' and on those who 'denied their Jewish origin' (2004: 435).[105]

However, this considers the community from the outside: even though a group may have been Jewish in the eyes of the outsiders this does not necessarily represent their communal positionings; it is possible that they were Jewish to the outsiders; but at the same time had stepped too far in the eyes of other Jewish groups. Early Christian communities would have been identified as Jewish for a number of reasons, not least because of their symbolic universe and devalving the Greco-Roman culture, both inspired by Jewish cultural models. It is possible that they had liturgical similarities, if they still read the same scrolls, spoke about their God and his Messiah, etc. Yet at the same time, despite Jewish cultural elements, their discourse could make such radical statements as dismissing the Mosaic covenant. Therefore it is more plausible that the distance from Jewishness is ideological and community-shaping (Lieu 1996: 13; Lustiger-Thaler 1996: 207) rather than a reconstruction of Jewish-Christian relations at the time of writing. As Iser notes, 'although the text may well incorporate the social norms and values of its possible readers, its function is not merely to present such data, but, in fact, to use them in order to secure its uptake. In other words, it offers guidance as to what is to be produced, and therefore cannot itself be the product' (1978: 107). The text may also be intentional and influencing, incorporating guidance through selective or even fictional reflections of social reality, although such factors would not be directly representative of those experienced by either the author or the implied audience. In other words, the discourse reflects what the social entrepreneurship regards as important, providing direction rather than social commentary.

Bringing the discussion of Ephesians 2.15 to a close I conclude that the reader's role in the processing of the meaning of the text is crucial not only for the interpretation of the passage, but also for imagining its possible influence upon its recipients and any conclusions drawn about early Christianities and their relation to Law observance. Ephesians is clear that as far as the community goes, Christ had abolished the Law. The Torah did not play a decisive part in their communal experience and group identity processes. In my view, these factors make it unlikely that the Ephesian community was in close connection with other Jewish groups or

---

105   For a fuller discussion of Domitian's reign and Jewish groups see Wilson (1995: 11–16). Emerging Christian identity led to the development of radical responses to Imperial ideology and culture, because early Christ-followers were not allowed to have multifaceted identity, both Greco-Roman and Christian, but were encouraged to realign their loyalties heavenward. For a fascinating discussion of early Christianities in the Roman Empire, see Middleton, who argues that it was impossible to be both Christ-follower and loyal citizen of the Empire (2006: 40–70), and for sociological discussion of martyrdom, see DeSoucey et al. (2008: 99–121).

synagogue networks, despite other aspects of cultural similarity. Without Jewish relations, Ephesians' thought could brew and develop without immediate conflicts experienced by the Pauline communities; and even its distance from Jewish traditions could go unnoticed in a non-Israelite community if it had little or no relations with other Jewish groupings, who would have challenged social or ideological reforms. Therefore, I suggest that the non-Israelite location was as crucial for the successful social entrepreneurship as the compelling and persuasive articulation of the discourse itself.

As I have noted before, the interpreter's task in reading Ephesians as early Christian discourse is 'to elucidate the potential meanings of a text' (Iser 1978: 22). In the end, having wandered between different hermeneutical positions, first, considering taking the 'abolition of the Law' as a removal of the requirement of Torah observance from upon non-Israelites, while Israelite observance of the Law is sustained; and secondly, discussing its socio-ideologically radical meaning, as a denouncement of the Law in its entirety, it seems that the meaning of the text depends a great deal on the reader, and his or her underlying assumptions and the way 'gaps in the text are filled'. This confirms the importance of the socio-ideological preferences of a reader in discussing meaning(s) of a text: at least in the case of such an elusive text, the meaning is a product of an interpretive process, of a dialectic interaction between the text and its readers, and their socio-ideological environment – not a faculty of the text.[106] In my view, the meaning of Ephesians is arrived at – not discovered hidden under textual components or layers of tradition. It is about selection and deselection, discussing and dismissing textual perspectives, and dialogue with intratextual and extratextual factors. For instance, it is altogether unlikely that any reader would arrive at 2.11-22 without social and ideological preferences. The reader (or an ancient listener) connects the textual perspectives and interacts with its symbolic universe according to whatever ideological framework he or she subjectively deemed as the most suitable based on textual components, constraints and other factors. In the case of Ephesians 2.15 the reader will decide whether the text leans in the direction of the new perspective continuity with Paul, or whether it projects distinctive Christianness and a movement further away from Jewishness. It is these preferences that determine how one deals with the gaps in the text, or its difficulties. It is the filling of these textual gaps, or explaining where and why the text is silent that are crucial for the meaning making, because once the reader has

---

106   Naturally the meaning(s) are not completely random, but as Iser suggests, there are textual factors that 'precondition the composition of the meaning' (Iser 1978: 22), as discussed through the course of the chapter.

filled the gaps the text appears complete, the gaps disappear and a coherent reading rises from the text.

To conclude, in my view Israel is the most significant gap in the text in the sense that her status alongside the community of Christ-followers is not explored. While it is clear that Israel in 2.12 represents God's providence in the past, her present status and future are left unexplained. Therefore one can imply either a sympathetic attitude to Israel and read Ephesians in the light of this idea; or assume a reading position that is more critical to Israel and it is Christianness, not Jewishness, that rises to the fore in Ephesians. Consequently, Israel, her covenant and the Law can be dismissed from the life of the Christian community. As Iser noted, when 'the unsaid comes to life in the reader's imagination, so the said "expands" to take on greater significance than might have been supposed' (1978: 168). Therefore the same discourse may become a battleground for contrary interpretations; the filling of textual gaps becomes formative to the reading as differences between this study, and Yee's for instance, demonstrate. This insight explains how, for instance, Yee, on one hand, has filled the gaps of the text with Jewishness and hails Ephesians 2.11-22 as an example of how 'new perspective' Ephesians is. On the other hand, this study highlights the extent of cultural reforms – not presence of traditions. One reading may be more plausible than another, but this, again, rests with the reader.

3. *Ephesians 2.15, Ephesians' Jewishness and Shaping the Reputation of Christ*

It is important to proceed beyond discussion of the reading process and hermeneutical observations in the twenty-first century and to consider what kind of social orientation the text promotes for its original audience. Ephesians' challenge on the Torah observance is part of the discourse manoeuvres that shape ingroup identity by legitimating certain aspects of identity and culture, and invalidating others. Locating the removal of the Law on the cross loaded with salvific and transformative efficacy demonstrates how collective remembering may link the needs of a particular community with the past events and figures. Ephesians' remembering of Jesus (2.11-22) along with remembering Paul's 'unique revelation' (3.1-9) installs ideological beliefs in the memory of communal founders and at the core of their identity. Reputations and memories are part of a competitive social discourse that may be even in direct contrast with other groups: what is remembered by one group may be exactly the event that another group seeks to forget. Similarly, the adaptation of a certain historical figure in communal dialogue does not mean that such a figure is 'exclusively owned' by a given group. The 'ownership' of prototypes and exemplars can be contested in social negotiations and different, even competing groups may try to convince their members of the correctness of their collective memories and the relevance of the figure for their particular collectivity.

In his discussion of a constitution of collective memories Lustiger-Thaler speaks of 'mnemonic exchanges', or 'memory agencies' that are capable of reframing absent pasts (1996: 207). He stresses how we remember not only socially, but through social constructs, such as class, ethnic groups and other collective frameworks of remembrance (1996: 207–8). Such collective frameworks are cultural and ideological as communities remember selectively according to their communal agenda and values, as, for instance, a comparison of contrasting attitudes of Jesus in Ephesians 2.15 and Matthew indicates: the Matthean Jesus points out that he has not come to abolish the Law, and those who encourage a liberal view to Torah observance are belittled in the discourse – and the Kingdom of God (5.17, 19). Comparing Matthew and Ephesians demonstrates that they clearly operate with different socio-ideological frameworks, as if Ephesians is forcing dying Jesus to do something that he specifically said he was not going to.

Therefore, how the abolition of the Law is interpreted is an important part of how 'Jesus Christ' is remembered in Ephesians, stressing either his faithful Jewishness or reforms. Therefore, different projections on 2.15 either underline the shared identity or undermine it stressing its sectarian responses. On one hand, if 'the abolishing of the Law' meant denouncing Israelite ethnic chosenness while the Torah remains operative for Israelites, Christ would be remembered as 'the Saviour of the nations' who inaugurated eschatological reforms to proselyte policy. This view could maintain the continuity of Israel's faith while reforming what inclusion of non-Israelites meant, as the text could be seen as articulating separate terms of belonging. This reading finds continuity not only with Paul, but also with other contemporary Israelite groups in the concept of the 'righteous Gentile' possibly operative in some contemporary Jewish communities. Christ would therefore be seen as harmonizing the coexistence of different groups in one community marked by their shared religious experience, which is greater in significance than their diverse practices relating to the Torah.[107] However, although this view is very attractive, especially for Jewish-Christian and ecumenical perspectives, it suffers from a lack of legitimation in Ephesians. On the other hand, if one prefers a reading that 'the abolishing of the Law' spelled the end for Torah observance (from a viewpoint of this particular social entrepreneur) it must be noted that this interpretation implies a Messiah who is remembered as beginning to eradicate essential Jewishness and move

---

107   This view is closely representative of Yee (2005).

towards the construction of a 'new Israel' in later early Christian discourses. I am deliberately accentuating the contrast between 'the Saviour of the nations' and the law-abolishing Messiah, in order to emphasize the differences between the Jewishness of Jesus and who he has become in Christian imagination, largely due to early Christian social entrepreneurship, namely 'the founder of a new religion'. The latter (who exists in NT readings) was not about Israel's restoration, but the inauguration of a novel community of his followers, a new humanity and 'the church'.

Consequently, remembering Jesus in 2.11-22 has further social consequences, as well: it could be seen to essentialize the ethnic conflict in the discourse and foster negative views towards Jewish culture and 'the circumcised'. Such ideas have an unfortunate but undeniable presence in the early Christian thought, at least in the post-NT era. It would appear that the non-Israelite ideological and socio-ethnic location would have been decisive for the emergence of such views and their consequent dismissal of Jewishness. In closing, the idea of such 'non-Jewish Messiah' illustrates that remembering is subject to cultural change. As Halbwachs notes, remembering may include attaching new values into existing memories, 'society from time to time obligates people not just to reproduce in thought previous events of their lives, but also to touch them up, to shorten them, or to complete them so that, however convinced we are that our memories are exact, we give them a prestige that reality did not possess' (1992: 51). As Fine explains, 'reputations are grounded in the needs and the perspectives of those who put forward claims about those reputations' (2001: 20), and the reputation building is directed at typified audiences, personal or assumed (2001: 22).[108] It is notable that directing social entrepreneurship to non-Israelites results in commemorating the ethnic reconciliation and removal of the divisive Law as part of Christ's death. Therefore Ephesians' social entrepreneurship could be seen as tackling 1) Israel's ethnic covenant with God, as non-Israelites are elected and chosen 'in Christ'; and 2) their observance of the Torah and the status of Israel as God's holy people, as the community is imagined as holy without the boundary processes of the Law.

Ephesians' 'Jesus Christ' gave the non-Israelites citizenship rights and made them equal members in God's people, as if he forgot he was supposed to be Israel's Saviour and restore them – not abolish the Laws

---

108 Fine draws from Griswold's model of a cultural diamond, in which four corners of the whole metaphorically represent 'the interconnection of analytically distinct concepts: the cultural object (such as Jesus), the social world (here, of the non-Israelites), the creator (the social entrepreneur) and the receiver (the community)'. Each of these factors evolves and fluctuates over time and thus reputations, cultural objects, change reflecting the alterations in the structural factors or with the entrepreneur or the receiving community (2001: 17, cf. 17–23).

that preserve the group; or bring in 'migrants', facilitating their settlement by compromising well-established standards and operative legislation. This indicates that Israel was used for her legitimating symbolic universe and useful cultural models. While Pauline Christianness is quite conceivably seen as a reform movement, a group that remains within the larger community negotiating particular differences (Esler 1994: 13), Ephesians would seem to reflect different times and further developments as distancing is more evident and probably accentuated separation in the future as communal remembering focuses on the matters of ethnic differentiation, the role of the Law and on the social conflict with Israelites, in addition to remembering non-Israelite legitimacy through myths of election, adoption and membership.

This illustrates how various components of social entrepreneurship, communal legitimation, ideology and collective remembering are intertwined projecting the distinctiveness of the community through the memory of the cross. In my view this illustrates Hobsbawm's stimulating statement, 'if there is no suitable past, it can always be invented' (1998: 6). If we assume that the community did not obey the Law it becomes clear that it was important for the social entrepreneurship to explain why not. How better to resolve the matter but at the cross, the very heart of communal identity. Often the past is not entirely suitable, and therefore some embellished story telling or legitimation must take place (Hobsbawm 1998: 6). Here it is particularly the assumption of God's undertaking in these social, ideological reforms by 'Christ' that makes the discourse so compelling.[109]

Finally, Crossley draws attention to the function of the past in the present, or to 'the connections between the past and the lessons it inspires in the present' (2005: 17). He observes that 'the use of historical parallels might not show us a clear path to the future but on another level they can be used as a means of defying power, constructing identities or more generally as a way of living out/with the present, not least in religious traditions' (2005: 17). Similarly, the writer of Ephesians exercises social power by using his memories of the social conflict, non-Israelite difference and the death of 'Christ', in the construction of societal lessons for the communal present that provide a social and ideological framework for the group. This is an example of what Schwartz describes as shaping the past to reflect reality when past is interpreted 'in terms of images appropriate and relevant to the present' (2000: 18). If 'Christ' abolished the Law, he made the community incompatible with Law-observing Christianness and

---

109   Halbwachs ponders the power of the religious remembering which manages to resist change and convey divine legitimation so powerfully that faith community members' lives become controlled by doctrine (Halbwachs 1992: 113–14). He stated that 'religious doctrine is the collective memory of the church' (p. 112).

most likely with the wider Jewish movement, as well. Thus it could be argued that Ephesians may have triggered discontinuity rather than continuity. Not only does it challenge Israelite boundary processes and cultural performances in chapter 2, but the text immediately proceeds to pose another challenge for Israelite traditions by claiming to reveal a unique revelation.

4. *Conclusions*

In Ephesians 2 the discourse turns dramatically from celebrating the achievements of 'Jesus Christ' for the community (ch. 1) to the dark side of things, explaining the full significance of their membership against the background of sin, spiritual death, slavery to malevolent powers, alienation from God, enmity and ethnic hostility between people of the promise and outsiders. The social entrepreneurship reforms his Jewish symbolic universe by imagining 'Jesus Christ' at its centre and superimposing this ideological framework upon non-Israelites making reference to their past from an Israelite viewpoint. The discourse names the non-Israelites negatively as 'uncircumcised', 'strangers', 'aliens', 'hopeless', 'atheists' and separated from God, outside his covenant and promises. However, the negative labelling is overturned at the cross of 'Christ', which removes their alienation and welcomes them into the household of God. The text bears strong affiliation with Jewish traditions that were evaluated from two 'wandering viewpoints' to test the contours of Ephesians' ideological positionings. In my view, the Jewishness of Ephesians is best understood not in terms of continuity (contra Yee) but in terms of how it provides cultural models and how it is reformed to provide suitable social boundaries for the non-Israelite community. The ideological interpretations of the Christ-event expand and stretch traditional material so that the original meanings of ethnic Israel and her covenant fade (cf. Kunin 2005: 182–3).

Ephesians presents history and the communal present as an 'ordained' and structured series of events whereby God's salvific agent alters the covenantal basis of God's dealings with humanity and establishes new, cross-ethnic terms for his people. The legitimating discourse includes 1) positioning Israel as a symbol of God's covenant and joining non-Israelites into the people of God; 2) distancing the community from Jewish culture by using negative language of hostility and stressing conflicts involved in relations with the 'circumcised'; 3) removing markers of Jewish ethnic culture as socially harmful and hostile practices and setting Christ-followers free from the burden of Torah observance. This is achieved by shaping the reputation of 'Christ' as a reconciling agent for the non-Israelite saints. Therefore, I suggest that Israel and Jewishness are used to provide historical continuity and legitimation for the community as they are viewed in the light of the Christ-event and its processing as something socially and ideologically meaningful. In other words, Ephesians amalgamates Messianic convictions and principles of non-Israelite equality into a Jewish symbolic universe, providing the community a story of an ancient, benevolent deity. The author's dualistic worldview has been significantly altered as he distinguishes yet another group, 'new humanity'; and his loyalty has transferred to this third group, which indicates the new humanity represents neither Israelites, nor non-Israelites, but those who are reconciled in 'Christ'.

The reading of Ephesians 2 has demonstrated that remembering is inseparable from its socio-ideological setting as Ephesians selects a suitable element from the past and inscribes communal values and orientations into memories. Thus the discourse combines historical stories with the ideological beliefs and social needs of the present, as non-Israelites' status improvement and the removal of the Torah-code demonstrate. The writer does, as Schwartz puts it, make 'the past precarious, its contents hostage to the political conditions of the present' (2000: 16). An executed Palestine Jesus is remembered as transcendent cosmic saviour, who extended Israel's blessings to the nations and removed the Law. This is achieved by inventing traditions in order to remove social hostilities, despite the fact that other early Christian stories construct Jesus to whom keeping the Law was important.

Finally, can Ephesians be classified as a Jewish text, or a representative of Jewish Christianities? Does a Christian NT reader, theologian or critic have the right to argue that Ephesians should be classed as a Jewish text in the first place? Doesn't this involve 'our decision' about who is the Messiah and on which basis sacred traditions have been reworked? More specifically, is it right for us to insist on its Jewishness given that its promotion of Jewish values and beliefs is weak and its explanation for Israel's covenant and status is poor or altogether missing? I suggest that it may well have been the author's intention to revise proselyte policy and join the non-Israelites to God's people as newly accepted fellow-citizens, without dismissing Israel as the constitutive commonwealth and the core of the people of God. But if so, it was the failure of Ephesians' social entrepreneurship, a failure to guide the community to recognize the ongoing importance of Israel and her socio-cultural status that resulted in associating the text with Christian, not Jewish movements, or even Jewish Christianities. In my view, Ephesians can be classified as a Jewish text, but only when it is reasonable for us to decide on the Messiah, election et cetera, and only when it is reasonable to be Jewish without observing the Law.

Having considered the remembering of Jesus and what he is said to have achieved, a consideration of further communal legitimation in

Ephesians 3 and its shaping of the reputation of Paul is due. The reading now proceeds exploring how the reputation of Paul is constructed, and how this is used in communal legitimation: explaining and justifying the community and its distinctive construction of Christianness.

Chapter 4

READING EPHESIANS 3:
REMEMBERING PAUL AND COMMUNAL LEGITIMATION

To reiterate the goals of the chapter, the focus in reading Ephesians 3 is on how the reputation of Paul continues to develop the way Ephesians imagines the community as God's holy people by providing further legitimation for the group. I will also discuss what this means to the community and our understanding of Deutero-Pauline Christianities.

1. *Paul's Reputation in Ephesians Scholarship*

My study of Ephesians in general, its presentation of Paul and its treatment of non-Israelite inclusion, assumes the Jewishness of Paul in the light of the New Perspective scholarship.[1] The most relevant and significant contributions to the discussion of Paul's reputation in Ephesians are those of MacDonald (2000: 259–74) and Esler (2005b). MacDonald, to begin with, points to parallels between Pseudo-Pauline Ephesians (3.1-13) and Colossians (1.23-28). Colossians imagines that 'the gospel has been preached to every creature under heaven' (1.23; cf. Rom. 15.9), which is interesting reputational entrepreneurship, aiming to secure the reputation of the speaker (Paul) as an honourable man of authority and commission (MacDonald 2000: 76–7). Both Ephesians and Colossians develop the ideas of the apostolic authority and the role of the apostle as the one who reveals God's mystery (MacDonald 2000: 268). MacDonald's focus is particularly on the institutionalized presentation of the apostolic authority: there is no need to defend Paul's authority or make reference to 'his former life in Judaism' as in Galatians 1.13-17 (p. 269). Because Paul's authority is based on divine commissioning MacDonald suggests that this conveys divine, rather than conventional authority (p. 268). However, when we examine the shaping of the Pauline portrayal in the text, Paul's authority is based on claims of divine

---

1 Following e.g. Stendahl (1976); Sanders (1977); Dunn (1983; 1990); Wright (1991); Donaldson (1997); Nanos (1996; 2002); and others. For recent reviews of scholarship see e.g. Westerholm (2004); Campbell (2005).

commissioning and all we have is the discourse of power. This is especially important when we read Ephesians as Deutero-Pauline, which involves embellishing Paul with the divine credentials, and the portrayal of Paul in the text involves – not divine commissioning – but social entrepreneurship.

Paul's portrayal is not all about authority, though. MacDonald also discusses the sufferings of the apostle and its socio-cognitive significance for the recipient community. She uses de Boer's six images of the apostle in post-apostolic early Christian texts, stressing his role as (1) the apostle, (2) a mediator of the Gentile salvation, who (3) ministers to the whole world, (4) suffered greatly for his calling; and (5) as a redeemed persecutor of the Church now (6) ministers as the authoritative communal teacher (2000: 270).[2] Furthermore, although the apostle is portrayed as imprisoned, there is no shame involved but suffering is dressed in glory and his bondage is transferred to honour (p. 270).[3] Nevertheless, she regards the apostolic authority as the main feature of 3.1-13, exploring its social and cosmic significance in the light of the honour of the apostle's accomplishments for God and his charismatic authority (pp. 270–3).

On the contrary, Esler focuses on the post-Pauline images of the imprisoned apostle and the dramatic framework the image gives for the presentation of the apostle as their writer.[4] Esler discusses the images of the imprisoned apostle using social identity theory and collective memory research, as well as cognitive-scientific perspectives on autobiographical memory.[5] He engages with collective memory and social identity perspectives in the Deutero-Paulines, analysing how they enhance remembering of the apostle and create communal bonds. Esler suggests the 'autobiographical' material of Paul was probably of considerable importance shaping how the past was remembered and how the

2 De Boer discusses the images of Paul in the Acts as well as in Colossians, Ephesians and the Pastorals (de Boer 1980: 359–80).

3 Although the prison reference is often seen as an authentic witness to the final stages of the apostle's life, in my view the language of bondage that involves a social stigma is very adaptable for social entrepreneurship and discourse in the post-apostolic era, when the controversy regarding his fate has passed and the memory of his reputation supercedes any difficult reputation, such as being imprisoned. Otherwise a fuller explanation of the circumstances or legitimation of his innocence might have been required to legitimate him, despite social stigma.

4 My reading responds to Esler's conference paper given in Helsinki in 2005. Although I refer to an unpublished conference paper, it has subsequently been published in Luomanen et al. 2007.

5 Esler draws our attention to numerous passages in the Deutero-Paulines that either make a direct reference to Paul's imprisonment or contribute to the dramatic framework of his portrayal by reminding the readers of his sufferings and God's mighty protection of his servant: Col. 1.24, 25-27, 4.18, also 3-17; Eph. 3.1; 6.19-20; and 2 Tim. 1.8, 11-12, 13-14, 16, 17; 2.3, 8-9, 10-13; 3.11; 4.6, 7-8, 17-18.

communities interpreted their present experiences and identities, while memories of Paul would have become part of a 'culturally canonical narrative' (2005b: 18, 19). While Esler's discussion focuses on the imprisonment and sufferings of the apostle, this study seeks to further highlight the language of unique revelation and status of the apostle, and how this corresponds with the reputation of Jesus, as function to legitimate the community. In my view, although Jesus and Paul have experienced suffering, it is their exaltation and fulfillment of God's plans through them that raise them above others.

Esler links the ideas of imprisonment and suffering with more general persecution. This, he suggests, may have a significant bearing on the values and commitments of the group as well as heightening their sense of group-membership (2005b: 6–7). He believes that Christ-followers experienced harassment and persecution from the very beginning, and the imprisonment motif would have been part of the identity of the Christ-movement (2005b: 7). Although there is no direct reference to persecution in Ephesians and Colossians, Esler highlights the apostle's encouraging representation of a positive group identity (2005b: 9). The memory of the apostle offers an exemplar that reaches to the most difficult dimension of their social identity, preparing the believers to remain faithful at all costs, drawing encouragement from the memory of their heroic apostle (cf. 3.1; Esler 2005b: 10). In order to explore this fully, Esler combines theoretical insights on social remembering with the pseudo-Pauline authorship and advances Ephesians scholarship with interesting observations. He suggests that the pseudo-Pauline writers would augment, mould and redirect memories of the apostle to serve the needs of their communities facing at least an impending threat of social harassment (2005b: 11, 12, 17).[6] Thus memories of Paul are organized into a 'culturally canonical narrative' which encompasses reports of life events, as well as evaluative information making memories of Paul personally meaningful and part of their formative communal memory (2005b: 19, 21).

Esler's paper on Paul's reception in Ephesians is understandably limited in scope and length, and there are a number of points by which I seek to build on his observations. These include exploring how the Deutero-Pauline writer neutralizes the stigma of imprisonment and suffering. In my view, the imprisonment could simply provide the historical core for Paul's embellished reputation and the persecution assumption is not necessary for the passage to be socially relevant if we bear the need for communal legitimation in mind. The analysis of Paul's reputation in this study takes a different direction as I suggest that the key to Paul's

---

6 Parallel with the discussion of social remembering in this study. See theoretical frameworks in Chapter 2.

reputation is his apostleship and unique revelation, not his imprisonment or authority.

Having considered both Esler and MacDonald's work on Ephesians' apostolic portrayal I seek to offer a more extensive study of Paul's reputation as the traditional scholarship on Ephesians has not sufficiently explored the ideological colouring of Paul's portrayal in the letter or fully explored its contribution to identity and communal legitimating. The social memory and reputational entrepreneurship perspectives provide fresh theoretical frames for the task, which will focus primarily on the legitimating function of Paul's reputation, and how he provides ideological, social and historical explanations for the group, strengthening Christ-followers' identity. I will also discuss what bearing this has on Jewish-Christian discourse and intergroup relations.

2. *Reading Ephesians 3: Exploring the Construction of Paul's Reputation*

The study of Paul's reputation continues testing Ephesians' Jewishness and Christianness. As I have previously established, Ephesians imagines the community as God's holy people, inventing legitimating myths of their election, and covenant 'in Christ' (Ch. 1 above), and remembering 'Jesus Christ' provides legitimation on Jewish cultural performances (Ch. 3 above). Here remembering Paul builds on the previous ideas of God-legitimated non-Israelite Christianness and enhances the idea of distinctive communal identity. The social entrepreneurship involved in shaping Paul's reputation involves positioning Paul as God's agent, sent and empowered by him; neutralizing the stigma of the imprisonment and embellishing Paul's role in God's Eternal plans and setting him on a pedestal in the community as a servant as well as exemplar and model, as following readings will explore.

2a. *The Apostle Empowered by God*
As noted in the discussion of social memory theory (Ch. 2), collective memories often feature in the construction of communal identity. In Ephesians we find that remembering is used to explain the founding of the group as well as to provide it with a sense of purpose and destiny as God's people. Thus its social entrepreneurship is a synthetic activity which amalgamates ideological convictions (such as beliefs about 'Jesus Christ', God, his revelation to the community) and mnemonic components (remembering the non-Israelite past, Jesus' death and Paul's ministry), selecting and deselecting suitable elements from discourses and traditions.

First of all, the fact that Ephesians elaborates on Paul's reputation at all cannot be taken for granted or regarded as a necessity. The text could have made its claim for its apostolic verification simply by the opening statement, 'Paul an apostle of Christ Jesus by the will of God' (1.1).[7] Instead, it seems that Paul's reputation in 3.1-13 is geared towards explaining that the community fulfils God's eternal plans. According to Schwartz the task of a reputational entrepreneur is, 'to make an ordinary person great – or, more commonly – to bring the person's greatness to public attention' (2000: 67). Generally speaking, the NT documents lead us to view Paul as an enthusiastic member of a reform movement of Christ-followers; who, owing to his keen participation in communal life and discourse, oral and written, as well as enthusiastic involvement in the recruitment of new members, assumed a leadership role. However, this would not necessarily set him apart from other likeminded, active members of the movement.[8] Paul's self-positioning places him alongside recognized leaders of the movement as an independent and authoritative leader (e.g. Gal. 2.1-10); not only as equal but possessing a superior understanding of the Gospel. He could subject even the most senior authorities to rebuke (Gal. 2.11-14). It may be his life-changing encounter with the risen Christ (Gal. 1.13-16) that led him to extensive travelling, composing letters and gaining wide influence within the wider network of early Christian communities. However, it is social entrepreneurship that later post-Pauline texts, such as Ephesians, established his reputation in subsequent generations of the movement, beyond the limits of his time and influence, and engraved his reputation into early Christian literature and history (e.g. Acts 9–28).

Exploring the portrayal of Paul through the lenses of reputational entrepreneurship presumes the following assumptions. Paul's reputation in Ephesians is a representation of the past: based on 1) historical events extracted from the stories of the apostle, and 2) commemoration, which adds communal value and shape to the selected stories (Schwartz 2000: 9). The text of 3.1-13 demonstrates how these are intertwined, while the underlined phrases highlight how extensively remembering Paul relies upon the idea of divine legitimation to enhance his existing reputation and put him on a pedestal in the communal discourse:[9]

---

7   This would have placed the letter regarding Paul's 'charismatic authority' and tradition (MacDonald 2000: 194).

8   Consider, for instance, Peter, Barnabas, Silas, Timothy, Titus, Apollos, Priscilla and Aquila, or, for instance, Sopater (Acts 20.4) and Sosthenes (1 Cor. 1.1) in the Acts of the Apostles and Pauline letters.

9   This study explores particularly posthumous reputation construction and remembering Paul by later Christ-followers. In contrast, e.g. MacDonald's work suffers a methodological lapse when she talks about 'self-praise' in her discussion of the portrayal of Paul: 'Ephesians 3.1-13 functions rhetorically as an exercise in self-praise even if (as being argued in this commentary) it was written in Paul's name' (2000: 271). She explores Plutarch's treatise 'On Praising Oneself Inoffensively' and proceeds to highlight noble goals of self-praise. She

[1] This is the reason that I Paul am the prisoner for Christ Jesus for the sake of you non-Israelites – [2] for surely you have heard of *the commission of God's grace that was given me for you*, [3] and how *the mystery was made known to me by revelation*, as I wrote above in few words,[4] a reading of which will be enable you to perceive *my understanding of the mystery of Christ*. [5] In former generations this *mystery* was not made known to humankind, as it *has now been revealed* to his holy apostles and prophets by the Spirit: [6] that is, the non-Israelites have become fellow heirs, members of the same body, and sharers in the promise in Christ Jesus through the Gospel. [7] Of this gospel *I have become a servant* according to *the gift of God's grace that was given me by the working of his power*. [8] Although I am the very least of all the saints, *this grace was given to me to bring to the non-Israelites the news of the boundless riches of Christ*, [9] and *to make everyone see what is the plan of the mystery hidden for ages in God* who created all things; [10] so that through the church the wisdom of God in its rich variety might now be made known to the rulers and authorities in the heavenly places. [11] This was *in accordance with the eternal purpose* that *he has carried out in Christ Jesus our Lord*, [12] in whom we have access to God in boldness and confidence through faith in him. [13] Therefore I pray that you may not lose heart over my sufferings for you; they are your glory.

Social memory perspectives on reputations typically assume that the construction of a reputation is an activity of somebody else who manipulates memories of the past and explains the relevance of the past figure to the present context. Fine's insight into the shaping of heroes and villains is particularly relevant to remembering Paul in Ephesians 3. He suggests that 'heroes and villains may derive from numerous spheres, but in each case, the presentation of a hero or a villain is to be employed for a social end, as part of a prestige system that is used for social control' (2001: 20). In my view, this is evident in Ephesians' construction of Paul's reputation which makes use of previously established concepts of the non-Israelite inclusion (3.6, 8; cf. 2.13-14, 16-18, 19-22) and the fulfilment of the eternal plans of God in Christ and in the life of the community (3.9-10; cf. 1.4-5, 9-10; 2.10) in order to link the communal hero with key aspects of the communal discourse disclosed to the community by the apostle.

highlights that it was culturally acceptable to indulge in self-praise where the honour of the person is linked with his accomplishment to the Gods, where a person's fault is mentioned or where emphasis is given on the endurance of much hardship and danger (2000: 271). These are all highly relevant to Ephesians. However, MacDonald combines these with her general view on the tribulations the audience was facing and suggests that self-praise was driven by fear and hence there was a need for encouragement (2000: 271). Although her discussion of self-praise is valid and interesting, and it may explain the cultural appropriateness of the rhetoric, reading Ephesians 3 as reputational entrepreneurship draws our attention to other discursive goals and social causes.

This makes Paul's role integral to the community and her self-understanding in terms of being a bearer of divine revelation and agent of non-Israelite inclusion.

This study regards Paul's legacy as posthumous mnemonic engineering. With this in mind it is significant that it is specifically Paul's legacy as a spokesperson for non-Israelite inclusion which is selected from among all possible memories of Paul.[10] The construction of his reputation does not develop the events dominating his reputation in the Acts of the Apostles: such as his dramatic encounter with the Lord on the Damascus Road, his exciting travels around the provinces of the Roman Empire or any events taking place during his expeditions; his two-year establishment in Ephesus, the legendary escapes from death and danger. There are no echoes of Paul's ongoing association with the synagogue network or temple, or their importance to both his faith and his mission. Similarly, Ephesians dismisses concerns that overshadowed his letters; his conflicts with other Jewish Christian agents of the non-Israelite recruitment, the terms of his mission agreed with other apostles that guaranteed an outreach to both Israelites and non-Israelites, his teaching on the future salvation of Israel or his view on communal worship and leadership explored in other epistles. It is not assumed that the writer of Ephesians would have had access to any of these writings, but they provide examples of stories of the apostle, of which the author of Ephesians may well have been aware. They illustrate the wide range of traditions and stories about Paul that the author deselected in his shaping of Paul's reputation.

This indicates that Paul was recalled and remembered in Ephesians as a God-made hero of the non-Israelite movement – not because his story was of essential importance – but because his assumed character, interest and achievements resonated with the concerns of the later Christianness seeking further legitimacy in building social and ideological distance to other groupings and previous social networks (cf. Schwartz 2000: 297). Therefore, Paul's reputation in Ephesians is an example of how the later generation finds the image of the past leader suitable for their interests. It is parallel to what happened in the development of President Lincoln's reputation analysed by Schwartz. He found that a later generation 'legitimates changing social realities by retaining its original identity as it adapts to new conditions, instead of pressing his reputation selectively to their own service' (2000: 299).

---

10 It is assumed that the audience probably knew (at least something of) the apostle's story and probably represent the mission of his followers. However, his reputation is made of the memories that the author selects and deselects, and their social meanings.

2b. Neutralizing the Stigma of Paul's Imprisonment

The Pauline portrayal is launched with the image of the 'prisoner for Christ Jesus for non-Israelites' (3.1) which is then extended into explaining his reputation, who he was, and what he has achieved. This is achieved by explaining the uniqueness of his position and the magnitude of this eternal mystery of God.[11] Paul is presented as the prisoner for Christ, a paradigmatic prisoner for Christ-followers (MacDonald 2000: 260, 270; Esler 2005b: 4). He is 'a man of God' who is imprisoned for his non-Israelite mission (3.1), and suffers for their sake (3.13).[12] This provides 'a dramatic framework' for the remembering of Paul (Esler 2005b: 1).[13] Its textual presentation implies correspondence between Paul and Christ as God's agents who faced rejection and suffering in the world. Both illustrate the transformation of a difficult memory into honourable and exemplify the social amplification of a contested reputation (Schwartz 2000; Fine 2001). While Paul's reputation in the eyes of outsiders would have probably been tarnished by the very fact of imprisonment, the community is drawn to admire him for this as it is presented as demonstrating his commitment to his God-given task and to their

---

11   The image of the imprisoned is repeated at the very end of the epistle in another autobiographical(ly constructed) statement that reiterates the themes of apostleship and the mystery of the gospel, 'for which I am an ambassador in chains' (6.20). This section highlights the urgency of the Gospel as a God-revealed mystery before the closure of the epistle that positions the text with Tychicus (6.21-24).

12   MacDonald focuses on the issues of leadership as well as structural and institutional development of early Christianities and concluding on the importance of apostolic authority is the main feature of the passage (2000: 273). The reading offered here is not in disagreement with MacDonald's view, although my focus is on socio-ideological manoeuvring that creates the illusion of the apostolic authority.

13   According to Esler, 'Remember my fetters', the key to Paul's portrayal is encouragement and the inspiration it provides to the suffering audience. He accepts the historical basis of early Christian accounts of early persecution in NT texts, such as in Mark 4.17; 13.9, Acts and 1 Thess. 2.14 (2005b: 7). Similarly, MacDonald discusses the considerable likelihood of social hostility the community probably faced in their late first-century Graeco-Roman environment. The image of apostolic, exemplary suffering would have boosted the identity of believers when external forces threatened and early Christians faced tribulations (MacDonald 2000: 271, 273). However, Esler notes the absence of specific persecution references in Colossians and Ephesians. He suggests that this could be due to the fact that these are early Deutero-Pauline texts that were either written before a persecution had become common or that the authors were deliberately sensitive avoiding anachronisms of either positioning the persecution into Paul's date or even having him make reference to a phenomenon that was not characteristic of his time (2005b: 7). While these are very interesting observations they do suffer a slight problem of probability: such 'anachronistic sensitivity' is not necessarily the writers' concern as it is ours, given that he could, for instance, project criticism on the Law into early Christianness, although it seems uncharacteristic of Paul, and further beyond, to the cross (Eph. 2.15; cf. Col. 2.14).

community (3.1, 13).[14] While Paul (and Jesus') reputation may have been contested in the wider social networks effecting Jewish communities and Jewish Christianities at the time of writing, its presentation in Ephesians is a communally oriented subgroup discourse. It represents a subcultural reputation (Fine 2001: 11).[15] Therefore this reading is sensitive to not offering a study of Paul's reputation as such, but Paul's reputation in Ephesians, among early Christ-followers preconditioned to accept his embellished story.

The label of a prisoner would naturally result in a stigmatized identity, which, however, is here ideologically transformed to a positive reputation. It is highly significant that this is not achieved by deflecting any criticism in explicit discussion or counter-arguments (Fine 2001: 243), but enshrining the virtues of Paul's character, perseverance and godliness, and by underlining God's role in his mission.[16] Countering the social stigma of his captivity is not based on any attempt of apology or blame on the authorities either, but solely on the divine legitimacy of his mission. The stigma of the imprisoned may be beneficial to the letter. Katz notes that 'stigmatized persons will be evaluated more positively than nonstigmatized persons when both display socially desirable qualities, and more negatively when both display socially undesirable qualities' (1981: 81). Consequently, stigmatizing Paul in the discourse makes him more, not less, attractive to the community, given that he displays qualities that are socially desirable, such as the revelation of God, obedience to his call and partaking in the mission (cf. 1.9, 17, 18; 2.10; 4.7, 12-16).

Giving the apostle the label of 'the imprisoned' consents to the existence of the stigma attached to his story or his socially contested identity.[17] However, the labelling is manipulated very skilfully in Ephesians: while the negative label is retained the apostle is given a positive reinterpretation and positive values are attached to his reputation in the subsequent

14   Following Fine, reputational entrepreneurship is seen as serving the interests of a collective (not individual) creation of *shared images* that reflect and shape ideology and social orientation of both their creators and their communities (Fine 2001: 24).

15   Subculture is similar to what Bruner and Feldman describe as 'miniculture', proximal group(s) of one's cultural location (1995: 294). This highlights the subjectivity of both remembering and group membership, as well as a plurality of possible affiliations and groupings available.

16   To a NT reader the idea of the fierce opposition that Paul faced is easily implied into remembering Paul, exalting his role further, although Ephesians does not make reference to contested aspects of Pauline mission.

17   The labelling is subject to a number of social flexibilities and contextual factors. As Katz explains, 'Whether a given act or personal quality will be labelled by others as deviant will depend primarily on contextual variables – particularly, the power or resources of the individual, the social distance between the labeler and the labelee, the tolerance level in the community, and the visibility of the deviant behaviour or characteristic' (1981: 121).

discourse. These new qualities immediately empty the label 'prisoner' of any negative value judgment that might be evoked by it, and provide it with an ideological significance instead. This is very compelling: what we have at the end of the passage is the image of a faithful and humble God-empowered bearer of the eternal divine revelation and the pioneering spirit of the non-Israelite inclusion into God's people.[18]

The process of stigmatization involves assigning a deviant label and inferior status to individuals (Katz 1981: 118). A typical reaction would involve taking note of the negative label and the social attribute it implies and, consequently, disvalue their possessor in social interaction (1981: 118). However, in Ephesians' social entrepreneurship the deviant label is completely overturned and its bearer is exalted and celebrated. This is how positive reputational entrepreneurship works. Compelling positive reputation construction could result from the fact that the critical influencers are not about at all (due to non-Israelite location of the discourse) or they represent outsiders who do not gain the same favourable reception as the intra-communal discourse does (cf. Schwartz 2000: 73). It is particularly when the reputational entrepreneurs share the culture of their audience that they are able to utilize communal language, values, existing beliefs and norms, and thus they are better equipped to successfully influence the community than outsiders (Fine 2001: 22). In such cases the communal social entrepreneur will also benefit from the ingroup orientation, as group processes may involve a continual tarnishing of reputation and credibility of outsiders. This is exceedingly relevant for Ephesians which fosters the ingroup orientation by presenting Paul in the line of apostolic leadership as reliable witnesses for the plans of God: 'in former generations this mystery was not made known to humankind, as it has now been revealed to his holy apostles and prophets by the Spirit' (3.5). In addition, the discourse seeks to pre-empt any influence of the outsiders by their negative portrayal and explicit warning that the community would not be immature and doctrinally instable, 'We must no longer be children, tossed to and fro and blown about by every wind of doctrine, by people's trickery, by their craftiness in deceitful scheming' (4.14).[19]

---

18   Similarly in 2.11-22 where the discourse retains the negative label of 'uncircumcision', the social entrepreneurship transforms the naming with new interpretations and communal beliefs, so that the negative label becomes virtually insignificant in comparison to magnificent discourse manoeuvres and new community descriptors that follow. I suggest that the use of the divisive and thus negative labels provides the text with a sense of historical continuity, otherwise the historical positioning of the discourse is rather unspecific in terms of the description of its recipients and the circumstances that promoted the writing.

19   The warnings in 4.1-16 are more likely to deal with the doctrinal matters, communal core beliefs, as the context of unity and maturity suggests. Elsewhere the text expands warnings of the delusion and deceitfulness of the outsiders that threatens believers and even their salvation.

In my view Paul's reputation is constructed in the likeness of what we now perceive as a political prisoner, somebody who is oppressed for representing a just cause and faces the opposition of an unjust society (by the virtue of his imprisonment). He could be likened to a precursor of social or ideological change, who might not have been celebrated during his imprisonment, or even his life, but is then retrospectively recognized as somebody who was 'ahead of their time' and one of the pioneering critics of the dominant structures or values of the society, which the later generations may subsequently expand upon and give their views deeper historical roots. So, for example, Ephesians projects later social values on Paul, who becomes essentially linked in the abolishing of the law, although this is a later development possibly formulated by the author of Ephesians. Furthermore, the apostle, although imprisoned, is protected by the positive construction of his reputation: he is not like a villain that should be disregarded and rejected, despite the obvious judgment of the society and governing authorities upon his mission. Instead, the audience is led to hold him in the highest regard for proclaiming the non-Israelite inclusion and making God's mystery widely known (3.6, 8-11).

There are a number of possible motivations for social entrepreneurship to use the image of a suffering, imprisoned apostle. First, the motivation could be simply historical, moving from well-established historical facts to their spiritual and ideological embellishment, in terms of decorating the apostle with divine legitimation and purpose. Positioning the writing during the imprisonment, at the end of Paul's life, could add continuity with the apostle (Meade 1986: 153) and increase the validity of the text as representing the culmination of his thought. Esler suggests that remembering Paul's imprisonment was significant, in terms of inventing a body of tradition that would be accepted as a 'historical memory' of the apostle (2005b: 12), lodging both information and argument in their memories (16).[20] Developing from Esler, the reputation of Paul in Ephesians suggests that the writer regarded the unique revelation of the non-Israelite

20   This, according to Esler, had great potential of being of personal interest to the audience: portraying Paul as an exemplar of suffering for the sake of Christ would be of direct relevance to the turbulent social conditions of the early Christians (Esler 2005b: 17). The conversations about the past have at least two functions, sharing information and in case of joint remembering or reminiscing, creating interpersonal bonds and strengthening connections that depend on shared history (p. 17). Remembering of the imprisoned apostle is therefore about the transfer of information and making it part of the abiding collective memory among the members of the Christ-following movement (p. 18). It is an example of what Fivush and Reese describe as a 'culturally canonical narrative': conveying a series of events as well as contextual information (how these memories relate to the lives of others) and evaluative information (how they convey meaning and significance) (p. 19). Esler concludes that the distinctive message that the apostolic portrayal conveys to the community, along with the status of the apostle, presents Paul as 'very negative in relation to the Judeans and their Law' (p. 21).

inclusion and Paul's role as its spokesperson as the core of Pauline legacy, and key components of his 'historical memory'. This highlights the ideological construction of his reputation: who he is believed to be in God's economy is more important than historical details of his story, which are virtually missing from Ephesians.[21]

Secondly, the social circumstances of the audience could provide the motivation if, for instance, the author felt that the strong ingroup orientation, and its counterpart, distancing from Jewish and Greco-Roman social environments, was likely to lead to social conflict. Therefore stressing the undertaking of God in remembering 'Christ' and Paul contributes to communal legitimation as the discourse leads the community to believe that the community is closely related to the supreme God and benefit of his power and revelation. This is where we are faced with the fact that Ephesians' social entrepreneurship is clearly subcultural. For instance, all other deities except the God of Israel are denied existence; there are no other gods, just opposing spirits and inferior spiritual powers (1.21; 2.2; 6.12).[22]

Therefore, placing Paul, the ideological leader of the community, on a pedestal of a unique divine revelation provides not only an example of their suffering leader, but it also includes a challenge to the readers. This applies not only in terms of his suffering, as Esler and MacDonald suggest; but perhaps more importantly, it implies an obligation of loyalty to the 'god given' doctrinal/ideological framework of the letter. The idea of divine empowerment and transformation is implied in the reference to Paul's weakness 'as the very least of all the saints' that contrasts with God's magnitude that made him great in the eyes of the community (3.8-11).[23] Similarly, the audience may draw inspiration from having 'boldness

---

21　As noted before, this is typical of character positioning in Ephesians' symbolic universe: non-Israelite audiences also lack any ethnic or specific social description, and the story of Jesus is also missing. Ephesians' fictional characters serve the purposes of the discourse, as their origins and lives are of secondary importance to what they represent.

22　A critical reader could find Ephesians somewhat arrogant or intolerant as other cultures are unrepresented and their traditions and values dismissed.

23　Hoehner sees here the signs of true apostolic origin [and humility assumed his true characteristic], 'this is not false modesty but true humility' and he argues 'such deprecation likely would not have been expressed about Paul by a pseudonymous author' (Hoehner 2002: 452; cf. Barth 1974: 363; Bruce 1984: 318–19; contra Lincoln 1990: 183). On the contrary, this could have indeed been the case as Perkins explains; the reference to Paul's low status is a rhetorical ploy to magnify God, following the rules of the use of 'self-praise': 'By having Paul deprecate his own achievement, Ephesians has him magnify the graciousness of the divine benefactor who has given him the task of preaching the gospel' (Perkins 1997: 84; cf. Schnackenburg 1991: 136; MacDonald 2000: 265). However, in the study of literary construction of his reputation we are not dealing with the humility of the apostle or the egotistical stress of his own role – but consider how Paul's reputation is constructed paying attention to textual as well as social and ideological elements of that construction (even if

and access [to God] in confidence through faith in him, Christ' (3.12; cf. 2.18). This echoes the political language of a citizen's freedom of speech (MacDonald 2000: 266–7; Hoehner 2002: 465) and therefore reminds the community of their heavenly citizenship (2.19). This counter-political metaphor suggests a status that implies rights, benefits and privileges.[24] The reputation of the apostle, therefore, links him with the non-Israelites not only in terms of his mission and their role as its recipients, but also in terms of their corresponding positioning before God.[25]

Thirdly, the motivation could be ideological, which again opens up further alternatives. For instance, the text could be aiming to strengthen the social power of the likeminded apostolic leadership (cf. 3.5-6).[26] Therefore it would be the apostles and prophets associated with the Torah-free mission that would benefit from this legitimation of their role as recipients of God's revelation. Esler's research on the construction of autobiographical memory leads him to suggest that in the construction of the apostle we see a reflection of the pseudonymous writers, 'writing of Paul, the exemplary Christ-follower, they were also writing of themselves' (2005b: 20). Building on this further, it could be argued that the structural components for the construction of Paul's reputation were 1) the writer's ideological concern for the non-Israelite fellow-heirs; 2) their equality as bearers of promise in 'Christ',[27] and 3) the legitimacy of the leadership that can be traced back to the great apostle. While the theory of the

---

regarded as Pauline). It is not about anybody's self-esteem or sense of worth, but of giving Paul merit whilst underlining God's empowering activity in making that happen. Perhaps, then, like Perkins suggests, followed by MacDonald, it is not about diminishing Paul – which is clearly not going on in the passage – but glorifying God, which receives much rhetorical flare in Ephesians' extravagant and flamboyant language.

24   As citizenship (*politeia*) of Israel's does in Ephesians 2.12. The counter-political language would also include connotations to privileged Roman citizenship, more relevant to a non-Israelite audience.

25   Boldness and confidence are also key values in Mediterranean culture, superimposing honour on the apostle as well as on the recipients (MacDonald 2000: 267). As Reese points out, the social entrepreneurship takes the interpersonal values as an image that defines human-divine relations (1993: 9). In terms of the Mediterranean idea of limited goods (Malina 2001), we find that while Ephesians credits honour to the community it is reduced from the opponents shamed in the discourse: the text honours the believers and dishonours ungodly outsiders.

26   For instance, Meade argues in his evaluation of the Deutero-Pauline characteristics of Ephesians that Paul is presented as a messenger of God's mystery, an archetype of teaching and ethics, orthodoxy and orthopraxis (1986: 116–57). He suggests that the writer is concerned with securing the heritage of Paul, particularly in terms of the ecclesiology of the letter (pp. 149–51).

27   The fact that Ephesians describes Israelite *politeia* as having 'covenants of promise' (2.12) but the non-Israelites are not said to partake in these, but are co-sharers 'in the promise in Christ Jesus through the Gospel' (3.6), is another significant pointer for newness of the communality Ephesians imagines.

legitimation of subsequent leaders is attractive, it is also somewhat speculative as the text does not legitimate any followers of Paul by naming them, with the exception of Tychicus, who is positively associated with the apostolic mission (6.21). It is possible that Tychicus outlived the apostle, was known to the community and could have still been in the position of leadership and influence at the time of writing to the benefit of the legitimation.[28]

Alternatively, the portrayal of the apostle could have been designed to further validate the ideological position adapted by the community in terms of their claim for equal membership in the people of God alongside the Israelites. This is seen as the mystery of God: 'the non-Israelites have become co-heirs, co-members of the same body, and co-sharers in the promise in Christ Jesus through the Gospel' (3.6; cf. 2.15-20). In my view, the possibility of alternative voices forces the social entrepreneurship to legitimate Paul as well as 'Christ': Ephesians' interpretation of the Christ-event is presented as originating with Paul and therefore the apostle must be validated as the true spokesperson of God so that his message, i.e. the ideological positioning of the community, could not be (or should not be) challenged or overturned. This leads me to the following topic of discussion.

2c. *Embellishing Paul's Role in God's Eternal Plans*

The analysis of 2.11-22 alongside 3.1-13 is appropriate not only for their suitability for the use of social memory theory, but evaluation of the connection between these sections is pertinent and beneficial because of the textual links between Christ's reconciliation and the Pauline mission.[29] First of all, this is seen in the use of the unusual phrase *toutou charin* in the statement that introduces the apostle: 'for this reason I Paul am a prisoner for Christ Jesus for the sake of you Gentiles' (3.1). The phrase 'for this reason' is generally understood as providing more than a mere literary connection between two sections of the text; it has a thematic function as well as exploring what God has achieved in 'Christ' and sets the tone for Paul's portrayal and construction of his reputation. Paul's imprisonment

28 Interestingly, Tychicus is only mentioned in the Deutero-Paulines and the Acts of the Apostles, which suggests that he represents Paul's associates at the later stages of his life (MacDonald 2000: 351) and the second generation of Christian leaders (cf. Acts 20.4; Col. 4.7-8; 2 Tim. 4.12; Titus 3.12).

29 The core to Ephesians' embellished apostleship and its divine authorization derives from Paul himself, and from his experience of God's call (e.g. Gal. 1.1, 15-16; Rom. 1.1-6; 1 Cor. 1.1, 17; 9.1; 1 Thess. 2.4) which is a standard basis of his reputation in early Christian texts (cf. Acts 9.15; 13.2; 22.14-15; 25.22-23; 26.17-18; Col. 1.24-29). For a similar connection between the crucified and his apostolic role see, for instance, 1 Cor. 4.1-13 which describes the ministry of the apostles, 'as servants of Christ and stewards of God's mysteries' and 2 Cor. 6.3-11 for the personal cost of the ministry of reconciliation as service to God.

is presented as a consequence of the egalitarian message of ethnic reconciliation in 2.11-22.[30] Therefore this little phrase is far from insignificant in the ideological and social positioning of the letter as it explains the non-Israelite inclusion as the cause of Paul's suffering. Secondly, the same connection between ideology and social reality is also evident in the further reference to the apostle and his enduring mission for the Gentiles. It is interesting that the text makes only two references to the sufferings of Paul and both are linked to 'bold speech' and non-Israelite mission (Perkins 1997: 81): 'I pray therefore that you may not lose heart over my sufferings for you; they are your glory' (3.13); and 'Pray also for me so that when I speak, a message may be given to me to make known with boldness the mystery of the gospel, for which I am an ambassador in chains. Pray that I may declare it boldly, as I must speak' (6.19-20). These two verses clearly explain that the uncompromised proclamation of his revelation, non-Israelite equality and their membership in the people of God are Paul's God-given mission and his destiny. Thereby, the shaping of Paul's reputation makes him a successor of 'Jesus Christ' who boldly proclaims what he achieved at the cross. At the same time, Ephesians places the Pauline dispute over the terms of non-Israelite inclusion at the cross, where 'Christ' is believed to have 'abolished the Law'. Thus Ephesians exceeds Paul's critique of the Law and makes even greater ideological manoeuvrings that changed the way later Christ-followers understood the death of Jesus.

Therefore the discourse takes the negotiation of communal boundary processes of non-Israelite Christ-followers – that they ought not to obey the Law – and links it, not only with the cross, but also with the apostle, his imprisonment (and death). In my view, this is a highly significant act of communal legitimation that conveniently relates the 'abolition of the Law' with the memory of earlier Pauline controversies. In other words, Ephesians takes what Paul was associated with (according to his own writings) and legitimates it at the cross. By doing so the discourse grants a twofold divine verification on communal ideology and social processes, as both 'Christ' and Paul seem to 'sing from the same hymn sheet'. Consequently, the communal legitimation has two interesting nuances: a) legitimation of distinctive Christianness: abolishing of the Law and positioning the community as the people of God; b) legitimation of the ideological Deutero-Pauline developments. This is an example of how the author of Ephesians shaped 'Christ' and Paul's reputations by adapting stories of his apostolic commissioning and mission, and controversy with other Jewish Christians. Therefore the elements for Ephesians' reputational entrepreneurship were found in the legacy of Paul, which provided

30   Cf. Lincoln 1990: 172; Perkins 1997: 81; Best 1998: 294; MacDonald 2000: 260; Schnackenburg 1991: 130; and Hoehner 2002: 418.

a suitable basis for adapting these according to the ideological orientation and social needs of the later community.

The legitimation of textual social entrepreneurship – identity, shared ideology and social orientation – in Ephesians means explaining how the group fulfils God's plans and operates on the divine warrant.[31] The factors in the legitimating function of Paul's reputation are *the* divine commissioning and divine revelation. The discourse assumes the audience to be familiar with beliefs reinforced in the text: 'for surely you have already heard of the commission of God's grace that was given me for you' (3.2); and 'how the mystery was made known to me by revelation' (3.3). Thus Paul is a prophet-like figure who is raised by God for a specific purpose and exercises divine revelation. Stressing the divine origin of his legacy and his unique revelation raises him above a potential social contest and enhances his reputation.[32] Thereby the community is justified socially, ideologically and historically: socially, as it boasts of the apostolic connection (through the receipt of the discourse); ideologically, as the communal beliefs are God-given revelations of his eternal mystery; and historically, as the community claims to be (the) heir of Israel's benevolent God.

The mystery made known to Paul is God's eternal plan of non-Israelite inclusion (3.6); a plan that has been waiting for its time and the Christ-event, 'hidden for ages in God who created all things' (1.9; 3.9). Although Ephesians has a very strong non-Israelite focus, and there is no explicit reference to a Jewish constituency in the implied community, the mystery is specifically a non-Israelite inclusion, not invasion. As noted before, the non-Israelites are co-heirs, co-members of one body and co-recipients of the promise (3.6).[33] More importantly, although this reading argues for

---

31 MacDonald points to different types of communal legitimation in a post-apostolic context:

'The social situation in the earliest days of community-building was different from the social situation resulting from the death of Paul and the incorporation of a new generation. For his associates who wrote Colossians and Ephesians, the goal was not so much to legitimate the formation of the sect, as to ensure its continued existence – to stabilize community life in the absence of the apostle. Standing within the Pauline symbolic universe, they appealed to aspects of the symbol system, which could remain relevant in the light of new social situations. The symbolic universe simultaneously expanded and was transformed in relation to new circumstances' (MacDonald 1988: 236).

In addition, the need for communal legitimation intensified as the movement grew and increasingly dissociated herself from the synagogue context and Jewish groupings. These factors enhanced, not diminished, the need for communal legitimation.

32 It is also significant that Ephesians positions no other associates: the letter is not written by Paul and his co-workers (contra 1 Cor. 1.1; 2 Cor. 1.1; Phil. 1.1; 1 Thess. 1.1; 2 Thess. 1.1; Phlm. 1.1) except Tychicus (6.21-22).

33 See discussion of non-Israelite inclusion in reading Ephesians 2 in the previous chapter.

the construction of Christianness that positions itself as distinctive from Jewish groupings by abolishing the Law, the mystery is not that 'Christ has abolished the Law'; or that the *ekklēsia* would have taken over or that Israel would stand condemned. The mystery is a rhetorical code for divine legitimation but it is not used to legitimate the beliefs or social processes of the community as such. Instead, it is used to legitimate the status of non-Israelites among the people of God. The mystery is that the non-Israelites have become 'fellow-heirs, members of the same body, and sharers in the promise in Christ Jesus through the gospel'. This further indicates that for Ephesians the status of the community is more important than its boundary processes, which remain implicit and rather un-detailed in the discourse. The boundary processes are no longer as contested as they were in Paul's day, especially when writing Galatians. Instead, the legitimacy of increasingly independent *ekklēsia* is celebrated as a cosmic manifestation of God's wisdom and its positioning as the fulfilment of his eternal plan reinforced (3.10-11).[34]

Although the idea of divine mystery conveys privilege, it is anything but a communal or exclusive secret, revealed only to some chosen initiates. Instead, it is to be revealed for the whole cosmos and its spiritual powers (3.9-10).[35] Ephesians uses the language of revealing divine mystery to

34   The accentuation of the status of the non-Israelites is likely to be linked with the writer's ideal of a distinctive community, ideologically separated from both Jewishness and its Greco-Roman environment. This would explain Ephesians' use of political language to construct counter-reality where the real God is served; his eternal plans are known and the peace of 'Jesus Christ' reigns (Faust 1993). Faust likens Ephesians' language to the rhetoric of the Empire and suggests that Ephesians responds to Jewish war with the counter-ideological language of the peace of Christ (1993: 226). There could be an explicit comparison between Christ and the Emperor (pp. 324; 378ff.); although it cannot be known with any certainty as to what extent the status of the community is inspired by Scriptural ideas of God's might expressed in his people, and to which extent it might reflect Imperial social context.

35   So Hoehner (2002: 429, 433). The term *mustērion* is used in the book of Daniel for Nebuchadnezzar's dream (LXX 2.18, 19, 27, 28, 29, 30, 47) and for pagan cults in apocryphal texts (Wis. 12.5; 14.15, 23). Other Hebrew texts use different terms to describe heavenly council (Job 1–2; 15.8; Pss. 82, 89) and secret council (Ps. 25.14; Amos 3.7; Jer. 23.18, 22) that have their bearing on the use of 'mystery' in Jewish and NT texts. Jesus traditions uses *mustērion* to describe secrets of God undisclosed from unbelievers (Mt. 13.11; Mk 4.1; Lk. 8.10). It appears in Revelation (1.20; 10.7; 17.5, 7) where its use echoes the book of Daniel, where the symbolic mystery is given an explanation. It is used 20 times in the Pauline/Deutero-Pauline corpus (Rom. 11.25; 16.25; 1 Cor. 2.6, 7, 10; 4.1; 13.2; 14.2; 15.51; cf. Col. 1.26-27; 2.2-3; 4.3; 2 Thess. 2.7; 1 Tim. 3.9, 16). For a more detailed examination of the term and its linguistic parallels in Jewish texts see Hoehner (2002: 428-34). In Ephesians it is used as a legitimating code for non-Israelite inclusion as God's grand plan in 1.9; 3.3, 4, 9; for its proclamation in 6.19; and it describes the union of Christ and the *ekklēsia* in 5.32, where the intimate union between a husband and a wife is likened to spiritual union of the Saviour and his people. It is more likely that its use in Paul and in Ephesians reflects its Jewish, rather than Greco-Roman, roots. Hoehner makes the following five observations when comparing

legitimate non-Israelite inclusion. While the non-Israelite inclusion and equality was probably a socio-ideological innovation, it is presented as an eternal concept, imagined as a deliberate concealing of divine secrets till the appointed time (3.5, 11). Given that the Law was also inaugurated by God it could hardly be removed by communal leaders' reasoning, but Ephesians confirms that he approves Christ's death, and by implication, its consequences. Similar cultural superiority operates here: the non-Israelite inclusion is presented as a superior divine knowledge as Ephesians positions the community superior in terms of knowledge of God's plans. What is even more striking is that the deselection of other Jewish groupings and everybody else is explicitly pointed out: 'in former generations this mystery was not made known to humankind' (3.5a). Consequently, by knowing and embracing Ephesians' message of the non-Israelite transformation and Torah-free Christianness, the community is in possession of a divine plan of utmost importance. One can only imagine that this had a communally self-enhancing function, yet the contested nature of both of these claims is equally obvious.

Similarly, the idea of divine revelation builds Paul's reputation, not only as one of the chosen generation of apostles and prophets (3.5b) but also as the servant of the gospel personally responsible for its proclamation (3.7-9). Both factors shape his reputation: it is important that he is positioned among 'apostles and prophets' as this makes him a 'regular' representative of the servants of God, which reduces the conflict over the exact terms of the gospel that this apostle fervently upheld. In other words, although Ephesians appears to be a post-Pauline development of

---

Jewish and NT references to 'mystery': 1) The concept of mysteries known only to God is common in Jewish literature (esp. apocalyptic and Dead Sea Scrolls; cf. Eph. 3.9. 2) The Jewish materials place more emphasis on the vindication of the saints and judgment of the wicked in the last days (cf. Gospels and Revelation). While the Jewish literature elaborates on the Elect One who will reveal mysteries in the last days, in contrast, the presentation of Christ, the NT equivalent to the Elect, does not focus on the mystery parallel to the Elect in other Jewish texts. However, in my view Hoehner overlooks the parallels of revealing the mystery by the Elect to an enraptured seer in heavenly splendour, which is similar to divine revelation entrusted to Paul and saints. 3) In Jewish literature the mysteries were typically disclosed only to the members of the closed community by the seer, which seems to be different from Ephesians' mystery, which is to be made known across cosmic spheres. 4) While Jewish mystery texts were usually focused on the future, the NT increasingly interweaves mystery teaching with the present realities. Similarly, the Jewish texts emphasize God's reign in heaven and its realization on earth; NT passages focus on God's reign on earth, albeit this has a future fulfilment. 5) Finally, Jewish literature puts more emphasis on God's holiness and wrath, vindication and judgment, while the NT is mainly concerned with God's redemptive act for humanity (Hoehner 2002: 433). However, the idea of God's justice/ vengeance and the coming (or reappearing) of the Messiah are nevertheless standard early Christian convictions (cf. Halbwachs 1992: 96), and their absence from Ephesians is rather an anomaly than regularity.

the Pauline legacy, it is important for the acceptance of 'invented tradition' that it is accepted as genuine, as Ephesians' interest in apostolic foundation suggests (cf. 2.20; 3.5).[36] Therefore, presenting Paul among other recipients of the mystery does not reduce his status but legitimates him among other reputable leaders of the Christ-followers' movement. However, the discourse stresses the importance of his individual role by positioning him as the spokesperson of the gospel who makes 'everyone see what is the plan of the mystery hidden for ages in God who created all things' (3.9). Therefore Paul's reputation draws on the idea of a prophet in terms of knowing the will of God and making it known, although it deselects other prophetic characteristics, such as the miraculous deeds Paul is elsewhere known for.[37]

The legitimation of the innovative Deutero-Pauline ideology rests on the image of Paul's understanding of the mystery (3.3-4). Developing the image of prophet and God's people is another example of modelling the community after Israel, as seen in the explanation of Paul's ministry (3.1-13): the representative of the community is a chosen and empowered servant of God, a recipient of and a sole voice for the divine revelation.[38] However, although this sounds Jewish, the discourse is yet again more complicated than might first appear, if one asks where does this actually leave other Israelites? Without a prophet of God, unless they accept the revelation of Christ and non-Israelite inclusion, it seems. Furthermore, one might also ask, how Jewish is Paul's understanding of the mystery? Although he is portrayed as a prophet adapting the memories of great men of God known from the Hebrew Scriptures,[39] the discourse takes yet

36   Although 'prophet' could suggest continuity with the history of Israel's prophets (so e.g. Faust 1993: 195) one must note that Ephesians does not remember any prophets of old nor do the prophets have any function that suggests direct continuity with Jewish faith. Instead they are explicitly linked with Christ and the Christ-following community (2.20; 3.5; 4.11).

37   Miracles are a fascinating part of Paul's reputation in the Acts of the Apostles, along with his persuasive rhetoric. See, for instance, the retelling of Paul's mission in Ephesus: 'God did extraordinary miracles through Paul, so that when the handkerchiefs or aprons that had touched his skin were brought to the sick, their diseases left them, and the evil spirits came out of them' (19.11-12).

38   Note that other apostles and prophets are allocated the operations of communal training and supervision of the mission (4.11-12). Paul's unique revelation adapts the idea of Paul's prophethood, best explained in Gal. 1.15-16, where the apostle boasts of being set apart before his birth, and called through God's grace who was 'pleased to reveal his son to me, so that I might proclaim him among the Gentiles ...'

39   However, as noted before, this is an example of adapting Paul's heritage within the Jewish cultural framework, which in the first instance, is meaningful to the author, not to his non-Israelite audience. However, it is plausible to assume that if/when non-Israelite Christ-following communities had (at least for some time) Jewish communal leaders and influencers, they were socialized in Hebrew traditions to some extent. The early Christian acceptance of

another Jewish concept, the voice of God, and uses it in the service of redefined Jewishness or non-Israelite Christianness. The divine revelation has now been revealed to the representative of the community of Christ-followers and God's eternal mystery is the transformation of non-Israelite status.[40]

In my opinion, there are two factors that make the idea of the continuity of Israel in the community of believers and thus the Jewishness of Paul's reputation less likely. First, the text as a whole, the components of its symbolic universe and the status reversal are legitimated upon 'Jesus Christ' (and the apostle's revelation). Given the contested nature of Jesus' Messiahship and its rejection by many Jewish groupings, the fact that Ephesians positions the exalted 'Christ' alongside God, without any explanation of either non-believing Israelites or a chosen remnant of believers, is difficult. Secondly, the claim for the unique revelation implies a certain discontinuity with the past. Along with the creation of 'new humanity' (2.15), it conveys distinctiveness and difference.

As previously established, the discourse implants the community in the symbolic universe that assumes continuity with Israel's heritage, deity and providence; and the invented traditions receive a stamp of divine approval. The antiquity of communal legitimation is important to Ephesians; it rather anachronistically predates the election of non-Israelites before Israel's election as God's chosen people 'before the foundations of the world' and raises the communal prophet, Paul, above the prophets of Israel, as the bearer of 'the eternal mystery of God' (1.4; 3.5-10). The traditions invented in Ephesians go back to eternity and provide the community with a past as well as with a present identity, a sense of importance, and a future as God's people. This demonstrates the social entrepreneur's ability to provide an existing community with identity, purpose and legitimacy, tapping into his cultural heritage, and use its resources creatively. It is obvious that textual social entrepreneur-ship is a rather complex task and we cannot assume that people are always seeking to legitimate their present interests by appealing to the past; or seeking to 'overturn' established concepts. These might be secondary to other motivations; as Schudson suggests, people may 'seek to know what is right, what is true. They seek some kind of direction when they are

the Hebrew Bible – even if as 'the old testament' – is an important example of such resocialization as the Christ-followers embraced the sacred Israelite texts and began to claim for their rightful ownership.

40 Paul's commissioning is to proclaim the inclusion and equality of non-Israelites. Although there is continuity with universalism that appears in the Hebrew Bible, it is significantly more prominent here as it is articulated as God's plan and the reason for Paul's assignment. Notably, the terms of Paul's project do not include the restoration of Israel, contra Rom. 9–11. This, in my view, is another 'gap' in the text that evokes different explanations and processing of meaning based on other ingredients in the text and beyond.

aimless. They seek in the past some kind of anchor when they are adrift' (1992: 213).[41] These are possible motivations for Ephesians, given that the community would have naturally maintained their Greco-Roman cultures and beliefs. Ephesians negotiates both Jewish and Greco-Roman cultural frameworks and shapes a different communal identity, achieved by anchoring the community in Jewish traditions, reforming its unwanted cultural performances and boundary processes, as well as rejecting non-Israelite culture, condemned as a futile and 'alienation from the life of God' (4.17, 18).

Although the discourse is a subjective response to how the social entrepreneur perceived the ideological and social needs of the community, reflecting his choices and predispositions and prejudices to provide direction for the community, it is adorned as a new, superseding revelation from God himself (3.5). Dressing a later idea as a superior revelation is typical of the religious phenomena, ancient (as seen in early Christianities) and modern. As Halbwachs suggests, this is part of the universal religious rhetoric:

> ... every religion refers to the revelations and supernatural facts that marked its appearance as its true source. But we could argue that it is not only the source, in a sense that the whole of religion is so constituted. The role of the fathers of the Church, of the councils, theologians and priests, was in every successive period simply to better understand all that was said and done by Christ and by the Christians of the first centuries. Where we believe we see *an* evolution determined by the milieus in which Christianity was practiced, the church asserts that there was only a development. It is as if by concentrating their attention and their thoughts on such remembrances, the faithful had distinguished new details from century to century, and had better understood their sense as time went on. (Halbwachs 1992: 185)

Therefore, contextualizing beliefs to later generations and different social circumstances is often bolstered with a claim to divine revelation, where communal ideology allows it.[42] Here the social entrepreneur uses such validation strategies by constructing communal memories of Paul and

---

41   Therefore, when this reading describes the legitimation of the community it cannot be known with certainty to what extent this was an intended skilful design, and to what extent it resulted in discussing the past with some other motivation. The stress in this study is deliberately laid on the social constructions and manoeuvrings of the social entrepreneur in the light of the chosen socio-scientific theoretical framework and with a view to an overarching goal of communal self-enhancement when the past validates the present.

42   For Ephesians, knowing God's will is an essential part of religious persuasion as seen e.g. in the (pseudo) apostolic prayers for spiritual revelation by 'a spirit of wisdom and revelation' (1.17) and that the 'eyes of their hearts' would be 'enlightened' (1.18). The second prayer in 3.14-19 reiterates the importance of a deeper saturation in communal spirituality: 'strengthening of the inner being(s) with power by his Spirit'; indwelling of Christ in their

positioning his views (in Paul's persona) as superior to alternative interpretations of faith and traditions, expressing theological and spiritual vantage points for modified Jewishness and emerging Christianness. At a time when apostolic authority mattered, it was called upon using a phenomenon of pseudonymous writing, and the message 'from Paul' was reinforced further with the claim of possessing the ultimate revelation from God. This shapes Paul's reputation by stressing his exceptional power and the divine origin of his role and provides further legitimation for other culturally radical claims of the letter.[43]

At times posthumous reputational entrepreneurship makes use of 'reputational residue' which earlier generations have left behind, which could be picked up by later generations as the chronological distance increased (Schwartz 2000: 103). Schwartz argues that it was because President Lincoln's supposed character and achievement echoed the concerns of later society that he became so formative in the forging of national identity (2000: 297). A corresponding process seems to take place in Ephesians' remembering as the community of Christ-followers gained ideological strength and distance from Jewish culture. For instance, 'Jesus Christ' gained a firm footing and new meanings in Ephesians, which is seen in the 'abolition of the Law'.[44] Similarly, Ephesians exploited the vital residue of commemorative symbols and stories of earlier Christians, and embellished Paul's reputation above other early Christian leaders (3.3, 8, 9).

Schwartz suggests that socially shaped reputations involve both sustaining the past heroes and revision of their memory relating them with the needs of changing values (2000: 298). However, sometimes reputations seem unsuitable for further adaptation and historical reputations lose their position in the communal remembering to new figures, who better represent its changing values (Schwartz 2000: 299–303). Consequently, it is possible that the Deutero-Pauline emphases in Ephesians might have represented the ideology of an increasingly non-Israelite Christ-following movement, and its lack of interest in maintaining close relations with the Jewish Jesus-believing communities; but it was

---

cognitive and emotive faculties; comprehending the dimensions of Christ's love that 'surpasses knowledge' and being 'filled with all the fullness of God'. Thus knowing the will of God is also a socio-ethnic safeguard and communal defence (cf. 5.17).

43   Paul's commissioning resembles Weber's 'charisma', which 'sets its own limits, and its bearer seizes the task for which he is destined and demands that others obey and follow him by virtue of his mission' (Weber 1978: 1.241; 3.1112–3). However, Polaski points out that Weber's concept fails to provide proper attention to Paul's role as a messenger of Christ (1999: 28–35, esp. 34).

44   Yet it was later than Ephesians or other NT texts that Jesus' reputation turned into that of the creedal 'Son of God', as later generations saw him through different lenses (cf. Schwartz 2000: 107–8).

inconceivable to replace Paul's authoritative tradition by a later writer. If the Christ-following communities held on to apostolic legitimation as a non-negotiable feature of authoritative tradition, the replacement of Paul with his follower would have been inconceivable. Nevertheless, it seems that the social changes had already begun to take effect: it is rather likely that the explicit articulation of Ephesians 2.15 that 'Christ had abolished the Law' would have caused uproar in Paul's context.

Nevertheless the social associations with Jewish groups are not so formative to the movement/writer of Ephesians as they were for St Paul, as we can reliably assume from Paul's undisputed letters. This is evident in the novel ideology that has found its way to the Jewish symbolic universe in Ephesians: the social entrepreneur uses both 'Jesus Christ' and Paul in leading the community to imagine that 'the Law has been abolished' (2.15) and non-Israelites have a full citizenship status granted by Israel's God. By making both figures divine agents the past becomes God's work, which provides the legitimating traditions for the present; and therefore present beliefs and practices resist social contestation. If Paul was a prominent campaigner for non-Israelite inclusion without the Law, this historical core of his reputation could explain why Ephesians has an adaptation of Paul's reputation and not his replacement by someone else. Hence Paul is decorated with badges of divine revelation and purpose: a controversial Pharisee is celebrated as the God-empowered apostle, who could 'make everyone see what is the plan of the mystery hidden for ages in God who created all things' (3.9). The past, then, is not 'a foreign country' for the writer of Ephesians, but a familiar territory: its people are not strangers, but as the reputational entrepreneur explains, they and their values are known to the community.

This leads me to conclude that Ephesians' reputations are in many ways reconstructions of historical figures. Such reconstruction may or may not derive from 'historical facts', that is, widely approved historical memories. Schwartz suggests that there are at least four possible ways for reconstructing a reputation: it may be 1) invented; 2) constructed from historical facts that are exaggerated, subdued or transformed; 3) patterned from historical facts but so selectively that the picture is distorted; or 4) modelled upon some attitudes seen as deriving from the historical person (2000: 6). There is plenty of textual evidence to suggest that these elements are intertwined in Ephesians' reputation shaping. First, there are invented elements that are claims beyond historical verification, like 'Christ abolished the Law' (2.15); or that he removed ethnic hostility (2.14-16) or that God gave a special revelation to Paul or the Deutero-Pauline writer (3.2-3, 5, 7-9). Secondly, there are elements of historical recon-struction as the text adapts historical Israelites, Jesus and Paul, in the discourse, exaggerating their Christianness and distance from their cultural origins for the purposes of the approval of non-Israelite, non-

Torah-observant communal processes. Thirdly, some elements of reputations are patterned corresponding to popular historical narratives, like
the life and death of the Jewish Jesus on the cross (2.16). However, his
reputation is badly distorted due to its focus on the reconciliatory effects
of his death and subsequent resurrection and exaltation; ignoring a large
part of his historical reputation, such as stories of his life and interactions,
which might be, as witnessed in some other documents, critical to non-
Israelites (e.g. Mark 7.27). Fourthly and finally, the reputations of both
Jesus and Paul reflect attitudes seen as connected to these historical
figures. For instance, the discussion of Torah observance was probably
part of remembering 'Christ' and Paul from a very early stage in Christ-
following movements that incorporated non-Israelites, regardless of how
accurate the reflection of their attitude(s) to the Torah might have been, or
whether it was a misrepresentation of the person, as is quite likely.[45] These
attitudes were part of remembering the person.

According to Schwartz, 'ordinary men cannot represent great and
powerful nations; elitist strongmen cannot represent democracies' (2000:
256). In my view, this illustrates why non-Israelite Christianness required
Torah-critical founders and why Ephesians remembers 'Jesus Christ' and
Paul as radical Jews who act on God's warrant, include 'others' and
reform the traditions. More specifically, it is the interpretation of Christ as
a Law-abolishing communal founder of the non-Israelite collectivity in
Ephesians 2 that builds the strong link between 'Jesus Christ' and the
(probable) historical core for Paul's Law-critical reputation. Finally, not
only are 'Jesus Christ' and Paul remembered together as founding figures
of the non-Israelite community, but one strengthens the reputation of the
other, and vice versa.

These factors provide further evidence for the assumption that
Ephesians does not engage in biographical remembering of either Jesus
or Paul, but that they have been reconstructed for communal purposes.
Interestingly, not only is 'Jesus Christ' transcendent but also Paul's
reputation in Ephesians 3 implies a prototypical connection with the
divine: he has been granted a special revelation only given to the chosen
pioneers of the movement; he knows God's plans and has on his shoulders
the ministry of the gospel; he bears the resulting suffering with exemplary
courage, and confidently enjoys his position that represents God's will,
empowering and grace. This makes him an epic hero that transcends time
and cultural change, and retains his relevance to further generations of
Christ-followers. Paul, just some Jew from Tarsus with a history of
controversy and dispute, could not represent non-Israelite Christianness,

---

45   The Deutero-Pauline and subsequent early Christian thinkers may have been taking
transferring Paul's Torah-critical statements out of their original context of negotiating the
non-Israelite inclusion among the Jewish people of God, to reflection of the Torah in general.

which is envisaged as the locus of God's might (3.10) – neither could his anonymous follower – but the apostle, commissioned by God as the voice of God's eternal mystery, could. Croly saw similar self-enhancing notion in the admiration of the President Lincoln: later generations 'continued to disguise flattery of themselves under a form of reverence for him' (1920, quoted in Schwartz 2000: 256). Similarly, the non-Israelite Christianness has continued to admire herself, as God's treasured possession, and Paul as its symbol.

Given that heroes typify those who put them on a pedestal, so does Paul in Ephesians: the text shapes remembering of Paul as that of a hero who excels in spiritual power and unrivalled status in God's economy and the community also enjoy his predestination, empowering and blessing. Heroes also have the legendary potential to maintain their status from generation to generation. Schwartz illustrates this with the cartoon of the President Lincoln (Figure 1), who is elevated above his contemporaries and gains a mythical status that transcends time (2000: 261).

In my view, Ephesians portrays Paul, metaphorically speaking, 'towering over' other apostles and prophets, although modestly sketched as their contemporary. Furthermore, just like Lincoln in the cartoon, the figure of the Apostle transcends time, beyond the lifespan of his contemporaries, even beyond his disciples, and remains as a communal exemplar and inspiration through Christian generations to date, reflected against the contemporary landscape of the twenty-first century. He remains of paramount importance in Christian thought and an exemplar to many Christ-followers, as does Jesus himself, whose reputation similarly transcends time and cultural barriers due to ongoing social entrepreneurship in various forms of public life, including Christian art.[46]

Although Paul's reputation is that of an empowered servant of God, it skilfully balances humble servitude and authoritative leadership. Why this is important becomes clear when we consider Paul's reputation as a communal prototype that embodies the values and behaviours of the group (Turner 1991: 76–8; Esler 2005b). First, Paul is presented as accepting captivity and suffering (3.1, 13) and his role is presented as 'a stewardship of the grace of God' (3.2). He is further described as *diakonos*, 'a servant of the gospel' (3.7) and he relies on God's initiative, revelation, grace and empowering (3.2, 3, 7). However, the discourse does

---

46 Paul is projected as a relevant contemporary to twenty-first-century life in various Christian discourses, texts and preaching which draw from his story as a culturally relevant resource for present-day Christians. It is due to compelling and persuasive reputational entrepreneurship, as in Ephesians 3, that he became a chief landmark in early Christian thought. Paul's reputation provides paradigms for ongoing Christian identification and remembering of the distant past. The topic of ongoing reputational entrepreneurship of Jesus, Paul and other saints in popular culture would be a very interesting topic to explore further and is on my list of future projects.

Figure 1: Lincoln and his contemporaries. *Chicago Tribune*, 12 February 1913. Courtesy of the Library of Congress

refer to 'his understanding of the mystery of Christ', which implies there could be alternative interpretations (3.5) and emphasizes Paul as the representative of 'non-Israelite inclusion' (3.8).

The divine commissioning and revelation function like a pedestal, upon which Paul is elevated despite his human ordinariness (3.7-8). Although both 'Christ' and Paul are communal heroes, their presentation differs: Paul is presented as an exemplar of the community that faithfully exercises servanthood, i.e. ministry that rests upon God's grace and his empowering. The exemplary role of Paul's divine commissioning is a significant part of his reputation: he is not 'worshipped' like 'Christ' but in him the community finds inspiration for their own ministry that everybody is expected to partake. In my view, Ephesians' remembering of Paul is an important part of its cultural program, that is, ingroup orientation that mobilizes the spiritual resources of the community, reinforces their predestined role as God's holy people (2.10), and challenges them to faithful following of God (5.1-2).[47] The text makes an explicit link between Paul's commissioning described as a 'gift of God's grace' (3.7) and the gifting of the subsequent community members, who all possess 'grace according to the measure of Christ's gift' (4.7).[48] This 'grace' could refer to leadership roles alone (4.11), but on the basis of the verbal repetition of *charis* and *dōrea* it seems to refer to communal gifts given to each member.[49] The 'saints' are 'equipped for the work of ministry' by their leaders (4.12),[50] and it is when 'each part of the whole body' is 'working properly' that the community body grows (4.16). Finally, God's

47 Mobilizing the community for mission is an important part of social entrepreneurship. It is presented as an essential, God-ordained part of the identity of the saints (2.10; 3.10; 4.7-16; 6.10-19). The mission, however, seems to be lifestyle oriented, where faithful following of Christ is more important than evangelism; there is no emphasis on 'winning converts' while the holiness dominates the discourse, as Chapter 6 will explore in more detail.

48 'Grace' is a standard description for Paul's apostolic commission in the undisputed letters (Rom. 1.5; 12.3, 6; 15.15; 1 Cor. 3.10; 15.10; Gal. 2.9). Its adaptation in the Deutero-Paulines is an example of maintaining a standard terminology with a similar meaning. Its Deutero-Pauline use, of course, has a different nuance (cf. Col. 1.23-29). In terms of construction of social memory it is an example of retaining the historical detail and ideology of the communal founder. The view to gifting and function of the community is very similar to the plurality of gifts in Rom. 12.3-8, given according to the 'measure of faith that God has assigned', while each member has a different function, just like parts of a human body have different functions. The same thought is expanded in 1 Cor. 12, where the gifts have a more 'spiritual' flavour in comparison to ministry-related giftings in Romans and their non-elaborate mentioning in Ephesians. Nevertheless all three passages contain the idea of a necessity of diverse gifts granted by the divine power to the community of Christ-followers.

49 So, for instance, MacDonald (2000: p. 289). It is of social and ideological importance that Christ (not God) gives gifts of grace to leaders and community members; this is a significant Deutero-Pauline development and also a pointer of the Christianness of the discourse (cf. Rom. 12.5-8 and 1 Cor. 12.4-7, 27-28). In the NT both *dōrea* and *charisma* refer to gifts of the Holy Spirit given to the believers (cf. Acts 2.38; 8.20; 10.45; 11.17; Rom. 12.6; 1 Cor. 12.4). Here *dōrea* refers to the gifts of Christ, distributed according to the 'measure of Christ', which allows for diversity of giftings within the community (4.13, 16). However, despite the differences in terminology the point of 4.11-16 retains the Pauline thought that all gifts are required for the proper functioning of the body (Rom. 12.3; 1 Cor. 12.11).

50 Ephesians regards the leaders responsible for mobilizing the whole community in a lifestyle of ministry. This could to be an example of a transfer from the charismatic itinerant leaders, apostles and prophets, who are seen as foundational to Christian communities, to the resident leadership, strengthening the authority of evangelists, pastors and teachers (MacDonald 2000: 299). The 'equipping' uses a unique *katartismos*, a *hapax legomenon*, that gives the leaders a very practical task of training and preparation of the *diakonia*. MacDonald's work on the Pauline churches defines the development of early Christianities reflected in Colossians and Ephesians as a 'community-stabilizing institutionalization' as these documents continue to solidify and modify the symbolic universe. She provides a

empowering links the reputation of Paul with the life of the community. The operation of God's power in and for the community members is a recurring theme in Ephesians: they are marked by the Holy Spirit (1.13) and God's great power is working for them and in them (1.19; 3.20). Therefore the grace given to Paul is echoed in the gifting and empowering of the members and his reputation is shaped as an exemplar of a God-empowered servant (3.7; cf. Col. 1.23, 25) just as all saints take part in works of service, building up the body of 'Christ' (4.12, 16).[51]

However, the discourse positioning of Paul also conveys social power, presenting Paul as an apostle par excellence, who by his revelation and divine commissioning provides direction to the community. In fact, when reading Ephesians as pseudonymous both Paul and the writer seem to be socially influential; the former is granted an influential position in the communal remembering and ideology, while the latter operates influentially in shaping the discourse and its authoritative Pauline legacy. One of Paul's legitimating functions is the creation of communal stability. It is worth considering the function of early Christian communities for their members. It seems that Christ-following groups were 'positive reference groups' for their members, as they provided guidelines for norms and behaviours, as (pseudo)Paul does in Ephesians 4–6. John Turner defines such positive reference groups as associations that 'one privately accepts or aspires to belong to, that one identifies with, is attracted to and feels psychologically involved with' (1991: 5). On the contrary, a negative reference group is 'one that one privately rejects or "dis-identifies" with, i.e. that one uses to define who one is not and what one does not want to be' (1991: 6). Therefore positive and negative reference groups are parallel to ingroup and outgroup, while the former terms place more emphasis on the social processes involved in different 'reference groups'. Social integration of members in 'positive reference groups', such as the group of Christ-followers addressed in Ephesians, gives rise to and reinforces shared social norms and orientations that provide order, coherence and stability (Turner

---

compelling explanation as to how the next generation adapted the communal norms, ministry structures, ritual forms and beliefs established by the apostolic mission during the early Pauline institutionalization (MacDonald 1988: 84–122).

51 The reputation of Paul makes a point of his 'servanthood' in most English translations. However, in order to understand the activities of social actors in the text, we must reconstruct 'the sociological facts governing their actions' and 'the symbolic forms and social arrangements of which their world was constructed' (Petersen, 1985: 4). The expression takes the idea of servanthood that sounds rather modest to modern critics. Nevertheless in its original context it may have implied more authority: in the antiquity *diakonos* was used for an agent of a high-ranking person, who acted on his behalf as an intermediary (MacDonald 2000: 264). Furthermore, being a 'mediator of the Gospel' and a 'steward of the grace of God' (3.2) are by no means mediocre positions. Instead they convey God's authority and a level of social power, too, in contrast with the less empowered community members; cf. 4.7-16 in Chapter 6 below.

1991: 16).[52] Such factors are important to Ephesians discourse, which has
an explicit concern for mature Christianness that involves a unity of beliefs
and taking a positive, functional role within the community (cf. 4.1-16).

The construction of the reputation of Paul, as in most parts of the letter,
predominantly utilizes informational influence that operates on providing
a correct and compelling interpretation of social life and its ideological
constraints, not on building social pressure to compliance.[53] This is seen in
the role Paul is given in communal proclamation. He is portrayed as a
God-appointed communal prophet who reveals and interprets God's
mysteries to the community: he provides the reliable information on
which social orientation and ideological dogma are based (3.3-4, 8-9).[54]
This model also highlights how Paul's example as God-commissioned,
God-empowered and God-gifted provides followers of 'Jesus Christ' with
a long-lasting motivation. This is seen, for instance, in the construction of
motivational examples, as, for instance, the participation of the saints in
ergon diakonias of 4.12 and in the description of their general orientation
toward God in grateful loyalty: 'therefore be imitators of God, as beloved
children, and live in love, as Christ loved us and gave himself for us, a
fragrant offering and sacrifice to God' (5.1-2). The language of identity

52   The desire to conform to group norms is inherent in communities and can occur even
without any coercion or pressure for agreement. Cognitively and socially motivated
uniformity is a basic group process motivated by the desire for perceptual structure or a
desire to explain things or to fit in with one another (Turner and Giles 1991: 16).

53   Ephesians' social entrepreneurship applies the language of both voluntary and
coercive social influences: the social influence takes both informational (predominantly) in
chapters 1–3, 6, and normative forms in 4.17–5.20 (cf. Chapter 6 below). Therefore the two
levels of social influence are rhetorically located in different sections of the discourse for the
maximum effect on identity construction and social orientation. Turner's discussion of
different types of influence is helpful here. On one hand, the informational influence is about
accepting information from a socially significant person as reliable evidence about objective
reality. It creates a desire to conform that is motivated by 'the desire to form an accurate view
of reality and to act correctly' (1991: 35). It is 'true' influence that leads to its acceptance,
internalization and long-lasting attitude change (p. 37). Normative influence, on the other
hand, is a coercive influence that conforms to the expectations of another (p. 34). It is
compliance, which may involve resistance as 'one conforms outwardly but not necessarily
inwardly' to the expectations of others under social pressure to do so (p. 37). It is based on
the power of others to reward and punish; and the motivation to conform is to gain approval
and acceptance as well as to avoid punishment or the negative consequences of deviance on
expected norms (p. 37).

54   The discourse is a social process that allocated authority to Paul and verifies his role
of social influence. The unique commission of the apostle implies an extensive social
authority as seen, for instance, in the platform for the apostolic mission: Paul takes the
message 'to the nations' (lit.) and makes 'everyone see what is the plan of the mystery hidden
for ages in God who created all things'. The vocabulary of other nations, reaching out to
'everyone' and the description of God as the 'creator of all things', conveys the totality of his
constituency and projects him in global mission as God's representative to people and the
spirit world (3.10).

that highlights the characteristics of those who are 'in Christ' also helps in moulding a communal mind-set that serves God in obedience and voluntarily shuns evil, because of their love for God and 'Christ'; and loyalty to them. The reputation of Paul as a minister of God for non-Israelite Christianness thus creates a sympathetic orientation for the rest of the discourse, its description of a united, yet diversified, active community and lifestyle appropriate for the people of God.

3. *Conclusions*

Reading Ephesians 2 and 3 has demonstrated the remarkable extent to which the discourse is founded on two Israelite figures with contested reputations, Jesus and Paul. Their stories are adapted to inaugurate distinctive Christianness, designed by God 'before the foundations of the world' (1.4), and now revealed to Paul, the unique bearer of God's mystery (3.7-9). Like the remembering of 'Jesus Christ' Paul's reputation is constructed in a way that legitimates non-Israelite Christianness: it ignores narratives of his travels, mighty deeds and mission to synagogues. Instead it is about proclaiming the message of non-Israelite Christianness, and as such it embodies the values and behaviours of the community (Turner 1991: 76–8). For instance, Paul is the only character to embody the communal values of possessing divine empowering and knowledge, instruction, unwavering commitment and being faithful in ministry. Positioning Paul in the highest position of spiritual power due to his unique revelation amidst diverse religious groups at the time of writing is highly significant. It shapes Paul's reputation by stressing his exceptional power and the divine origin of his role (Weber 1978: 1.241; cf. MacDonald 2000; Polaski 1999). The explicit textual claims for uniqueness use Paul's reputation to legitimate inter-communal dialogue and the negotiation of boundaries. This has severe consequences for self-positioning because Paul's revelation receives divine legitimation and, by implication, so does everything else in the discourse. Consequently, reforms on Jewishness, construction of Christianness and its essential component of non-Israelite resocialization are all expressions of God's will.

It is also worth noting that post-Pauline authorship makes the portrayal of Paul even more interesting: if pseudonymous, then the reputation of Paul in Ephesians with its highly significant strategy of legitimation steers remembering the apostle in the direction of present communal interests. The naming of Paul as the imprisoned author in 3.1-13 is a momentous act of power that puts Paul simultaneously in chains and on a pedestal due to his unique revelation of God's eternal mystery (3.6), although any stigma of his imprisonment is transformed by stressing Paul's role in the non-Israelite mission. Consequently the reader is steered away from Paul's contested memory as he is positioned in the lineage of the reliable apostolic authority (3.5) although he is portrayed as 'the very least of all the saints' (3.8) it hardly challenges his status as the ultimate spokesperson for God, but adds 'humility' into Paul's portfolio of prototypical values along with the perseverance and unyielding commitment of continuing the mission despite the chains.

Therefore, Ephesians links the inclusion of the non-Israelites and ideological reforms to the death of 'Jesus Christ' and with the other communal hero, Paul. The way in which Paul's reputation is shaped contributes further to the socio-historical as well as ideological legitimation. First, it places him alongside the 'holy apostles and prophets' who exercise their mandate of proclaiming the message of Ephesians 2, the inclusion of the non-Israelites; and secondly it raises him above his contemporaries by stressing his particular role in proclaiming the eternal mystery of God. This is significant for the communal dialogue, as the discourse leads the group to believe that they possess a unique revelation from God, and therefore, any opposing views are incorrect or lack full understanding of God's plans.

In summary, Paul's reputation adds to the legitimating language of Ephesians 2. The idea of the unique revelation is an umbrella covering the pseudonymous claims of the epistle, for example, that the election and status of Israel as God's people is now extended to the community of foreigners 'in Christ', and that their boundary processes are not defined by the Law. It is most likely that these issues were key concepts in the ongoing identity negotiation of early Christianities in the second half of the first century CE. In my view, instead of strengthening social networks and ideological resources to ensure peaceful relations with other Jewish groupings, Ephesians seems to contribute to social processes and ideological resources that led to the development of non-Israelite Christianness. I suggest that Ephesians offers, in rudimentary form, some of the basic elements of what would become an emerging constitution of a separate movement (cf. Zetterholm 2003), as it develops ideological resources for distancing without the explicit condemnation of 'the Jews'. This would explain the reformist social entrepreneurship, the silencing of Israel in the text, and why Ephesians does abolish the Law. Therefore it seems that the construction of Christianness in Ephesians is more developed and non-Israelite oriented than that of the undisputed Paulines, and yet not hostile toward Israel as the early Church Fathers of the second century. Having invented traditions of Jesus' Messiahship and Paul's prophethood, Ephesians continues to model the community after Israel in chapters 4–6, to which we now turn for a discussion of communal social orientation in Part Three.

PART THREE

POSITIONING IDENTITY

Chapter 5

THEORETICAL FRAMEWORK FOR
EXPLORING COMMUNAL SOCIAL ORIENTATION

1. *Introduction to Reading Ephesians 4–6*

Having explored the construction of the community and the positive
ingroup identity (Chapter 1), established how the discourse legitimates the
group as 'the people of God' inventing traditions and shaping legendary
reputations for 'Christ' and Paul (Chapters 2–3), this chapter will
conclude the study of Ephesians' social entrepreneurship by examining
how the writer uses previously established ideological principles in the
shaping of communal values, which provide practical instructions for
communal lifestyle in the second half of the letter. So far we have explored
how the discourse has celebrated the ingroup and her status in 'Christ',
and commemorated the founders of the community; but in the latter
chapters the writer turns his gaze to the community and surrounding
world, as the writer considers the key characteristics of the community
against outsiders' separation from God, warning the group to maintain a
safe distance from 'others' and manifest the counter-cultural holiness
expected of God's people. This section explores how the language of social
orientation and ideological motivations is intertwined; demonstrates how
group processes and norms go together with the writer's ideological
positionings; and discusses how chs 4–6 complete Ephesians' social
entrepreneurship. It is regrettable that this section is rather short in
comparison to readings of chs 1–3, but nonetheless it will reflect on theory
and outline what I consider key social manoeuvres of the author and their
connection to ideological discourse.

Ephesians 4–6 transports its reader to cultural boundaries, where
different values and cultural performances are compared. This is an
important part of social entrepreneurship as it is precisely at the cultural
boundaries where communities become aware of their distinctiveness as
communal culture heightens their awareness of their difference from
outsiders (Cohen 1982: 20; 1985: 50, 70). Consequently, setting communal
boundaries and models for appropriate cultural performances is crucial
for the identity and ongoing process of societal identification, as this
strengthens their distinctiveness and thus contributes to group survival.

Cohen defines culture as 'the community as experienced by its members' (1985: 98). It follows that in order to understand a community 'we have to consider its constituent social relations as repositories of meaning for its members, the community exists in the minds of its members', not in social structures or sociographic facts (Cohen 1985: 98). In other words, culture is the real expression of identity: it is about being and positioning oneself in a certain way, and about association as well as about disassociation. I regard Cohen's model of the symbolic community (that which is meaningful for insiders only) useful in exploring Ephesians, particularly due to its distinctively symbolic language of identity.[1] The 'symbolic construction of community' has made a positive contribution to Jenkins' (1996; 2004: 110–16) and Pickering's (2001: 79–84) views on communal social processes. Jenkins likens cultural meanings of communality with the virtual aspects of identification that essentially flow from its cognitive, nominal aspects, and make the real difference in the lives of its members (2004: 76–78; 112–16).

According to the SIT, 'us' and 'others' are equally important aspects of identity, and accordingly their difference is vital for social orientation, too. In Ephesians 4–6 the discourse constructs stereotypical examples of both 'us' and 'others'. First, the ingroup members are united in faith and function according to their diverse giftings (4.1-16); maintain harmony in socially unequal positions (5.22–6.9) and spiritual ideology (6.10-20). Secondly, the non-members are the 'significant others', who provide antitypes for the discourse of identity and communal values (4.17–5.20). Their characterization involves stereotypical prejudice and negative labelling that constructs the sinful 'non-Israelites' as the antitype for positive ingroup identity. Therefore, these chapters are crucial for understanding the full scale of Ephesians' social entrepreneurship, because it is in this section where the discourse develops both prototypical and antitypical language, which not only provides examples for what Christianness means, but also how it maintains cultural scepticism which influences group processes and intergroup relations.

This chapter will proceed to survey previous literature on social orientation of Ephesians 4–6. A brief literature survey will be followed by a theoretical framework, which discusses relevant models for exploring how the social entrepreneurship transfers the ideological paradigms to social orientation. The theoretical discussion considers perspectives for understanding ingroup orientation, cohesion and deviance, as well as prejudice against outsiders and a variety of functions of naming and stereotyping. The reading of Ephesians 4–6 considers textual construction of communal prototypes and antitypes in four different passages. First, the self-enhancing prototypical behaviours are discussed in three separate

1 Despite its criticisms, cf. Cohen (2002: 165–70).

discourse units: 1) outlining the cohesion and diversity of giftings (4.1-16); 2) explaining the relationship between communal equality and hierarchical household relations (5.21–6.9) and 3) using symbolic language to evoke spiritual resistance (6.10-20). Secondly, the negative portrayal of non-Israelite 'otherness' (4.17–5.20) is examined to demonstrate that communal antitypes and the discourse of deviance are equally important for identity construction and setting the paradigms for social experience.

1a. *Literature Review*

In terms of Ephesians' social orientation, its teaching on household relations has probably received the widest scholarly attention. Amy-Jill Levine's edited collection, *A Feminist Companion to the Deutero-Pauline Epistles* (2003) offers two critical contemporary readings that contribute to the understanding of Ephesians' social orientation within ancient households. The Feminist Companion's analysis of Ephesians' social entrepreneurship is careful and insightful as the readings perceptively highlight the interconnectness of communal ideology and social life and members' behaviour. First, Virginia Mollenkott argues that both traditional and feminist readings of Ephesians 5.21-33 fail to notice its emancipative elements. She suggests that there are three significant liberating principles of equality that characterize Ephesians' view to marriage: the mutual submission of marital partners (5.21); husbands' self-sacrificial loving of their wives (5.25);[2] and the interdependence of marital partners just as the church as a body of Christ is an interdependent union (5.23) (2003: 45–53).[3] In agreement with Mollenkott, it is clear that Ephesians maintains social hierarchy; but it gives traditional social positions new meanings, so that values, roles and behaviours do not seem to derive from traditions or values of the corrupted society, but from 'Christ' and the egalitarian ideology of the community. In my view, such ideological Christ-centred resocialization characterizes all aspects of Ephesians' guidance; not only in its household relations, but also in that the instructions for social living are ideologically driven.

Secondly, Elna Moulton's essay complements Mollenkott's readings as it engages with the ideological core of communal values and ethics, discussing how the household code reinterprets its patriarchal structure from the Christological perspective (2003: 69). Moulton uses van

---

2 Mollenkott takes this as 'self-emptying' (*kenosis*) or 'self-sacrifice' following Christ's example in Phil. 2.5-8 (2003: 48).

3 In contrast to, for example, Elizabeth Schüssler Fiorenza's readings that argue for constant support for male dominance in the New Testament teaching on household relations (1983: 269; 1998: 119, 148) and Elizabeth Johnson, who argues that Ephesians suppresses the interest of women in the service of religious vision doomed as over-idealistic as well as serving the interests of the male (1998: 428–32).

Gennep's anthropological concept of ritual 'liminality', which refers to ceremonies and rites performed in different stages of life to highlight the transition from one stage to another (such as adolescence, marriage, parenthood, old age, death). These involve three kinds of rituals that provide interesting parallels to Ephesians' identity processes. These are separation, a departure from an original stage; transition, during which previous 'roles, regulations, structures and certainties may be relativized and fundamentally rearranged'; and incorporation, when members are reintegrated and reconstituted into new roles and groups (p. 61). Moulton proceeds to discuss the rhetorical strategies for the transformation of non-Israelite believers from being 'outsiders' to being 'in Christ', and the liminality of the journey. She suggests that the images of communal head (1.10; 4.15-16; 5.23, 29-30), body (4.12-16; 5.29-30) and fullness (3.19; 4.13; 5.18) stress the incorporation of the believers, their process of growth and ever increasing reflection of fullness of Christ (2003: 65).

According to Moulton, Ephesians seeks to reorient both 'Jews and Gentiles, and both men and women' by disclosing a new way of looking at things and offering new roles for them to assume (2003: 72). This is achieved by the liminal dynamics of identification, alienation and reorientation that view human existence in the light of the Christ-event (2003: 78). Her model for the transformation processes illustrates how different parts of the letter correlate, and how different components of identity provide a coherent reading of the letter. In addition, her attention to reorienting 'both Jews and Gentiles' exemplifies integration of different parts of the letter. It is similar to what Asano describes as a 'recreated worldview' of innovative Pauline enterprise that also challenges the Jewish commonwealth with its orientation to non-Israelite incorporation (2005: 104, 178). This concept deserves further attention in the subsequent readings.

Finally, Darko's 2008 monograph offers a recent study of shared ethical values in Ephesians, discussing the 'rhetoric of differentiation' and social function of the *Haustafel* (4.17–6.9). In terms of the his contribution to the household code readings, Darko outlines the bearing of fictive kinship language and demonstrates how this 'engenders a strong sense of belonging and solidarity' (2008: 101); and considers a wide range of parallel moral discourses form the antiquity, concluding that the distinctiveness of the *Haustafel* is in its Christological motivations, while there is nothing novel about its moral instruction (2008: 106). His reading of 4.17–5.21 surveys ancient literature to test the innovation of the discourse of differentiation between insiders and outsiders, to which 4.17 sets the tone (and gives the book its title phrase). He argues that Ephesians reflects typical ancient elite in their discussion of virtuous life and those who live up to its expectations won't significantly differ from the cultural elite, except on rhetorical and ideological level (2008: 67, 68).

In my view, Darko's reading, which stresses the unity of 'the church', could be further nuanced by discussion of ethnic differentiation that continues in Ephesians 4–5. This is linked to the very essence of the 4.17 claim, 'You must no longer live like the Gentiles live . . .' and causes me to question, if the author was consciously reflecting on elite moral discourses as Darko interestingly demonstrates, this would imply that he valued such rhetoric and – by default – non-Israelite contribution to moral discourse; so what then does 4.17 mean? In my view there is some distinction between the material Darko explores and Ephesians' attitude to non-Israelite culture, which could be explored further. Where Darko compares Ephesians' detailed discourse with ancient literature, I argue for the Jewishness of Ephesians' imagination as an overarching model, suggesting that the basic idea for 'Gentile lifestyle' derives from Israel's holiness, i.e. holiness of God's people which Ephesians seeks to now replicate. In my view, the model of the writer's Jewishness explains why the social orientation uses language of ethnic differentiation, instead of just 'then – now', and 'them – us' comparisons to differentiate between insiders and outsiders. If this was the case there would have been no need to say 'do not live like the Gentiles', but 'godless', 'unbelievers', or 'those who are in the darkness' could have been used instead. This could be connected to his terminology as he frequently uses 'the church' for Ephesians' community, which could indicate that what 'the church' has become provides some of the gap fillers for study of social construction of the early Christian movement. For instance, ethnic differentiation and prejudice would not be accepted in today's churches (or they should not be) but our values of political correctness and love toward one's neighbour despite ethnicity could be read into the text triggered by a suitable code, such as unity in Ephesians. However, it is not so clear that Ephesians was a community 'regardless of ethnicity' (p. 66) and a community that 'transcends ethnic boundaries' (p. 110), given that 'don't live like Gentiles' characterizes its attitude to social relations.

MacDonald's contribution to understanding Ephesians' social motivations is again very insightful and theoretically informed. She identifies the sharp, uncompromising distinction from the outsiders as the most striking feature of 4.17–5.20 (2000: 321) and follows Perkins focusing on key themes of introversionist tendencies and sectarian mechanisms of identity construction (321; cf. Perkins 1997: 118). As Perkins correctly observes, Ephesians' vision of social distance is different from, for instance, the Essene separation from the 'sons of darkness' as Ephesians does not develop the genre of rival interpretations of the sacred texts, the alternative ritual calendar and so forth (1997: 118).[4] It is also very

---

4 The Deutero-Paulines seem to be dismissive of ritual aspects of Jewish culture, like Ephesians, or outright negative, as for instance Colossians (2.16-17, cf. 18-23).

interesting that Ephesians does not significantly develop the language of (re)interpretation of the Law by a communal leader, unlike other contemporary Jewish subgroups (Perkins 1997: 121).[5] Similarly, the dissociation from the non-Israelite world is somewhat ambiguous: the text adamantly requires separation from sinful lifestyle, but does not detail its social, political or economical implications. Nor does it explain how to maintain social networks within the society in which worship of various gods was a prominent part of the social life and cultural performances, and not constricted to a 'religious' component that could easily be classified and rejected.

In the absence of any specific detail about the implied audience and the recipient community it may be assumed that the lists of vices and virtues are not context-specific but provide cultural models. However, MacDonald has identified what appears to be a key issue in these lists: it is particularly where Ephesians departs from traditional moral teaching,[6] where it reveals a community specific issue, namely a concern for the unity of the group against external pressure (2000: 320–24). She recognizes how Ephesians interrelates communal ideology and identity; for example, using ecclesiological motivations in avoiding falsehood is linked with close communal networks, 'since we are members of one another' (4.25); and the constructive dialogue for communal up-building (4.29) connects the vices and virtues with the previous teaching on communal unity in 4.1-16, thus expanding the concern for unity which reoccurs throughout the letter (MacDonald 2000: 320). Closer examination of such distinctive developments reveals that they are either Christ-centred legitimations, fundamental to the ideology of the community, or communal motivations deriving from 'Christ'. All in all, MacDonald arrives at an important conclusion endorsed in this study: the omission of ritual boundary markers associated with Judaism has led to a greater attention to ethical boundaries, in the fear of assimilation with the surrounding society in the absence of protective (Jewish) boundary markers (2000: 322).

The following readings of Ephesians will focus particularly on the function of negative language against the non-Israelites in the communal text. The antagonism against the 'non-Israelite other' is often linked with the causality of extratextual factors. For instance, MacDonald argues that Ephesians' emphasis on the identity of the Church reflects a transitional

---

5   Although it assumes superior insight of Paul (ch. 3) neither his nor Jesus' role is expanded in terms of a teacher. For other parallels see 5.10; 6.2-3; Perkins, 1997: 121) and MacDonald 2000: 321–22).

6   Such as parallels in Colossians, Pauline literature, the Dead Sea Scrolls, other Jewish ethical teaching and Greco-Roman moral codes cf. Lincoln (1990: 271–6, 293–9, 319–20, 339–40); Perkins (1997: 104–10, 112–21, 122–5) MacDonald (2000: 238) and Darko (2008: 31–7).

post-Pauline situation when external threats, 'menacing spiritual powers and increasingly hostile reactions from the outside world' mounted up against the community (2000: 298, 299).[7] Hence she regards that Ephesians composes a defensive stance, encouraging internal cohesion by expanding on its purpose (4.1-16) and rejecting the outsiders' lifestyle (2000: 298, 319–20). However, the extent of external pressure in pre-text social context cannot be known with any certainty. As noted before, there is a strong tendency in the NT studies to regard detecting 'textual context' as a key task in the interpretive process.[8] In my view this should be done in terms of outlining generic influences if the explicit 'data' is missing; and in every case, mindful of the fact that such 'data' is also socially and ideologically constructed and positioned in a certain way. Discussion of the historical context should also acknowledge the (potential) difference between fictional characters of the text and how they are positioned in social life, and the context or the writer and the community addressed. It is possible that the text gives reasonable indication that it takes an objective stance. But often an analysis of intentionality and author's motives reveals that the positioning the discourse characters indicates that they serve the 'ideas of the writer' and they are discursively positioned for particular purposes, which makes reconstruction pointless or inaccurate.

In the light of the social entrepreneurship model, it is possible that the

---

7   Ephesians makes explicit reference to spiritual beings and powers hostile to God (2.2; 3.10; 6.10-22). God's power is exemplified in Christ at his resurrection and exaltation (1.20-21) and his dominion (1.22-23, cf. 1.10). The letter also implies conservative reflections of social power relations as it maintains existing social structures (5.21–6.9) and relates social power with the power of Christ who makes leadership appointments. Clinton Arnold sees these powers as particularly connected with the worship of the Ephesian Artemis (1989 123–4, 167–72). This may be particularly appealing for readers who maintain the Pauline authorship of and its historical connection with the Acts narrative, despite textual difficulties involved with the 'Ephesus' location (1.1). Although the dynamics of power are an interesting dimension of the text, the 'powers' do not, like Arnold admits, sufficiently account for the purpose of the letter or its 'theological peculiarities' (1989: 168), which are better explained by identity processes. Cf. Schnackenburg (1991: 34); Lincoln (1990: lxxxvi); O'Brien (1999: 56–65); and Hoehner (2002: 102–6).

8   According to Elliot the social-scientific criticism 'studies the text as both a reflection of and a response to the social and cultural setting in which the text was produced. Its aim is the determination of the meaning(s) explicit and implicit in the text, meanings made possible and shaped by the social and cultural systems inhabited by both authors and intended audiences' (Elliott 1995: 8). However, my reading of the NT texts as socially influential presumes that texts can be formative and world-shaping, and inspired by cognitive reflections as well as by actual social circumstances. For instance, given that Israel is a formative model for the people of God this alone would be sufficient to explain Ephesians 4–6. Given that the text or its author is positioned in a Greco-Roman social setting (I mean, not in monastic isolation, for instance) both life and text were, of course, socially influenced too, and not written in a vacuum. Therefore a threat or harassment was possible, but in the absence of specific evidence, secondary to cultural models.

writer reacts to social circumstances affecting the group; but it is equally possible that it shapes the social life because it does not value certain other social connections nor does it allow alternative cultural models avoiding dispute and deviance. In my view, the latter is more likely as it features explicitly in the discussion; without excluding the possibility of the former. It is also possible that Ephesians' strong ingroup orientation leads to a deliberate weakening of other social networks in the community, if the social entrepreneurship pre-empted the problems its ideological positionings were likely to cause by promoting ingroup orientation.[9] When discussing Ephesians' social setting scholars often observe that Ephesians somehow assumes a general conflict.[10] For instance, despite his interest in the social setting of Ephesians, Esler takes 'persecution' as a general phenomenon (2005b: 6–7) and fails to note that Ephesians' cultural reforms on Judaism and distance it demands from other cultures could actually provide resources for inflaming socio-ideological conflict and encourage social distancing. In this reading the focus is upon the dynamics of the discourse that contribute to social conflict, which are largely unexplored by the previous scholarship. I will discuss the problematics embedded in the text, without assuming that the text was born as prompted by external threats. Instead, it may be the persuasive social entrepreneurship that confidently envisions culturally distinctive Christianness to which the discourse gives birth, and potentially leads itself to social conflict if its values were contested.

2. *Theoretical Framework*

In order to critically engage with Ephesians' social entrepreneurship in chapters 4–6 one must be informed of both positive, self-enhancing group dynamics and their negative counterparts that construct 'the prototypical ingroup model' and 'the ultimate other' which both feature in the positioning of the discourse at the cultural boundaries. The following theoretical perspectives will now be outlined in brief: self-enhancement, stereotyping, social prejudice and social exorcism, while other important concepts of naming and positioning have been outlined in Chapter 1.

---

9   The distinctiveness of Ephesians' construction of Christianness was likely to intensify social conflicts with both Israelites and non-Israelites. It is possible that the writer anticipated further conflicts and thus embedded the idea of building distance from both Israelite and non-Israelite groupings into the discourse. In other words, the text involves an element of a self-fulfilling prophecy, as it both generates increasing social distancing and provides discourse elements that legitimate such separation.

10   Cf. e.g. MacDonald (2000: 320) and Hoehner (2002: 99–100).

2a. *Self-enhancement*

The theoretical frameworks for understanding Ephesians' social orientation build on the basic elements of SIT assuming that group processes are based on self-definition and strengthening the sense of positive distinctiveness. The letter contains both guidance for intra-communal relations and communal relations with outsiders. The simultaneous operation of these two underlying identity processes, categorization and self-enhancement is elementary to group processes. Hogg defines these as follows:

> *Categorization* ... clarifies intergroup boundaries by producing group stereotypical and normative perceptions and actions, and assigns people, including self, to the contextually relevant category. Categorization is a basic cognitive process which operates on social and non-social stimuli alike, to highlight and bring into focus those aspects of experience that are subjectively meaningful in a particular context.
>
> *Self-enhancement* ... guides the social categorization process such that ingroup norms and stereotypes are largely ingroup favouring. It is assumed that people have a very basic need to see themselves in a relatively positive light in relation to relevant others (i.e. have a positive self-concept), and that in group contexts self-enhancement can be achieved through evaluatively positive social identity in relation to relevant outgroups. (1996: 67, italics in original)

According to Tajfel it was a psychological requirement that groups would provide their members with a positive ingroup identity that derives from comparative observations between social groups (Tajfel 1972 in Turner 1996: 16). He observed that intergroup comparisons focus, not on objective evaluations of the groups or diversity of social life, but on maintenance and bolstering of positive distinctiveness and group identity (Turner 1996: 16).[11]

Consequently, the theoretical framework for exploring group processes in Ephesians 4–6 is entirely dependent on this basic assumption of the SIT. It regards the interplay of internal similarity and external difference as a central part of the identification of 'us' and 'others' (Jenkins 2004: 89); and a fundamental part of both intra- and intergroup dynamics. Furthermore, cultural similarity is an essential component of the sense of common identity, as well as of ingroup social orientation and the negotiation of communal boundaries. Therefore the ingroup similarity and difference from others is not only part of the members' cognitive and emotive dynamics, but also fundamental for the discursive processes of

---

11   As discussed in the literary review previously, this is fundamentally important for the study of the social dynamics of early Christian texts, which are all too often approached with the method of 'mirror reading', assuming that the text responds to and/or reflects social circumstances outside the text, or that a community and its social counterparts can be reconstructed form the text.

the group. It is fundamental for social identity construction that, 'groups distinguish themselves from and discriminate against other groups in order to promote their own positive social evaluation and collective self-esteem' (Jenkins 2004: 89).

Jenkins' distinction between nominal and virtual identifications, between bearing a certain label and what it means for its bearers, is helpful here (2004: 76–8). The nominal is how the group or category is defined, and the virtual is how its members behave or are treated on the basis of their collective identification (2004: 86).[12] Furthermore, defining 'us' simultaneously defines 'others' (Jenkins 2004: 79). In other words, ingroup membership and what it means in practical everyday life is discussed at the cultural boundaries, that is, at the point of separation and identification, where the social entrepreneur helps the community to discover who they are and what they do.[13] My focus is on what identity seems to mean to the writer and how the writer conveys the virtual aspects, i.e. practical meanings of the ingroup identity. It must be recognized that although the reading seeks to understand how the text construes identity through communal culture, values and social orientations, my readings will be chronologically distanced outsider's responses to how the social processes of particular community are construed in the ancient text, mindful of its complexities.

Finally, the construction of a socially charged discourse is connected to its social goals. The social identity theory assumes that individuals or groups that have a deficient sense of identity may seek to restore or acquire a more positive status and identification via social mobility, assimilation, creativity or competition (Brown 1995: 180–81; Jenkins 2004: 89–90). Given that Ephesians generally promotes positive aspects of belonging it seems, in the light of SIT, that it projects an insufficient identity and is geared towards encouraging and generating those cultural choices and social processes that increase their conformity to group values and behaviours. This is also reflected in the encouragement of cultural assimilation and resocialization as the text provides new, countercultural values and promotes distancing the community members from their cultural context, which is interpreted negatively, in order to undervalue

---

12   Cf. A. Cohen, (1985), for the discussion of the idiosyncratic aspects of collective belonging in ingroup rhetoric.

13   The understanding of group processes in this study is influenced by Barth, who emphasizes the difference and intercommunal boundary processes that negotiate internal similarity and external difference (1969; 2000); as well as by Cohen, who emphasizes the collective similarity and how these manifest in intracommunal processes (1985; 1994; 2000: 145–69).

prior culture and reinforce communal belonging and the social networks of the group.[14]

2b. *Stereotyping*

As noted above, Ephesians' different social processes are interlinked with and derive from identity. For example, naming follows identification and begins the construction of identity with a nominal classification of people into different groups, exaggerating similarity and difference in the social life. Other group processes build on initial identification, naming and positioning, intensifying similarities and differences and expanding them with virtual identifications.[15] This could involve discourses of coherence or deviance, which will be explored shortly. Or, for instance, stereotyping, which is used for a variety of social purposes. Stereotyping refers to the creation of simplified images of peoples and groups that typically exaggerate intergroup differences and minimize intragroup differences (Tajfel 1969: 83).

Although stereotypes are strongly associated – both in popular perception and in social-scientific literature – with the negative simplification involved in external categorization processes, they are also part of ingroup identification and positive self-enhancement. Thus alongside naming, stereotypes facilitate both ingroup communal and wider social processes, as they can be used in both idealizing and demonizing (Pickering 2001: 40). They typically accentuate positive aspects of the ingroup and amplify negative traits of outsiders, as Ephesians demonstrates. Tajfel explains, '[stereotypes] introduce simplicity and order where there is complexity and nearly random variation. They can help us to cope only if fuzzy differences between groups are transmuted into clear ones, or new differences created where none exist' (1969: 82). In other words, stereotyping can accentuate existing differences or assume a significant difference where none might exist.[16] This explains why stereotyping frequently contributes to the construction of 'the ultimate other', projecting stark discontinuity with the ingroup and what they have in common. The construction of 'the ultimate other' is another elementary

14 The understanding of resocialization relies on Tajfel's concept of 'assimilation', referring to 'the processes by which culturally generated norms, values and content of stereotypes are transmitted to individual members of society' by the socially influential (cited in Turner 1996: 13).

15 Although I discuss different processes that usually begin with identifications I do not suggest that these would happen in a particular order, or that I would engage with all relevant identity and group processes in Ephesians.

16 For instance, Ephesians attributes negative stereotypes to non-Israelite immorality, although it has previously seen moral decline as part of a common human problem. Thus it both accentuates and constructs difference.

social process which is often regarded as a primary component of social identity (F. Barth 1969: 11–13).

In literature, stereotypes are value-loaded devices that convey the writer's attitudes toward those stereotyped. They describe the disposition of the author rather than different individuals or groups and they can be used in idealistic self-enhancement, as well as a negative disposition and prejudice toward the 'other'. On one hand, stereotypes are used in the prototypical construction of a person or values that typify group values and the ideal position of the group (Turner 1991: 76–9). On the other hand, they also feature in providing social guidance toward 'the other'. According to Elizabeth Bronfen, '[t]he stereotype of the Other is used to control the ambivalent and to create boundaries. Stereotypes are a way of dealing with the instabilities arising from the division between self and non-self by preserving an illusion of control and order' (1992: 182). Consequently, stereotyping is understood here as 'a process for marking, maintaining and reproducing norms of behaviour, identity and value' (Pickering 2001: 174).

This leads me to conclude that stereotypes are *not explanations* but *rather exaggerations* used to guide and direct social orientation. Rupert Brown makes an important point arguing that stereotypes have a self-fulfilling quality and they create expectancies that bias judgments (2000: 307). Complementing, positive stereotypes may provide motivation to become what the stereotyping suggested, for example, virtuous, hard-working and so forth. Negative stereotypes may be equally self-fulfilling if they create disagreement that leads to predictable ways of behaviour to a given individual or group; or if they are contested, the stereotyped continues in their normal way, and thus fulfils the stereotype's self-fulfilling prophecy in the eyes of the critical observer. Both Ephesians 'saints' and 'sinners' could function in this way.

Furthermore, as Pickering's compelling metaphors illustrate, stereotyping 'tends to freeze-frame our thinking about others. It fossilizes representation and excludes alternative ways of seeing and understanding' (2001: 43).[17] Therefore, they lead us to conceal or forget (Pickering 2001: 20) and guide and legitimate people's behaviour, which is why they may contribute to the construction of social inequalities (Brown 2000: 307).

2c. *Social Prejudice, Social Exorcism*

It has been widely acknowledged that group membership may attribute social bias as a negative counterpart for positive ingroup identity, without any practical justification for its negative stance towards outsiders, except

---

17 Pickering develops two of Ostendorf's ideas, namely 'social exorcism' and 'fossilized representation' (Ostendorf 1982: 29).

appreciation of communal togetherness.[18] This is particularly relevant for the use of stereotypes in communal discourses, as stereotyping involves compelling cognitive 'mechanics' that involve a diffusion of hostile and potentially derogatory social images (Tajfel 1981: 4, 9, 143; Pickering 2001: 37–8). Consequently, when a community internalizes such discourse values it simultaneously adopts its polarized view to social diversity. While this may be self-enhancing, it could be, at the same time, disastrous and lead to hostility, as the Holocaust or more recent examples of ethnic cleansing demonstrate.[19] It is particularly significant when a discourse has power to cause its readers to 'switch off' critical evaluation of the discourse (say, for example, if it was 'word of God').[20] Tajfel describes this as a

> spiral effect in which the existence of prejudice at large not only provides additional support and rewards towards hostile judgments, [but] also removes the possibility of a 'reality check' for these judgments which then feed upon each other and become more and more strongly entrenched in the form of powerful social myths. (1981: 134).

Therefore a communal discourse which is strongly geared towards ingroup promotion may turn social boundaries and prejudice into cognitive models that facilitate stereotyping (Barth 2000: 33; Jenkins 2004: 165). In the same way, ingroup awareness and communal dialogue provide a fertile breeding ground for discriminative thought (Pickering 2001: 30), as they heighten members' awareness of their difference with outsiders, while stereotypes accentuate these features (Oakes 1996: 97). Hence groups could be responsible for fostering negative and socially divisive attitudes as part of their group identity maintenance (Tajfel 1969: 85).

The stereotypes are frequently used to demonize others, making them unattractive, untrustworthy or even dangerous, which may significantly hinder the development or maintenance of functional interpersonal connections. So Pickering, who suggests that stereotypes are a form of social exorcism; that is, a symbolic expulsion of certain social counterparts, or othering the different into the periphery and distancing them from the communal core (2001: 48, 49). He argues that

18 SIT offers plausible explanations for a variety of communal processes that bolster ingroup orientation, especially when the ingroup orientation and its counter side, negative attitudes to outsiders, are without any specific causes. See Brown's discussion of ingroup harmony and intergroup conflict (2000: 309–60).

19 Hostility fuelled by a (religious) discourse may range from silent and personal disapproval to extreme cases of, for instance, assassinations, terrorism or religiously motivated warfare (sadly history is full of examples). In moderate forms rhetoric of hostility in subcultural discourses may lead to stronger communal affiliation and self-enhancement but at its extremes it may lead to unlawful acts, terrorism, genocide and war.

20 See Penner (2008: 429–55) and Crossley (2008) for critical assessments of NT scholarship and cultural bias.

> As a rhetorical strategy of exclusion, made in the interests of a unified
> collective identity, stereotypical othering seeks to deny not only its
> historical basis but also its basis in dependency on that which it casts
> out into the periphery. It attempts to separate and distance itself from
> the subjugated Other... [and] to contain the Other in its place in the
> periphery. (2001: 49)

This illustrates how the socially excluded stand in danger of being
scapegoated and being excessively charged with a negative symbolic value
(2001: 183). By doing so it is not only their difference that is accentuated,
but they seem to personify the negative end of a moral continuum as
scapegoating involves 'the symbolic identification and isolation of a social
problem in a single individual or stereotyped category of a person' (2001:
183). Consequently, what is symbolically rejected as deviant and
stereotypically scapegoated defines the limits within the prototypical
and makes the normative steadfast (2001: 200).

Prejudice and scapegoating may not be attractive perspectives to reading
Ephesians if it is seen as 'Christian theology', but the traces for negative
counterparts of identity processes should also be tested in the light of SIT,
as the social entrepreneur exercises his (self-acclaimed) social power to
classify, symbolize, ordain and exclude.[21] Similarly, as Sallie Westwood
reminds, it is important to remember that communal texts, including the
religious, are discourses of power – as well as sacred texts and their
interpretations, I would hasten to add (2002: 134). Similarly, Ephesians is a
discourse of power that exemplifies social realities and gives voice to
viewpoints and orientations filtered according to the social and ideological
agenda of the writer exercising his prerogative. The social entrepreneur is
responsible for the discursive construction of Christianness, and the
worldview that considers 'others' as a deviant, subordinate type, pushed to
the periphery of communal life (Pickering 2001: 75).

Having outlined key theoretical perspectives for exploring the complexity of Ephesians' social orientation and how the text provides
paradigms for social life, we will now proceed to apply these theories in
the reading of Ephesians 4–6.

---

21 Although this reading does not allocate much scope for social power and influence,
power relations are seen as underlining features in the discourse and a vital part for its
history. Power is intrinsic to the communal discourse, just as it is intrinsic to all social
interactions, whether actual, fictional or textual (Giddens 1984: 14). Depending upon the
perspective, the social orientation of Ephesians can be viewed as either actual, fictional or
textual: actual, if it is approached as evidencing historical early Christian movement;
fictional, if its reflection of historical social circumstances are seen as contested and
considerably modified to the extent when it moves from actual or historical to creative and
fictional; or textual, which is its obvious dimension, but nevertheless, challenged or dismissed
by those readers who prefer its actual and historical (or fictive) dimensions.

Chapter 6

READING EPHESIANS 4–6:
PROTOTYPES AND ANTITYPES: PARADIGMS FOR SOCIAL ORIENTATION

This chapter seeks to demonstrate that social entrepreneurship provides a useful heuristic model to demonstrate how the communal self-enhancement and socio-ideological positioning continue throughout the discourse. Furthermore, examining the author's social manoeuvrings gives a broad understanding of what Christ-followership means to the non-Israelite community, spiritually, ideologically and socially. Bringing the readings of Ephesians to a close in this chapter demonstrates that the letter forms a coherent literary unit, whereby its latter half (chapters 4–6) develops the pragmatics of the legitimating identity discourse (chapters 1–3) and explains how this particular social orientation conforms to the ideological core of the community.[1] In continuity with earlier readings, I attempt to demonstrate that Ephesians provides ideologically motivated guidance for social life designed to generate appropriate cultural performances. As Jenkins writes, 'identification is never just a matter of name or label: the meaning of an identity lies also in *the difference that it makes* in individual lives' (2004: 77). I will explore how Ephesians constructs both nominal and virtual identity, continuing to imagine non-Israelite Christ-followership according to Jewish cultural models for Israel's separation and ingroup orientation. The following readings explore communality and difference, and how the identification of 'us' and 'others' reinforces cultural and value distinctions,[2] focusing particularly on those aspects of identity which have been insufficiently discussed by the previous scholarship: first, examining the relationship between the construction of

1   The basic categories of cognitive and pragmatic identity processes characterize the division of the letter into two sections that, first, establish communal identity, and secondly, outline its consequences for cultural performances, intra- and intergroup relations. The paraenetic elements in Ephesians 4–6 are interwoven with Christological motivations explaining how the community can lead a life worthy of their calling (4.1) that links the two main sections of the letter, as commonly acknowledged (cf. Moulton 2003: 66).

2   The polarization of insiders and outsiders runs throughout the letter. Although it could be explained as dynamics involved in non-Israelites to the Jewish community, it seems that the importance of membership 'in Christ' is formative despite ethnic priority given to Israel in Ephesians' positionings.

communal ideology, ingroup culture and socially restrictive attitudes to non-members; and secondly, analysing how stereotyping and social prejudice are used in communal self-enhancement, strengthening communality and identity. I will first outline elements of prototypical discourse and contrast these with the communal antitypes, although this takes me out of reading sequence with regards 4.17–5.20.

1. *Communal Prototypes: The Holy, The Conservative*

1a. *Ephesians 4.1-16: Unity, Diversity, Cohesion and Communal Goals*
Having legitimated the community as 'the people of God' and the manifestation of his eternal plan, the social entrepreneurship turns to outlining what consequences this counter-cultural identity has for the non-Israelite members. Although this section is more pragmatic, the social entrepreneurship continues to position the social discourse in the symbolic universe which informs the connection between communal beliefs and social life. This is evident in placing a reminder of the apostolic authority (4.1-3) and key communal beliefs (4.4-6) in the beginning of the discussion of values and behaviours.

> [4.1] I therefore, the prisoner in the Lord, beg you to lead a life worthy of the calling to which you have been called, [2] with all humility and gentleness, with patience, bearing with one another in love, [3] making every effort to maintain the unity of the Spirit in the bond of peace. [4] There is one body and one Spirit, just as you were called to one hope of your calling, [5] one Lord, one faith, one baptism, [6] one God and Father of all, who is above all and through all and in all. [7] But each of us was given grace according to the measure of Christ's gift. [8] Therefore it is said, 'When he ascended on high me made captivity itself a captive; he gave gifts to his people.' [9] When it says, 'He ascended', what does it mean but that he had also descended into the lower parts of the earth? [10] He who descended is the same one who ascended far above all the heavens, so that he might fill all things. [11] The gifts he gave were that some would be apostles, some prophets, some evangelists, some pastors and teachers, [12] to equip the saints for the work of ministry, for building up the body of Christ, [13] until all of us come to the unity of the faith and of the knowledge of the Son of God, to maturity, to the measure of the full stature of Christ. [14] We must no longer be children, tossed to and fro and blown about by every wind of doctrine, by people's trickery, by their craftiness in deceitful scheming. [15] But speaking truth in love, we must grow up in every way into him who is the head, into Christ, [16] from the whole body, joined and knit together by every ligament with which it is equipped, as each part is working properly, promotes the body's growth in building itself up in love.

The new identity Ephesians constructs for the non-Israelite Christ-followers requires new culture and cultural remodelling. Christ-follower-ship is here explained as a harmonious orientation and confessional unity, and likened to a physical union of its different members of the body to the divine head, 'Christ'. In other words, Christianness is here imagined as an ideological unity and cultural similarity among Christ-followers, using prototypical language which makes any suggestion of discord or deviance intensely harmful for the corporate body-image. This brings together three important communal theses: social unity, ideological conformity and lifestyle of holiness characterized by ingroup orientation and organic relationship with its other members, leaders and the spiritual head. Although cohesion may be like the cement that links and joins community members together (Schachter 1951), Ephesians' organic imagery itself provides excellent ways of imagining communality. While the body imagery in 4.7-16 allows for diversity it also requires ongoing membership as each member requires the connection to survive.

The plea of the apostle in 4.1-6 reiterates the core beliefs of the community: one body, one spirit, one hope of their calling, one Lord, one faith, one baptism and one God and Father of all, which link together communality and belief.[3] It is quite possible that this is another Deutero-Pauline expansion of the early connection between baptism and believers' unity (Gal. 3.27-28; 1 Cor. 12.13; cf. Lincoln 1990: 240). These verses highlight their unique beliefs and communal belonging that separated them at the boundaries of these values.[4] These ideological values, and their sub-communal meanings in particular, highlight their difference from the surrounding world and constitute their community. It is also important for the communal survival that the distinctiveness behind these key words becomes socially formative as socially integrated lives require common culture and group cohesion. This is evident from Ephesians, which calls the Christ-followers to 'eagerly maintain the unity' (4.3).[5] This builds on the complementary address of the audience, praised for their faith and 'love toward all the saints' (1.15) as thus they have modelled

---

3   The articles of faith echo previous teaching on 'one body' (2.16; 3.6); the spirit (1.13, 18); hope (1.12, 18, cf. 1.9, 10; 3.9, 10); Lord (1.10, 17, 20-23; cf. 4.10, 15, 16); faith (1.13, 15; 3.16-17); and father God (1.3-10; 17-23; 2.4-7, 10, 18-22; 3.2, 7, 9-10, 12, 14, 20-21). Interestingly, although baptism was in all likelihood of key ritual importance as the initiation rite into community membership, it is only mentioned in 4.5. Despite this, commentators often associate liturgical and hymnic elements with baptismal allusions (cf. 1.11-14; 2.1-6; 4.22-24, 30; 5.25-27 in e.g. MacDonald, 2000: 287–8); contra Lincoln (1990: lx, lxxix).

4   Cf. Boyarin, (2004: 22); as well as Beard, North and Price (1998: 249).

5   No wonder there is a lot of stress on unity as the reconciliation took place at the cross where hostility was killed by Jesus (2.14-16); and it would be difficult to explain why hostility would rise again. In my opinion, ethnic hostility was not killed, but some aspects of differentiation clearly are alive, and further conflicts were likely.

their prototypical values.[6] However, whether this is a true reflection of their ingroup orientation or a rhetorical applause to encourage harmonious cohesion remains unknown (cf. Brown 2000: 46).

The language of God's intervention is used throughout the letter in order to make the discourse more compelling: it is a rhetorical key for the divine authenticity of the message and legitimation of the community, which here reminds them of the apostle's example and his authority, a prototypical person who exemplifies the ingroup values. The cultural discourse opens and closes with the image of an imprisoned apostle who persuades the community members to 'lead a life worthy of the calling' they have received (4.1; 6.19-20). This reminds the community of Paul's status in the sub-cultural communal discourse (3.1-13; cf. Cohen 1985); and the symbolic and spiritual status of the believers, expressed in the myth of their election and adoption according to God's eternal purpose (1.4, 5; 4.4) and urges for a faithful response.

Ephesians' use of divine legitimation continues throughout the letter, justifying and explaining the community, as well as its distinctive identity and culture. Here we find that the social orientation is also legitimated by God as the demand for resocialization is anchored on God's calling (4.1). The 'divine calling' is a loaded expression in early Christian rhetoric that links Ephesians 4–6 with the earlier discourse where their inclusion and status was legitimated.[7] Here the social entrepreneur begins to explain the practical implications of imagining the Christ-following community as God's holy people; modelling the community after Israel as God's people. God's calling sets the community apart and requires positioning the community in a socially and culturally different place. It involves resocialization, new beliefs and culture, particularly as it involves bringing in 'cultural others' into God's people.[8] The non-Israelites would have to undergo a radical change of symbolic universe, distancing themselves from their previous culture and accept new beliefs, values and worldview, which includes retrospective reinterpretation of the past and new forms of communal remembering. As Zetterholm and MacDonald have noted, distancing from the local cultic context is particularly relevant, but an

---

6   Ephesians does develop on the character or values of prototypical Paul as, for example, in Phil. 1.15-18. Paul's reputation includes exemplary characteristics of hope, mission-orientation, humility, endurance and so forth; his reputation is geared towards his mission and message. Otherwise the ideals of gentleness, love and tolerance are typical values in the NT imagination (cf. Rom. 12; 13.8-10, 12-14; 14; 15.1-9a; Gal. 5.22-23; 6.1-2; 1 Cor. 13).

7   See for instance Eph. 1.18; 4.4; Rom. 8.29-30, 11.29; 2 Thess. 1.11; and Heb. 3.1.

8   Ephesians' prototypical social orientation and value of one's calling also includes counter-cultural elements, such as humility (4.2) and ingroup orientation that ensures internal harmony (4.3). Humility is usually associated with servitude and not with honourable behaviour (Lincoln 1990: 235–6; MacDonald 2000: 286).

often neglected area of studies in early Christianities.[9] In the light of the SIT Ephesians' discourse seems to offer resources for socio-ideological mobility if one's identity is perceived as insufficient, which could result from any possible psychological, social or economic reasons, while confident Ephesians, for the sake of speculation, could have quite well contested Ephesians' identity building and its ethno-cultural notions, in particular.

Achieving social and ideological cohesion is one of the key tasks in social entrepreneurship. Communities require at least 'minimal individual submission to collective routines' (Jenkins 2004: 162), even if they may not detail actual rules for conduct and processes for dealing with possible misconduct. Having appealed to the members' sense of loyalty to God (4.1) the social entrepreneurship continues to shape group cohesion using models for appropriate roles. The first and most formative social value positioned in the fictional community-body is virtuous and harmonious ingroup orientation, as the social entrepreneur imagines the community living in 'humility, gentleness ... and patience, bearing with one another in love' (4.2).[10] The key values, 'gentleness' (cf. Gal. 5.23; 6.1; Col. 3.12) and 'patience' (cf. Gal. 5.22, 2. Cor. 6.6; Col. 3.12) and 'love' (cf. 1 Cor. 13), draw from early Christian traditions of the prototypical 'Jesus Christ' (MacDonald 2000: 287). These values reinforce the reconciliation that 'Jesus Christ' of the group as 'one body, one Spirit (that operates in all), having one hope' (4.4). It is socially significant that Ephesians provides models that encourage harmonious relations. This is particularly import-ant as unity belongs to remembering of the cross (2.15); and therefore harmonious life honours the memory of the Saviour's death.

The focus then turns to the social aspects of unity, as Ephesians calls the

---

9   Zetterholm suggests that it was particularly the Christ-following communities that restricted non-Israelite engagement with the *polis*, unlike other Jewish communities who were less restrictive to ethnic affiliates (Zetterholm 2003: 222–3). Despite differences in cultural responses between Ephesians and texts Zetterholm considers, Ephesians typifies the attitude demanding socio-ideological distance. MacDonald notes that Ephesians remained integrated within the urban fabric of its Greco-Roman setting although it shows a strikingly negative orientation towards the surrounding world (MacDonald 2004: 422–32).

10   *Peripatein*, literally: 'walk worthy of your calling ...', which summons the community to act honourably. The term 'walk' is used for a previous life in sin (2.2) and for encouraging lifestyles that demonstrate the honour of the community and her heavenly calling (2.10; 4.17; 5.2, 8, 15). Constructing *halakhah* for non-Israelite Christ-followers in Ephesians 4–6 makes use of the Jewish genre of instruction, explaining to non-Israelites how to behave as the people of Israel's God. The lifestyle discourse in Ephesians can be divided into the following parts based on the repetition of *peripatein* in chs 4–6. These instructions include: walk in unity (4.1-16); walk in holiness (4.17-32); walk in love (5.1-6); walk in light (5.7-14); and walk in wisdom (5.15–6.9); which are followed by encouragement for partaking in the spiritual warfare (6.10-20) and the letter conclusion (Hoehner 2002: vii). I have examined some of these together, for their thematic purposes.

community members to make 'every effort to maintain the unity of the Spirit in the bond of peace' (4.3); mindful of the unity of their confession (4.4-6). While the previous discourse explored the ideological and spiritual aspects of membership, that is, being united by God in 'Jesus Christ' (2.11-22) here the writer calls for a lifestyle that will both cherish and maintain what 'Jesus Christ' has brought together and reconciled with God. Ephesians brings together the Lord and his community in the confession 'One Lord, one faith, one baptism' (4.5). The unity of the group is essential for communal life and survival and Ephesians manipulates the discourse skilfully, merging ideological and social cohesion. Furthermore, unity is experienced on dual levels; with 'Christ' and within the group.

Although unity is only mentioned in 4.3 and 4.13 (Kreitzer 1997: 131), it is the underlying thought of communal ideology and social orientation, brought about by 'Jesus Christ' (2.11-22). It is presented as a non-negotiable characteristic of the community, likened to 'one body (of Christ)', 'one new person' and being united as God's dwelling in other images that stress communal belonging (1.23; 2.15, 20-22; 5.25-30). It is typical of communal self-enhancement to accentuate differences between categories and assimilate differences within categories, homogenizing variety focusing on commonality of identification (Brown 2000: 306). This is evident in the positive ingroup stereotypes that emphasize commonality and ingroup orientation towards one another in love and harmony, loading Christ-followership with prototypical values of blessedness and the unity of pious saints. This demonstrates how the social entrepreneurship entwines previously established communal ideology with its social orientation, while the former legitimates the latter. Furthermore, the fictional community is presented as prototypical and united, in order to evoke the members to replicate it in their social experience.

The reinforcement of communal beliefs also confesses belief in one God (4.6). In the examination of 4.4-6 scholars' focus tends to fall on either monotheism of the creedal confession (Lincoln 1991: 240; Best 1998: 370; MacDonald 2000: 289) or its Trinitarian reference (Reumann 1991: 121; Hoehner 2002: 516, 518, 521), which is typically related to how readers position Ephesians on a Jewish-Christian continuum. From a Jewish point of view, the confession may echo Israelite monotheism or its Pauline modifications (cf. Deut. 6.4; 1 Cor. 8.6; cf. Gal. 4.6; Rom. 8.14-17); but its boundaries are stretched extensively to accommodate placing 'Jesus Christ' at the centre of the Jewish symbolic universe. For example, Ephesians adds other beliefs alongside faith in 'one God' in verses 4–6. As a consequence, the monotheistic confession is transformed almost beyond recognition, as the creedal confession affirms belief in 'one Lord', non-Israelite calling and baptism together with 'one God', although the belief in one universal God provides the basis for the unity of ethnicities and different people in 'Christ' (Lincoln 1990: 241; Meeks 1983: 165–8). Furthermore, although Ephesians reflects typical NT belief of 'God as the Father of Lord Jesus Christ' (Schnackenburg 1991: 168) the communal confession uses a different formula, which installs a more communal creed into the discourse, in 'One God and Father of all'. These two factors typify Ephesians' reforms on Jewishness in light of the present values of Christ and non-Israelite inclusion, which seem to reinforce cultural and ideological connections with later Christianness rather than earlier Jewishness. The former characterizes Ephesians' values and beliefs, while the latter has to make room for 'Jesus Christ'. However, what often goes unmissed in Ephesians' scholarship is that the belief in 'One God' is immensely radical for non-Israelites, and it probably meant abandoning all others, whom Ephesians does not recognize as God(s). This alone would be hugely consequential for non-Israelites, their social life and networking in the Greco-Roman context.

The intertwining of ideological and social cohesion is an important motivational resource as it creates a desire to conform. According to Brown, ingroup conformity is typically motivated by dependence on others for information and legitimation, as well as by the achievement of group goals and the need for approval (2000: 165). In Ephesians the textual social entrepreneurship establishes conformity both socially and ideologically; mobilizing social processes that encourage 'togetherness' and reinforce the importance of cohesion to apostolic instruction, and by reiterating ideological convictions that legitimate the lifestyle discourse.[11] Social-scientific literature demonstrates that communal processes that encourage ingroup cohesion are often compelling and guide the members to redefine their behaviours in the light of the required standards in order to enhance their identification that brought them together in the first place (Pickering 2001: 177). Ephesians achieves this by linking communal ideology and lifestyle instruction, that is, by linking the divine election and the members' beliefs with their values.[12] Consequently, it is rather plausible that the community that was ideologically predisposed would also be socially predisposed to accept the social implications of the communal beliefs. All the more so, given that prototypical values that

---

11 Here the audience is encouraged to keenly uphold unity while the discourse provides the ideological reasons or motivations for this (cf. 4.11-16). Later the writer encourages social processes that reinforce ingroup norms, e.g. dissociation from the deviant (5.7-8) and exposing wicked deeds for communal correction (5.11-14).

12 For example, the cultural discourse in chs 4–6 is saturated with ideological reminders and motivations that build upon the previously established idea of pre-ordained sainthood (1.4; 2.10) and being God's 'masterpiece' (*poiēma*), his handiwork that like creation itself proclaims his glory (3.10; cf. Pss. 9.14; 14.25; Rom. 1.20).

draw from 'Christ' are positioned in the argument as essential aspects of what being 'in Christ' means (cf. 4.1, 20-24, 30; 5.1, 8-10).[13]

Ephesians' language of divine gifting explains communal hierarchy and spurs all of its members to action. In addition to unity and internal cohesion, the second fundamental characteristic of the prototypical ingroup model is the idea of divine gifting.[14] Having stressed the importance of unity the text provides divine legitimation for the diversity of communal roles, thus legitimating divergent social positions within the community (4.7-16).[15] The language of divine gifting has very interesting social consequences, as it (1) legitimates communal leadership structures, placing them beyond challenge or conflict as initiated by 'Christ'; and (2) imposes the requirement of active participation in the function of the community upon each of its members, as every member is responsible for the faithful operation of God's gift. This means that Ephesians' social entrepreneurship disguises both leadership structures and the requirement of cohesive participation in the ministry of 'Christ' as divine gifts: 'Christ' gave gifts to each member (4.7); and he also gave to 'some apostles, some prophets, some evangelists, some pastors and teachers' (4.11).[16] As noted

13   In the reading of 4.17–5.20 below I will proceed to discuss how the lifestyle of the faithful is contrasted with the sinners' slavery to malevolent powers and misdemeanour, while the communal discourse aims to transform non-Israelite believers into united and ideologically sound saints characterized by virtue and God's approval.

14   Divine gifts are not received by the ritual of apostolic laying on of hands (cf. 1 Tim. 4.14; 2 Tim. 1.6; Acts 6.6). Ephesians does not explain when or how the giving of gifts occurs, or whether this would be ongoing indefinitely, as assumed by charismatic Christianities. The verbs describing giving are, in fact, in the past tense (*edothē* in 4.7, *edōken* in 4.11), but the giving of gifts to each believer suggests that gifting might still be ongoing, just as the body of Christ could still be regarded as alive and growing, assuming that it continues to incorporate today's Christians. The use of 'Christians' for contemporary believers is deliberate, to highlight their different culture and weight of traditions in comparison to the Christ-followers of the early Church.

15   The reading focuses on key social functions of this passage excluding discussion of other interesting factors, such as the role of Ps. 68.18 in 4.8, although it would be relevant to Ephesians' Jewishness. See for instance Harris (1996); Lincoln (1990: 241–8), and Hoehner (2002: 523–38).

16   It is commonly thought that 'apostles and prophets' describe the first-generation leaders, while other roles refer to the existing communal roles. This is quite possible, given that 'holy apostles and prophets' are discursively positioned with Paul as 'recipients' of God's mystery, 'the revelation of non-Israelite inclusion' in God's people (3.5). This seems to refer to the early days of the movements and the ministry of Paul (and others) who laboured to make this 'mystery' known. These positions are discussed as a past phenomenon when Christianness 'was built upon the foundation of the apostles and prophets' (2.20). There is much internal evidence in the text to assume that this period has lapsed, as the absence of any conflict relating to these matters and the 'abolition of the Law' suggest. The differences between the structural leadership positions of Ephesians and spiritual gifts outlined in the undisputed Paul are also notable, and could witness a different Christianness (cf. Rom. 12.6-8; 1 Cor. 12, 14). While Ephesians recommends being 'filled with the spirit' the text gives no

in the discussion of shaping Paul's reputation, the exemplary apostle is portrayed as embodying God's empowering and gifting which is explicitly linked with the gifting of individual believers (3.7; 4.7).[17]

In my view, the discourse constructs an implicit hierarchy whereby Paul holds the supreme position (3.1-5), and communal leaders operate their gifting mobilizing the whole community in the transformation into Christ-likeness and maturity, while all are gifted by 'Christ'.[18] It should not be surprising that the whole community enjoys divine gifting, as it is 'the body of Christ' – if not, the body would be weaker and less able. This is similar to earlier claims that God's power exerted in the resurrection now energizes the members (1.19-20) and that they are symbolically exalted in the heavenly realms (2.6). In other words, being 'in Christ' results in sharing in his likeness, power and mission. It is also very interesting that here the members' identity is explicitly linked with the founding figures, 'Christ' and Paul, as the believers share in the gift of God's grace, given by 'Jesus Christ' and associated with Paul's unique ministry (MacDonald 2000: 289).

The egalitarian language of gifting stresses the importance of the participation of all members in the ministry, adding value to ordinary members of the community and reducing in some sense the hierarchical positioning of 4.11. Furthermore, it enhances their belief in a connection with 'Jesus Christ' who is here depicted as (the imaginary) communal leader, actively engaged in the life of the community. This makes a significant addition to the social remembering of 'Christ': he is not only the God-appointed Saviour of the communal past, but he is imagined to be actively involved with the life of the community in terms of appointing its leadership and sustaining the body of believers linked to 'Christ' and to each other, 'from whom the whole body, joined and knit together by every ligament with which it is equipped as each part is working properly, promotes the body's growth in building itself up in love' (4.11, 15-16).

Furthermore, the language of inauguration of ministerial positions by 'Christ' in 4.11 is similar to 2.11-22 and 3.1-13 (also 5.21-6.9, to which I

---

guidance for other charismatic experience, unlike e.g. 1 Corinthians. See for instance Lincoln for further discussion of Christ's gifts (1990: 248–53); and MacDonald for the discussion of Pauline leadership, later hierarchical developments and the transitional period reflected in Ephesians (2000: 298–9). Hoehner represents evangelical readings that maintain that these gifts are still operative in the Church, except he doesn't believe in prophecy in our context, but still maintains that missionaries are modern-day apostles (Hoehner 2002: 545–7).

17 Similar to Schnackenburg (1991: 174–6), and Kreitzer (1997: 124–5); contra Kitchen (1994: 75).

18 Maturity and Christ-like perfection are key metaphors for communal cohesion and ingroup orientation. Ephesians uses distinctively idealistic terms, challenging 'the corporate Christ-body' to match the perfection of Jesus Christ (Bruce 1984: 350–1; cf. Eph. 1.23; 3.19), although it has to be said, what is ideal is the imagined community in the text and its Jesus.

will return later), as it offers divine legitimation for communal life. This is hugely significant as the structures, leaders and activities of the community are granted divine legitimation; just as 'Christ abolished the Law' earlier he also authorized the leaders of the movement. Just as disregarding the Torah and socially contestable communal heroes 'Jesus Christ' and Paul, communal leaders are also divinely appointed and positioned beyond social contest. The community should regard their influence as a gift (4.7, 11ff.). This does not leave much room for a critique on their performance or character, but in a typical Ephesian fashion, consequential pronouncements relating to the life of the community are made as if complexities could not arise. Here the social entrepreneur grants power to the communal leaders, as does their positioning together with 'apostles and prophets', who have a particular role in the founding of the movement (cf. 2.20; 3.5). This is remarkable as Ephesians grants them an unlimited scope to exercise their influence: it neither sets paradigms for their authority nor does it describe appropriate leadership styles or explain what the community could expect from them or possible further appointees. Comparison with other Deutero-Pauline parallels is also interesting, as for instance, the Pastorals provide more detailed information about appropriate leaders and culturally appropriate leadership styles.[19] This illustrates again how the distinctiveness of Ephesians' social entrepreneurship is missed when it is interpreted in light of the rest of the NT.

The divine gifting is believed to facilitate the operation of the community as the leaders equip the saints (4.12); so that all members strive to achieve cohesion and maturity (4.13-14); and work together, ensuring the growth of the body of 'Christ' (4.16). The idea of the supernatural gifting of each communal member (4.7) and their spiritual empowering (1.19; 3.16) are not just 'mere rhetoric' but contribute to cohesion; explaining members' active participation in the community as a God-intended group ethos. What, then, are the communal goals to which members ought to direct their energies and potential? At least some of the roles could imply participation in communal recruitment.[20] The saints ought to partake 'in the work of ministry', which cannot completely exclude recruitment of non-members, as Ephesians refers to bringing

19   Cf. 1 Tim. 3.1-7, 8-13; 5; and Titus 1.5-9; 2. See also Stepp (2005: 111–91.

20   If 'apostles and prophets' refer to the founding figures of the Christ-following movement, the evangelists were probably itinerant recruitment agents, while the pastors and teachers would have represented localized leadership who explain traditions and gear the communities to cohesive belief and culture. The 'evangelist' and 'pastor' do not have equivalents in the undisputed Paulines, but seem to appear later (Acts 8.5, 40; 21.8; 2 Tim. 4.1-5; cf. Acts 20.28 and 1 Pet. 5.2). They are particularly associated with functioning as exemplars and social entrepreneurship safeguarding the community against deviance and ideological alternatives.

people to 'learn Christ' (4.20) and proclaim the Gospel of peace (6.15). However, Ephesians never launches a conversionist missionary sect or explains its recruitment ethos or practice. The passionate presence of the apostle and his urgency for mission are absent (Lincoln 1990: lxiii). Although the ministry of proclamation in 6.19-20 is particularly associated with the apostle, the members must, nevertheless, enthusiastically embrace proclaiming the gospel (6.15). However, the community seems to have a rather spiritual emphasis, as the ultimate mission of the church is to manifest God's wisdom to spiritual powers (3.10) and fight in the spiritual combat zone (6.10-20).

So the communal goals are not expansion or recruitment oriented (Lincoln 1991: lxiii; MacDonald 2000: 266), but the text is predominantly geared towards internal growth, articulated in terms of corporate development, described as 'building up the body of Christ' unto 'unity of faith', 'knowledge of the Son of God', 'maturity to the measure of the full stature of Christ' and 'growing into Christ' (4.12-15).[21] This leads me to assume that the 'equipping of saints for ministry' (4.12) is likely to involve teaching of communal values and beliefs to produce cohesion and motivation. In my view, these are likely to be the actual social goals behind the spiritual language of a unified confession and spiritual maturity in 4.1-16. Therefore it seems plausible to me that the real-life equivalent of 4.11 leaders are the operative social entrepreneurs of the community, who guide the members into required communal thought and culture. It is notable that there is no requirement to honour or obey them, but this is probably implied.[22]

Positive ingroup orientation boosts communal growth. There is considerable evidence that Ephesians' positive presentation of communal matter is focused on values, behaviours and social processes that strengthen the group and its members' networks within the group. There is, however, one possible exception in an earlier discourse that must be briefly considered when discussing the community lifestyle here. Previous ideological discourse proclaimed that the community is preordained for a lifestyle of good works (2.10), typical of Deutero-Pauline worldview.[23] This may have been motivated by ingroup processes to

---

21 What does God's power do in the community as there is no discourse of miracles or spiritual gifts, as in the undisputed Paulines? It seems that all power and influence is geared towards spiritual maturity and cohesion (cf. 1.17-23; 3.14-21).

22 Robert Goss makes a fascinating point that the writer neither expects submission to leaders, nor does the text actually state that they represent God (2006: 635). In my view, this could be linked with the fact that Ephesians does not discuss conflicts or complications, because if it did, perhaps submission to communal leaders would require explicit mention. However, this is unusual in comparison to household roles, where the submission of the inferior is non-negotiable. See reading 5.21–6.9 below.

23 Cf. 2 Tim. 2.21; 3.17; and Titus 3, who actively encourage 'good works'.

bolster commitment and cohesion; but it is equally possible that a kind and virtuous lifestyle may have had external functions, such as enhancing the reputation of the group. Rodney Stark's influential work on the rise of Christianity highlights the importance of social networks for the growth of the early Christian movement (1996). It is possible that communal love and kindness to non-members would have enhanced the reputation of early Christian communities and attracted potential new members. Stark suggests that a charitable and kind orientation of Christian communities would have drawn the attention of socially mobile sections of the population, immigrants, in particular, as the communal ethos offered security and hope to socially displaced people particularly, as they were in the process of establishing new social networks (1996: 74–5; 161–2). All the more importantly, he proposes that an actual conversion and new affiliation would take place when the attachments to members of the group outweigh their attachments to non-members; and groups would grow fast within existing social networks (1996: 18; 55).

Despite the fact that Ephesians makes no actual reference to its recruitment base or related strategies, Stark's view of communal growth suggests that the positive ingroup orientation, unity and 'good works' could have been influential in the growth of the community. Although 'good works' might have drawn positive attention to the group, it is possible that they are mainly displayed within the ingroup, given that the other language of recruitment and winning new members is absent. However, if the group manifested harmony, unity and kindness toward one another, it is quite possible that such values spilled beyond communal bounds. This could have enhanced the reputation of the group and made it socially more attractive to outsiders, especially as strong polemic against particular trends in their social context is not part of Ephesians' worldview and the discourse does not provide specific resources to hinder social relations, despite the author's generic cultural stereotypes. Openness towards social interaction is possible given that Ephesians does not promote strict separation, but we can plausibly assume that ordinary social networks remained in operation. However, on the other hand, Ephesians does recommend separation from the sinful (5.6-7) and the stronger the internal-external dialectic of comparison was the more the community members may have started to view non-members as potentially corruptive. Speculation aside, it is certain that Ephesians' social entrepreneurship is geared internally, providing little or no resources for communal recruitment. Instead, it is intended for promoting the identity of the people of God, their cultural change and safeguarding communally beneficial features, rather than expansion.[24] Furthermore, the text is only

___

24 As Lincoln has observed, it is the role of the leaders in the 'transmission and interpretation of the apostolic gospel and tradition that will prove especially constructive for

concerned with internal growth in 'Christ', when 'each part is working properly' and the body grows so 'building itself up in love' (4.16). In terms of the growth of the community, the body of Christ either thrives or shrivels depending on how compelling the discourse is in resocializing the members into a culturally and ideologically cohesive unit.

Nevertheless, the social entrepreneur imagines the threat of dissension, mindful of his or her social competition. The positive language of Christ-given gifts is accompanied by a negative warning of being ideologically unsound (4.14).[25] Immaturity is the opposite of cohesion and a major threat for social entrepreneurship: social dissonance could make the group unstable or break it up, and ideological immaturity would make the community vulnerable to the influence of unwanted, competing social entrepreneurs.[26] Therefore the positive instruction for communal growth is followed by the warning, 'we must no longer be children, tossed to and fro and blown about by every wind of doctrine, by people's trickery, by their craftiness in deceitful scheming' (4.14). This is reiterated later in 5.6 'let no one deceive you with empty words' (see 4.17–5.20 below). The constantly evolving early Christianness was by default a diverse socio-ideological location, where different traditions, cultures, beliefs and values flourished, and different identities were being formed and reformed. The NT bears witness to the phenomenon in numerous warnings against false teachings in different texts. For instance, both pseudo-Pauline Ephesians and Colossians contrast growing into 'Christ' with its antitype, being influenced by adversaries (Eph. 4.14; 5.6-7; Col. 2.16-19). Some social judgments were placed on the lips of Jesus (Mt. 24.4; Mk 13.5; Lk. 21.8) and others demonize sinful and ungodly people (1 Cor. 6.9) or lament one's own temptations (Jas 1.16). I suggest that because most of 'us' (readers of the NT) are theologically conditioned or positively predisposed, scholarship is all too often immune with regards negativity towards outsiders in the Bible (first testament and the second),[27] but such labelling and stereotyping is of enormous significance in the study of the social

---

the rest of the body' (Lincoln 1990: 255). The relationship between understanding the Scripture and the lifestyle of holiness and unity was a commonplace in early Pauline Christianness. Paul and Deutero-Pauline writers saw a connection between ideology and the social life of the group: the Christian identity that springs from communal Christ-centred values was seen as correctly understood when it was transformed into a harmonious and godly lifestyle in the group (cf. Rom. 15.4-6; 1 Tim. 6.11-12; 2 Tim. 3.16-17).

25   This introduces the pattern of entwined encouragement and warnings, which will dominate 4.17–5.20.

26   Such metaphors for immaturity seem to be common in NT thought, as e.g. infants in 1 Cor. 3.1ff and the pairing of the wind and waves in James 1.6-8 demonstrate.

27   Following renaming of the 'sacred canons' in the Queer Bible Commentary (Goss 2006).

attitudes of texts and their characters. So I would not assume their divine correctness but explore their cultural positionings and intentionality.

It is equally problematic that such warnings and stereotyping evoke mirror reading. For instance, Schnackenburg compares Ephesians with Ignatius' response to a 'spiritual crisis': diverse false doctrines, schisms, lessened enthusiasm for gatherings of the Christ-following movement and a reduced passion for its cause (1991: 35).[28] Similarly, Neyrey describes the world of early Christianities as a world of deception, hypocrisy and disguise, which caused early Christian leaders to demand their followers to be alert and not be deceived (1993: 42). Rather than explaining the warning by assuming a conflict (like Schnackenburg) or deliberate deceitfulness (like Neyrey), I propose that such warnings are examples of stereotypical othering of possible social competition, when diverse cultural positions, or even fellow Christ-followers with different socio-cultural views, were deemed socio-ideologically threatening and demo-nized in the discourse. In my view this is a rare glimpse into socio-ideological positions of early Christian authors, who categorized 'others' negatively for the purposes of self-enhancement of their particular point of view. For instance, Ephesians does not even give any explanation of what exactly the harmful ideas are (4.14, cf. 6.11), which is rather disappointing. This is an example of social exorcism on some unknown ideological grounds (cf. Pickering 2001: 38–46).

Warnings do not necessarily mean that a community was in conflict with particular groups or ideologies, or that their social environment was particularly deceitful, hypocritical or fraudulent (contra Neyrey 1993). Instead, one must remember competitiveness of early Christian ideo-logical positionings and shaping the discourse to promote particular ideas, whether we are considering fictional character in the texts or real authors and their communities. Similarly, the world of early Christianities was, 'religiously speaking', a pluralistic and polytheistic environment, where different philosophies were contemplated, and multiple identities and voluntary associations were a common place in diverse cultures. Consequently, given that Christ-followership originated among a Jewish minority, and developed as a further subgroup within it, culturally and ideologically foreign in the Greco-Roman context; it is then entirely possible that communal social entrepreneurs were simply socially aware and negotiated plurality of their environment, and the possibility of social competition as by default. Given that Christ-movement made bold claims and manifested social inflexibility towards other beliefs and cultures, the basic stance of the movement was vulnerable for competition and would have required ongoing social entrepreneurship to firmly establish itself. To

---

28   Schnackenburg refers to Ign. Eph. 5.3; 13.1 and Rev. 2.4; 3.15ff., for the letter to Ephesus and Laodicea.

push my point even further, it is possible that social entrepreneurs used positive ingroup orientation as a fertile feeding ground for sowing seeds of suspicion towards anything that represented outsiders' influence for the purposes of communal self-enhancement, particularly if they had no particular warnings to resound (like Ephesians).

Furthermore, it is important to consider the function of communal discourse in reinforcing ingroup orientation and intracommunal social networks. While persuasive ingroup rhetoric reinforces cultural sameness, cognitive and emotive aspects of identification, it mobilizes resources for identity negotiation and discourse with outsiders. Such resources are communally important as the success of ingroup social entrepreneurship relies on the ability to produce cultural sameness and socio-ideological cohesion, which hopefully result in strengthening the communal predisposition to guard the community against outsiders (cf. Fine 1996: 1182; Schwartz 2000: 254). Warnings against dissonance in 4.13-14 demonstrate yet another key feature of social entrepreneurship, illustrating what SIT refers to as the internal-external dynamic of comparing 'us' and 'others' (Jenkins 2004: 117). This means comparing and contrasting 'us' and 'them'; virtues and vices; good examples and bad. Demonizing the outsiders may also help; at least many NT writers add this to their discursive techniques, as does Ephesians. For instance, Ephesians uses the word *panourgia* for deceitful outsiders in 4.14. In 2 Corinthians it is used for the cunning serpent that misguided Eve in a similar context of ideological dispute over correct beliefs (11.3, cf. 1-6; cf. 1 Cor. 3.19). 2 Corinthians offers fascinating polemics, inventing 'another Jesus' and 'super apostles', as well.[29] Furthermore, stereotypical othering of external influencers also builds on the previous discourse which explained that Paul represents the divine revelation and correct understanding of 'the mystery of Christ'. This implies a contrast between the ingroup influencers and those outside: while communal leaders produce cohesion and facilitate the growth of the body into unity and maturity, the outsiders bring confusion and instability, and they are cursed (5.6-7).[30]

---

29   Cf. Schnackenburg (1991: 187). In addition, the book of Revelation is particularly strong in demonizing others: for instance, the letters to the seven churches speak about 'false apostles' (2.2); 'false Jews' and the 'synagogue of Satan' (2.9; 3.9); 'the devil' (2.10); personification of Satan (2.13); villains from the Hebrew Bible story (2.14); Jezebel, a 'self-acclaimed' female prophet, is accused of leading people into immorality and ritual uncleanness by violating sexual conduct and food Laws (2.20-23); and 'satanic' teaching (2.24). The seven letters use the prototype/antitype comparison with spiritual/Christological motivations, similarly to Ephesians, as reading of 4.17–5.20 will explore.

30   Cf. Gosnell (2000: 135–43); and Hoehner (2002: 561).

In addition to warnings and stereotypical othering of alternative views, Ephesians 4–6 develops different values and norms to frame communal social experience. Norms have a variety of functions, regulating the culture and social existence of the group; reinforcing group goals and contributing to their achievement; and enhancing and maintaining the identity of the group (Brown 2000: 60). While norms regulate behaviours by providing boundaries, it is typically supplemented in communal discourses with values that provide motivation for observing the norms. Both norms and values are expressions of ideology which ultimately determine the social direction of the group and thus establishing effective prototypical ingroup norms is important for the community, to provide 'frames of reference through which the world is interpreted' (Brown 2000: 59). In 4.13-14 we find that Ephesians gives such frames of a cohesive, mature, Christ-oriented community for social experience. Furthermore, prototypical maturity is contrasted with antithetical instability: cohesion is contrasted with being childlike, unstable, 'blown about by every wind of doctrine' and susceptible to being deceived by harmful views (4.14). Both adverse metaphors have a common denominator: establishing a positive ingroup orientation that strengthens positive communal association, cohesion and interpersonal bonds within the group. The community imagines 'Jesus Christ' as a divine agent, who is positioned at God's right hand in the majestic position of favour, victory and power (1.20). Positioning 'Christ' in this manner charges him with authority and boosts the identity of the community, who is imagined in a vital relationship with their Lord.

Ephesians' self-enhancement continues in two passages that broaden the textual construction of a prototypical community with stereotypical behaviours that derive from the ideological values of the community. The household relations (5.21–6.9) and the spiritual warfare (6.10-20) illustrate further aspects of the social and spiritual orientation of the community, providing further resources from the communal ideology to their worldview and negotiation of both social realities and spiritual beliefs.

1b. *Ephesians 5.21–6.9: Communal Household Relations*
The instructions for household relations are a significant addition to the construction of communal social paradigms and therefore cannot be dismissed from the discussion of ideological and social manoeuvrings of the text, although their discussion here is regrettably limited to key observations on how the household instructions fit into the communal social orientation, and how the social entrepreneurship positions itself with regard traditional, hierarchical structures of the society. It is commonly acknowledged by the scholarship that Ephesians' household instruction integrates traditional social roles in order, harmony and unity

(Brown 1988: 57).[31] The instructions reinforce a socially conservative communal cohesion strengthened by motivations drawn from the communal ideology and the sense of unity in 'Christ'. While on one hand, Ephesians demands countercultural distancing from the surrounding non-Israelite world and its impurity, it does, on the other hand, encourage conservative acceptance of social hierarchy and patriarchal models typical of the surrounding social world. Therefore, I suggest that unlike the reforms on Jewishness or distancing from non-Israelite culture, household relations are not countercultural, but insist on maintaining order and honour within established hierarchical positions.[32]

Like other parts of the letter, the discussion of households intertwines firm instructions with the ideological motivations reiterating Christ-followers' communal values. Although Ephesians opens the section with an idea of Christian servitude to one another, 'be subject to one another out of reverence for Christ' (5.21), nothing radical follows, as the social entrepreneur maintains the traditional social structures and power-relations between wives and husbands (5.22-33), children and fathers (6.1-4) and slaves and their masters (6.5-9).

> [5.21] Be subject to one another out of reverence for Christ. [22] Wives (be subject) to your husbands as you are to the Lord. [23] For the husband is the head of the wife just as Christ is the head of the church, the body of which he is the Saviour. [24] Just as the church is subject to Christ, so also wives ought to be, in everything, to their husbands. [25] Husbands, love your wives, just as Christ loved the church and gave himself up for her, [26] in order to make her holy by cleansing her with the washing of water by the word, [27] so as to present the church to himself in splendour, without a spot or a wrinkle or anything of the kind – yes, so that she may be holy and without blemish. [28] In the same way, husbands should love their wives as they do their own bodies. He who loves his wife loves himself. [29] For no one ever hates his own body, but he nourishes and tenderly cares for it, just as Christ does for the church, [30] because we are members of his body. [31] 'For this reason a man will leave his father and mother and be joined to his wife, and the two will become one flesh'. [32]

---

31   For discussion of parallel texts see Darko (2008: 75–81), and MacDonald for a more detailed socially interested discussion of the household relations in Colossians, Ephesians and in other early Christian texts (MacDonald 2000: 152–70; 324–42). MacDonald follows the work of David Balch on the NT Household codes as the ancient *topos* of household management (Balch 1981; 1988: 25–50; 1992: 380–411). For perceptive and relevant perspectives on women's role in early Christian antiquity, see Osiek, MacDonald and Tulloch (2005), esp. ch. 6, 'Ephesians 5 and the politics of marriage', particularly in conjunction with Darko (2008).

32   Although instruction is admittedly optimistic and naïve, providing yet another example of how social entrepreneurship dismisses conflicting scenarios, which are probably of particular concern for contemporary readers. For a discussion of domestic complications see Thistlethwaite (1985: 96–107); Mollenkott (2003); and Moulton (2003: 59–87).

This is a great mystery, and I am applying it to Christ and the church. [33] Each of you, however, should love his wife as himself, and wife should respect (lit. fear) her husband. [6.1] Children, obey your parents in the Lord, for this is right. [2] 'Honor your father and mother' – this is the first commandment with a promise. [3] 'So that it may be well with you and you may live long on the earth.' [4] And fathers, do not provoke your children to anger, but bring them up in the discipline and instruction of the Lord. [5] Slaves, obey your earthly masters with fear and trembling, in singleness of heart, as you obey Christ; [6] not only while being watched, and in order to please them, but as slaves of Christ, doing the will of God from the heart. [7] Render service with enthusiasm, as to the Lord and not to men and women, [8] knowing that whatever good we do, we will receive the same again from the Lord, whether we are slaves or free. [9] And masters, do the same to them. Stop threatening them, for you know that both of your have the same Master in heaven, and with him there is no partiality.

The subordinate is always addressed first but both inferior and superior binary positions are challenged to consider and respect one another. The traditional structures are merely enhanced with communal motivations as the discourse provides a godly incentive for both the powerful and the less powerful. However, although Ephesians is culturally radical when it comes to legitimating the community, and the writer is happy to renegotiate Jewish identity and cultural boundaries when it comes to the Law obedience, similar radicalism is not manifest in the positioning of the members in social relations. Although reforms on the Torah seem socially motivated in order to reform culturally unattractive initiation along with other restrictive cultural elements such as purity laws, Sabbath and food laws, there is no corresponding radicalism with regards household hierarchy. I cannot argue whether Ephesians' household code was in any way unjust or unequal in its ancient setting. Therefore I do not want to read my criticisms into the antiquity or judge social positions then, but rather I reflect upon the passage with twenty-first-century concerns in mind, processing its meaning in my setting.

If the social entrepreneur was culturally flexible for the benefits of his community, perhaps the community had a vocal presence of the dominant members (male, married with children, slave owners) and it was in the communal interests to maintain their position. Or perhaps the writer did not identify with female, children and/or slave members, or they did not have (or voice) any concerns. It is typical of Ephesians not to identify with the positions potentially regarded socially unattractive, given the stereo-typing of them as culturally suspicious. So, Ephesians reinforces the dominant positionings and turns the submission of the less powerful into spiritual matter, illustrated with their submission to Christ: 'wives, be subject to your husbands as you are to the Lord ... wives ought to be, in everything [subject] to their husbands' (5.22, 24); 'children, obey your parents in the Lord' (6.1); [33] and 'slaves, obey your earthly masters with fear and trembling ... as you obey Christ' (6.5).[34]

Despite providing ideological motivations towards fair treatment of the minor, Ephesians clearly reinforces the pattern of subordination, submission and the inequality of women, children and slaves (Schüssler Fiorenza 1983: 269). For instance, given that the text compares wives' submission to their husbands to Christ-followers' submission to their Lord, it is hard to imagine that its view of marital relations would be egalitarian: 'husband is the head of wife ... and just as [surely as] the Church is subordinate to "Christ", wives should be subject to their husbands in everything' (5.23-24). As if this was not already clear, the social entrepreneur returns to remind us that 'the wife should revere [lit. fear] her husband' (5.33). The metaphors that compare 'Christ' and husband speak of promise and provision. Therefore, the emancipative elements of 5.21-33 rely on the ability or willingness of the husbands to be 'Christ-like', caring, loving and exemplary, as the discourse portrays.

In my view, Ephesians falls short of the emancipative Christianness of, for instance, Galatians, where ethnic, social and gender divisions are disproved, as Paul imagines that 'all are one in Christ Jesus' (3.28). In other words, in Ephesians' world equality is a mind-set inspired by Christ, not an ideological or social basis for being 'in Christ' (contra Mollenkott 2003). Typically to Ephesians, in an ideal world, things would be perfect: women would have Christ-like husbands, children kind fathers who are not too harsh and slaves would have fair masters and nobody would be treated unfairly; and they would return joyous submission to the slave

33   The instruction for children and their fathers is very Jewish, reiterating, first of all, the fourth of the Ten Commandments, the principle that respectfulness to one's parents will result in God's favour (Exod. 20.12). Furthermore, instruction to the fathers encourages them to bring up their children 'in the discipline and instruction of the Lord' which probably refers to communal values. This seems to be Ephesians' equivalent for the Hebrew Bible's instruction to impress the Exodus events firmly into the social memory of the growing generations from the early age (Deut. 11.18-21).

34   The opening instruction in 5.21: 'be subject to one another out of reverence for Christ' is taken to introduce a new section and provide the key verb 'be submissive' to the following instruction (MacDonald 2000: 326). The introductory imperative turns the focus from a wider social context (4.17–5.20) to household dynamics between socially unequal members, explaining how communal ideology is contained in socially imbalanced positions. The instructions are typically naïve and disallow complications in mixed households consisting of both believers and unbelievers, and further social entrepreneurship was probably required to provide specific guidance to community members in diverse situations and circumstances (cf. 1 Cor. 7). It is regrettable that discussion in this study does not fully engage feminist scholarship owing to the constraints of space. For discussion on 'love patriarchalism' see Schüssler Fiorenza (1983: 233), and MacDonald (1988); for women's position in the *ekklēsia* see Økland (2004); as well as Osiek, MacDonald and Tulloch (2005).

masters, fathers and husbands. As usual, Ephesians discusses only social orientation, not complications, offers no discussion to address any complications, if, for instance, Christological motivations do not work: women are stuck with abusive husbands, or harsh fathers to their children, and slaves' only hope is the blessing that God has promised for their enthusiastic service, rendered as to God himself. Or if women, children or slaves are continually difficult or disobedient towards behavioural guidelines outlined in the pericope. It seems, like Schüssler Fiorenza states,

> The author was not able to Christianize [the household] code. The 'gospel of peace' had transformed the relationship of Gentiles and Jews, but not the social roles of wives, children, and slaves within the household of God. On the contrary, the cultural social structures of domination are theologized and thereby reinforced. (1983: 270)

She notes that such discourse cements the inferior positions with Christological motivations (1983: 270). This is highly significant. Similarly, Goss argues that 'Christ's headship is an oppressive model' and reasons that the image of self-giving love has never taken a strong interpretive hold in Christianity (2006: 635). In my view, there is further irony; the husband's dominance is likened to 'Christ' (5.23, 33).[35] Fair enough, one might think 'love one another as I have loved you ...' (John 15.12-13); but Ephesians imagines 'Christ' as exalted and holding all authority (1.20-23). I cannot help but ask, isn't comparing husbands to an exalted 'Christ' strange? In fact, the social entrepreneur could not have given any higher position to husbands in Ephesians' symbolic universe than likening them to 'Christ' – apart from comparing husbands to God.

Perhaps there is no better description for a deep commitment and binding covenant than that of marriage (cf. MacDonald 2000: 327; Hosea; Ez. 16.8-14).[36] Brown proposes an alternative motivation from Greco-Roman society, suggesting that marriage spoke of stability and order in a way that non-Israelites could understand (1988: 57). The fact that Ephesians included a household code (unlike Paul) resembling later NT writers, suggests that the social entrepreneur possibly had socially conservative interests in mind, and wanted to ensure a good reputation for the community, or appealed to its members as a reputable group that

---

35 Literally 'headship' (cf. 1 Cor. 11.2-16). It is also used for the dominion of the Emperor over Roman Empire (Goss 2006: 635).

36 Obviously, Ephesians' rhetoric is typically idealistic. But it is interesting that when we read Ephesians' comparisons of marriage, Christ and the *ekklēsia*, we tend to eliminate the idea of a covenant breaking down, as I am led to believe, also happened in antiquity (Mt. 5.31-32; 19.3-12; Mk 10.1-12; Lk. 16.18; 1 Cor. 7.10-11; Deut. 24.1-4). Could then covenant between Christ and his people could be annulled if, for instance, the conditions of Eph. 5.6-7 were fulfilled? The threat does not specify what would happen to the deviant Christ-follower, as opposed to the 'genuine outsider'.

embraced common conventions.[37] However, it is more plausible that the Diaspora Jews had similar cultural conditioning in what Brown sees as belonging to the 'pagan world'; and consequently, Ephesians' household discourse could reflect a common civic arrangement, not particular tailoring its values to please non-Israelites.

So while the writer is perhaps not a social activist, the discourse does provide ideological resources to cope with social circumstances and interpret reality in the light of an alternative ideology, for example, being mindful of spiritual rewards (6.8).[38] Most importantly, for the purposes of social entrepreneurship, the household code offers a sense of value for members, drawing countercultural values from spiritual realities not social relations. Thus the discourse provides dignity and humanity to lesser members in social relationships (Moulton 2003: 69), and challenges the superior to consider their position as subject to greater spiritual authorities and their responsibility to care for the members of the communal body (5.25, 28; 6.4, 9). This may have transformed the lives of the community members if idealistic harmony transformed social experience. Therefore, consistently to other sections of the letter, the communal ideology and remembering 'Christ' in the household instruction provides the basis for the communal social model, guiding the community to socially honourable behaviours and roles, whilst maintaining the framework of household relations acceptable in the eyes of the wider society.[39] In other words, 'Christ' is 'a vision of transformation' that provides a renewed social orientation of maintaining traditional forms which have been given new meaning (Moulton 2003: 87). In my view, Ephesians' Christianness gives the socially inferior 'something to feel good about', even if they could not expect their social conditions to improve.

In my opinion, this could be a further example of the writer's stereotypes that fossilize social relations and exclude alternative ways of thinking. Thistlethwaite has identified this function of Ephesians' social entrepreneurship and correctly points out that 'tying marriage to the divine-human relationship clearly divinizes male superiority in the relationship' (1985: 107). Readers engage with the text differently and readings of Ephesians' household code continue to elucidate both critical and positive readings, as well, like Moulton (2003), Osiek and MacDonald

---

37   Cf. Col. 3.18–4.1; 1 Pet. 2.18–3.7; Tit. 2.1-10.

38   For similar motivations to slaves in other NT texts see Col. 3.22-25; Tit. 2.9-10; 1 Pet. 2.18-25. Without passing judgment on their authors in a different world, nonetheless they appear unjust in today's social climate. For recent evaluation of slavery in Pauline scholarship see Byron (2008).

39   For the discussion of the persuasive power of the Christ-metaphors in the household code see Moulton (2003: 76-8). She concludes that '[B]y inviting humankind to assume its honourable status in Christ, Ephesians offers its readers a new self-understanding, leading to a new ethos, new attitudes and actions' (p. 78).

(2005), demonstrate, discussing emancipative elements and empowering language surrounding the image of the female body. Ephesians' social entrepreneurship organized social relationships, expecting respectful communal relations where men, fathers and slave owners rule over women, children and the enslaved. As divergent readings illustrate, the text may have enhanced communal cohesion in patriarchal households, reduced conflicts and prevented uprisings that might have endangered the reputation of the group. But it also sanctified oppression, of slaves in particular. This is an example of how social entrepreneurship uses Christianness and its various ideological components to legitimate communal norms, behaviours and social structures. And these norms have in turn shaped the social experience of so many people, and continue to do so, sometimes offering inspiration, motivation and hope for one's effort to lead a virtuous life in the spirit of loving one's neighbour, but all too often sanctioning injustice.

Finally, and very briefly, a comment on Ephesians' intimate image of 'Jesus Christ' as the husband figure for the communal bride. In my opinion, this is the most striking feature of the household relations, not their socially conservative, communally motivated respect and servitude (Darko 2008), but the use of a female body as an image for the community of Christ-followers (5.22-23) and the image of spiritual union as an illustration for marital relations (5.24-33).[40] As NT readers 'we' typically brush over any notions of intimacy in the imagery by, for example, implying that the purest love – *agapē* of God – must be the deepest love, and therefore comparisons to marital relations that are normally expected to be otherwise intimate, make perfect sense.[41] Not so Mollenkott, who que(e)ries the transvestite notions in Ephesians' imagery, which mixes images of the 'bride of Christ' (presumed female) and 'body of Christ' (presumed male).[42] Imaginations aside, this adds a new aspect into 'remembering Jesus Christ': apart from the saving and reconciling hero, and exalted ruler, Ephesians also imagines 'Christ' as a husband, who is

---

40   See Osiek, MacDonald and Tulloch (2005).

41   Just as 'Song of Songs' is about God and Israel; or Christ and the Church, not about erotic poetry and desire; or the wedding of the Lamb is a perfectly appropriate metaphor (Rev. 19.6-10).

42   Mollenkott continues, 'And if Christ's body is assumed to be a male body (as the power structures of the church still seem to indicate), yet the church itself is assumed to be female (as the numbers in the pews would still seem to indicate), then the church itself is a he/she, a transgender entity. Furthermore, since the men in Ephesus were called Christ's bride – and by extension, all Christian men were called Christ's bride – then the New Testament has used imagery of a same-sex marriage in which a "male" Christ marries not only Christian women but millions of male brides.' (Mollenkott 2001: 110). Similarly, Stuart who notes the transgendered images of Christ (male with a female body) and Church (female with a male head) which easily go unnoticed in traditional readings (2000: 32). See also Økland (2004: 51–7).

mystically (in the absence of a better word) joined to his people, loves them and cares for them. However, he also expects his covenant partner to be a picture of perfection; splendid, without spot or wrinkle, or any imperfection (5.25-32).

1c. *Ephesians 6.10-20: Social Orientation and Ideological Resistance*
The metaphor of spiritual warfare brings the discourse into conclusion and reiterates the language of spiritual awareness that underlines Ephesians' worldview. In the beginning of the discourse the establishing of the community was celebrated as the victory of 'Jesus Christ' (1.20-22), who rescued the people from spiritual oppression, and 'made them alive' for God, so that they would be his 'spiritual temple' and celebrate his grace and their status improvement with a life that fulfils God's plans (2.1-10, 19-22). It is highly significant that the letter closing calls the community for a spiritual – not political or social – battle as Ephesians imagines conflict in spiritual terms, not as political or social oppression (6.11-12). Alternatively, it could imagine spiritual oppression behind any socio-political conflict. Furthermore, given that sin is associated with evil powers and spiritual darkness (2.1-3; 5.3-16), the language of spiritual resistance seems to be another literary device to reiterate communal ideology, calling to embrace communal teaching and norms. The rhetoric implies that a failure to equip oneself with all God's armour, and withstand spiritual opposition, would be a victory for spiritual opposition.

> [6.10] Finally, be strong in the Lord and in the strength of his power. [11] Put on the whole armour of God, so that you may be able to stand against the wiles of the devil. [12] For our struggle is not against enemies of blood and flesh, but against the rulers, against the authorities, against the cosmic powers of this present darkness, against the spiritual forces of evil in the heavenly places. [13] Therefore take up the whole armour of God, so that you may be able to withstand on that evil day, and having done everything, to stand firm. [14] Stand therefore, and fasten the belt of truth around your waist, and put on the breastplate of righteousness. [15] As shoes for your feet put on whatever will make you ready to proclaim the gospel of peace. [16] With all of these, take the shield of faith, with which you will be able to quench all the flaming arrows of the evil one. [17] Take the helmet of salvation, and the sword of the spirit, which is the word of God. [18] Pray in the Spirit at all times in every prayer and supplication. To that end keep alert and always persevere in supplication for all the saints. [19] Pray also for me, so that when I speak, a message may be given to me to make known with boldness the mystery of the gospel, [20] for which I am an ambassador in chains. Pray that I may declare it boldly, as I must speak.

I suggest that the language of spiritual opposition is a rhetorical masterpiece that calls for communal obedience using a variety of illustrations of symbolic armoury and a fictional enemy.[43] The imagery of the spiritual battle positions the community as the army of 'Jesus Christ' who has overcome the enemy, but departed from the conflict zone to await a further strategic moment, when his rule will be enforced (1.20-23). The members must resist the devil, being 'strong in the Lord and in the strength of his power', so that they can stand firm in their commitment (6.10, 13). The image of the spiritual battle is defensive, rather than offensive, as it is geared to defending what God has achieved for them, rather than advancing into new territory with aggression. Similarly, the equipment is protective armour for a close combat (Hoehner 2002: 819-54). At the time of writing Ephesians the Roman military presence was a constant demonstration of the Imperial power, and the Roman world was 'saturated with the symbols of Imperial power' (MacDonald 2004: 424, 343). Therefore Ephesians' use of the battle imagery led by the one who is above 'all rule and authority and power and dominion' (1.21) is counter-political and highly charged, as it leads the Christ-followers to imagine themselves as somehow superior to Roman forces.

Social entrepreneurship proclaims the victory of 'Christ', drawing upon ancient ideas of the armour of a divine warrior (Isa. 11.5; 59.16-17; cf. Neufeld 1997; Gombis 2005). It combines traditional elements from the Pauline instruction of putting on the 'armour of light' and 'the Lord Jesus Christ' in moral resistance of evil, whilst accepting the socio-political power of the authorities (Rom. 13.1-7); and uses a similar idea of a battle against spiritual strongholds as 2 Corinthians (10.3-6). Nevertheless, in terms of military language, Ephesians' battle imagery is undeveloped, as it focuses only on the armour and does not imagine a battle scene, victory of the believers or triumphant return of the victors. The battle does not involve aggression or rough metaphors. Most importantly, the battle has already been fought and won by 'Jesus Christ' and the spiritual battle is about defending oneself against the devil and hostile powers (6.11-12).

The community must withstand and persevere, despite the spiteful activities of the enemy, the devil and the evil one (6.11, 16).[44] It is not explained what the devil wants, or how exactly he would harm the members, but the battle metaphors imagine a faithful and unyielding

---

43   See Neufeld (1997) for a detailed discussion of the passage and the Divine Warrior motif; Arnold (1989) for a detailed discussion of powers and spiritual beings in the antiquity of Asia Minor and their bearing on Ephesians' language of warfare; Faust (1993) for ancient parallels of battle-talk by generals to their troops; and Hoehner (2002: 817-66) for detailed analysis of parallels in other ancient texts, including DSS and LXX.

44   Ephesians regards the world as dominated by evil and it is most likely that the imagery describes a general attitude of ongoing readiness, although an eschatological battle is a possibility (6.13; cf. 1 Thess. 5.2-8; cf. 5.16).

community that takes to battle in their God-given armour, standing firm and victorious (6.13, 14ff.). This is a further example of how the social entrepreneur implants key communal values through various discursive manoeuvrings and metaphors. For instance, like their salvation and communal growth, the ability to withstand opposition relies upon divine empowering. Furthermore, the divine equipping involves a number of metaphors that reinforce their communal values as the elements of the spiritual battle equipment reinforce the core elements of their ideology. These include truth (6.14; cf. 1.13; 4.21, 24, 25; 5.9); righteousness (6.14; cf. 5.8-9); readiness to proclaim the 'the gospel of peace' (6.15; cf. 1.13; 2.14, 15, 17; 4.3);[45] faith (6.16; cf. 1.15); the assurance of salvation, experience of the Spirit and the word of God (6.17; cf. 1.13-14, 19).

The battle is fought in prayer which is a spiritual ritual that strengthens the members' commitment to God, which in all likelihood had an identity reaffirming the community cohesive function (6.18-20). Earlier social entrepreneurship included two prayers in which Paul is imagined to intercede with the audience (1.15-23; 3.14-21). These intercessions are immersed in symbolic language, petitioning for fuller experience, knowledge and assurance of communal ideology (beliefs about God and 'Jesus Christ'). Elsewhere in Ephesians spirituality involves thanksgiving and being 'filled with the Spirit' (cf. 5.18-20) and the letter closes reiterating the memory of the prototypical apostle who in chains requests for intercession (6.18-20). The imprisoned apostle spurs the community on in prayer, which is the demonstration of communal disposition: it involves an ongoing vigil, intercession and supplication on behalf of all saints, keeping spiritually alert, and in prayerful reverence of the apostle.

The battle symbolism reiterates the positioning of the community as God's people, in opposition to the hostile spiritual realities. The devil and his troops are positioned in direct opposition to 'Christ and his people' (Hoehner 2002: 828). Here Ephesians' social entrepreneurship makes an explicit point of discouraging political resistance and channels the community to focus upon spiritual matters, not in a battle against social structures or political rule, which are accepted as given. This illustrates, yet again, how social entrepreneurship avoids discussion of social complications and concentrates on ideological reaffirmation, without guidance on how to negotiate social relations; or how to respond to dominant culture and, for example, worship of Greco-Roman deities or the imperial cult.

The social function of the 'putting on the armour of God' is, in essence,

---

45   This is among the few references to communal recruitment in the discourse. While the apostolic mission is geared to the establishing of the community and negotiating the 'mystery of the gospel', i.e. the non-Israelites' inclusion in the people of God (6.19-20), the members themselves ought to be prepared to share the gospel, that is, the communal ideology.

similar to putting on the '*new anthrōpos*' 'created according to the likeness of God in true righteousness and holiness' (4.24), as the spiritual readiness reiterates concepts of the spiritual transformation taking place in their lives. In terms of social entrepreneurship, both metaphors highlight the importance of re-anchoring one's identity in a different symbolic universe. Therefore, it does not need to demonstrate any stronger social separation or sectarian stance than the language of identity negotiation elsewhere, given that it explicitly draws on same communal values, despite the fact that the letter climaxes in gazing at a soldier dressed for a battle ready to fight for his life. In my view, although Ephesians clearly imagines the surrounding social context as evil and gives ideological resources for social distancing, the social entrepreneurship is too ambiguous to be a deliberately constructed sectarian rhetoric.

Ephesians' social entrepreneurship is calling for a socially conservative resistance. In the same way as household relations gave new meanings to traditional social structures, the language of spiritual warfare offers a spiritual interpretation for social factors that problematize the lives of the believers. In other words, it does not promote political resistance or monastic separation. Instead the language of spiritual interpretation may actually calm sectarian notions, as the battle is not 'against enemies of blood and flesh', in other words, not against prevailing social or political order. In the same way, the battle tactics are those of determined resistance and defence, defending oneself spiritually. The key for the battle imagination, in my opinion, is that the language of battle is geared to reinforce the God-given provision of 'spiritual resources', which are socio-ideological resources that cause the believers to stand firm, realizing the effectiveness of their spiritual gear, despite any opposition they may face. Fictional positioning of members as divine warriors provides a compelling image of God's provision for them, which within Ephesians' symbolic universe, can only lead to victory. The battle image completes Ephesians' imaginary positioning of the community members in various situations, in order to explain further aspects of identity; here determined stance of resistance and spiritual vigilance.[46]

---

46 Non-Israelites began to value Christianness with increasing allegiance, even to the point of exclusive commitment and martyrdom in favour of maintaining their traditional cultural values. Lieu, among others, has discussed the stigmatization of the Christian movement and the social cost of membership and the causality of these factors in the forging of Christian identity. She discusses both accusations of early Jewish persecution and the strength of identification with Christ that led martyrs to an uncompromising loyalty to their confession in a hostile environment capable of the execution of ideological convicts (cf. Lieu 2002a: 135–50, 211–31). Lieu draws attention to the early Christian determination to reject other possible identities and to the reconfiguration of former social affiliations and structures (2002a: 229). She outlines how the early Christian martyr's identity is a self-description of conviction, protest and opposition: 'the exclusivity built into the martyr's confession and its

It is notable that in Ephesians believers are not sent to conquer, as victory has already been achieved by 'Jesus Christ' (Hoehner 2002: 818). This provokes the question that what is believers' warfare then about? Or can 'Christ's' victory be overturned? Although 'Jesus Christ' has conquered all cosmic and spiritual enemies and God has surrendered cosmic reign to him (1.10, 20-22) the fulfilment of his triumph is positioned in the future. This leaves the believers in an ongoing battle with the malevolent powers. Nevertheless, the battle is defensive and there is no need to wage war to change cosmic or spiritual realities. The social entrepreneur brings the discourse to a close by addressing his troops like a general,[47] channelling them into a socially conservative spiritual mode of resistance, where their main function is to safeguard their loyalty and 'be strong in the Lord' (6.10).

The discussion of prototypical models may be brought to a close concluding that the social entrepreneur uses prototypical discourses to reposition the Christ-followers in three ways: 1) communally oriented, as a cohesive and united group in which each participant is organically connected to the community, and gifted by God (4.1-16); 2) socially conservative, maintaining traditional positions whilst leading virtuous lives conscious of one's responsibility to do so before God in loyalty to 'Christ' and communal members; and 3) spiritually vigilant, politically moderate, oriented in faithful spirituality in the presence of opposing powers. Having outlined how the prototypical models of a harmonious community in 4.1-16 install a sense of cohesion and purpose (Lincoln 1990: 269), I will now turn to consider how social entrepreneurship constructs communal antitypes naming and stereotyping sinful non-Israelites. While the previous discourse has established and legitimated the distinctive identity of the community and their prototypical orientation in 4.17-5.20, the prototypical values of ideological steadfastness, holiness and function of the community are contrasted with the outsiders projected as antitypes for the community. The social entrepreneurship contrasts the required resocialization of the members by portraying non-Israelite heritage as spiritually negative and communally disruptive.

---

consequences coalesces with the opposition to society and to the world' (2002a: 229). This is achieved by constructing alternative values and configuring symbols that invert the familiar ones, inscribing a subversive identity (2002a: 229). See also Middleton for idealization of martyrdom in early Christian literature (Middleton 2006).

47   Lincoln offers an insightful interpretation of 6.10-20 as a *peroratio*, that is, an emotion-stirring and challenging conclusion that had a number of rhetorical purposes: 1) ensuring that the audience was positively disposed toward the speaker; 2) ensuring that they were ill-disposed toward the opposition; 3) exciting the emotional response, where the manipulation of facts was not uncommon; and 4) reinforcing the construction of formative memories by recapitulation (Lincoln 1990: 432).

2. *Communal Antitypes: The 'Gentiles', the Deviant*

This section provides most direct comparison of 'us' and 'them' in Ephesians constructing both communal identity and otherness. Ephesians 4.17–5.20 illustrates how social groups may utilize negative language and evoke negatively oriented social processes to achieve their societal goal of ingroup self-enhancement. This has been widely acknowledged in the SIT which assumes that biased intergroup comparisons and negative attitudes to outgroups are stimulated by the desire to improve self-perception and ingroup identity (Brown 2000: 334–6). Therefore, as Cohen suggests, communal culture is inherently antithetical (Cohen 1985: 115); and perhaps nowhere more so than in religious texts that polarize outsiders as condemned sinners, subject to God's wrath (Eph. 2.1-2; 5.3-6). I will explore how Ephesians repeats negative non-Israelite and outsider stereotypes which were used to characterize the audience and expands them with further description of non-Israelite otherness.

Figure 2 demonstrates the deliberate social entrepreneurship of inter-twining prototypical and antitypical language (left and right columns). The use of negative language is in **bold italics** to highlight the extent to which the instruction uses negative language or warnings, even in phrases otherwise describing lifestyle appropriate for the community members.

Figure 2: Construction of communal antitypes and prototypes in Ephesians 4.17–5.20

COMMUNAL ANTITYPES Non-Israelite lifestyle & deviance	COMMUNAL PROTOTYPES The lifestyle appropriate for the community
[4.17] Now this I affirm and insist on in the Lord: you must no longer live as the non-Israelites live, *in the futility of their minds.* [18] *They are darkened in their understanding, alienated from the life of God because of their ignorance and hardness of heart.* [19] *They have lost all sensitivity and have abandoned themselves to licentiousness, greedy to practice every kind of impurity.*	
	[4.20] That is not the way you learned Christ! [21] For surely you have heard about him and were taught in him, as truth is in Jesus.
[4.22] You were taught to put away *your former way of life, your old self, corrupt and deluded by its lusts,*	

COMMUNAL ANTITYPES	COMMUNAL PROTOTYPES
Non-Israelite lifestyle & deviance	The lifestyle appropriate for the community

	[4.23] and to be renewed in the spirit of your minds,[24] and to clothe yourselves with the new self, created according to the likeness of God in true righteousness and holiness.[25] So then, putting away *falsehood*, let all of us speak the truth to our neighbours, for we are members of one another. [26] Be angry but do not *sin*; do not let the sun go down on your *anger*,
[4.27] and *do not make room for the devil.* [28] *Thieves* must give up *stealing*; rather let them labour and work honestly with their hands so as to have something to share with the needy. [29] Let no *evil talk* come out of your mouths, but only what is useful for building up, as there is need, so that your words may give grace to those who hear. [30] And do *not grieve the Holy Spirit of God*, with which you were marked with a seal for the day of redemption. [31] Put away from you all *bitterness* and *wrath* and *anger* and *malice*, [32] and be kind to one another, tenderhearted, forgiving one another, as God in Christ has forgiven you.	
	[5.1] Therefore be imitators of God, as beloved children, [2] and live in love, as Christ loved us and gave himself up for us, a fragrant offering and sacrifice to God.
[5.3] But *fornication* and *impurity* of any kind, or *greed*, must not even be mentioned among you, as is proper among saints. [4a] Entirely out of place is *obscene, silly, and vulgar talk*,	
	[5.4b] but instead, let there be thanksgiving.

COMMUNAL ANTITYPES Non-Israelite lifestyle & deviance	COMMUNAL PROTOTYPES The lifestyle appropriate for the community
5.5 Be sure of this, that no *fornicator* or *impure person*, or one who is *greedy* (that is, an *idolater*), has any inheritance in the kingdom of Christ and of God. 6 Let no-one *deceive* you with empty words, for because of these things the *wrath of God* comes on those who are *disobedient*. 7 Therefore do not be associated with them. 8 For once you were *darkness*.	
	5.8b but now in the Lord you are light. Live as children of light. 9 For the fruit of the light is found in all that is good and right and true. 10 Try to find out what is pleasing to the Lord.
5.11 Take no part in the *unfruitful works of darkness*, but instead expose them. 12 For it is shameful even to mention what such people do secretly; 13 but everything exposed by the light becomes visible, 14 for everything that becomes visible is light. Therefore it says, "Sleeper, awake! Rise from the dead, and Christ will shine on you!"	
	5.15 Be careful then how you live, not as *unwise* people but as wise, 16 making the most of the time, because the days are evil
5.17 So do not be *foolish*, but understand what the will of the Lord is. 18 Do not get *drunk* with wine, for that is *debauchery*;	
	5.18b but be filled with the Spirit, 19 as you sing psalms and hymns and spiritual songs among yourselves, singing and making melody to the Lord in your hearts, 20 giving thanks to God the Father at all times and for everything in the name of our Lord Jesus Christ.

The use of non-Israelite deviance in stern warnings indicates the writer still thinks through ethnic categories. This challenges scholarship that concludes with the ethnic discourse in harmonious 2.19-22, emphasizing how Ephesians embraces ethnicities without differentiation (Yee 2005: 32; Darko 2008: 66, 110). While the opening charge makes explicit reference to non-Israelites and expands on their difference (4.17-19), and the second echoes the language of alienation from 2.1-2 (4.22), most of the stereotypes then address deviance and communally harmful behaviours more generally. Thus Ephesians demonstrates that self-enhancing communal discourses typically offer highly charged and polarized reflection of outsiders. Intergroup negotiation does not consider all the relevant data objectively, or take external opinions into account; but projects outsiders through lenses of communal ideology.

Barth points out that identity 'implies a series of constraints on the kinds of roles an individual is allowed to play ... the partners he [or she] may choose ... and defines the permissible constellation of statuses, or social personalities, which an individual with that identity may assume' (1969: 17).[48] The guidance for Christ-followers' lifestyle illustrates the Jewishness of Ephesians as the writer uses halakhic metaphor of walking (*peripateō*) translated with 'live' accompanied by a reference to a required lifestyle (4.17; 5.2, 8, 15; cf. 2.2; 4.1).[49] Thus Ephesians imagines the Christ-following community in Jewish terms, outlining here a lifestyle fitting for members of God's people, offering his own parallel to proselyte discourses that set the paradigms for affiliation of outsiders. This indicates that the writer adapts Jewish cultural models for sub-communal purposes, in the light of distinctive values of 'Jesus Christ' and full non-Israelite membership 'in Christ'. Consequently, believers whose primary cultural environment was Greco-Roman were faced with a radical resocialization and cultural change (Lieu 2004: 40).

The imperatives that use the *peripatein*: formula are: 1) 'you must no longer live as the non-Israelites do'; 2) 'Live in love, as Christ loved us'; 3) 'Live as children of light'; and 4) 'Be careful how you live'. The text explains the essentials of identity in very practical terms. These imperatives reiterate the key components of identity established earlier in the letter; namely the dissimilarity of believers with the surrounding non-Israelite world, their transformation and close relationship with God, and the responsibility of living according to God's plan. These instructions

---

48   Although Barth speaks of ethnic identity in particular, the wider aspects of his identity discourse process is more generally applicable. For a reflection on his earlier model of ethnic identity see Barth's later work (F. Barth 2000: 17–36) and its evaluation in Jenkins 2004: 104–7).

49   This is another example of Ephesians' strong affiliation with Jewish literature in general, and as Perkins suggests, the Dead Sea Scrolls in particular, which used 'walking in good works' to highlight the causality of knowing God with the godly lifestyle that results (Perkins 1997: 63–4). Further evidence of its widespread metaphorical use is found in Paul, who uses the term metaphorically in both negative and positive contexts (cf. 1 Cor. 3.3; Rom. 6.4; Gal. 5.16) as well as in other Deutero-Paulines (Col. 3.7; 2 Thess. 3.11).

highlight what is central to their identity as each *peripatein* clause is accompanied by a separate motivation: an explanation of the non-Israelites'/sinners' spiritual separation from God (4.18-19); imitating God, as beloved children (5.1); the transformation from the past darkness to light (5.8, cf. 2.1-6; 2.11-13); and finally, the examples of unwise and the wise people (5.15). The discourse signals appeals to the *peripatein* formula and uses it to reiterate key ideological concepts of the letter. It is also used to evoke their communal remembering by introducing a reminder of their transformation and, finally, it is used in the final appeal for the making of wise, not foolish decisions.

The non-Israelites' otherness is essentialized as the communal identity is enhanced. Ephesians 4.17–5.20 demonstrates that the construction of identity requires communality as well as difference against which similarity is outlined and the meaning of the group thus enhanced.[50] The reference to the ingroup and outsiders is an indication of the construction of identity at the boundaries. It is at the boundaries where people become aware of – and in terms of textual social entrepreneurship, are made aware of – their culture and its relation to others (cf. Cohen 1985). It is at these socially and discursively constructed borders (Bhabha 1994: 13) that identities and categories receive more detailed attention.

As previously established, Ephesians interacts with social reality through the discourse in which various aspects of ideological and social commonality and otherness function to construct the in-group and its significant others.[51] Given that 'names' or 'labels' are rhetorical extensions of categorization, they may be highly subjective and biased, as for instance the categorization of social actors in Ephesians demonstrates. Ephesians ignores the ethnic heritage of its community and projects them stereotypically as coming from 'the nations' (*ta ethnē*). Their otherness is formative both for shaping a new identity and the construction of 'the ultimate other': previously Ephesians used the non-Israelite otherness to construct a new identity 'in Christ', by projecting the former life of non-Israelites 'without God and Christ' (2.11-12), and the members' transformation as 'a new humanity created in Christ' (2.15). Here the otherness of the nations is reiterated and used to construct the 'ultimate other' for

---

50   For instance, Ephesians' constitution of Christianness makes reference to both Israelites and non-Israelites, reflecting the cultural matrix. For a discussion of Christian identity negotiated at the borderlines see Lieu (2004); and Boyarin (2004), who both discuss the social competition of emerging Christianness negotiated.

51   As established before, Ephesians categorizes people into three groups on the basis of their ethnic origin and religious affiliation: Israelites, those 'in Christ', and non-Israelite sinners. Having examined the relation of believers and Israelites in the previous chapter, our attention is now on the intergroup relations of saints and non-Israelite sinners.

Christian identity.[52] This is significant, for while 2.11-22 established the idea of discontinuity achieved by 'Christ', here in 4.17–5.20 the audience is challenged to ensure the discontinuity prevails and to realize the social dimensions of what 'Christ' had achieved on a spiritual level. In other words, the discourse presumes that Christ-followers no longer identify themselves according to their previous identity (dismissed by the social entrepreneur as 'foreign') but that they identify themselves as God's holy people and, consequently, position themselves appropriately in the social experience.

The 'essentialized otherness' of the nations is explained using negative stereotypes (Pickering 2001: 48). First and foremost, their otherness is theorized as a conscious distance from God:

> Now this I affirm and insist on in the Lord: you must no longer live as the Gentiles live, in the futility of their minds. They are darkened in their understanding, alienated from the life of God because of their ignorance and hardness of heart. They have lost all sensitivity and have abandoned themselves to licentiousness, greedy to practice every kind of impurity. (4.17-19)

This reminds us of an earlier description of the community, which was similarly positioned as alienated from God in chapter 2 (2.1-3, 13, 19). This betrays a crucial characterization of the audience: it seems that in the eyes of the author the non-Israelites have a socio-cultural default setting that causes them to 'live like non-Israelites'.[53] The ethnic reference suggests to me that Ephesians has not reconciled ethnic conflict, as such, but simply legitimated non-Israelite Christ-followers. His attitudes are still coloured by the stereotype that ethnically different is culturally different. This is very interesting as 'the nations' are discursively fixed into a subordinate status, characterized by impurity in the following antitypes which repeatedly contrast the lifestyle appropriate for saints with the ways of the ungodly. It seems that such stereotyping reinforces primary identification as Christ-followers and mobilizes group processes to strengthen Christianness further. It encourages structuring boundaries of identity and constructing limits and boundaries for what is acceptable and what is deviant (Dyrberg 1997: 173, 178). In other words, the social

---

52   The terminology in 4.17-25 corresponds to Rom. 1.21-29 (Hoehner 2002: 584). The idea of humanity separated from God derives from the writers' Jewish culture. Although Ephesians does not explicitly use the stereotype of 'Gentile sinners' like Paul in Gal. 2.15, the non-Israelites are discursively positioned as a negative example for those saved among their midst.

53   This could seem inconsistent with the fact that in 2.1-3 sinfulness was regarded as a universal problem (cf. Rom. 3.23; 11.32; Gal. 3.22). Ephesians' treatment of the nations in 4.17ff. is stereotypical othering as the writer reverts back to stereotyping considering the distance of non-Israelites from God.

entrepreneurship forces the community to the point of conscious decision that connects their nominal and virtual identifications, discovering what their identity is, and what it means in practical terms (Jenkins 2004: 76-78).[54] This is socially influential because it is when the identification is actualized in cohesive social behaviour that a community endures and maintains its distinctiveness.

Similar warnings against the corruption of the nations have been resounded in other Jewish communities, too.[55] For instance, Jubilees also contains warnings against walking 'after the Gentiles, and after their uncleanness, and after their shame' (Jub. 1.9 quoted in Lieu 2004: 281). Lieu discusses the use of the 'abhorrent Gentile' label for insiders in Jubilees and in the Halakhic Letter of the Dead Sea Community and Jewish texts othering deviant practices (2004: 281). She points out that one cannot know with certainty who is behind the mask of otherness, but somebody could be labelled 'Gentile' if their compromised standards suggested greater distance from God (2004: 281). This illustrates the imaginative entrepreneurship involved in the labelling of 'others'. Furthermore it also demonstrates how important 'the other' is in identity dialogue as stereotypes are used for rhetorical purposes despite their inaccuracy. Communal (even prejudiced) motivations are rhetorically more important than descriptive accuracy, as seen in Matthew's gospel, where a deviant (presumably Jewish) Christ-follower is socially exorcised as 'a Gentile and a tax collector' (Mt. 18.17). In other words, negative labelling and stereotyping is used to identify, condemn and eliminate deviance. So, for instance, Ephesians 4.17-19 translates the cultural difference of the nations into otherness and deviance, making it rhetorically unattractive, in the interests of communal norms, power and control (Pickering 2001: 204). This implies that Ephesians' social entrepreneurship is highly focused on the normative cohesion that the antitype of the non-Israelite other is designed to produce.

The comparison of these two groups, the nations fixed into a

---

54 Previously all people, even Israelites, were seen as sinners led astray by the malicious powers and passions of the flesh (2.3), but in chs 4–5 stereotypes return to the idea of the ethnic otherness of non-Israelites without Christ. This poses a challenge upon the non-Israelite believers: they must demonstrate with their conduct that they belong to Christ and they are not – like all other non-Israelites – futile and alienated from God (4.17). I suggest that Ephesians 4.17 demonstrates the writer's Jewishness while 2.3 indicates his Christianness. When remembering the Christ-event he concludes that all people need salvation in Christ. However, he considers the ethical implications of his ideology and lifestyle issues, but still stereotypically maintains that non-Israelites are the 'real sinners'. This could be prejudice, or just a rhetorical ploy. However, in terms of social entrepreneurship the devaluation of a subgroup identity would be a dangerous activity, unless the common identity (here, Christianness) is persuasively established (Esler 2003).

55 See Niehoff (2001), for discussion of Egyptians as 'the ultimate other' for Israelite identity.

subordinate status and the Christ-followers, is achieved using a discourse positioning in which each group is given stereotypical roles. These follow from identification processes and correspond with the polarized assumptions of communal ideology that shape communal behaviour and social orientation.[56] The social entrepreneurship uses the rhetoric of dualistic opposition constructing 'sinners' and 'saints', both formative to understanding what constructs the honourable behaviour expected of the community, as Figure 2 demonstrates. The alternating negative and positive voices, warnings and encouragements contrasts God's people with those awaiting his wrath and punishment. The instruction uses negative language widely, not only descriptively characterizing outsiders, but providing warnings within the discussion of the lifestyle of saints, too. The frequency of reference to deviance is significant: as the discourse intertwines the ideas of good and evil, alternating virtues and vices throughout. This suggests that the separation from non-Israelite lifestyle is fundamental to the social orientation of the letter because of their cultural difference and the threat that could pose to the community. The cultural reorientation is non-negotiable, as the introductory formula 'Now this I affirm and insist on in the Lord' suggests.[57]

Ephesians imagines non-Israelites 'greedy to practice every kind of impurity' (4.19) and the discourse betrays the writer's concern with the threat of deviance. The prejudiced view to other cultures is masked in the language that projects resocialization as an essential component of the new identity. As for all Ephesians' social entrepreneurship, the imagined divine legitimacy is fundamental to the prejudiced treatment of non-Israelites, too. The demonizing of the cultural other leads to pronouncement of God's wrath that awaits them (5.5-6). The distance Ephesians requires from non-Israelite cultures is often taken as given by NT readers, but was socially highly significant for early Christianities. As Lieu points out, 'the apostle to the Gentiles' made no effort to create continuity with

---

56 As previously established, the believers' common denominator is Christ-followership, and the interpretation of the Christ-event is central to the identity and culture it produces. Common faith also excludes non-believers and Christ becomes a symbolic boundary defining insiders and outsiders, constructing the community as a social minority group. For collective identification and communal boundaries see e.g. Jenkins (2004: 79–123), and Turner and Giles (1991: 48–79).

57 Ephesians uses *marturomai* which is a loaded term associated with the core of the gospel (MacDonald 2000: 301; Hoehner 2002: 582). The urge for resocialization and distance from 'Gentile sinners' is very similar to 1 Thess. 2.12, which describes how Paul and his associates were appealing to believers, 'urging and encouraging you and pleading that you lead a life worthy of God, who calls you into his own kingdom and glory'. More importantly, it reinforces the plea of Eph. 4.1, where the appeal for holiness of God's elect began. Although SIT perspective acknowledges that identity is fluid and negotiable, this is not how identities are presented in communal discourses, particularly of minority groups, who need to legitimate their position.

Greco-Roman cultures and identities, which are typically rejected and portrayed negatively in de-paganizing Christian literature (2004: 129).[58]

Once again the idea of divine authority rationalizes the socio-ideological manoeuvres of Ephesians; in this case, the use of 'nations' to provide communal antitypes of deviance and explaining the need for social distance, reinforcing ingroup values (e.g. 4.17; 5.5, 6) is reflected as God's judgment upon them and such values. Consequently, the stereo-typical othering jeopardizes non-Israelites' social relations with the ingroup (cf. Pickering 2001: 5, 49). This is an example of how stereotypes can function as social exorcism, maintaining the boundaries by fossilizing representation of others in a negative position (Pickering 2001: 43). The non-Israelite other becomes desanctified as their deviance is amplified and essentialized as the discourse transforms them into a subordinate type, serviceable for the discourse of identity (Pickering 2001: 76). This is, in some sense, the inevitable consequence of idealistic ingroup portrayal, which is often supplemented with the discussion of difference of others, just as self-enhancement goes together with discrimination of outgroups (Brown 2000: 306). In Ephesians we encounter positive communal stereotypes that enhance the ideals of holiness and virtue, and their antitype is similarly exaggerated, as utterly corrupted and wicked.

Ephesians seems to reflect a multi-ethnic 'diasporic space' where ethnic differentiation and polarization was commonplace (Westwood 2002: 42, 43). In my view, it is an example of colonial thought that travels to a new cultural environment, but devalues its diversity and seeks to eliminate the difference and the different, and operate under norms established in a previous social location. Although Ephesians disputes the Hebrew tradition of God's ethnic community creating '*new anthrōpos*' in 'Christ' (2.15),[59] the discourse, nevertheless, returns to a familiar basic assumption that non-Israelite culture is inferior. It assumes that ethnic outsiders require resocialization so that they would conform to the writer's norms and ideals, that is, separation of the righteous from the nations.[60] Furthermore, while Ephesians 2 explains the ideological meaning of the transformation in 'Christ' and discontinuity between past and present, here the discourse returns to the very ideas which were connected with the hostility and social conflict, and stresses the need for social discontinuity and cultural realignment. The text develops a set of instructions and examples, taking a negative view on non-Israelite culture, and points out

58   This is seen, for instance, in 1 Cor. 6.11; Col. 1.21-22 and in Eph. 4.17–5.20.

59   This contrasts both the Israelite idea of the ethnic covenant of God's holy people and Paul's in-grafting of non-Israelites into a cultivated olive tree (Rom. 11.13-24).

60   Parallel to Eph. 2.11-12 where the writer superimposed a culturally foreign collective memory upon its audience, demanding them to 'remember' their foreignness and cultural alienation.

the dangers of affiliation with 'the disobedient' (5.6). For instance, deviance is associated with 'darkness': those who are 'light', and 'children of the light', must shun darkness and avoid its 'unfruitful works' and produce 'the fruit of light' which is 'all that is good and right and true' instead (5.8-11). The darkness leads to secrets too shameful to mention (5.12) but the saints must bask in the light of 'Christ' (5.14).[61]

Ephesians could be encouraging performative racism. If identity, like Jenkins suggests, involves more than bearing a label, if 'the meaning of the identity is the difference it makes' in the lives of people (2004: 77) then 4.17–5.20 is of crucial importance for understanding the construction of identity in Ephesians. It is in this section where the meaning of identity is discussed on a very different level in comparison to other parts of the letter, characterized by self-enhancing harmony and unity of God's people. It is only in 4.17–5.20 that we fully appreciate that Christianness would have been a socially costly and demanding identity for its non-Israelite bearer in the late first century CE given their need for resocialization.

Sociological studies have also shown that the community members are drawn to conformity to normative attitudes, especially when the group is seen to be under pressure or threat from the outsiders (Brown 2000: 201–212). Painting the Greco-Roman cultural environment negatively may have contributed to non-Israelite believers' desire to resocialize, and to embrace virtual meanings of following Israel's Messiah. The fact that the community members were socially mobile and ideologically as well as culturally open is apparent in the fact that they had acquainted themselves to emerging Christianness, despite its cultural peculiarities, and Israelite history. Having attached themselves with the originally Jewish Christ-following movement they faced increasing social pressure to assimilate to new cultural forms, as Ephesians demonstrates.

Perhaps social entrepreneurship was successful in terms of implanting an idea of insufficient identity, which typically results in attempts to bolster one's identity. If so, then the Christ-followers could be likened to those who experience disadvantage due to their unenviable negative identity and as a result may seek to abandon their current social identity and join a more prestigious group, adopt new values and achieve a better status (Tajfel and Turner in Brown 1995: 180–1). This provides a plausible model for how the text was received by its non-Israelite audience in the original context. The favourable receipt implies receptiveness to the social influence of the text, which suggests they embraced the representative(s) of the movement as revealing the mysteries of the supreme God and operating on his commission, which could explain their willingness to

---

61   Ephesians' language of 'darkness' and 'light' in 5.8-14 echoes sectarian language of the Qumran literature (Perkins 1997: 117–18; MacDonald 2000: 313).

extensive ideological and social changes. Although the text provides the non-Israelites with spiritual and symbolic benefits, they are also disempowered by the discourse as they are compelled to reorientate their lives in accordance to foreign culture and new identity. This involves devaluing previous culture and social networks, accepting culturally foreign traditions to characterize and undervalue their past, as well as embracing a new symbolic universe and modified Israelite traditions as a basis of their identity. In my view, such colonizing attitude could be an example of what Westwood describes as performative racism (2002: 55). It is clear that the discourse positioning of ethnicities carries ethnic preference. Although the writer expands his or her cultural traditions to facilitate the inclusion of others, this comes with a price, as they have to accept cultural re-positioning themselves, in order to align their world-view, beliefs, memories and behaviours with communal ideology and social orientation. Therefore the devaluation of non-Israelite cultural heritage as well as social networks sets the Christ-followers in a counter-cultural opposition to the surrounding Greco-Roman cultural matrix. Therefore, in the social entrepreneurship of Ephesians, the difference that the identity makes in the lives of the believers involves a spiritual, ideological and social re-orientation of non-Israelite members.

Ephesians makes use of stereotypes to explain, predict and control social life. In my view, Ephesians uses stereotypes as 'powerful social myths' (Pickering 2001: 43), for the purposes of communal self-enhancement.[62] Stereotypes are useful as simplified, socially 'shared images' of categories of people that reduce complication in social interaction (Turner 1996: 14). They are not descriptions, but 'hypotheses about the world', which function like mental shortcuts for social judgments (Brown 1995: 96, 103). Stereotyping imposes what Pickering calls 'disciplinary power over people, the responsibility not to be deviant, not to cease patrolling between legitimacy and danger' (2001: 175). This is clearly taking place in Ephesians, which assumes a disciplinary power over its audience, and uses the stereotypical mode to restrict and limit people's behaviour, and influence their selection of social counterparts. For instance, behaviours that would threaten the harmony of the group, such as falsehood, anger, stealing, inappropriate talk, as well as bitterness, wrath, and malice, are

---

62 Pickering's explanation of the social function of stereotypical othering is worth quoting in full: 'The definition offered at the outset was made in the light of this critical difference between "self" and "other" in the stereotyping process, for stereotypes operate as distancing strategies for placing others in such a manner that will serve to point up and perpetuate certain normative boundaries of social conduct, roles and judgments, separating what is seen as threatening and disturbing from what is regarded as acceptable and legitimate' (Pickering 2001: 174).

disapproved of (4.25-31; 5.4), as well as maintaining networks with deviant people (5.6-7).[63]

Communal membership also limits their sexual experience by condemning some practices as 'fornication' and 'impurity' (5.3, 5). These are accompanied by 'greed' in 5.3, which are closely associated in Jewish ethical teaching. MacDonald reasons that Ephesians might be concerned with seeking economical benefits using networking with non-Israelites, cultivating relations with pagans for economical gain leading to compromising their standards (2000: 311). Although this is less convincing, she makes a further important observation on the nature of deviance in Ephesians: the discourse seems particularly concerned about the verbal and sexual pollution that would cause a loss of honour and reputation to the group and violate the boundaries of the holy community (2000: 315).[64] Some things are even too vulgar to expand upon in the discourse (5.11-12).[65] Ephesians also maintains that communal members themselves are responsible for maintaining boundaries for appropriate behaviours and they must be prepared to actively confront deviant members exposing their error (5.11).[66] Therefore stereotypes are used to promulgate

63   In other words, Ephesians condemns associations that would threaten Christianness, whether that be deviant communal members, who challenge strict norms and resocialization, or outsiders, who might challenge the culturally distinctive movement (cf. 2 Cor. 6.14–7.1).

64   Peculiarly, it is particularly the claims of communal secrecy and the sexual promiscuity of early Christian communities that drew the attention of second-century pagan critics of the movement (MacDonald 2000: 315). This is intriguing, given that Ephesians condemns immorality using stereotypes of pagan otherness, while later pagan critics make the very same accusation of Christ-followers. Interestingly, when comparing Ephesians and Paul's use of 'shameful' *aischros*, Paul's concerns seem rather innocent, as Paul regarded as 'shameful' particular women's hairstyle in vogue and their partaking in public communal discourse (1 Cor. 11.6; 14.35). In contrast, Ephesians warns about shameless people who 'having ceased to care, they have given themselves to licentiousness for every work of impurity with greed' (ET by MacDonald 2000: 303). Paul, of course, was equally unimpressed by a 'pagan's moral deprivation' (Rom. 1.24; cf. Col. 3.5). For a discussion of Pauline and Jewish attitudes to pagan immorality see Lincoln (1990: 276–9); MacDonald (2000: 303, 312).

65   Now this hardly refers to business dealings, contra MacDonald above.

66   Perhaps the resident communal leaders provide further instruction in matters the discourse leaves unexplained. Cf. basic moral instruction, referred to in 4.21-24. Confronting people of sin has a rather evangelistic tone of bringing about conviction of sin in 1 Cor. 14.24. But, as usual, Ephesians is less interested in winning over other or communal expansion. Perkins believes that the believers' role as 'moral agents in their world' extends to outsiders, which implies a possibility of leading them into conversion, like that undergone by the members themselves earlier (Perkins 1997: 118–19). Although Perkins correctly notes that their initiation presumes that processes of conversion are in place, nevertheless, Ephesians seems less concerned in solving wider social problems. In my view, the strategy of promoting strict countercultural communal norms and behaviours seems an unlikely recruitment strategy. It is more likely that Ephesians focuses on the internal affairs as the members are told to confront and oppose deviance.

boundaries, accentuate differences and to identify dangers and threats.[67] Therefore, Ephesians' stereotypes are not only socially shared, but also socially influential as they affect social processes and group relations (Tajfel 1981: 144–7).

In my view, stereotyping deals with complex social realities from a particular vantage point, with a particular agenda. They combine social characteristics with the fictive and imaginary, and with particular ideological or social motivations, such as social enhancement of the ingroup, or prejudice against the other. Ephesians uses stereotyping to project what being 'the people of God' means, constructing prototypical sainthood. First, Ephesians uses a direct comparison of prototypical and antitypical examples that provide rhetorical counterparts, contrasting appropriate and improper behaviours. For instance, what is 'fitting for the saints' provides the counterpart for pagan immorality (5.3); thanksgiving for inappropriate communication (5.4); and the experience of being filled with the Spirit is recommended instead of getting drunk with wine (5.18). Secondly, prototypicality manifests itself in ideologically loaded descriptions for the community, which include 'a new self, created in the likeness of God in true righteousness and holiness' (4.24); being 'neighbours and members of one another' (4.25); 'marked with the seal of the Holy Spirit' (4.30); 'forgiven by God in Christ' (4.32); 'imitators of God' and 'beloved children' (5.1); 'loved by Christ, who sacrificed himself for us' (5.2); 'children of light' (5.8); and finally 'wise people, who make the most of the time' (5.15-16); and 'a thankful, worshipping community filled with the Spirit' (5.18-20).

Ephesians' prototypical norms derive from the writer's Israelite traditions and adapting Israel as a model for what being 'people of God' involves. This further demonstrates how Ephesians imagines that believers 'in Christ' function in the position usually assumed by Israel in Jewish literature. Hebrew traditions are reformed removing the ethnic exclusiveness of Torah observance, but the distance from 'the nations' and outsiders is maintained.[68] Thereby, Ephesians condemns both the Law and lawlessness, using stereotyping to simplify social life and highlight what are seen as the essential characteristics of each group, namely a

---

67 See Pickering (2001: 174). For Esler's evaluation of the social function of Paul's stereotypes in Galatians see Esler (1998: 55–7). The language of the apostle is highly polarized and ideologically divisive, reinforcing identifications of, for example, 'Gentile sinners' (2.15), 'sons of Abraham' (3.67), 'sons of God' (3.26), 'those led by the Spirit' (5.16) and 'those of Christ' (5.24). Stereotyping creates socially shared imaginations that combine the cultural heritage of the apostle with his judgment of social affairs, as for instance, 'children of the free woman' and 'children of the slave girl' (4.31) demonstrate.

68 The distance from 'the nations' was a central feature of Paul's Israelite identity, too: cf. Gal. 2.15.

relationship with God and distance from the unholy and ungodly.[69] It uses intertwined good and bad stereotypes: those that *idealise* the ingroup and those that, as Pickering puts it, 'in the interest of order and control, *demonise* [others], making them figures of fear and derision' (2001: 40).[70]

Finally, stereotypes affect not only people's attitudes to themselves and towards outsiders, but also their reception by others and their social interaction.[71] If, as Pickering suggests, 'the purpose of the stereotype is to endorse the social or cultural norm from which it is alleged to depart' (2001: 176), then the stereotypes of non-Israelite sinners reinforce the cultural norms of the community of Christ-followers. The stereotypical non-members emphasize the idea of their otherness and the threat this poses to the group. Pickering continues,

> The satisfaction of thus fulfilling the norm is jeopardized by that which is projected outward as the departure of it. That which is made to inhabit the border zones of normality continually poses the threat of arriving back within its heartland as a subversive force, leading to further waves of expulsion as the only way to contain the danger once again. (2001: 176)

This has a significant bearing on the social relations of Christianness projected in Ephesians. The sinner is made to live at the periphery and the community should reject such people. Stereotyped outsiders are portrayed as threatening the virtuous communality (5.5-7).

It seems that the intensity of the non-Israelite cultural heritage greatly concerns the social entrepreneur; he seeks to exclude both the deviance and the deviant, as repeated instructions seek to ensure that deviant behaviours are not fostered among the community members. In my opinion, the social entrepreneur's concern about deviance provokes the question whether he doubted the intensity of resocialization that the transformation of believers in Christ involves?[72] This could be an example

---

69   Ephesians' social entrepreneurship presents both groups, the community and non-members, stereotypically, erasing variance and accentuating their key characteristics. Both prototypical community and antitypes for outsiders are discursively constructed and imagined, rather than actual signifiers of the groups and individuals they consists of.

70   In my view, Kitchen goes beyond textual evidence suggesting that the depiction of 'Gentile sinners' is 'one of pity which issues in compassion' (Kitchen 1994: 85). Such psychoanalytical speculation is unnecessary, and given that motives of correction and extending saving grace to non-Israelites are missing, it is also highly unlikely.

71   See Jenkins for further discussion of the consequences of stereotyping upon individual lives (Jenkins 2004: 168–71).

72   The writer does undoubtedly use powerful metaphors to illustrate the cultural gap, which seems to be a combination of spiritual slavery (2.2-3) and culture itself (4.17-19), unless the former is a metaphor for the latter. However, in the light of positioning Israel as 'children of wrath' (2.3) this is unlikely. In my view, just as the writer regarded humans 'slaves to sin' unable to break free from their condition that included certain behaviours, so too the cultural

of stereotyping due to loss of control (Gilman 1985: 20, quoted in Pickering 2001: 41). Pickering's model of social exorcism provides an interesting perspective on Ephesians' communal rhetoric (2001: 38–46). He suggests:

> Stereotyping always operates in relation to what is culturally ambivalent and thematically contrary within everyday life, and does so as a common-sense rhetorical strategy of naturalizing order and control. Stereotypes operate as socially exorcistic rituals in maintaining the boundaries of normality and legitimacy. (2001: 45)

The social entrepreneur responds to the threat of a deviant lifestyle by cursing the wicked and stressing their spiritual otherness (4.17-19; 5.5-7, 8-14, 15-17). The discourse of Ephesians not only demonizes sinners, projecting them as slaves to evil powers and subject to the wrath of God; it also exorcizes them, demanding saints have nothing to do with them.[73]

It cannot be known with any certainty if social entrepreneurship echoes frustration resulting from first-hand experience of cultural diversity or whether it derives simply from deeply embedded cultural stereotypes. For instance, the discursive voice betrays a mix of identifications and emotions:

---

heritage of a person may be likened to some kind of a bondage in a sense that a person is always biased and usually unable to critically assess their culture, or its faults and vices unless being exposed to other cultures or relevant ideas, otherwise a person would remain unaware of their 'bondage' to cultural heritage.

73   It is important to note that stereotypes may erode and lose their effectiveness. All stereotypes, like Ephesians' 'non-Israelites' are context specific. Although these were socially and rhetorically loaded when Christianness was emerging, they were soon replaced by Israelites who were stereotypically demonized and exorcized in second-century Christianness (see Lieu 2004; Boyarin 2004). In addition, it explains why Ephesians' 'Gentile stereotypes' might be little more than meaningless for today's reader, who is likely to strongly associate Christianity [deliberate use of term that would be anachronistic in the discussion of early Christianities] with non-Israelites by default; and on the contrary, struggle to perceive the Jewishness of early Christ-following movements. Pickering explains,

> [Stereotypes] have a historical basis. Despite appearances to the contrary, in common sense, such a basis is prone to change ... [t]heir rhetorical vibrancy and force is undercut by the contingent historical basis on which they depend ... Stereotyping is always a part of ongoing cultural processes and shifting symbolic relations. It is because of this that a stereotype may lose its common-sense value when it crosses into a succeeding period of different social group to the one in which it achieved wide circulation. Conflicting meanings may then come to the fore, or its own formerly unquestioned qualities be turned against it. This may help to undermine its previously effective exorcistic functioning, permitting individuals to see stereotypes as stereotypes and so "hold them lightly", allowing them to do their play rather than applying them aggressively or as absolute truth. It is because stereotyping processes are part of ongoing symbolic life that the ritualistic exorcism of any low-Other is never guaranteed for all time. (Pickering 2001: 45)

> Be kind to one another, tenderhearted, forgiving one another, as God in Christ has forgiven you. Therefore be imitators of God, as beloved children, and live in love, as Christ loved us, and gave himself up for us, a fragrant offering and sacrifice to God. But fornication and impurity of any kind, or greed, must not be even mentioned among you, as is proper among the saints. (4.32–5.3)

The writer seems concerned that his audience might ruin communality by deviance. This is strange as they were said to have been raised by 'Christ' from spiritual death to life (2.1-6) and one could assume that those so gloriously transformed and exalted by 'Christ' would not 'die spiritually' again. How could those that 'Christ' has brought near, in forgiveness and reconciliation (2.16-19), be alienated from God again (4.18-19)? How could those who have been sealed by God be lost again (1.13-14)? How could those who have been 'raised into heavenly places' (2.6) lose their inheritance in 'the kingdom of Christ and God' (5.6)? Or, if God's power now operates in the believers (1.20; 3.20) how would the spirit that 'works among the disobedient' take over again (2.2)? I suggest that sin is deviance to communal norms (4.17, 22). The text reveals an urgent concern that either habitual deviance or other more tolerant social entrepreneurship might gain footing in the community.

However, after negative stereotypes, Ephesians returns to discuss the novelty of a harmonious community and how wonderful households would be (5.21ff.) if everybody respected one another as members of the same body (and caused no social conflict by challenging the established social structures of the society).[74] It is as if remembering the work of 'Christ' (in the motivation clause 5.13-14) helps the writer to recompose himself and the tone of thanksgiving and focus on 'Christ' gradually returns, as the discourse moves from deviance, foolishness, drunkenness and debauchery to being filled with the spirit, singing and thanksgiving 'at all times and for everything in the name of our Lord Jesus Christ' (5.14-20; cf. 5.21–6.24). It seems that Ephesians' challenge of resocialization was socially costly for the non-Israelites as demand for the distance appears rather difficult and socially alien in the polytheistic Greco-Roman context in which Ephesians' social entrepreneurship presumably operated.[75] This demonstrates that Ephesians reinvents God's people and creates an inversion of the surrounding society modelled reflecting Israel's holiness and separation from the 'nations'. Consequently, holiness as God's people and separation from the unholy typify Ephesians' construction of Christianness throughout the epistle.

---

74 See discussion of 5.21–6.9 and 6.10-20 above.

75 See, for instance, Halbwachs' discussion of cultural foreignness of Christianity [sic] and how it superimposed new practices, like the eucharist and spiritual exercises upon its affiliates (Halbwachs 1992: 297).

Therefore Ephesians' Christianness is not ideologically novel, but it is a Jewish reform movement that gave new meanings to established concepts adopted from the Israelite cultural heritage of the earliest communal leaders. Therefore Ephesians' politics of identity involve 'a symbolic reversal of normality', when the writer re-evaluates non-Israelite cultural heritage in the light of the new ideological principles (Cohen 1985: 62–3).[76] In Ephesians 2.15 the reversal of normality involves a rejection of a dominant Jewish communal praxis, without their explicit replacement by counter-norms; but a symbolic reversal of normality in 4.17–5.20 involves quite a contrary move of transplanting Israelite culture norms into the life of non-Israelites, as the non-Israelite community is forced to reassess their heritage in the light of Israelite values, categorizing them as deficient (also in 2.1-3).[77] The symbolic reversal of normality, i.e. reversing values and practices outside the community, develops a distinctive 'we-ness' further, providing a contrast to outgroups characterized by other types of Jewish culture or non-Israelite, predominantly polytheistic worldviews.

Despite revisions to Israelite traditions, it is specifically in 4.17–5.20 where Ephesians betrays the author's Jewishness, which provides the model of othering 'nations'. In my opinion, the change of tone from 'being a sacrifice to God' to 'fornication, impurity and greed' is sudden and powerful, if not bizarre. It seems that the writer – who has spent a considerable time (1.1–4.16) in awe of God and 'Christ', remembering their achievements for the benefit of the believers – loses the spiritual-ideological momentum used to explain Christianness up to this point. Having just explained how the community body operates according to the divine giftings in unity and harmony, it is as if he all of a sudden, 'remembers' how detestable or difficult the non-Israelites actually are (according to his socio-ideological conditioning, that is); and the polemical discourse of sinful culture and alienation from God begins. The model of separation between the people of God and others is embedded in Jewish heritage and literature, as Judith Lieu explains:

> The Hebrew Bible has also been seen as archetypal in its construction of otherness as utterly alien and beyond negotiation, for it assumes that all other ways are false, alien to Israel's understanding of the true God and to her unique covenantal role in God's purposes. That 'the LORD your

---

76   Reversing 'normality' (dominant social forms or cultural expressions) can be used to emphasize and reassert norms, and to reject and replace them by asserting another norm to replace the dominant concepts (A. Cohen 1985: 63).

77   Further evidence for the reversal of Jewish normality is seen in the inclusion of non-Israelite Christ-followers and their chosenness in Ephesians 1 and 2. According to Jewish traditions non-Israelites were forbidden from entering the Israelite temple, but in 2.19-22 the writer sees them transformed and exalted, and transcending the sacred space of ordinary temples and synagogues by becoming 'God's dwelling'.

God has chosen you out of all the peoples on earth to be his people, his treasured possession' can become a licence to utterly destroy 'the many nations' who threaten the integrity of the people (Deut. 7.1–6). (2004: 279–80)

The cultural conditioning of the Hebrew traditions on Jewish (and Christian) discourse demonstrates that Israel's scripture has deeply embedded the idea of a uniform mask of otherness upon other nations (2004: 280). Furthermore, the scriptural language of non-Israelite otherness typically describes their impurity, pollution, uncleanness, abomination, and infection (Lieu 2004: 285). Furthermore, it also reinforces the alienness of the other and recognizing the threat it poses for the community of the righteous (Lieu 2004: 285). The prejudice against other nations is a highly significant factor in the ideological positioning of the text: the othering of non-Israelites seems to have more in common with Jewish polemical discourse than later Christianness. For instance, in the second-century Christian texts stereotypical othering reconfigures both categories of 'Jew' and 'Gentile': the former becomes loaded with negative aspects, while the latter is seen as the recruitment base for the Christ-movement, and the concept of the third race gradually emerges (Lieu 2004: 286–97).[78]

Here Ephesians seems to typify what Stark describes as a culturally revitalizing new movement that removes certain social problems associated with the affiliation of non-Israelites with the Jewish groupings. He regards Christianity as a 'revitalization movement within the [Roman] empire' that offered 'a coherent culture that was entirely stripped of ethnicity' (1996: 213). It may be the case that the Christ-movement accepted members from among any ethnic group and it may have been a more cosmopolitan and universalistic movement than, for instance, Jewish communities who had significant ethnic barriers and restrictive practices (Stark 1996: 213–14). However, in my view Ephesians is not 'completely stripped from ethnicity', as prejudice against non-Israelites betrays. Most importantly, although Ephesians has redefined common Israelite beliefs, it is, nevertheless, the non-Israelites, other ethnicities and nations that are constructed as the ultimate other in Ephesians' social entrepreneurship.

---

78 Therefore it seems plausible that a changing Christian discourse would reflect the changing circumstances and the antitype language seems to betray what was considered a threat to the movement. Thus it could be proposed that the process of gaining independence from Israelites resulted in antagonism reflected in the discourses of the period, while the popularity of the movement among non-Israelites would explain the reconfiguration of 'Gentiles' from sinners to the 'we Gentiles' of Justin Martyr (Dial. 41.3 quoted in Lieu 2004: 289).

3. *Social Entrepreneurship in Ephesians 4–6*

Ephesians' social entrepreneurship may have been compelling in its original setting, explaining how and on which terms non-Israelites are given the benefit of being counted among the people of Israel's God.[79] However, a critical examination of its social entrepreneurship suggests that spiritual and ideological dynamics are perhaps somewhat optimistic. It could be naïve to assume that a positive disposition toward 'Jesus Christ' would result in the spiritual transformation described in Ephesians 1, let alone in the social transformation required by the writer. Both spiritual and social consequences of the value disposition are interesting: Christ-followership could repel malevolent spiritual powers (2.2-3; 5.8) and give believers a new status as 'God's own people', which comes with spiritual resources (1.13-14, 19; 3.16, 17, 20; 6.13f.). When being 'in Christ' is seen not only as transforming spiritual dynamics, although it may provoke etic speculation and secular scepticism, it essentially positions itself beyond empirical verification. However, it is particularly when being 'in Christ' is projected as socially transforming that it invites closer examination. Ephesians offers counter-ideology geared to making non-Israelite primary socialization unattractive, so that non-Israelites' heritage and social networks would become unattractive and less consequential. However, it seems to me that even the author himself is unsure as to what extent the spiritual transformation, or the counter-ideology, or both, can guarantee a successful resocialization, as evident in his repeated warnings and negative language. If the believers were simply transformed from one 'regime' to another, from the slavery of 'evil' spirits and sin to being God's holy, empowered and gifted people, little or no caution or further persuasion would be required. However, Ephesians ensures that the communal discourse provides ideological resources to confront deep-rooted primary socialization and its powerful emotional and cognitive factors.

Finally, one more sociological model is required to illuminate the complexity of Ephesians' treatment of the non-Israelites. Pickering's sociology of the stranger provides an interesting theoretical perspective for understanding how non-Israelites were received in early 'Jewish

---

79 The appeal of a self-enhancing discourse is unquestionable: it seems reasonable that if offered a beneficial opportunity people are likely to accept any legitimation, within certain cultural and ideological paradigms, that makes them recipients of the available advantage. Consequently, if it was beneficial (spiritually or socially) for the non-Israelites to be counted among the followers of Israel's Messiah, Ephesians offers just the kind of modification that made the association more appealing by extending the blessings of Israel to nations without the inconvenience of Torah observance, the social ostracism it may cause or the pain of circumcision.

Christianities'.[80] The sociology of the stranger distinguishes between others and strangers: the relations of belonging are unsettled because strangers are ambivalent, neither central nor peripheral, and they exist in the contact zone between belonging and unbelonging (Pickering 2001: 204, 211–12). Strangers might have both negative and positive character-istics due to their location at the social boundaries (2001: 205). For instance, the non-Israelites are strangers due to their cultural otherness; although they are insiders, they are 'different' because of their cultural dissimilarity. They are labelled as saints, but doubt remains if they are willing and/or able to live according to communal norms. Therefore the social entrepreneur seems to endeavour to fully ensure that they will be properly, culturally as well as ideologically insiders, that they 'no longer live like the non-Israelites do' (4.17). The non-Israelites are, like strangers, difficult to position because they are 'neither socially peripheral nor symbolically central, but somewhere peculiarly in between' as they inhabit an anomalous, hybrid position which may upset fixed communal positionings (2001: 204). Furthermore, non-Israelite strangers are intrin-sically ambivalent: as they exist 'in the contact zone between belonging and unbelonging', as they resemble both 'us' and 'others' and they are 'neither Other nor not-Other' (2001: 204). This is why they become a target of stereotyping and a cause of social entrepreneur's concern.

Furthermore, Ephesians' degree of negative stereotyping suggests that 'non-Israelite-saints' are like strangers that the author accepts into the community, but not without reservations. He aims to resocialize the members to deepen their cultural assimilation and ensure their cohesion to appropriate values and norms that reflect Israel's traditions. Like strangers, the non-Israelites are not necessarily different, but they generate doubt inside the boundaries of identity. This is manifested in frequent appeals and warnings.[81] Ephesians regards non-Israelites as embodiments of evil or 'folk-devils': futile, ignorant, hard-hearted, licentious, corrupt and deluded' (4.17, 18, 22).[82] This aptly illustrates Pickering's description

80 Bauman describes strangers as 'undesirables', who 'bring outside to inside, and poison the comfort of order with suspicion of chaos' (1991: 56). The sociology of the stranger has developed in the studies of modernity and metropolitan urbanization. Simmel developed the notion of the stranger that preserved social distance in an urban environment where material distance had dissolved. For further discussion of metropolitan strangerhood see Pickering (2001: 205–9), and pp. 212–17 for evaluation of Simmel and Bauman.

81 Although there are no specific charges and accusations, but the vices seem to be rather general and stereotypical. However, those readers of Ephesians who prefer a more reconstructive method or mirror-reading would typically assume that the community struggled with liars, internal arguments, thieves, fornicators and the like (4.25-28, 31; 5.3-5).

82 See Pickering's discussion of 'folk devils' and 'moral panic theory' (Pickering 2001: 182–97). In my view, the ethnic prejudice in the accusing voice of the author betrays his cultural stance is suspicion of non-Israelites and concern about deviance they may introduce to communal life.

of strangers as an 'enemy within', who cannot be trusted without reservations (2001: 213): they are treated with some suspicion although theoretically seen as equal. For instance, Ephesians reapplies negative attitudes that its previous discussion tried to disarm, recalling the negative traits that separated non-Israelites from God. It is striking that 4.17 virtually repeats ethnic antagonism, pointing to non-Israelites as 'alienated from the life of God' (2.12), who are futile and their understanding is – not illuminated by the Spirit of God (cf. 1; 3), or by the relationship with God (2.12) – but darkened, because of their ignorance and hardness of heart (2.1-3). Ephesians may seek to forget ethnic hostility but it remembers non-Israelite otherness.

It is not surprising that a communal discourse would be suspicious of the culturally different, who exist between 'us' and 'them', similar, but different and thus they resist the very functions of cohesive identity discourse. In my view, Pickering's idea of 'the aggressive manoeuvres against strangers' arrives at the very heart of social entrepreneurship in Ephesians 4.17–5.20: the basic options on how to deal with strangers are those of assimilation and exclusion (2001: 213). The former is geared to elimination of the strangerness: removing the difference and assimilation into a similarity that resembles us; while the latter is about elimination of the strangers from social interaction to ghettoized spaces where they are beyond social engagement (Pickering 2001: 213). These strategies seek to transfer the strangers into either insiders or outsiders, and therefore, eliminate their strangerness and classify them according to their exposed characteristics that lie beneath the ambiguous strangers' persona, as they either become known or reveal themselves. Ephesians operates both of these options, promoting cultural assimilation, but retaining a threat of exclusion if assimilation fails (4.17; 5.5).

In my view, there is no textual evidence to suggest that Ephesians' negative attitude to outsiders would be based on conflicting goals or social competition between rival groups.[83] Instead, it seems that Ephesians' negative orientation toward non-Israelites is cultural suspicion or prejudice which featured in his Israelite traditions, in order to accentuate Israel's difference from the surrounding nations. Furthermore, it is all the more striking that such cultural characteristic is spiritualized and legitimated in the discourse as 'God's viewpoint'. Cultural stereotypes are clearly very persistent as most of us know from personal experience.

---

83 In his discussion of prejudice Brown suggests that conflicting goals and intergroup competition are significant causes of prejudice (Brown 2000: 245–52) and that superordinate, common goals do therefore ease intergroup tensions (2000: 252–7). While the latter provides a useful general model to accompany, for instance, Esler's discussion of superordinate identities for multiple subgroups of early Christ-followers (Esler 2003), Ephesians does not explicitly reflect competing groups.

When it comes to Ephesians, it is quite likely that its stereotyping was socially divisive. The idea of morally questionable non-Israelite cultures, which are without protective standards of Israelite tradition, poses a threat to a community that rejects Israelite Law but desires the purity it ensured. Curiously, what is rejected in Ephesians then is both the Law and Lawlessness.

4. *Conclusions*

The analysis of societal discourse in the second half of Ephesians (chapters 4–6) demonstrates that these chapters are essential for the textual construction of identity as they provide the paradigms for virtual identification, explaining what Christianness means for the community. Ephesians' social paradigms are based on the primary assumption that the community members must replicate Israel's holiness and distance from 'the nations'. This is achieved by simplifying the complexity of social life in terms of the 'we-ness' of the ingroup and otherness of outsiders. These identifications are then stereotypically embellished, resulting in the construction of a prototypical ingroup model, and its negative counterpart for non-Israelites as 'the ultimate other'. These are designed to lead the audience to assume that Christ-followers construct a holy community that is distinctive from the sinful otherness of the surrounding social world that awaits God's judgement. This explains why Ephesians disapproves the Lawlessness of nations and seeks to ensure that deviance is clearly identified and condemned in the communal discourse.

The social entrepreneur uses prototypical language to exemplify the positive behaviours of the ingroup, who must live a life 'worthy of their calling' (4.1). The first prototypical section portrays a socially and ideologically cohesive, harmonious community that benefits by divine gifting and grows toward maturity (4.1-16). Secondly, social entrepreneurship deals with ancient households and provides traditional hierarchical structures with communal values that derive from 'Christ' (5.21–6.9). There is no egalitarianism or radical reforms of traditional roles, but the discourse cements hierarchy of patriarchal households in the language of its divine sanctioning. Instead, the discourse provides countercultural motivations and thereby installs a sense of mutuality and submission to God, a reminder that the socially powerful and powerless are both servants of God and recipients of his blessing and retaliation. The third and final prototypical community model refocuses the group ideologically and spiritually, as the letter closes with the image of communal spirituality that reiterates key terms that remind of communal ideology (6.10-20). Although it uses military language it has a pacifying social effect as it turns the attention from political context and Roman Imperial reign to the reign of 'Christ', who has conquered the ultimate enemies, hostile spiritual powers. More importantly, the image of a faithful soldier, equipped by God, reminds us that communal identification is based on spiritual matters that provide the basis for ideology, social identity and the appropriate lifestyle.

While the prototypical ideals for communal life encourage commitment to group values and goals, Ephesians demonstrates that internal-external dynamics are important for identity construction. This is demonstrated in the construction of 'us' and 'others' with particular reference to the surrounding other cultures. Reflecting against non-Israelites in setting the social paradigms of the group suggests that communal links to Greco-Roman culture are probably more tangible than networks with Jewish groupings: social entrepreneurship does not make any reference to communal relations with Israelite groups, but instead, shows strong concern about how to distinguish the community from the nations, as the boundaries of Christianness are drawn against the non-Israelite world.

In order to explain what Christianness is and what it is not, the negative antitypes become a vital component of Ephesians' identity construction which intertwined positive and negative examples. First of all, communal cohesion and growth towards maturity is contrasted with immaturity in 4.13-14. This launches a series of motivations and warnings that construct the prototypical group and the ultimate other in 4.17–5.20. This is based on the dualistic ideology that people and cultures are divided into godly and ungodly. The negative stereotypes include condemnation of non-Israelite lifestyles characterized by futility, alienation from God, ignorance and stubbornness, and surrendering themselves to licentiousness, greediness for anything wicked (4.17-18). 'Former selves' are corrupted and lustfully deluded and therefore urgently require resocialization (4.22). Further deviant behaviours relate particularly to sexual immorality and communally disruptive behaviours that would threaten cohesion and harmony (4.23–5.20).

Ephesians imagines social life in terms of stereotypical dualism, which involves seeing things in 'black and white'. It could also lead to positive ingroup preference and a prejudiced othering of non-members. Thereby the social entrepreneurship seeks to turn non-Israelite Christ-followers into a cohesive community of God's people who manifest his holiness. This involves their resocialization, so that they would adapt a different socio-ideological framework, and an elimination of their cultural difference, so that the community would not be threatened by deviance. It seems that Ephesians treats the non-Israelite believers like strangers, who resemble both insiders and outsiders; the former by their identification as those who are 'in Christ' and the latter by their cultural heritage, which the social entrepreneurship regards as having a strong tendency to deviate from what is expected of God's people. The discourse operates a twofold strategy for dealing with non-Israelite strangers: first, the elimination of the strangerness: removing the cultural difference and its threat of deviance and assimilation of the dubious into a prototypical community model; and secondly, the elimination of the outsiders from social interaction to ghettoized spaces, beyond social engagement. In terms of social entrepreneurship it is highly significant that the text seems to complicate intergroup relations. First, the abolishing of the Law positions the community in conflict with the essential Jewishness of its day, and its language of unique revelation probably did the same (Eph. 2–3). Secondly, a negative view of non-Israelites would have complicated relations with Greco-Roman society (Eph. 4–5).

In the light of the previous discussion it seems fair to conclude that for Ephesians, Christianness is a primary identification that ought to characterize both values and behaviours of community members. The discourse defines social roles and positions that community members may assume, depicting belonging and otherness. Ephesians' social orientation, therefore, is characterized by a prototypical model of Christianness, empowered by God and devoted to his service in holiness in a strongly cohesive, closely knit community, where hierarchical leadership operates and traditional social disproportions are maintained. The community is constructed against the antitypes of outsiders and the deviant, who are portrayed as being far from God, stubborn at heart and corrupted by the evil they are keen to commit. The holy are contrasted with the deviant, as the salvation is contrasted with those who will perish.

Chapter 7

Conclusions

1. *Reading Ephesians and Exploring its Social Entrepreneurship*

This study has attempted to advance Ephesians scholarship by a methodical evaluation of the construction of identity and community, long acknowledged to be formative to the thought of the letter. Although Ephesians seems strongly concerned with identity and life of the believers, actual references to the community addressed are rather artificial as there are no specific references to any community members or discussion of circumstances of the community or its social setting. Therefore I have deliberately rejected a reading strategy which would seek to reconstruct the community from the letter or assume that communal circumstances would be mirrored in the text. The lack of detailed reference to Ephesians' community could result either from authorial intention to focus on matters considered more important or from social reasons, if the relationship between the writer and the community is rather superficial. Therefore we applied the model of social entrepreneurship, examining the shaping of social orientation of its recipient community, how the fictional community is positioned in the text and how this provides them socio-ideological resources and guidelines.

Given that Ephesians is a discourse that explains what being a non-Israelite Christ-follower means or should mean, the readings of Ephesians in this study have focused on the text and its discursive manoeuvrings testing its cultural contours, its Jewishness and Christianness.

Exploring Ephesians' social entrepreneurship was based on the hypothesis that each section of the letter contributes to the shaping of social orientation and ideological paradigms. It was further assumed that the social identity theory (SIT) provides the basic social-scientific framework for the discourse. This involves 1) a socially shared primary identification, Christ-followership; 2) self-enhancing discourse that strengthens primary identification and outlines its meanings and consequences for the community of Christ-followers; and 3) cultural renavigation that adapts Israelite models and rejects other cultures and traditions.

The study has demonstrated that Ephesians projects Christ-followership as a primary identification and simultaneously differentiates the

Christ-followers from 'others' who do not identify with this communal core belief, upon which all its social meanings are based. This would have had important societal functions when Ephesians was written, stressing the social consequences the belief in Jesus as Israel's Christ (and Saviour of the nations) is seen to involve. Such community-shaping discourse was particularly important for the emerging Christ-movement in the post-Pauline era as the movement developed and grew. The need for clear primary identification, together with consequential communal ideology and boundaries, was pressing for two reasons. First, Christ-followers' ideological convictions, such as messianic identification of Jesus and the inclusion of nations in God's chosen people in 'Christ', were presumably highly contested among Israelites, but curiously popular among non-Israelites, such as those addressed in Ephesians. Therefore the text engages in communal legitimation in order to provide a compelling explanation for the community, its role as God's people and distinctive-ness from others. Secondly, the writer sought to firmly establish Christ-followership among other ethnicities, providing cultural models for worshipping Israel's God and 'Christ'. This is seen in the resocialization of the non-Israelites so that they would internalize the story of Israel's god and the symbolic universe it requires, rejecting their cultural origins that contrasted with Israelite understanding of holiness.

Part One explored the construction of a positive communal identity in Ephesians 1, in the light of social identity theory. The construction of communal identity is achieved by drawing from Israel's traditions and beliefs relating to 'Jesus Christ' as exalted Lord and the saviour of the nations (1.15-23). The writer does not only use 'Jewish language' but maintains his cultural traditions and positions 'Jesus Christ' and his non-Israelite followers in a Jewish symbolic universe, celebrating their election in 'Christ' 'before the foundation of the world' (1.4) and covenant with God (1.13-14). Ephesians' construction of identity and socio-ideological meanings is achieved by positioning the fictional community in a symbolic universe, designed to inform and influence the ingroup, avoiding discussion of the recipient community and their actual social experience. Therefore the opening chapter reinforces communal identification and sense of togetherness using a language of divine legitimation and silencing any challenge to its contestable ideology. This is evident in positioning the discourse onto different symbolic universe, which provides counter-cultural resources for community building as the discourse invents non-Israelite Christ-followers a myth of divine chosenness. Ephesians' social entrepreneurship then revolves round this centre, explaining various ideological and social consequences of the Christ-event.

Part Two explored use of social memory to explain how the group fulfils God's plans and operates on the divine warrant, and what consequences this has to its members. As discussed in Chapters 3 and 4, this is achieved by remembering key communal figures, 'Jesus Christ' and Paul, who are used to justify communal beliefs and social positioning. Remembering is ideologically coloured by the need for communal legitimation and self-enhancement. For instance, Ephesians 2 legitimates Christianness which no longer obeys the Jewish law, shaping the reputation of 'Jesus Christ' so that it conveniently provides divine legitimation for communal culture. Thereby Ephesians distances itself from Pauline controversy on Law observance and positions the negotiation of Torah observance (anachronically) as already taking place at the cross. This discourse positioning dismisses the debate over terms of non-Israelite inclusion and alternative cultural paradigms for their membership in God's people.

One of the key aims of this study was to explore Ephesians' Jewishness and Christianness. The claim that 'Christ abolished the law' in 2.15 was seen as a test case for socio-ideological orientation of the discourse and its interpretation decisive to whether the text is seen as reflecting continuity with Israel, Paul and Jewish Christianities, or as a voice for increasingly distinctive Christianness that began to argue extensive reforms on Jewishness that eventually led to separation of the Christ-following movement from Israel groups. The meaning of 2.15 was considered using 'wandering viewpoints' in order to examine different reading positions and presuppositions; and how these lead to different interpretations and observations.

First, it is possible to read Ephesians in continuity with the hermeneutical position of 'New Perspective on Paul', stressing its Jewishness. According to this view that 'Christ has abolished the law' means a rejection of ethnic division expressed in cultural symbols of membership, like circumcision; while Israelite Torah observance was still retained. Consequently 2.15 and Ephesians is about negotiating non-Israelite inclusion and their new identity as members in God's household, to whom Israel's blessings are extended. Reading Ephesians from this position allows for two covenants, one for Israel and another for non-Israelites 'in Christ'. Similarly, it allows for diverse identities of God's people, whilst the 'newness' in 'Christ' (2.15) provides an overarching common denominator. However, one of the key weaknesses of this reading is that Ephesians lacks legitimation of ethnic Israel and stresses the need of 'Christ' to all people.

Alternatively, reading 2.15 from a different position highlights how the text promotes Christianness and speaks for the newness of all people, both Israelite and 'other'. This view acknowledges Israel's covenant, but this is seen both extended and reformed and the new base for membership in the 'new humanity' created at the cross, is 'Christ'. Reading Ephesians' social entrepreneurship from this angle highlights that relations with Israel do not seem consequential to the discourse: the Torah observance is portrayed negatively and 'Jesus Christ' inaugurates cultural reforms for his followers. This means that if Ephesians intended to project the people of God in terms of ethnic Israel nations in 'Christ', at least some aspects of its social entrepreneurship have failed as the text became associated with Christ-movement and new identity, increasingly unaccommodating for Jewishness. However, the weaknesses of this include that Ephesians refers to some Israelites in the language of reconciliation, making explicit reference to non-Israelites' inclusion into Israel's covenant, not her replacement.

The reading of Ephesians 2 also demonstrated that remembering 'Christ' is ideologically coloured and serves particular communal purposes. 'Jesus Christ' is remembered for the ethnic reconciliation as he reformed Jewishness and joined his non-Israelite followers into God's people as equal members. Thus his reputation is reflected in the light of the concerns of the writer, fixated with the idea of a non-Israelite blessedness. Consequently, Ephesians installs an idea of culturally reformist 'Jesus Christ' into communal memory, remembering a Law abolishing reformer of Israelite traditions, despite the fact that other early Christian stories remember Jesus as one for whom keeping the Law was important (Mt. 5.17-19). Therefore, Ephesians can provide an early, subtle example of later Christian texts that are 'engaged in a process of creating a difference between Judaism and Christianity' (Boyarin 2004: 27). Despite Ephesians' relatively early date, it seems that the writer stood at the inter-religious boundaries, intrinsically aware of his Israelite culture and heritage, yet drawn to redefine them, challenging the exclusivity of Israel's ethnic covenant, because he envisioned the election of the nations in 'Christ' before the world began. According to (t)his revelation, the community forms a spiritual dwelling for God: outside are the non-Israelites, with their sinful lifestyle, and the circumcision group with their particularism and social exclusivism.

Ephesians 3 provides the community social legitimation linking the group with the apostle and his teaching, although their relationship is not historically expanded upon. However, remembering Paul offers ideological legitimation as it invents traditions of Paul's supreme prophethood and unique revelation, contrasting Ephesians' revelation of God with Israel's former prophets and traditions. This provides divine legitimation for the community, which is thus assumed to be the chosen bearers and fulfilment of God's eternal plan. In my view, the memory of Paul's unique revelation functions as an umbrella covering the pseudonymous claims, for example, that the election and status of Israel as God's people are now extended to the community of foreigners in 'Christ' and that the law was abolished at the cross. Thereby, Ephesians anchors both 'Jesus Christ' and Paul in the myth of eternal God as both figures represent God's intervention in history and inauguration of the community.

The third part of the study explored the shaping of communal social orientation in Ephesians 4–6. Ephesians' social entrepreneurship culminates in providing the community with prototypical ingroup values that explain how the non-Israelites should 'be' Christ-followers and God's people. The social entrepreneurship fosters a strong ingroup orientation that provides communal togetherness and the discourse develops different models for 'living a life worthy of their calling' (4.1). This is achieved by intertwining positive and negative stereotypes that construct prototypes and antitypes for the community typifying virtuous and deviant behaviours. These are combined with ideological motivations such as reflecting Christ's love and forgiveness, 'being imitators of God' and children of light, not darkness, which reiterate construction of identity earlier in the discourse. The social entrepreneurship links communal ideology (belief) with social orientation (values and behaviours) throughout the letter, enhancing communal identification and togetherness.

Ephesians 4–6 contains three prototypical sections which outline appropriate functions and behavioural models for the community and one antitype discourse, where virtuous and deviant behaviours are contrasted, which I explored thematically starting with the models for communal life. The first prototypical section calls for unity and socio-ideological coherence which is extremely important for the survival of the community (4.1-16). This section also legitimates the divine appointment of group leaders, and implies a call for obedience. Secondly, the social entrepreneurship provides instructions for households, addressing wives and husbands; children and fathers; and slaves and masters (5.21–6.9). Although Ephesians makes bold cultural reforms in Ephesians 2, the household roles are conservative: traditional social hierarchy is maintained, although the text provides Christological motivations and promises God's reward for correct behaviour to children and slaves, despite social inequalities. Thirdly and finally, Ephesians rekindles the spiritual language that also opened the letter in the symbolic battle imagery calling for spiritual resistance (6.10-20). This closing section reiterates key components of communal ideology and pacifies any extremism or counter-political activism that may arise in response to Greco-Roman environs. The prototypical discourses demonstrate that Ephesians' social entrepreneurship seeks to produce a socially and politically conservative community which reflects their spiritual transformation. This demonstrates that despite denouncing the Law, Ephesians also denounces lawlessness, and mimics Israel in constructing a community which is sacred and set apart for God.

Ephesians also re-engages in ethnic reasoning projecting non-Israelites as culturally precarious due to their distance from Israel's God, suggesting that Christianness is not comfortably nested within Greco-Roman life, but resocialization. Ephesians imagines other cultures as communal antitypes in 4.17–5.20. The negative stereotypes result from discourse positioning at the cultural boundaries, which highlight both similarity and difference as the section compares appropriate and inappropriate behaviours. Furthermore, Ephesians 4–6 demonstrate that the social entrepreneur is not interested in conversion, but on normative cohesion: the discourse is not about making the group attractive and attracting outsiders to join, but keeping the group within certain cultural parameters and making the group socio-ideologically cohesive.

2. *Reading Ephesians and Exploring Emerging Christianness*

Reading Ephesians in this study has focused on shaping of emerging Christianness in the post-apostolic situation. While we can understand something of the early Christian movement reflected in the text, its relations with Jewishness and emerging Christianness, we are, nevertheless, faced with the silence the text leaves on some of the most challenging aspects of social life, which are left unexplained. We are left wondering how relations with Israelites might be conducted from their reformist viewpoint, which does not provide ideological resources to appreciate Israel apart from 'Christ'. Similarly, the community is not instructed as to how they should deal with the Greco-Roman world either. For instance, while the discourse imagines holy and harmonious community it provides no guidance for how to make this work in the diverse environs and social networks, despite denouncing both Jewish Law observance and lawlessness of other cultures.

Finally, having explored Ephesians' social entrepreneurship, it seems that the community was not threatened or persecuted – and there is little evidence to suggest it was – but the movement was socio-ideologically vulnerable to currents of thought and belief (4.14) and required legitimation in its challenging social climate. The language of divine legitimation was important to the group because it imagined possessing the ultimate revelation from God (3.5-6), despite the fact that all its core beliefs would have been contested minority positions. Ephesians' social entrepreneurship targets all key areas of communal ideology: 1) the belief that Jesus is Israel's Messiah and this is of consequence to non-Israelites; 2) its social consequences, that in 'Jesus Christ' non-Israelites are reconciled to Israel and join the people of God, and the law is abolished; and 3) cultural inflexibility, that required non-Israelite resocialization so that they would be separated from their culture and reflect Israel-like holiness. Ephesians responded to its diverse cultural matrix by self-enhancing discourse and compelling imagination which invented traditions of Jesus' Messiahship and non-Israelite election and led its readers imagine blessedness and God's favour.

BIBLIOGRAPHY

Biblical Literature

Novum Testamentum Graece, Aland, B. and Aland K. (eds), 27th edn, Stuttgart: Deutche Bibelgesellschafts, 1993.

The Holy Bible, New Revised Standard Version, San Francisco: Harper Collins, 1989.

Septuaginta: Id est Vetus Testamentum graece iuxta LXX interpretes. Rahlf, A. (ed.) Stuttgart: Deutsche Bibelgesellschaft, 1979.

Other Literature

Adam, A. K. M. (ed.) (2000), *Handbook of Postmodern Biblical Interpretation.* St Louis: Chalice Press, pp. 8–13.

——(2000) 'Author' in *Handbook of Postmodern Biblical Interpretation.* St Louis: Chalice Press.

Adams, E. (2000), *Constructing the World: A Study in Paul's Cosmological Language.* Studies of the New Testament and Its World. Edinburgh: T&T Clark.

Amit-Talai, V. (ed.) (2002), *Realizing Community: Concepts, Social Relationships and Sentiments.* London: Routledge.

Amit-Talai, V. and C. Knowles (eds) (1996), *Re-situating Identities: The Politics of Race, Ethnicity, Culture.* Ontario: Broadview Press.

Anderson, B. (1991), *Imagined Communities: Reflections on the Origin and Spread of Nationalism.* Revised edn of 1983 original. London and New York: Verso.

Appadurai, A. (1981) 'The Past as a Scarce Resource.' *Man* 16: 201–19.

Arnold, C. E. (1989), *Ephesians, Power and Magic: The Concept of Power in Ephesians in the Light of its Historical Setting.* SNTSMS 63. Cambridge: Cambridge University Press.

Aronowitz, S. (1992), *The Politics of Identity: Class, Culture, Social Movements.* New York and London: Routledge.

Asad, T. (2003), *Formations of the Secular: Christianity, Islam, Modernity.* Stanford: Stanford University Press.

Asano, A. (2005), *Community-Identity Construction in Galatians: Exegetical, Social-Anthropological and Socio-Historical Studies.* JSNTSup 285. London and New York: T&T Clark International.

Ashton, J. (2000), *The Religion of Paul the Apostle.* New Haven and London: Yale University Press.

Assman, J. (1995), 'Collective Memory and Cultural Identity'. *New German Critique* 65 (Spring–Summer): 125–35.

——(1997), *Moses the Egyptian.* Cambridge, MA: Harvard University Press.

Augoustinos, M. (1998), 'Social Representations and Ideology: Towards the Study of Ideological Representations' in U. Flick (ed.), *The Psychology of the Social.* Cambridge: Cambridge University Press, 156–69.

Aune, D. E. (ed.) (1988), *Greco-Roman Literature and the New Testament: Selected Forms and Genres.* SBS 21. Atlanta: Scholars Press.

Avery-Peck, A. J., J. Neusner, B. Chilton (eds) (2001), *Judaism in Late Antiquity, Part Five, the Judaism of Qumran: A Systematic Reading of the Dead Sea Scrolls. Vol. 1: Theory of Israel.* Leiden: Brill.

Balch, D. L. (1981), *Let Wives be Submissive: the Domestic Code in 1 Peter.* SBLMS 26. Atlanta: Scholars Press.

——(1988), 'Household Codes' in D. E. Aune (ed.), *Greco-Roman Literature and the New Testament: Selected Forms and Genres.* SBS 21. Atlanta: Scholars Press, 25–50.

——(1992), 'Neopythagorean Moralists and the New Testament Household Codes'. *ANRW* II, 26.1, 380–411.

Banks, R. J. (1980), *Paul's Idea of a Community.* Exeter: Paternoster.

Barclay, J. M. G. (1987), 'Mirror-reading a Polemical Letter: Galatians as a Test Case'. *JSNT* 31: 73–93.

Barclay, J. and J. Sweet (eds) (1996), *Early Christian Thought in its Jewish Context.* Cambridge: Cambridge University Press.

Barth, F. (1969), *Ethnic Groups and Boundaries: the Social Organisation of Culture Difference.* Oslo: Universitetsforslaget.

——(2000), 'Boundaries and Connections' in A. P. Cohen (ed.), *Signifying Identities: Anthropological Perspectives on Boundaries and Contested Values.* London: Routledge.

Barth, M. (1959), *The Broken Wall: A Study of the Epistle to the Ephesians.* Valley Forge: Judson.

——(1974a), *Ephesians. Introduction, Translation and Commentary on Chapters 1–3.* Anchor Bible. Garden City, NY: Doubleday.

——(1974b), *Ephesians. Introduction, Translation and Commentary on Chapters 4–6.* Anchor Bible. Garden City, NY: Doubleday.

Barthel, D. (1996), *Historic Preservation: Representing the Past in Great Britain and United States.* New Brunswick: Rutgers University Press.

Bauman, G. (1999), *The Multicultural Riddle: Rethinking National, Ethnic and Religious Identities*. New York and London: Routledge.

Bauman, Z. (1990), *Thinking Sociologically*. Malden and Oxford: Blackwell.

——(1991), *Modernity and Ambivalence*. Cambridge: Polity Press.

——(1997), 'The Making and Unmaking of Strangers' in T. Werbner and T. Modood (eds), *Debating Cultural Hybridity: Multi-Cultural Identities and the Politics of Anti-Racism*. London: Zed Books.

——(2001), *Community: Seeking Safety in an Insecure World*. Cambridge: Polity Press.

Baumgarten, A. (1997), *The Flourishing Jewish Sects in the Maccabean Era: An Interpretation*. SJSJ 55. Leiden: Brill.

Bhabha, H. K. (1994), *Location of Culture*. London: Routledge.

Beale, G. K. (2004), *The Temple and the Church's Mission: A Biblical Theology of the Dwelling Place of God*. New Studies in Biblical Theology. Downers Grove: Apollos, InterVarsity Press.

Beard, M., J. A. North and S. R. F. Price (1998), *Religions of Rome*. Cambridge: Cambridge University Press.

Becker, A. H. and A. Y. Reed (eds) (2003), *The Ways that Never Parted: Jews and Christians in Late Antiquity and the Early Middle Ages*. TSAJ 95. Tübingen: Mohr Siebeck.

Ben-Yehuda, N. (1995), *The Masada Myth: Collective Memory and Mythmaking in Israel*. Madison: University of Wisconsin Press.

Berger, C. R. and J. J. Bradac (1982), *Language and Social Knowledge: Uncertainty in Interpersonal Relations*. London: Edward Arnold.

Berger, K. (2003), *Identity and Experience in the New Testament*. ET by C. Muenchow. Minneapolis: Fortress Press.

Berger, P. (1969), *The Sacred Canopy: Elements of Sociological Theory of Religion*. Garden City, NY: Doubleday.

Berger, P. and T. Luckmann (1966), *The Social Construction of Reality: A Treatise in the Sociology of Knowledge*. London: Penguin Books.

Berlinerblau, J. (2005), *The Secular Bible: Why Nonbelievers Must Take Religion Seriously*. Cambridge: Cambridge University Press.

Best, E. (1992), 'Ephesians 2.11-22: A Christian View of Judaism' in Robert P. Carroll (ed.), *Text as Pretext: Essays in Honour of Robert Davidson*. JSOTSup 138. Sheffield: Sheffield Academic Press.

——(1993), 'Ephesians: Two Types of Existence'. *Interpretation* 48: 39–51.

——(1998), *A Critical and Exegetical Commentary on Ephesians*. International Critical Commentary. Edinburgh: T&T Clark.

Bieringer, R., D. Pollefeyt and F. Vandecasteele-Vanneuville (2000), *Anti-Judaism and the Fourth Gospel: Papers of the Leuven Colloquium, January 2000*. Jewish and Christian Heritage series 1. Assen: Royal Van Gorcum.

Blanton, W. (2007), *Displacing Christian Origins: Philosophy, Secularity, and the New Testament*. Religion and Postmodernism. Chicago: Chicago University Press.

Blasi, A. J. (1991), *Making Charisma: The Social Construction of Paul's Public Image*. New Brunswick: Transaction.

Bockmuehl, M. (1989), *Revelation and Mystery in Ancient Judaism and Pauline Christianity*. WUNT 2.36. Tübingen: Mohr Siebeck.

Bockmuel, M. (ed.) (2001), *The Cambridge Companion to Jesus*. Cambridge: Cambridge University Press.

Bodnar, J. (1992), *Remaking America: Public Memory, Commemoration and Patriotism in the Twentieth Century*. Princeton: Princeton University Press.

Boer, M. C. de (1980), 'Images of Paul in the post-apostolic period'. *CBQ* 42: 359–80.

Boyarin, D. (1994), *Paul: A Radical Jew*. Berkeley: University of California Press.

——(2004), *Border Lines*. Philadelphia: University of Pennsylvania Press.

Brennan, C. (1997), *Max Weber on Power and Social Stratification*. Aldershot: Ashgate.

Bronfen, E. (1991), *Over Her Dead Body: Death, Femininity and the Aesthetic*. Manchester: Manchester University Press.

Brown, P. (1988), *The Body and Society: Men, Women and Sexual Renunciation in Early Christianity*. New York: Columbia University Press.

Brown, R. (1995), *Prejudice: Its Social Psychology*. Oxford and Cambridge, MA: Blackwell.

——(1996), 'Tajfel's Contribution to the Reduction of Intergroup Conflict' in P. W. Robinson (ed.), *Social Groups and Identities: Developing the Legacy of Henri Tajfel*. International Series in Social Psychology. Oxford: Butterworth Heinemann, 169–89.

——(2000), *Group Processes: Dynamics Within and Between Groups*. 2nd edn. Malden, MA and Oxford: Blackwell.

Bruce, F. F. (1984), *The Epistles to the Colossians, to Philemon, and to the Ephesians*. NICNT. Grand Rapids: Eerdmans.

Bruner, J. and C. F. Feldman (1995), 'Group Narrative as Cultural Context of Autobiography' in D. C. Rubin (ed.), *Remembering Our Past: Studies in Autobiographical Memory*. Cambridge: Cambridge University Press, 291–317.

Buell, D. K. (2005), *Why This New Race: Ethnic Reasoning in Early Christianity*. New York: Columbia University Press.

Burke, T. J. and J. K. Elliott (2003), *Paul and the Corinthians: Studies on a Community in Conflict*. SNT 109. Leiden: Brill.

Butler, J. P. (1997), *Excitable Speech: A Politics of the Performative*. New York: Routledge.

Byron, J. (2008), *Recent Research on Paul and Slavery*. Recent Research in Biblical Studies, 3. Sheffield: Sheffield Phoenix Press.

Cameron, A. (1991), *Christianity and the Rhetoric of the Empire: the Development of Christian Discourse*. Berkeley: University of California Press.

Campbell, D. A. (2005), *The Quest for Paul's Gospel: Suggested Strategy*. London and New York: T&T Clark.

Campbell, W. S. (1992), *Paul's Gospel in an Intercultural Context*. Frankfurt: Peter Lang.

——(2006a), *Paul and the Creation of Christian Identity*. LNTS 322. London and New York: T&T Clark.

——(2006b), 'Unity and Diversity in the Church: Transformed Identities and the Peace of Christ in Ephesians'. Unpublished conference paper, SBL Annual Congress, Washington DC.

Carroll, J. T. (2002), 'The God of Israel and the Salvation of the Nations: the Gospel of Luke and the Acts of the Apostles' in A. A. Das and F. J. Matera (eds), *The Forgotten God: Perspectives in Biblical Theology*. Louisville and London: Westminster John Knox, 91–106.

Carroll, R. P. (ed.) (1992), *Text as Pretext: Essays in Honour of Robert Davidson*. JSOTSup 138. Sheffield: Sheffield Academic Press.

Castelli, E. A. (1991), *Imitating Paul: A Discourse of Power*. Louisville: Westminster John Knox.

Castells, M. (1997), *Power of Identity*. Oxford: Blackwell

Chalcraft, D. J. (ed.) (2007), *Sectarianism in Early Judaism: Sociological Advances*. London and Oakville: Equinox.

Cinnirella, M. (1998), 'Exploring Temporal Aspects of Social Identity: the Concept of Possible Social Identities'. *European Journal of Social Psychology* 28: 227–48.

Clark Wire, A. (2000), 'Response: Paul and Those Outside Power' in R. A. Horsley (ed.), *Paul and Politics: Ekklesia, Israel, Imperium, Interpretation. Essays in Honor of Krister Stendahl*. Harrisburg: Trinity Press International, 224–26.

Cohen, A. P. (1982), 'Belonging: the Experience of Culture' in A. P. Cohen (ed.), *Belonging: Identity and Social Organisation in British Rural Cultures*. Manchester: Manchester University Press.

——(1985), *The Symbolic Construction of Community*. London: Tavistock.

——(1994), *Self-Consciousness: An Alternative Anthropology of Identity*. London: Routledge.

——(2000), 'Peripheral Vision: Nationalism, National Identity and the Objective Correlative in Scotland' in A. P. Cohen (ed.), *Signifying Identities: Anthropological Perspectives on Boundaries and Contested Values*. London and New York: Routledge, 145–69.

——(2002), 'Epilogue' in V. Amit (ed.), *Realizing Community: Concepts, Social Relationships and Sentiments*. London: Routledge, 165–70.

Cohen, A. P. (ed.) (1982), *Belonging: Identity and Social Organisation in British Rural Cultures*. Manchester: Manchester University Press.

——(ed.) (2000), *Signifying Identities: Anthropological Perspectives on Boundaries and Contested Values*. London and New York: Routledge.

Cohen, S. (1989), 'Crossing the Boundary and Becoming a Jew'. *HTR* 82.1: 13–33.

——(1999), *The Beginnings of Jewishness: Boundaries, Varieties, Uncertainties*. Berkeley: University of California Press.

Condor, S. (1996), 'Social Identity and Time' in W. P. Robinson (ed.), *Social Groups and Identities: Developing the Legacy of Henry Tajfel*. Oxford: Butterworth Heinemann, 285–315.

Cormack, M. (1992), *Ideology*. Batsford Cultural Studies. London: B. T. Batsford.

Cornell, S. and D. Harman (1998), *Ethnicity and Race: Making Identities in a Changing World*. Thousand Oaks, London and New Delhi: Pine Forge Press.

Coser, L. A. (ed.) (1992), *Maurice Halbwachs on Collective Memory*. The Heritage of Sociology. ET and Introduction by L. A. Coser. Chicago and London: University of Chicago Press.

Cosgrove, C. H., H. Weiss, K.-K. Yeo (2005), *Cross-Cultural Paul: Journeys to Others, Journeys to Ourselves*. Grand Rapids and Cambridge: Eerdmans.

Countryman, W. L. (2003), *Interpreting the Truth: Changing the Paradim of Biblical Studies*. Harrisburg and London: Trinity Press International.

Crossan, J. D. (1998), 'Part II: Memory and Orality' in *The Birth of Christianity: Discovering What Happened in the Years Immediately After the Execution of Jesus*. San Francisco, CA: HarperSanFrancisco, 45–89.

Crossley, J. G. (2005), 'Defining History' in J. G. Crossley and C. Karner (eds), *Writing History, Constructing Religion*. Aldershot and Burlington: Ashgate, pp. 9–29.

——(2006), *Why Christianity Happened: A Sociohistorical Account of Christian Origins 26–50 CE*. Louisville: Westminster John Knox.

——(2008), *Jesus in an Age of Terror*. London: Equinox.

Crossley, J. G. and C. Karner (2005), 'Writing History. Constructing Religion' in J. G. Crossley and C. Karner (eds), *Writing History, Constructing Religion*. Aldershot and Burlington: Ashgate, 3–8.

Dahl, N. A. (1978), 'Interpreting Ephesians: Then and Now'. *Currents in Theology and Mission* 5: 133–43.

——(1991), 'The Messiahship of Jesus in Paul' in D. H. Juel (ed.), *Jesus*

the Christ: the Historical Origins of the Christological Doctrine.
Minneapolis: Fortress Press, 15–25.

——(2000), *Studies in Ephesians: Introductory Questions, Text- and Edition Critical Issues, Interpretation of Texts and Themes.* D. Hellholm, V. Blomqvist and T. Fornberg (eds). Tübingen: Mohr Siebeck.

d'Anjou, L. (1995), *Social Movements and Cultural Change: the First Abolition Campaign Revisited.* New York: de Gruyter.

Darko, D. K. (2008), *No Longer Living as the Gentiles: Differentiation and Shared Ethical Values in Ephesians 4.17–6.9.* LNTS 375. London and New York: T&T Clark.

Das, A. A. and F. J. Matera (eds) (2002), *The Forgotten God: Perspectives in Biblical Theology.* Louisville and London: Westminster John Knox.

Davis, L. J. (1987), *Resisting Novels: Ideology and Fiction.* London: Routledge.

Dawes, G. W. (1998), *The Body in Question: Metaphor and Meaning in the Interpretation of Ephesians 5.21-33.* Biblical Interpretation 30. Leiden: Brill.

Day, J. (ed.) (2005), *Temple and Worship in Biblical Israel.* JSOTSup 422. London: T&T Clark.

DeSoucey, M., J.-E. Pozner, C. Fields, K. Dobransky and G. A. Fine (2008), 'Memory and Sacrifice: an Embodied Theory of Martyrdom.' *Cultural Sociology* 2: 99–121.

Diel, P. (1985), *Symbolism in the Bible: The Universality of Symbolic Language and its Psychological Significance.* ET by N. Marans. San Francisco: Harper & Row.

Dodd, C. H. (1952), *Social and Cultural Factors in Church Divisions.* Faith and Order Commission of the World Council of Churches. London: SCM.

Donaldson, T. L. (1997), *Paul and the Gentiles: Remapping the Apostle's Convictional World.* Minneapolis: Fortress Press.

——(2006), 'Jewish Christianity, Israel's Stumbling and the *Sonderweg* Reading of Paul'. *JSNT* 29.1: 27–54.

Duling, D. C. (2006), 'Social Memory and Biblical Studies: Theory, Method, and Application'. *BTB* 36: 2–4.

Dunn, J. D. G. (1983), 'New Perspective on Paul'. *BJRL* 65: 95–122.

——(1990), *Jesus, Paul and the Law: Studies in Mark and Galatians.* London: SPCK.

——(1991), *The Partings of Ways.* London: SCM.

——(1993), 'Anti-Semitism in the Deutero-Pauline Literature' in C. A. Evans and D. A. Hagner (eds), *Anti-Semitism and Early Christianity: Issues of Polemic and Faith.* Minneapolis: Fortress, 151–65.

——(1996) *The Epistles to the Colossians and to Philemon: A Commentary on the Greek Text*. NIGTC. Grand Rapids: Eerdmans and Carlisle: Paternoster.

——(1999), 'Who did Paul Think He Was? A Study of Jewish Christian Identity. *NTS* 45: 174–93.

——(2003), *Jesus Remembered: Christianity in the Making*. Vol. 1. Grand Rapids: Eerdmans.

——(2005), *A New Perspective on Jesus: What the Quest for the Historical Jesus Missed*. Grand Rapids: Baker Academic.

Dunn, J. D. G. (ed.) (1992), *Jews and Christians: The Parting of Ways AD 70 to 135*. WUNT 66. Tübingen: Mohr Siebeck.

Dyck, J. E. (1998), *The Theocratic Ideology of the Chronicler*. BIS 33. Leiden: Brill.

Dyrberg, B. (1997), *The Circular Structure of Power*. London: Verso.

Eagleton, T. (1976), *Criticism and Ideology*. London: NLB.

——(1991), *Ideology: an Introduction*. London: Verso.

——(2000) *The Idea of Culture*. Oxford: Blackwell.

Ehrensperger, K. (2004), *That We May Be Mutually Encouraged: Feminism and the New Perspective in Pauline Studies*. New York and London: T&T Clark International.

Eisenbaum, P. (1999), 'Paul as the new Abraham' in R. A. Horsley (ed.), *Paul and Politics: Ekklesia, Israel, Imperium, Interpretation*. Harrisburg: Trinity Press International, 130–45.

Elliott, J. H. (1982), *A Home for the Homeless*. London: SCM.

——(1995), *Social Scientific Criticism of the New Testament: An Introduction*. London: SPCK.

Eriksen, T. H. (1993), *Ethnicity and Nationalism: Anthropological Perspectives*. Anthropology, Culture and Society. London and East Haven: Pluto Press.

Esler, P. F. (1994), *The First Christians in their Social Worlds: Social-Scientific Approaches to New Testament Interpretation*. London and New York: Routledge.

——(1998), *Galatians*. New Testament Readings. London: Routledge.

——(2003), *Conflict and Identity in Romans: The Social Setting of Paul's Letter*. Minneapolis: Fortress.

——(2005a), *New Testament Theology: Communion and Community*. Minneapolis: Fortress.

——(2005b), '"Remember my fetters": a social- and cognitive-science approach to the memorialisation of Paul's imprisonment in the pseudo-Pauline letters'. Conference Paper, University of Helsinki, Finland, August 2005, published in P. Luomanen, I. Pyysiäinen and R. Uro (eds), *Explaining Christian Origins and Early Judaism: Contributions from Cognitive and Social Science*. Biblical Interpretation Series 89. Leiden and Boston: Brill.

——(2006), 'Paul's Contestation of Israel's (Ethnic) Memory of Abraham in Galatians 3, *BTB* 36.1: 23–39.

Esler, P. F. (ed.) (1995), *Modelling Early Christianity: Social-Scientific Studies of the New Testament in its Context*. London and New York: Routledge.

Exum, J. C., S. D. Moore (eds) (1998), *Biblical Studies/Cultural Studies*. Sheffield: Sheffield Academic Press.

Faust, E. (1993), *Pax Christi et Pax Caesaris. Religionsgeschichtliche, Traditionsgeschichtliche und Sozialgeschichtliche Studien zum Ephesebrief*. NTOA 24. Freiburg: Universitätsverlag and Göttingen: Vandenhoeck & Ruprecht.

Fine, G. A. (1996), 'Reputational Entrepreneurs and the Memory of Incompetence: Melting Supporters, Partisan Warriors, and Images of President Harding'. *American Journal of Sociology* 101: 1159–93.

——(2001), *Difficult Reputations: Collective Memories of the Evil, the Inept and the Controversial*. Chicago: University of Chicago Press.

Fiske, J. (1982), *Introduction to Communication Studies: Studies in Communication*. London: Methuen.

Flick, U. (ed.) (1998), *The Psychology of the Social*. Cambridge: Cambridge University Press.

Fortune, M. (1985), *Keeping the Faith: Questions and Answers for the Abused Woman*. San Francisco: Harper & Row.

Fowl, S. E. (1998), *Engaging Scripture: A Model for Theological Interpretation*. Challenges in Contemporary Theology. Oxford and Malden: Blackwell.

Fredriksen, P. (1988), *From Jesus to Christ*. New Haven: Yale University Press.

Gager, J. G. (1975), *Kingdom and Community: the Social World of Early Christianity*. Englewood Cliffs: Prentice Hall.

——(1983), *The Origins of Anti-Semitism*. Oxford: Oxford University Press.

——(1999), 'Christian Missions and the Theory of Cognitive Dissonance' in D. G. Horrell (ed.), *Social-Scientific Approaches to the New Testament Interpretation*. Edinburgh: T&T Clark, 177–94.

——(2000), *Reinventing Paul*. Oxford: Oxford University Press.

Gaston, L. (1987), *Paul and the Torah*. Vancouver: University of British Columbia Press.

Gathercole, S. J. (2002), *Where is Boasting? Early Jewish Soteriology and Paul's Response in Romans 1–5*. Grand Rapids and Cambridge: Eerdmans.

Giddens, A. (1984), *Constitution of Society: Outline of the Theory of Structuration*. Social and Political Theory Cambridge: Polity Press.

Glancy, J. A. (1998), 'House Readings and Field Readings: the Discourse of Slavery and Biblical/Cultural Studies' in J. C. Exum and S. D.

Moore (eds), *Biblical Studies/Cultural Studies*. Sheffield: Sheffield Academic Press, 465–82.

——(2003), 'Protocols of Masculinity in the Pastoral Epistles' in S. D. Moore and J. C. Anderson (eds), *New Testament Masculinities*. Semeia Studies 45. Atlanta: Society of Biblical Literature, 235–64.

Gnilka, J. (1971), *Die Epheserbrief*. HKNT 10.2. Freiburg: Herder.

Gombis, T. G. (2004), 'Ephesians 2 as a Narrative of Divine Warfare'. *JSNT* 26.4: 403–418.

——(2005a), 'The Triumph of God in Christ: Divine Warfare in the Argument of Ephesians'. Unpublished PhD thesis. University of St Andrews.

——(2005b), 'A Radically New Humanity: The Function of the Haustaufel in Ephesians'. *ETS* 48: 317–30.

Goodchild, P. (2005), 'On Religion: Speeches to its Cultural Despisers' in J. G. Crossley and C. Karner (eds), *Writing History, Constructing Religion*. Aldershot and Burlington: Ashgate, 49–63.

Gorman, M. J. (2004), *Apostle of the Crucified Lord. A Theological Introduction to Paul and his Letters*. Grand Rapids and Cambridge: Eerdmans.

Gosnell, P. W. (2000), 'Networks and Exchanges: Ephesians 4.7-16 and the Community Function of Teachers'. *BTB* 30: 135–43.

Goss, R. E. (2006) 'Ephesians' in Deryn Guest et al. (eds), *The Queer Bible Commentary*. London: SCM, 630–38.

Goss, R. E. and M. West (eds) (2000), *Take Back the Word: A Queer Reading of the Bible*. Cleveland: Pilgrim Press.

Gouldner, M. (1994), 'Vision and Knowledge'. *JSNT* 56: 53–71.

Grabbe, L. L. (2000), *Judaic Religion in the Second Temple Period: Belief and Practice from Exile to Yavneh*. London: Routledge.

——(2007), 'When is a Sect a Sect – or Not? Groups and Movements in the Second Temple Period' in D. J. Chalcraft (ed.), *Sectarianism in Early Judaism: Sociological Advances*. London and Oakville: Equinox, 114–32.

Guest, D., R. E. Goss, M. West and T. Bohache (eds) (2006), *The Queer Bible Commentary*. London: SCM.

Gunn, D. M. and P. M. McNutt (eds) (2002), ' "Imagining" Biblical Worlds'. *Studies in Spatial, Social and Historical Constructs in Honor of James W. Flanagan*. JSOTSup 359. Sheffield: Sheffield Academic Press.

Hacking, I. (1990), *The Taming of Chance*. Cambridge: Cambridge University Press.

Hakola, R. (2005), *Identity Matters: John, the Jews and Jewishness*. SNT 118. Leiden: Brill.

Halbwachs, M. (1925), *Les Cadres sociaux de la mémoire*. Paris: Presses Universitaires de France.

——(1950), *The Collective Memory*. Introduction by Mary Douglas. New York: Harper-Colophon Books.

——(1992), *Maurice Halbwachs on Collective Memory*. Ed. and trans. by L. A. Coser. Chicago: University of Chicago Press.

Harland, P. A. (2003), *Associations, Synagogues, and Congregations: Claiming a Place in Ancient Mediterranean Society*. Minneapolis: Fortress Press.

Harré, R. and L. Van Langenhove (eds) (1998a), *Positioning Theory*. Oxford and Malden: Blackwell.

Harré, R. and L. Van Langenhove (1998b), 'Introducing Positioning theory' in R. Harré and L. Van Langenhove (eds), *Positioning Theory*. Oxford and Malden: Blackwell, 14–31.

Harris, W. H. (1996), 'The Descent of Christ: Ephesians 4.7-11 and Traditional Hebrew Imagery'. AGJU 32. Leiden and New York: Brill.

Haslam, S. A. (2001), *Psychology in Organizations: The Social Identity Approach*. London, Thousand Oaks, New Delhi: Sage Publications.

Haslam, S. A., S. Reicher (2007), 'Identity Entrepreneurship and the Consequences of Identity Failure: the Dynamics of Leadership in the BBC Prison Study'. *Social Psychology Quarterly* 70.2: 125–47.

Hastings, A. (1997), *The Construction of Nationhood: Ethnicity, Religion and Nationalism*. Cambridge: Cambridge University Press.

Hay, D. M. (2002), 'All the Fullness of God: Concepts of Deity in Colossians and Ephesians' in A. A. Das and F. J. Matera (eds), *The Forgotten God: Perspectives in Biblical Theology*. Louisville and London: Westminster John Knox, 163–79.

Hays, R. B. (1989), *Echoes of Scripture in the Letters of Paul*. New Haven: Yale University Press.

——(1996), ' "The Gospel is the power of God for salvation to Gentiles only?" A Critique of Stanley Stowers' A Rereading of Romans'. *CRBS* 9: 27–44.

——(2002), 'The God of Mercy who Rescues us from the Present Evil Age: Romans and Galatians' in A. A. Das and F. J. Matera (eds), *The Forgotten God: Perspectives in Biblical Theology*. Louisville and London: Westminster John Knox, 123–43.

——(2005), *The Conversion of the Imagination: Paul as Interpreter of Israel's Scripture*. London and Grand Rapids: Eerdmans.

Hays, R. B. and E. F. Davis (eds) (2003), *The Art of Reading Scripture*. Grand Rapids: Eerdmans.

Hobsbawm, E. (1982), 'Introduction: Inventing Traditions' in E. Hobsbawm and T. Ranger (eds), *The Invention of Traditions*. Cambridge: Cambridge University Press.

——(1998), *On History*. Paperback edn of 1997 original. London: Abacus.

Hobsbawm, E. and T. Ranger (eds) (1983), *The Invention of Tradition*. Cambridge: Cambridge University Press.

Hock, R. F. (1980), *The Social Context of Paul's Ministry*. Philadelphia: Fortress Press.

Hoehner, H. W. (2002), *Ephesians: An Exegetical Commentary*. Grand Rapids, MI: Baker Academic.

Hogg, M. A. (1994), 'Intragroup Processes, Group Structure and Social Identity' in W. P. Robinson (ed.), *Social Groups and Identities: Developing the Legacy of Henri Tajfel*. International Series in Social Psychology. Oxford: Butterworth Heinemann, 65–93.

Holland, T. (2003), *Contours of Pauline Theology: A Radical New Survey of the Influences on Paul's Biblical Writings*. Fearn: Mentor.

Holmberg, B. (1978), *Paul and Power: The Structure of Authority in the Primitive Church as Reflected in the Pauline Epistles*. Lund: Studentlitteratur.

——(1990), *Sociology and the New Testament: An Appraisal*. Minneapolis: Fortress Press.

Horrell, D. G. (1993), 'Converging Ideologies: Berger and Luckmann on Pastoral Epistles'. *JSNT* 50: 85–103.

——(1995), 'The Development of Theological Ideology in Pauline Christianity: a Structuration Theory Perspective' in P. F. Esler (ed.) *Modelling Early Christianity: Social-Scientific Studies of the New Testament in its Context*. London and New York: Routledge, 224–36.

——(1999a), 'Leadership Patterns and the Development of Ideology in Early Christianity' in D. G. Horrell (ed.), *Social-Scientific Approaches to New Testament Interpretation*. Edinburgh: T&T Clark.

——(2005), *Solidarity and Difference: A Contemporary Reading of Paul's Ethics*. London: T&T Clark International.

——(2006), 'Disciplining Performance and "Placing" the Church: Widows, Elders and Slaves in the Household of God (1 Tim 5.1–6.2)'. Unpublished Conference Paper, Social World of the NT, BNTC, Sheffield, September 2006.

Horrell, D. G. (ed.) (1999b), *Social-Scientific Approaches to New Testament Interpretation*. Edinburgh: T&T Clark.

Horrell, D. G. and C. M. Tuckett (2000), *Christology, Controversy and Community: New Testament Essays in Honour of D. R. Cathpole*. NovTS 99. Leiden: Brill.

Horsley, R. A. (ed.) (2000), *Paul and Politics: Ekklesia, Israel, Imperium, Interpretation. Essays in Honor of Krister Stendahl*. Harrisburg: Trinity Press International.

Huskinson, J. (ed.) (2000), *Experiencing Rome: Culture, Identity and Power in the Roman Empire*. London: Routledge.

Iser, W. (1978), *The Act of Reading: A Theory of Aesthetic Response*. English translation of 1976 German original. Baltimore and London: Johns Hopkins University Press.

——(1989), *Prospecting: From Reader Response to Literary Anthropology*. Baltimore and London: Johns Hopkins University Press.

——(1993), *The Fictive and the Imaginary: Charting Literary Anthropology*. Baltimore and London: Johns Hopkins University Press.

Jenkins, R. (2004), *Social Identity*. 2nd edn. London and New York: Routledge.

Johnson, E. E. (1998), 'Ephesians' in C. A. Newsom and S. H. Ringe (eds), *The Women's Bible Commentary*. Expanded edn. Louisville, Westminster/John Knox Press, 428–32.

Johnson, L. T. (1998), *Religious Experience in Earliest Christianity*. Minneapolis: Fortress.

Jokiranta, J. (2005), *Identity on a Continuum: Constructing and Expressing Sectarian Social Identity in Qumran Serakhim and Pesharim*. Academic Dissertation. Helsinki: Yliopistopaino.

——(2009, forthcoming), 'Sociological Approaches to Qumran Sectarianism' in T. Lim and J. Collins (eds), *Oxford Handbook of the Dead Sea Scrolls*. Oxford: Oxford University Press.

Juel, D. H. (ed.) (1991), *Jesus the Christ: the Historical Origins of the Christological Doctrine*. Minneapolis: Fortress Press.

Katz, I. (1981), *Stigma: A Social Psychological Analysis*. Hillsdale, NJ: Lawrence Erlbaum.

Kee, H. C. (1989), *Knowing the Truth: A Sociological Approach to New Testament Interpretation*. Minneapolis: Fortress Press.

Kelley, S. (2002), *Racializing Jesus: Race, Ideology and the Formation of Modern Biblical Scholarship*. London and New York: Routledge.

Kessel, B. (1998), *Suddenly Jewish: Jews Raised as Gentiles Discover their Jewish Roots*. Hanover and London: Brandeis University Press.

Kim, S. (1982), *The Origin of Paul's Gospel*. Grand Rapids: Eerdmans.

——(2002), *Paul and the New Perspective: Second Thoughts on the Origin of Paul's Gospel*. Grand Rapids and Cambridge: Eerdmans.

Kirk, A. and T. Thatcher (eds) (2005), *Memory, Tradition and Text: Uses of the Past in Early Christianity*. Semeia Studies 52. Atlanta: Society of Biblical Literature.

Kitchen, M. (1994), *Ephesians*. London and New York: Routledge.

Kittredge, C. B. (1998), *Community and Authority: The Rhetoric of Obedience in Pauline Tradition*. Harrisburg: Trinity Press International.

Kreitzer, L. J. (1997), *The Epistle to the Ephesians*. Epworth Commentaries. Peterborough: Epworth.

——(2003), 'The Messianic Man of Peace as Temple Builder: Solomonic

Imagery in Ephesians 2.13-22' in John Day (ed.), *Temple and Worship in Biblical Israel*. JSOTSup 422. London: T&T Clark International, 484–512.

Kunin, S. (2005), 'Ideological "Destructuring" in Myth, History and Memory' in J. G. Crossley and C. Karner (eds), *Writing History. Constructing Religion*. Aldershot and Burlington: Ashgate, 179–204.

Lapide, P. and P. Stuhlmacher (1984), *Paul: Rabbi and Apostle*. Minneapolis: Augsburg Press.

Lawrence, L. J. (2003), *An Ethnography of the Gospel of Matthew: A Critical Assessment of the Use of the Honour and Shame Model in New Testament Studies*. Tübingen: Mohr Siebeck.

——(2005), *Reading with Anthropology: Exhibiting Aspects of New Testament Religion*. Carlisle: Paternoster.

Levine, A.-J. (ed.) (2003), *A Feminist Companion to the Deutero-Pauline Epistles*. Feminist Companion to the New Testament and Early Christian Writings. London and New York: T&T Clark International.

Lieu, J. M. (1996), *Image and Reality: The Jews in the World of the Christians in the Second Century*. Edinburgh: T&T Clark.

——(2000), 'Anti-Judaism in the Fourth Gospel: Explanation and Hermeneutics' in R. Bieringer et al. (eds). *Anti-Judaism and the Fourth Gospel: Papers of the Leuven Colloquium*. Jewish and Christian Heritage Series 1. Assen: Royal van Gorcum.

——(2002a), *Neither Jew nor Greek? Constructing Early Christianity*. SNTW. London: T&T Clark.

——(2002b), 'Impregnable Ramparts and Walls of Iron': Boundary and Identity in Early "Judaism" and "Christianity"'. *NTS* 48: 297–313.

——(2004), *Christian Identity in the Jewish and Graeco-Roman World*. Oxford: Oxford University Press.

Lincoln, A. T. (1981), *Paradise Now and Not Yet: Studies in the Role of the Heavenly Dimension in Paul's Thought with Special Reference to His Eschatology*. Cambridge: Cambridge University Press.

——(1987), 'The Church and Israel in Ephesians 2'. *CBQ* 49: 605–24.

——(1990), *Ephesians*. Word Biblical Commentary 42. Dallas: Word.

——(1995), ' "Stand, therefore ...": Ephesians 6.10-20 as *Peroratio*'. *BibInt* 3: 99–114.

Lincoln, A. T. and A. J. M. Wedderburn (1993), *The Theology of the Later Pauline Letters*. New Testament Theology. Cambridge: Cambridge University Press.

Lindzey, G. and E. Aronson (eds) (1969), *Handbook of Social Psychology*. 2nd edn. Cambridge, MA: Addison-Wesley.

Lowenthal, D. (1985), *The Past is a Foreign Country*. Cambridge. Cambridge University Press.

Lukes, S. (2005), *Power: A Radical View*. 2nd edn. Basingstoke and New York: Palgrave Macmillan.

Luomanen, P. (1998), *Entering the Kingdom of Heaven*. WUNT 101. Tübingen: Mohr Siebeck.

Luomanen, P., I. Pyysiäinen and R. Uro (eds) (2007), *Explaining Christian Origins and Early Judaism: Contributions from Cognitive and Social Science*. Biblical Interpretation Series 89. Leiden and Boston: E. J. Brill.

Lustiger-Thaler, H. (1996), 'Remembering Forgetfully' in Vered Amit-Talai and C. Knowles (eds), *Re-situating Identities: The Politics of Race, Ethnicity, Culture*. Ontario: Broadview Press, 190–217.

MacDonald, M. Y. (1988), *The Pauline Churches: A Socio-Historical Study of Institutionalization in the Pauline and Deutero-Pauline Writings*. SNTSMS 60. Cambridge: Cambridge University Press.

——(1994), 'The Ideal of the Christian Couple: Ign. Pol. 5.1-2 Looking Back to Paul'. *NTS* 40:105–26.

——(1999a), 'Citizens of Heaven and Earth: Asceticism and Social Integration in Colossians and Ephesians' in L. Vaage and V. L. Wimbush (eds), *Asceticism and the New Testament*. New York: Routledge, 269–98.

——(1999b), 'Ritual in Pauline Churches' in D. G. Horrell (ed.), *Social-Scientific Approaches to New Testament Interpretation*. Edinburgh: T&T Clark, 233–47.

——(2000), *Colossians and Ephesians*. Sacra Pagina Series 17. Collegeville: Liturgical Press.

——(2004), 'Politics of Identity in Ephesians'. *JSNT* 26.4: 419–44.

Maier, H. O. (2002), *The Social Setting of the Ministry as Reflected in the Writings of Hermas, Clement and Ignatius*. ESCJ Studies in Christianity and Judaism. Waterloo, Ontario: Wilfrid Laurier University Press.

Malina, B. J. (2001), *The New Testament World: Insights from Cultural Anthropology*. 3rd rev. edn. Louisville: John Knox Press.

Malina, B. J. and J. H. Neyrey (1988), *Calling Jesus Names: The Social Value of Labels in Matthew*. Sonoma, CA: Polebridge Press.

Malina, B. and J. J. Pilch (2006), *Social-Science Commentary on the Letters of Paul*. Minneapolis: Fortress Press.

Martin, R. P. (1991), *Ephesians, Colossians and Philemon*. Atlanta: John Knox.

Meade, D. G. (1986), *Pseudonymity and Canon: An Investigation into the Relationship of Authorship and Authority in Jewish and Earliest Christian Tradition*. WUNT 39. Tübingen: Mohr Siebeck.

Meeks, W. A. (1983), *The First Urban Christians: The Social World of the Apostle Paul*. New Haven and London: Yale University Press.

——(2003), 'Assisting the World by Making (Up) History: Luke's Project and Ours'. *Interpretation* 57: 151–62.

Middleton, P. (2006), *Radical Martyrdom and Cosmic Conflict in Early Christianity*. LNTS 307. London and New York: T&T Clark.

Misztal, B. A. (2003), *Theories of Social Remembering*. Maidenhead and Philadelphia: Open University Press.

Mollenkott, V. R. (2001), *Omnigender: a Trans-Religious Approach*. Cleveland: Pilgrim Press.

——(2003), 'Emancipative Elements in Ephesians 5.21-33: Why Feminist Scholarship has (Often) Left Them Unmentioned, and Why They Should be Emphasized', in A.-J. Levine (ed.), *A Feminist Companion to the Deutero-Pauline Epistles*. Feminist Companion to the New Testament and Early Christian Writings. London and New York: T&T Clark International, 37–58.

Moore, S. D. and J. C. Anderson (eds) (2003), *New Testament Masculinities*. Semeia Studies 45. Atlanta: Society of Biblical Literature.

Moritz, T. (1994), *A Profound Mystery: The Use of the Old Testament in Ephesians*. SNT 85. Leiden: Brill.

Moulton, E. (2003), '(Re)describing Reality? The Transformative Potential of Ephesians Across Times and Cultures' in A.-J. Levine (ed.), *A Feminist Companion to the Deutero-Pauline Epistles*. Feminist Companion to the New Testament and Early Christian Writings. London and New York: T&T Clark International, 59–87.

Moxnes, H. (2005), 'From Theology to Identity: the Problem of Constructing Early Christianity' in T. Penner and C. Vander Stichele (eds), *Moving Beyond New Testament Theology? Essays in Conversation with Heikki Räisänen*. Publications of the Finnish Exegetical Society 88. Helsinki: The Finnish Exegetical Society and Göttingen: Vandenhoeck & Ruprecht.

Muddiman, J. (2001), *The Epistle to the Ephesians*. London: Continuum.

Mussner, F. (1982), *Der Brief and die Epheser*. Gütersloh: Gerd Mohn.

Nanos, M. D. (1996), *The Mystery of Romans: The Jewish Context of Paul's Letter*. Minneapolis: Fortress Press.

——(2000), 'The Inter- and Intra-Jewish Political Context of Paul's Letter to the Galatians' in R. A. Horsley (ed.), *Paul and Politics: Ekklesia, Israel, Imperium, Interpretation. Essays in Honor of Krister Stendahl*. Harrisburg: Trinity Press International, 146–59.

——(2002), *The Irony of Galatians: Paul's Letter in First-Century Context*. Minneapolis: Fortress Press.

Neufeld, T. R. Y. (1997), *Put on the Armour of God: The Divine Warrior from Isaiah to Ephesians*. JSNTSup 140. Sheffield: Sheffield Academic Press.

——(2002), *Ephesians*. Believers Church Bible Commentary. Scottdale: Herald.

Neusner, J. (1987), *Judaisms and their Messiahs at the Turn of the Christian Era*. Cambridge: Cambridge University Press.

Newsom, C. A. (2004), *The Self as a Symbolic Space: Constructing Identity and Community at Qumran*. Studies on the Texts of the Desert of Judah 52. Leiden: Brill.

Newsom, C. A. and S. H. Ringe (eds) (1998), *The Women's Bible Commentary*. Rev. edn. Louisville: Westminster/John Knox Press.

Neyrey, J. (1990), *Paul in Other Words*. Louisville: Westminster/John Knox Press.

——(1993), 'Deception' in J. J. Pilch and B. J. Malina (eds), *Biblical Social Values and their Meanings: A Handbook*. Peabody: Hendrickson, 38–42.

Ng, S. H. and J. J. Bradak (1993), *Power in Language: Verbal Communication and Social Influence*. Language and Language Behaviours 3. London: Sage.

Nichols, B. (1981), *Ideology and the Image*. Bloomington: Indiana University Press.

Nickelsburg, G. W. E. (2003), *Ancient Judaism and Christian Origins: Diversity, Continuity and Transformation*. Minneapolis: Fortress Press.

Nickelsburg, G. W. E. and G. W. MacRae (1986), *Christians Among Jews and Gentiles*. Philadelphia: Fortress Press.

Niehoff, M. R. (2001), *Philo on Jewish Identity and Culture*. Tübingen: Mohr Siebeck.

Nodet, É. and J. Taylor (1998), *The Origins of Christianity: An Exploration*. Collegeville: Liturgical Press.

Oakes, P. (1994), 'The Categorization Process: Cognition and the Group in the Social Psychology of Stereotyping' in P. W. Robinson (ed.), *Social Groups and Identities: Developing the Legacy of Henri Tajfel*. International Series in Social Psychology. Oxford: Butterworth Heinemann, 95–119.

O'Brien, P. T. (1999), *The Letter to the Ephesians*. Pillar New Testament Commentary. Grand Rapids: Eerdmans.

Økland, J. (2004), *Women in their Place: Paul and the Corinthian Discourse of Gender and Sanctuary Space*. JSNTSup 269. London and New York: T&T Clark International.

Osiek, C., M. Y. MacDonald and J. H. Tulloch (2005), *Woman's Place: House Churches in Earliest Christianity*. Minneapolis: Fortress.

Ostendorf, B. (1982), *Black Literature in White America*. Brighton: Harvester.

Patzia, A. G. (1984), *Ephesians, Colossians, Philemon*. Peabody: Hendrickson.

Penner, T. C. (2004), *In Praise of Christian Origins: Stephen and the Hellenists in Lukan Apologetic Historiography*. Emory Studies in Early Christianity. London and New York. T&T Clark.

——(2008), '*Die Judenfrage* and the Construction of Ancient Judaism: Foregrounding the Backgrounds Approach to Early Christianity'. SBL Annual Congress, Washington DC (2006), published in Patrick Gray and Gail R. O'Day (eds), *Scripture and Traditions: Essays on Early Judaism and Christianity in Honour of Carl R. Holladay*. Leiden: Brill, 429–55.

Penner, T. C. and C. Vander Stichele (eds) (2005), *Moving Beyond New Testament Theology? Essays in Conversation with Heikki Räisänen*. Publications of the Finnish Exegetical Society 88. Helsinki: The Finnish Exegetical Society; and Göttingen: Vandenhoeck & Ruprecht.

Perkins, P. (1997), *Ephesians*. Abingdon New Testament Commentaries. Nashville: Abingdon.

Petersen, N. R. (1985), *Rediscovering Paul: Philemon and the Sociology of Paul's Narrative World*. Philadelphia: Fortress Press.

Pickering, M. (2001), *Stereotypes: The Politics of Representation*. Basingstoke and New York: Palgrave.

Pietersen, L. K. (2004), *The Polemic of the Pastorals: A Sociological Examination of the Development of Pauline Christianity*. London and New York: T&T Clark International.

Pilch, J. J. and B. J. Malina (eds) (1993), *Biblical Social Values and their Meaning: a Handbook*. Peabody: Hendrickson.

Polaski, S. H. (1999), *Paul and the Discourse of Power*. Gender, Culture, Theory 8. The Biblical Seminar. Sheffield: Sheffield Academic Press.

Radford Ruether, R. (1993), *New Women, New Earth: Sexist Ideologies and Women's Liberation*. New York: Seabury.

Räisänen, H. (1986), *Paul and the Law*. WUNT 29. Tübingen: J.C.B. Mohr.

——(2005), 'Last Things First: "eschatology" as the First Chapter in an Overall Account of Early Christian Ideas' in T. C. Penner and C. Vander Stichele (eds), *Moving Beyond New Testament Theology? Essays in Conversation with Heikki Räisänen*. Publications of the Finnish Exegetical Society 88. Helsinki: The Finnish Exegetical Society; and Göttingen: Vandenhoeck & Ruprecht, 444–87.

Reese, J. M. (1993), 'Assertiveness' in J. J. Pilch and B. J. Malina (eds), *Biblical Social Values and their Meaning: a Handbook*. Peabody: Hendrickson, 9–11.

Reumann, J. (1989), *Variety and Unity in New Testament Thought*. Oxford Bible Series. Oxford: Oxford University Press.

Robbins, V. K. (1996), *Exploring the Texture of Texts: A Guide to Socio-Rhetorical Interpretation*. Valley Forge: Trinity Press International.

Robinson, W. P. (ed.) (1994), *Social Groups and Identities: Developing the Legacy of Henri Tajfel*. International Series in Social Psychology. Oxford: Butterworth Heinemann.

Rodriguez, R. (2004), 'From Difficult to Dominant: the Reputation of the Historical Jesus'. Unpublished Conference Paper, Social-scientific Criticism of the New Testament, SBL Annual Congress, San Antonio, USA.

——(2005), 'Discoursing Miracles: Jesus' Healings in Early Christian Memory'. Unpublished conference paper, Social-scientific Criticism of the New Testament, SBL Annual Congress, Philadelphia, USA.

——(2009), *Structuring Early Christian Memory: Jesus in Tradition, Performance*. LNTS. London and New York: T&T Clark.

Roetzel, C.J. (1983), 'Jewish Christian–Gentile Christian Relations: A discussion of Ephesians 2.15a'. *ZNW* 74.1/2: 81–89.

——(1999), *Paul: The Man and the Myth*. Minneapolis: Fortress Press.

——(2003), *Paul: A Jew on the Margins*. Louisville and London: Westminster/John Knox Press.

Rubin, D. C. (ed.) (1995), *Remembering Our Past: Studies in Autobiographical Memory*. Cambridge: Cambridge University Press.

Russell, L. (ed.), (1985), *Feminist Interpretations of the Bible*. Philadelphia: Westminster Press.

Sanders, E. P. (1977), *Paul and Palestinian Judaism: A Comparison of Patterns of Religion*. Philadelphia: Fortress Press.

——(1983), *Paul, the Law and the Jewish People*. Philadelphia: Fortress Press.

——(1992), *Judaism: Practice and Belief 63 BCE–66 CE*. London: SCM; Philadelphia: Trinity Press International.

Sanders, J. T. (1993), *Schismatics, Sectarians, Dissidents, Deviants: The First One Hundred Years of Jewish Christian Relations*. Valley Forge: Trinity Press International.

Schachter, S. (1951), 'Deviation, Rejection and Communication'. *Journal of Abnormal and Social Psychology* 46: 190–207.

Schlier, H. (1957), *Der Brief an die Epheser. Ein Kommentar*. 7th edn. Dusseldorf: Patmos.

Schnackenburg, R. (1991), *The Epistle to the Ephesians*. ET by H. Heron. Edinburgh: T&T Clark.

Schreiner, T. R. (1993), *The Law and its Fulfillment: A Pauline Theology of Law*. Grand Rapids: Baker.

Schudson, M. (1992), *Watergate in American Memory*. New York: Basic Books.

Schüssler Fiorenza, E. (1976), 'Cultic Language in Qumran and in the NT'. *CBQ* 38: 159–77.

——(1983), *In Memory of Her: A Feminist Theological Reconstruction of Christian Origins*. New York: Crossroad.

——(1994), 'Paul and the Politics of Interpretation' in R. A. Horsley (ed.), *Paul and Politics: Ekklesia, Israel, Imperium, Interpretation. Essays in Honor of Krister Stendahl.* Harrisburg: Trinity Press International, 40–57.

——(1998), *Sharing Her World: Feminist Biblical Interpretation in Context.* Boston: Beacon Press.

Schwartz, B. (2000), *Abraham Lincoln and the Forge of National Memory.* Chicago and London: University of Chicago Press.

——(2005), 'Christian Origins: Historical Truth and Social Memory' in A. Kirk and T. Thatcher (eds), *Memory, Tradition and Text: Uses of the Past in Early Christianity.* Semeia Studies 52. Atlanta: Society of Biblical Literature, 43–56.

Schweitzer, A. (1998), *The Mysticism of Paul the Apostle.* ET by William Montgomery. Baltimore: Johns Hopkins University Press.

Schwindt, R. (2002), *Das Weltbild des Epheserbriefes: Eine religions-geschichtlich- exegetische Studie.* WUNT 148. Tübingen: Mohr Siebeck.

Scott, J. (2001), *Power: Key Concepts.* Cambridge: Polity.

Scripture Project, The, (2003), 'Nine Theses on the Interpretation of Scripture' in Richard B. Hays and Ellen F. Davis (eds), *The Art of Reading Scripture.* Grand Rapids and Cambridge: Eerdmans.

Segal, A. F. (1990), *Paul the Convert.* New Haven and London: Yale University Press.

——(2000), 'Response: Some Aspects of Conversion and Identity Formation in the Christian Community of Paul's Time' in Richard A. Horsley (ed.), *Paul and Politics: Ekklesia, Israel, Imperium, Interpretation. Essays in Honor of Krister Stendahl.* Harrisburg: Trinity Press International, 184–90.

Segovia, F. F. (ed.) (1985), *Discipleship in the New Testament.* Philadelphia: Fortress.

——(2000), *Interpreting Beyond Boundaries.* Sheffield: Sheffield Academic Press.

Setzer, C. (1994), *Jewish Responses to Early Christians: History and Polemics 30–150 C.E.* Minneapolis: Fortress Press.

Shkul, M. A. I. (2000), 'An Evaluation of the Explicit References to Moses in the Christological Rhetoric of the Fourth Gospel'. Unpublished MA dissertation, University of Sheffield.

——(2006), 'The Law in the Negative Frames of Reference: Ephesians 2.15'. Unpublished conference paper, SBL Annual Congress, Washington, DC.

——(2008), 'Difficult Readings and Dialogue: Readers between Theology and Theory'. Unpublished conference paper, SBL Annual Congress, Boston.

Shulam, J. and H. Le Cornu (1997), *A Commentary on the Jewish Roots of Romans*. Baltimore: Lederer Books.

Smith, A. D. (2003), *Chosen Peoples: Sacred Sources of National Identity*. Oxford: Oxford University Press.

Smith, D. C. (1989), 'Cultic Language in Ephesians 2.19-22: A Test Case'. *ResQ* 31.4: 207–17.

Smith, E. R. and M. A. Zarate (1990), 'Exemplar and Prototype Use in Social Categorization'. *Social Cognition* 8: 243–62.

Spears, R., P. J. Oakes, N. Ellemers and S. A. Haslam (eds) (1997), *The Social Psychology of Stereotyping and Group Life*. Oxford, UK and Cambridge, MA: Blackwell.

Stark, R. (1996), *The Rise of Christianity: a Sociologist Reconsiders History*. Princeton: Princeton University Press.

Stark, R. and W. S. Bainbridge (1979), 'Of Churches, Sects, and Cults: Preliminary Concepts for a Theory of Religious Movements'. *Journal for the Scientific Study of Religion* 18.2: 117–33.

——(1985), *The Future of Religion: Secularization, Revival, and Cult Formation*. Berkeley and Los Angeles: University of California Press.

Stendahl, K. (1976), *Paul among Jews and Gentiles*. Philadelphia: Fortress Press.

——(1995), *Final Account: Paul's Letter to the Romans*. Minneapolis: Fortress Press.

Stepp, P. L. (2005), *Leadership Succession in the World of the Pauline Circle*. New Testament Monographs 5. Sheffield: Sheffield Phoenix Press.

Still, T. D. (1999), *Conflict at Thessalonica: A Pauline Church and its Neighbours*. JSNTSup 183. Sheffield: Sheffield Academic Press.

Stirewalt, M. L., Jr. (2003), *Paul the Letter Writer*. Grand Rapids and Cambridge: Eerdmans.

Stowers, S. K. (1994), *A Rereading of Romans: Justice, Jews, Gentiles*. New Haven: Yale University Press.

Stuart, E. (2000), 'Camping Around the Canon: Humour as Hermeneutical Tool for Queer Readings of Biblical Texts' in R. E. Goss and M. West (eds), *Take Back the Word: A Queer Reading of the Bible*. Cleveland: Pilgrim Press, 23–34.

Sumney, J. L. (1999), *'Servants of Satan', 'False Brothers' and Other Opponents of Paul*. JSNTSup 188. Sheffield: Sheffield Academic Press.

Swing, J. K. and C. Stangor (1998), *Prejudice: The Target's Perspective*. London: Academic Press.

Synnott, A. and D. Holmes (1995), 'Canada's Visible Minorities: Identity and Representation' in V. Amit-Talai and C. Knowles (eds), *Re-situating Identities: The Politics of Race, Ethnicity, Culture*. Ontario: Broadview Press, pp. 137–60.

Tachau, P. (1972), *"Einst" und "jetzt" im Neuen Testament: Beobachtungen zu einem urchristlichen Predigtschema in der neutestamentlichen Briefliteratur und zu seiner Vorgeschichte.* Forschungen zur Religion und Literatur des Alten und Neuen Testaments, Heft 105. Göttingen: Vandenhoeck & Ruprecht.

Tajfel, H. (1969), 'Cognitive Aspects of Prejudice'. *Journal of Social Issues* 25: 79–97.

——(1978), *Differentiation Between Social Groups: Studies in the Social Psychology of Intergroup Relations.* London: Academic Press.

——(1979), 'Social and Cultural Factors in Perception' in G. Lindzey and E. Aronson (eds), *Handbook of Social Psychology*, Vol. 3. 2nd edn. Cambridge. MA: Addison-Wesley. 315–94.

——(1981), *Human Groups and Social Categories.* Cambridge: Cambridge University Press.

——(1991), 'Social Stereotypes and Social Groups' in J. C. Turner and H. Giles (eds), *Intergroup Behaviour.* Oxford: Blackwell.

Tan, S. L. and F. M. Moghaddam (1999), 'Positioning in Intergroup Relations' in R. Harré and L. Van Langenhove (eds), *Positioning Theory.* Oxford and Malden: Blackwell, 178–94.

Tellbe, M. (2000), *Paul Between Synagogue and State: Christians, Jews, and Civic Authorities in 1 Thessalonians, Romans, and Philippians.* Coniectanea Biblica. NTS 34. Stockholm: Almquiest & Wiksell International.

Theissen, G. (1982), *The Social Setting of Pauline Christianity: Essays on Corinth.* Philadelphia: Fortress Press.

——(1999), *A Theory of Primitive Christian Religion.* ET by John Bowden. London: SCM.

—— (2003), *The New Testament. An Introduction.* ET by John Bowden. London and New York: T&T Clark.

Thistlethwaite, S. B. (1985), 'Every Two Minutes: Battered Women and Feminist Interpretation' in Letty Russell (ed.), *Feminist Interpretations of the Bible.* Philadelphia: Westminster Press, 96–107.

Tomson, P. J. (2005), *Presumed Guilty: How the Jews Were Blamed for the Death of Jesus.* ET by Janet Dyk. Minneapolis: Fortress Press.

Toye, R. (2008), 'The Churchill Syndrome: Reputational Entrepreneurship and the Rhetoric of Foreign Policy since 1945'. *British Journal of Politics & International Relations* 10.3: 364–78.

Trebilco, P. R. (1991), *Jewish Communities in Asia Minor.* SNTSMS 69. Cambridge: Cambridge University Press.

Trouillot, M.-R. (1995), *Silencing the Past: Power and the Production of History.* Boston: Beacon Press.

Tucker, J. B. (2007), 'Kinship-formation and the Foundation of the Christ-movement Identity in 1 Cor. 4.14-21'. Unpublished research paper presented at the University of Wales Lampeter, Theology and Religious Studies Postgraduate Seminar.

Turner, J. C. (1989), *Social Influence*. Buckingham: Open University Press.

——(1996), 'Henri Tajfel: an Introduction' in Peter W. Robinson (ed.), *Social Groups and Identities: Developing the Legacy of Henri Tajfel*. International Series in Social Psychology. Oxford: Butterworth Heinemann, 1–23.

Turner, J. C. and R. Y. Bourhis (1995), 'Social Identity, Interdependence and the Social Group: A Reply to Rabbie *et al.*' in W. Peter Robinson, (ed.) *Social Groups and Identities: Developing the Legacy of Henri Tajfel*. International Series in Social Psychology. Oxford: Butterworth-Heinemann, 25–63.

Turner, J. C. and H. Giles (eds) (1991), *Intergroup Behaviour*. Oxford: Blackwell.

Walsh, B. J. and S. C. Keesmaat (2005), *Colossians Remixed: Subverting the Empire*. British edn of 2004 original. Milton Keynes: Paternoster.

Wan, S.-K. (2000), 'Does Diaspora Identity Imply Some Sort of Universality? An Asian-American Reading of Galatians' in Fernando F. Segovia (ed.), *Interpreting Beyond Boundaries*. Sheffield: Sheffield Academic Press, 107–31.

Watson, F. (1986), *Paul, Judaism and the Gentiles: A Sociological Approach*. SNTSMS 56. Cambridge: Cambridge University Press.

——(1994), *Text, Church and World*. Grand Rapids: Eerdmans.

——(1997), *Text and Truth*. Edinburgh: T&T Clark.

Weber, M. (1978), *Economy and Society: An Outline of Interpretive Sociology*. 3 vols. Berkeley: University of California Press.

Weedman, G. E. (2004), 'Reading Ephesians from the New Perspective on Paul'. Conference paper, International Society of Biblical Literature Congress, Groningen, Netherlands.

Weeks, J. (2000), *Making Sexual History*. Cambridge: Polity Press.

Wenham, D. (1995), *Paul: Follower of Jesus or Founder of Christianity?* Cambridge and Grand Rapids: Eerdmans.

Werbner, T. and T. Modood (eds) (1997), *Debating Cultural Hybridity: Multi-Cultural Identities and the Politics of Anti-Racism*. London: Zed Books.

Westerholm, S. (1988), *Israel's Law and the Church's Faith: Paul and His Recent Interpreters*. Grand Rapids: Eerdmans.

——(2004), *Perspectives Old and New on Paul. The "Lutheran" Paul and His Critics*. Grand Rapids and Cambridge: Eerdmans.

Westwood, S. (2002), *Power and the Social*. London and New York: Routledge.

White, L. M. (ed.) (1992), *Social Networks in Early Christian Environment: Issues and Methods for Social History*. Semeia 56.

Wild, R. A. (1985), ' "Imitators of God": Discipleship in the Letter to the Ephesians' in F. F. Segovia (ed.), *Discipleship in the New Testament*. Philadelphia: Fortress.

Williams, D. J. (1999), *Paul's Metaphors: Their Context and Character*. Peabody: Hendrickson.

Williams, R. (2001), 'The History of Faith in Jesus' in Markus Bockmuehl (ed.), *The Cambridge Companion to Jesus*. Cambridge: Cambridge University Press, 220–36.

Wilson, B. R. (1975), *Magic and the Millennium*. St Albans: Paladin.

——(1982), *Religion in Sociological Perspective*. Oxford: Oxford University Press.

——(1990), *The Social Dimensions of Sectarianism: Sects and New Religious Movement in Contemporary Society*. Oxford: Clarendon Press.

Wilson, S. G. (1995), *Related Strangers: Jews and Christians 70–170 CE*. Minneapolis: Fortress Press.

Witherington, B. III (1994), *Paul's Narrative Thought World: The Tapestry, Tragedy and Triumph*. Louisville: Westminster/John Knox Press.

——(1995), *Conflict and Community in Corinth: A Socio-Rhetorical Commentary on 1 and 2 Corinthians*. Grand Rapids: Eerdmans; Carlisle: Paternoster Press.

Wright, N. T. (1991), *The Climax of the Covenant: Christ and the Law in Pauline Theology*. Edinburgh: T&T Clark; Minneapolis: Fortress Press.

——(1992), *The New Testament and the People of God*. London: SPCK.

——(1999), 'Paul's Gospel and Caesar's Empire' in R. A. Horsley (ed.), *Paul and Politics: Ekklesia, Israel, Imperium, Interpretation. Essays in Honor of Krister Stendahl*. Harrisburg: Trinity Press International, 160–83.

Yee, T.-L. N. (2005), *Jews, Gentiles and Ethnic Reconciliation: Paul's Jewish Identity and Ephesians*. SNTSMS 130. Cambridge: Cambridge University Press.

Zerubavel, E. (1997), *Social Mindscapes: An Invitation to Cognitive Sociology*. Cambridge, MA and London: Harvard University Press.

——(2003), *Time Maps: Collective Memory and the Social Shape of the Past*. Chicago and London: University of Chicago Press.

Zerubavel, Y. (1995), *Recovered Roots*. Chicago: University of Chicago.

Zetterholm, M. (2003), *The Formation of Christianity in Antioch: A Social-scientific Approach to the Separation between Judaism and Christianity*. London and New York: Routledge.

INDEX OF BIBLICAL SOURCES

INDEX OF BIBLICAL AUTHORS